Green Building *Illustrated*

Green Building *Illustrated*

Francis D. K. Ching
Ian M. Shapiro

WILEY

Contents

Disclaimer

While this publication is designed to provide accurate and authoritative information regarding the subject matter covered, it is sold with the understanding that neither the publisher nor the authors are engaged in rendering professional services. If professional advice or other expert assistance is required, the services of a competent professional person should be sought.

Preface

Green building is a relatively new field. Its goal is to substantially reduce the environmental impact of buildings, while providing a healthy environment within buildings. This book seeks to introduce the field of green building, explore a variety of fundamental concepts in green design and construction, and provide guidance to professionals engaged in the field.

Designing and constructing buildings is about making choices. It is the creation of choices at the beginning of a project, the evaluation of choices during the design process, the making of choices with the owner, the documentation of choices on drawings, and the implementation of choices through construction. In this book, we have attempted to provide a variety of choices for the design and construction of green buildings.

The book begins by exploring the goals of green buildings and by defining green buildings. It is strongly contextualized within the goal of reducing building-related carbon emissions to counter the increasing impacts of climate change. Various codes, standards, and guidelines are introduced, each of which sets forth requirements to give green buildings further definition.

A methodical exploration of green design is structured by working "from the outside in," from the community and site, through various layers of the building envelope, and proceeding to examination of the green aspects of lighting, heating, and cooling. Related topics are explored, including water conservation, safeguarding indoor environmental quality, material conservation, and renewable energy.

For energy-related discussions, a variety of first principles of physics are invoked, the combination of which is increasingly referred to as "building science." For example, first principles of heat transfer are applied to heat loss, and to reducing such loss. We explore aspects of illumination, relating to lighting energy use, and the human interaction and ergonomics of lighting. First principles of fluid dynamics lie behind a discussion of such building-related phenomena as "stack effect" buoyant airflow through buildings. First principles of thermodynamics are applied to the efficient generation and delivery of heat, the transport of heat away from buildings for cooling, and how to increase associated efficiencies in order to reduce energy use.

Detailed illustrations translate these principles and discussions into specific guidance for green building design and construction. A variety of best practices are offered, which are intended to be flexible enough for practitioners to design and construct the green building of the owner's dreams. The illustrations are also intended to be expansive, to offer a wide array of choices possible for green buildings.

Finally, a discussion of the practice of quality is used to explore how design and construction may most effectively deliver the goals sought for green design and construction.

The reader is advised to treat the methods covered in the book as tools. A building does not need to incorporate all the approaches suggested in this book in order to be green. The book is also a broad brush. It would be difficult to cover all the many emerging green building improvements, methods, and products. The focus is instead on underlying tools and strategies, from which professionals can create the choices necessary to design and construct high-performing green buildings.

Acknowledgments

First, thanks to Florence Baveye for research and concept drawings and to Marina Itaborai Servino for checking of facts and calculations. Further checking was done by Zac Hess and Daniel Clark. Double thanks to Roger Beck, for encouraging me to write 40 years ago, and for reviewing the manuscript 40 years later. Thanks go to Mona Azarbayjani of the University of North Carolina at Charlotte and to Jonathan Angier of EPA/Office of Water for reviewing the manuscript. Invaluable reviews and comments were also provided by my wife Dalya Tamir, my daughter Shoshana Shapiro, Susan Galbraith, Deirdre Waywell, Theresa Ryan, Jan Schwartzberg, Daniel Rosen, Shira Nayman, Ben Myers, Bridget Meeds, and Courtney Royal. Thanks to Lou Vogel and Nate Goodell for information on commissioning, to Javier Rosa and Yossi Bronsnick for information on structural design, and to Umit Sirt for information on modeling. Thanks to Nicole Ceci for energy analysis in the early going. Thanks to all my colleagues at Taitem Engineering for the research, observations, and discussions that are behind so much that is in this book. Thanks to Sue Schwartz for use of her apartment on Cayuga Lake, where I wrote. Thanks to Paul Drougas at Wiley for his thoughtful editorial input. Thanks to my family — Dalya, Shoshana, Tamar, and Noa, for their support throughout. Thanks to my mother, Elsa Shapiro, for being a sounding board each day, about the day's progress, over tea. And last, but really most of all, thanks to co-author Francis D.K. Ching, whose work is such a gift to the world. My colleague Theresa Ryan put it best: "We want to live in Frank's drawings." Frank's illustrations, guidance, layout, collaboration, and edits all made this book happen.
— Ian M. Shapiro

Metric Equivalents

The International System of Units is an internationally accepted system of coherent physical units, using the meter, kilogram, second, ampere, kelvin, and candela as the base units of length, mass, time, electric current, temperature, and luminous intensity. To acquaint the reader with the International System of Units, metric equivalents are provided throughout this book according to the following conventions:

- All whole numbers in parentheses indicate millimeters unless otherwise noted.
- Dimensions 3 inches and greater are rounded to the nearest multiple of 5 millimeters.
- Nominal dimensions are directly converted; for example, a nominal 2 x 4 is converted to 51 x 100 even though its actual 1 $\frac{1}{2}$" x 3 $\frac{1}{2}$" dimensions would be converted to 38 x 90.
- Note that 3487 mm = 3.487 m.
- In all other cases, the metric unit of measurement is specified.

1
Introduction

In the span of a few years, the planning, design, and construction fields have been swept up in a dynamic discussion of sustainability and green buildings. In design studios and on construction sites, we are learning to share new goals and new standards and even a new language. For many, our professional lives have been greatly enriched as we learn the meanings and means of this new language. For others, questions swirl: How did this all come about? What is it all about?

Sustainability is about the promises of things that will last—buildings with long and useful lives, forms of energy that are renewable, communities that endure. Green building is about turning the promises of sustainability into reality.

Parallel to the promises of sustainability, and even calling for their fulfillment, is the insistent reminder of scientists who caution about environmental hazards, hazards that are increasingly affirmed by our own observations. However, there is something deeply empowering in not shying away from these hazards, in turning and facing them, in weighing them collectively, and in developing strategies for addressing them. Ultimately, this may be the greatest promise of sustainability—the impetus to consider the environmental challenges we face, and to find ways to overcome them.

1.01 The fragility of life on Earth has been emphasized through views of the planet from space, such as the 1990 photograph from the *Voyager 1* spacecraft. The astronomer Carl Sagan describes Earth as the pale blue dot, "the only home we've ever known." (Source: NASA)

Facing Environmental Challenges

Several environmental crises are motivating us to reevaluate how we plan, design, and construct buildings. Air and water pollution resulting from fossil fuel use, fallout from nuclear power plant accidents, and the incipient and potential devastation of climate change all point to a critical need to reduce energy use. Human illness resulting from exposure to toxic chemicals compels us to re-examine their intensive use, especially in building materials.

Of particular concern is climate change. The Intergovernmental Panel on Climate Change (IPCC), which includes more than 1,300 scientists from the United States and other countries, reports that "warming of the climate system is unequivocal, as is now evident from observations of increases in global average air and ocean temperatures, widespread melting of snow and ice, and rising global average sea level." According to the IPCC, the impacts of climate change have already begun and are expected to only get worse. The consequences of climate change also include such extreme weather events as increased cyclone activity and longer, more frequent, and more intense heat waves; reduced snow cover and greater incidence of coastal and inland flooding; shifting plant and animal ranges and loss of biodiversity; and reduced water availability for human consumption, agriculture, and energy generation.

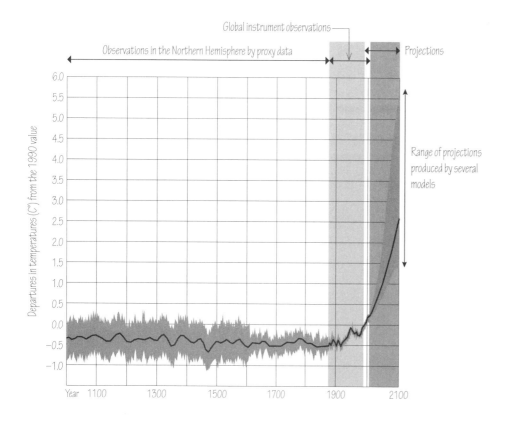

1.02 Variations in the Earth's surface temperature from the year 1000 to 2100. (Source: IPCC)

The major cause of climate change is the increasing concentrations of greenhouse gases (GHG) produced by human activities, such as deforestation, changes in land use, and especially the burning of fossil fuels. This finding is recognized by the national science academies of all major industrialized nations.

Greenhouse gases, primarily water vapor but including smaller amounts of carbon dioxide (CO_2), methane (CH_4), and nitrous oxide (N_2O), are emissions that rise into the atmosphere and act as a thermal blanket, absorbing heat and reemitting it in all directions. The downward portion of this re-radiation is known as the greenhouse effect and serves to warm the Earth's surface and lower atmosphere to a life-supporting average of 59°F (15°C). Without this natural greenhouse effect, life on Earth as we know it would not be possible.

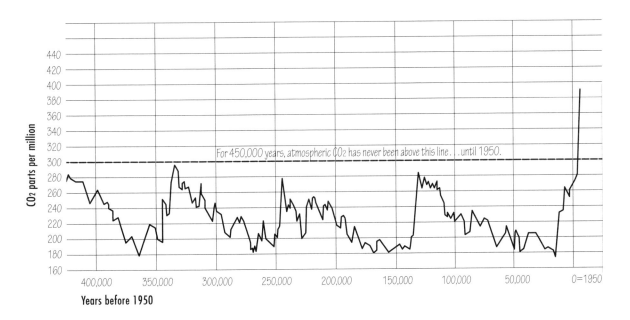

- While some of this infrared radiation passes through the atmosphere back into space, most is absorbed and reemitted in all directions by greenhouse gases in the atmosphere.

- Most of the solar energy reaching the Earth's atmosphere passes through and is absorbed by the Earth's land and oceans.

- The absorbed energy is emitted back toward space as infrared radiation.

The downward part of this infrared radiation is the greenhouse effect, raising the temperature of the lower atmosphere and the Earth's surface.

1.03 The greenhouse effect.

Beginning with the Industrial Revolution, however, the burning of fossil fuels in ever-increasing amounts has contributed to higher concentrations of carbon dioxide, methane, and nitrous oxide in the atmosphere, intensifying the natural greenhouse effect and contributing to global warming and climate change.

For 450,000 years, atmospheric CO_2 has never been above this line... until 1950.

CO₂ parts per million

Years before 1950

1.04 Atmospheric samples contained in ice cores and more recent direct measurements provide evidence that atmospheric CO_2 has increased since the Industrial Revolution. (Source: NOAA)

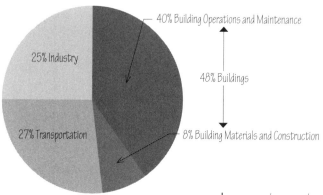

25% Industry

40% Building Operations and Maintenance

48% Buildings

27% Transportation

8% Building Materials and Construction

1.05 U.S. energy consumption by sector. Building-related energy use has been identified as one of the major causes of greenhouse gases, most significantly carbon dioxide. (U.S. Energy Information Administration)

Data from the U.S. Energy Information Administration indicates buildings are responsible for almost half the total U.S. energy consumption and greenhouse gas emissions annually; globally, the percentage may be even greater. What is relevant to any discussion of sustainable design is that most of the building sector's energy consumption is not attributable to the production of materials or the process of construction, but rather to operational processes, such as the heating, cooling, and lighting of buildings. This means that to reduce the energy consumption and GHG emissions generated by the use and maintenance of buildings over their life span, it is necessary to properly design, site, and shape buildings and incorporate efficient heating, cooling, ventilation, and lighting strategies.

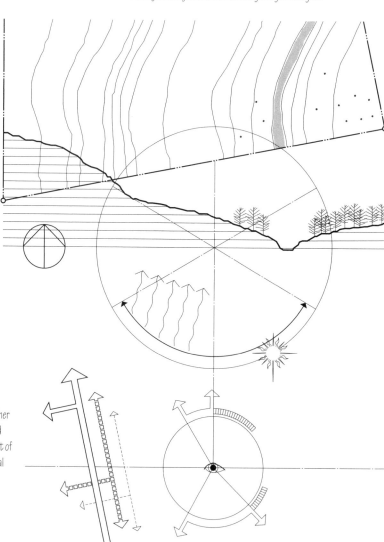

1.06 Well-sited and energy-efficient buildings could reduce carbon emissions in other sectors as well, by using less energy to produce and transport building materials and for people to be transported to and from buildings. Furthermore, the potential benefit of a future stream of reduced energy costs has been viewed as a way to offset the initial investment required to reduce carbon emissions.

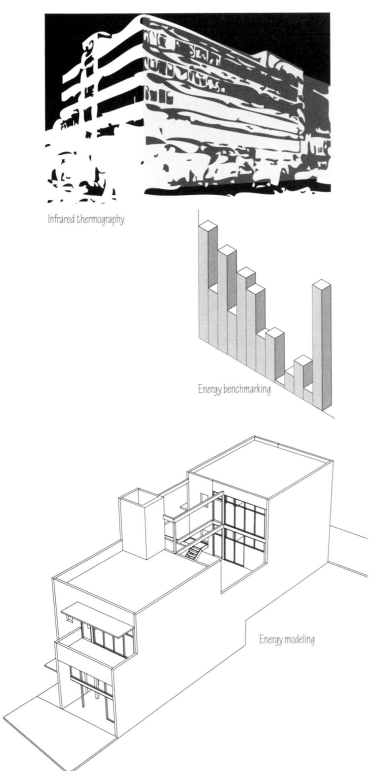

Infrared thermography

Energy benchmarking

Energy modeling

1. 07 Each year new approaches, new tools, and new products become available, offering ways to reduce energy and material use in buildings.

New Information, New Risks, New Opportunities

As knowledge of climate change and other environmental risks have been emerging, formal and informal research in buildings during the past few decades has given insights into how buildings work, how they can fail environmentally, and, as importantly, how such failures can be prevented. The converging demands of our multiple environmental crises and the relatively new information about how buildings perform and can be developed more sustainably offer opportunities for approaching the design of buildings in new ways. The field of green buildings is young and infinitely rich. New opportunities abound in design and construction to improve energy and resource efficiencies, to reduce the use of toxic chemicals, and to do so in a more affordable way.

However, there are many potential risks and pitfalls in green building design and construction. It is easy to be drawn to new products or approaches that claim to be green, but are in fact ineffective or are so costly as to prevent balanced investment in other, more cost-effective improvements. Our challenge is to use common sense, to reject token, showy, or ineffective building improvements, all while staying open to new, potentially valid ideas and tools. There is an urgent need both for critical thinking when scrutinizing new ideas and for flexibility when adapting to change that is occurring at a rapid pace.

Green building design need not focus solely on simply adding features to buildings to make them greener. While increasing thermal insulation values will improve the energy efficiency of a building and adding solar photovoltaic systems will reduce the need for electricity derived from nonrenewable sources, there is also much to be gained through judicious design that is not simply additive but rather more integrated and organic in nature. For example, we could select more reflective surfaces for interior finishes that would require fewer artificial light sources while delivering the same interior light levels. We could select building shapes that have less exposed surface area and so use less energy for the same floor area than more complex building shapes.

Being always mindful of the aesthetic nature of what we design and build, we might also ask: What is the effect of green design on the beauty of the built environment? Fortunately, beauty need not be sacrificed in order for buildings to be green. Green buildings may challenge conventional notions of what is beautiful, but the opportunity arises to reevaluate our notions of beauty, to reexamine how we define beauty in buildings, and to explore beauty in new architectural forms.

Trademarked Logo of the U.S. Green Building Council

Copyrighted Logo of the Forest Stewardship Council

1.08 Symbols for green materials, processes, and practices.

What Is a Green Building?

In this book, the question "What is a green building?" is repeatedly posed. This question takes many forms: Is a green building one that is greener than it could have been? Is a green building one that meets a green building standard? Is a green building one that has low or zero negative impact on the environment and on human health? Should all buildings be green? Are green buildings a passing fad? Do green buildings stay green over time?

The answer to "What is a green building?" is still evolving. Some buildings certified as green according to one of the green building standards have been found to be, in fact, high energy users or in some other way polluting. Conversely, many zero-energy or near-zero-energy buildings have been successfully designed and built but have not been certified as green by any rating system. This is not to question the environmental performance of all certified green buildings. Green building standards and certification systems have contributed immeasurably to the advancement of sustainable design and will continue to do so. However, we may still have a way to go before a green building certification guarantees a high level of energy efficiency or low level of pollution.

Parallel to the question "What is a green building?" is a similar but different question, "What is a greener building?" In many specific areas of building design, the relative merits of different approaches can be weighed by asking which of multiple available options is greener. This is not to advocate for small or incremental improvements in green design. The overall goal of a meaningfully green building remains paramount. However, when facing the many design decisions that need to be made in planning a building, "Is this approach greener?" can be a useful question—one that is often worthwhile asking, regardless of compliance with a specific green building code, standard, or guideline.

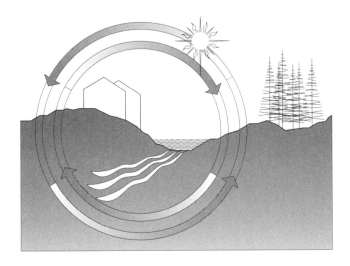

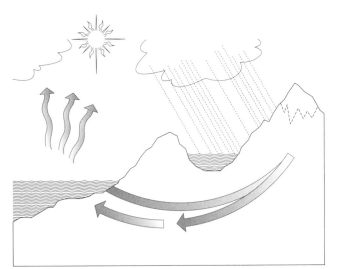

Green Building Goals

There are many goals that motivate the planning and design of green buildings.

Perhaps the most widely recognized goals address environmental degradation:

- Mitigate global warming through energy conservation, reduction of GHG emissions, and carbon sequestration through biological processes, such as reforestation and wetland restoration.
- Minimize environmental impacts resulting from the extraction of coal, natural gas, and oil, including oil spills; the mountaintop removal mining of coal; and the pollution associated with hydraulic fracturing for natural gas.
- Reduce pollution of air, water, and soil.
- Protect clean water sources.
- Reduce light pollution that can disrupt nocturnal ecosystems.
- Protect natural habitats and biological diversity, with specific concern for threatened and endangered species.
- Prevent unnecessary and irreversible conversion of farmland to nonagricultural uses.
- Protect topsoil and reduce the impacts of flooding.
- Reduce use of landfills.
- Reduce risk of nuclear contamination.

1.09 Mitigating environmental degradation through conservation, reduction of pollutants, and protection of water and natural resources and habitats.

Goals for green buildings include providing for improved human health and comfort:

- Improve indoor air quality.
- Improve indoor water quality.
- Increase thermal comfort.
- Reduce noise pollution.
- Improve morale.

Some goals might be considered economic in nature:

- Reduce energy costs.
- Improve productivity.
- Create green jobs.
- Increase marketing appeal.
- Improve public relations.

Some goals might be considered political in nature:

- Reduce dependence on foreign sources of fuel.
- Increase national competitiveness.
- Avoid depletion of nonrenewable fuels, such as oil, coal, and natural gas.
- Reduce strain on electric power grids and risk of power outages.

1.10 Improving environmental and economic health.

Some people broaden the goals of green buildings to include social or societal goals:

· Follow fair labor practices.
· Provide access for the disabled.
· Protect consumers.
· Protect parklands.
· Preserve historic structures.
· Provide affordable housing.

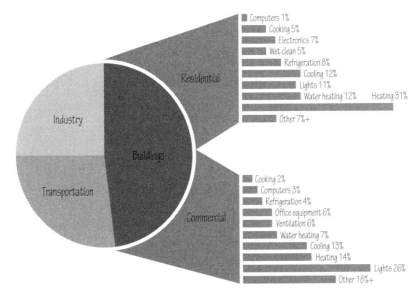

1.11 Meeting social and societal goals.

And some goals reflect the unique needs of the human spirit:

· Express deep connection to and love of the Earth and nature.
· Be self-reliant.
· Satisfy the quest for beauty.

Some goals may not be explicitly stated but represent some of our less nobler needs, such as the quest for status or prestige.

Regardless of how the stated goals are grouped, there is an ongoing and valid conversation to be had about what the goals are and how to prioritize them. In most instances, constructing green buildings supports one or more of the goals in a harmonious way. However, in some cases, conflicts may occur between two or more goals and the reconciliation of these conflicts represents a vital sorting-out of what is important to us as humans.

In the face of almost unanimous agreement among scientists about the consequences of climate change, and with impacts well under way, such as shifting plant and animal ranges, more frequent flooding of low-lying areas, and receding of polar ice, a major focus of the green building field will remain the reduction of energy consumption and associated carbon emissions.

1.12 Energy consumption in the U.S. (Source: DOE) Reducing energy consumption and associated carbon emissions remains of paramount importance in the way we plan, design, and construct buildings.

Approaches to Green Building

In green building design and construction, it often helps to use a common sense approach. Most of the energy- and water-efficiency tradeoffs of different technologies and strategies are readily quantifiable and so can guide decision-making. Hazardous materials are reasonably well-known and identifiable and so can be avoided. Common sense can also be helpful in addressing some of the more complex tradeoffs, guiding consideration of new technologies, and preventing design paralysis, which may arise when faced with the many choices and unknowns in green design and construction.

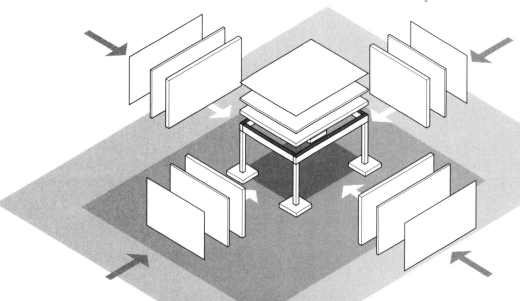

1. 13 Designing from the outside by incrementally adding layers of shelter.

In this book, we offer one approach to designing green buildings: *designing from the outside in.* A variety of benefits can be realized by designing from the perimeter of a building site, toward the building, through its envelope, and to its core. By incrementally adding *layers of shelter* and ensuring the integrity and continuity of each of these layers, various energy loads can be substantially reduced. In doing so, the accumulation of green building improvements can actually reduce construction costs, making possible buildings that not only use less energy, less water, and fewer materials, but are more affordable to construct.

Building on some of the notable, recent developments in building science, this book focuses on design strategies for green building rather than on compliance with specific requirements of any particular code, standard, or guideline. However, the principles and approaches presented are intended to be robust enough to meet or exceed the requirements of existing codes, standards, and guidelines, and be applicable to all types of buildings, whether they be wood-frame residences or high-rise structures of steel and concrete.

The various standards for green building design are generally consistent with the approaches suggested by designing from the outside in. However, many existing green building standards calculate energy savings relative to a hypothetical reference building or focus on energy use per unit floor area, and take the building shape as given. Green building standards tend not to question the floor area or the building shape itself. In designing from the outside in, everything is up for questioning, including the floor area and building shape.

Some approaches to green buildings take a particular building design, invest in improved construction (such as thicker walls with more insulation, tighter construction, more energy-efficient windows, or higher-efficiency heating), and have as a goal a building that uses perhaps 10%, 20%, or 30% less energy. While this approach is fully valid, it can be enhanced by a complementary approach, which is to design not an improved traditional building but rather a different type of building that meets the same human needs, for which the goal is to use significantly less energy or preferably net-zero energy and with an eye to affordability throughout.

1.14 We can trace a building's energy use through its utility bills.

Buildings leave a trace of their greenness in their utility bills, a trace that will last for decades to come. Increasingly, buildings are judged by this trace, as online databases in recent years track energy use in individual buildings and perform widespread comparisons of energy use between buildings. The judgment of history has already begun to weigh more heavily on buildings that waste energy, particularly buildings that claim to be green. The good news is that the tools to design and build energy-efficient buildings are increasingly available. The challenge lies in their application.

To architectural form and function, a new dimension in building design is presenting itself: performance. In addition to serving the needs of its occupants and appealing to the eye, mind, and spirit, a building must now perform well, and perform persistently well over time, consuming less energy and resources while providing a high level of comfort and conditions conductive to good health. On one hand, an added set of constraints has been placed on building design. On the other, an opportunity exists to clear a higher bar, do better work, and avoid wasteful and unhealthy buildings.

The reader is invited to join an exploration of the promise of
buildings that impact the environment as lightly as possible and use
significantly less energy, water, and materials than at present. Let
us explore the promise of buildings that could cost less than current
buildings while being more comfortable and conducive to human
health. Let us explore the promise of buildings that are more strongly
integrated into our human communities and the natural world. Let
us explore the promise of buildings that we can be proud of.

And then let us try to boldly deliver on these promises.

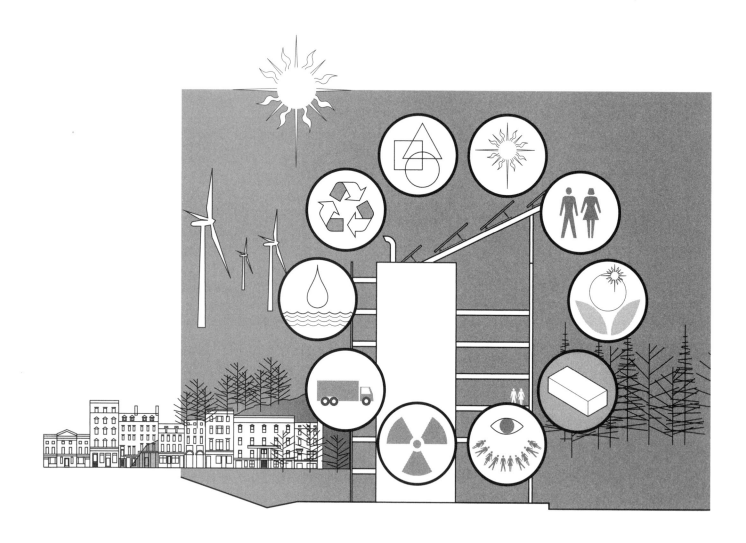

2
First Principles

What is a green building? In the Introduction, we examined the significant impacts of buildings on our natural environment and made the case for buildings that mitigate these effects, not only by lowering their use of energy and water but also reducing the amount of materials and resources used in their construction. Reducing their impact on the natural environment is a major goal of green buildings.

Is there anything else that makes a building green? In discussions of green building and the various green building codes and standards, we find some widely accepted goals that do not contribute directly to reducing the impact of buildings on the natural environment. These include such goals as improving indoor air quality, providing views from the building interior to the outdoors, and enhancing thermal comfort. And so we can and should broaden the definition of green buildings to include the design of indoor environments that are conducive to human health.

Let us begin with the following working definition: A green building is a building that has a substantially reduced impact on the natural environment and that provides indoor conditions conducive to human health.

However, other questions quickly arise. When we say "substantially reduced impact on the natural environment," how substantial does the reduction need to be? And, in order to know how substantial the reduction is, is there some way that we can measure the greenness of a building? And if so, what do we measure it against? Do we measure it in a relative way, against a hypothetical building of the same size and shape that would comply with some current code or standard? Or do we measure it against other buildings of a similar type?

Measuring the greenness of a building relative to:

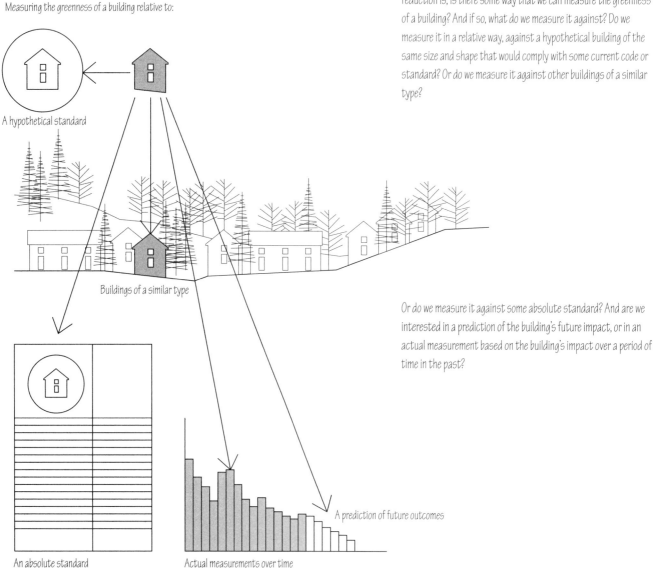

A hypothetical standard

Buildings of a similar type

An absolute standard

Actual measurements over time

A prediction of future outcomes

2.01 How should we gauge the greenness of a building?

Or do we measure it against some absolute standard? And are we interested in a prediction of the building's future impact, or in an actual measurement based on the building's impact over a period of time in the past?

These questions are good ones, with which the green building community is actively wrestling. And in our uniquely human way—full of debate and discourse—they are questions we may be slowly but steadily answering.

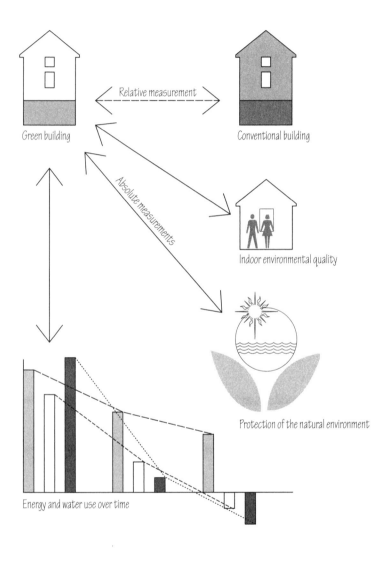

2.02 Relative versus absolute greenness.

Labels within figure:
- Green building
- Relative measurement
- Conventional building
- Absolute measurements
- Indoor environmental quality
- Protection of the natural environment
- Energy and water use over time

Relative and Absolute Green

For the question "What baseline should we use?," much can be gained by comparing a proposed green building to a hypothetical building of the same size and shape that might have been designed and built without any green features, but meets current building codes and generally accepted construction standards. Let us call this the relative approach to green building design. The goal here is to have a substantially reduced impact on the environment and provide substantially improved human health, relative to that hypothetical "same building without green building features." However, an important discussion is emerging about whether we should not also be examining absolute measurements of environmental impact and improved health, such as meeting specific goals of energy and water use per unit area of building, or even meeting a goal of zero energy and water use in the building.

In the areas of energy and water, a building's predicted future use has much value and can guide many decisions and standards. A consensus is also developing that actual energy and water use must also be measured, to actively demonstrate conservation rather than relying only on predictions.

Other areas, such as material conservation and indoor environmental quality, are slightly harder to define and measure than energy and water consumption, but we nonetheless have made strides to develop consensus on what constitutes being green in order to set goals and measure our progress toward these goals.

The answer to the question "What is a green building?" will continue to change and evolve, as long as our own standards of what impact on the natural environment is acceptable, and what level of human health is desirable. In fact, to effectively design and construct green buildings will likely always mean repeatedly asking "What is a green building?" and continually seeking consensus-based answers to the question.

The enterprise of designing and constructing a building is extremely challenging. Hundreds or even thousands of decisions are required to complete any single building, as tradeoffs of program, form, quality, cost, scheduling, and regulations are weighed. A green building presents even more challenges, with added constraints and often difficult performance goals to achieve. Designing and building an affordable green building—one that performs well in meeting the needs of its occupants, does not harm the environment, is conducive to good human health, and meets its owner's budget—is the ultimate challenge. Guiding principles can sometimes help to manage how we meet a challenge as large as this.

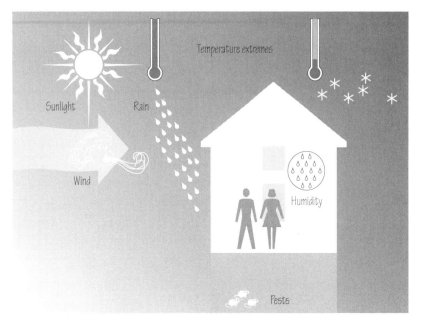

Loads and Layers

Buildings shelter their occupants from a wide variety of outdoor elements, which we might refer to as *loads*. These loads are in some ways stresses or pressures, both on our buildings and on our everyday lives. Important among these loads are temperature extremes, the reason we heat and cool buildings. There are loads other than temperature extremes from which we also seek shelter, such as blustery winds, driving rain, and the searing sun. We seek protection from the ultraviolet rays of the sun, which can contribute to skin cancer and deteriorate artwork and building materials. Some loads are more subtle in their effects, such as humidity, which can compromise human health and the integrity of our possessions. Some loads are simple, such as darkness. Some loads are living, such as insects, rodents, birds, and other animal life. And some loads result from human activity, such as noise, air, and light pollution.

2.03 Types of loads.

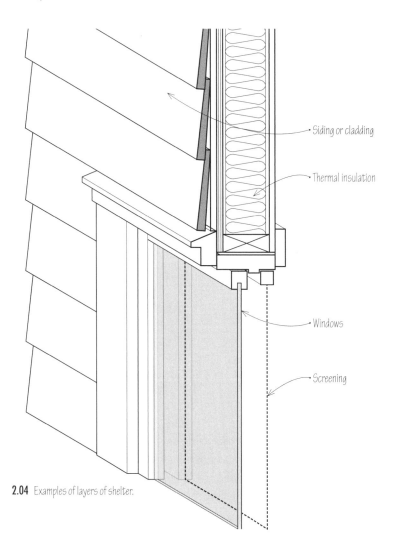

Siding or cladding

Thermal insulation

Windows

Screening

2.04 Examples of layers of shelter.

Buildings are important to us because they are the settings in which we live, work, teach, learn, shop, and congregate for social activities and events. We also recognize that a fundamental and functional role of buildings is to provide shelter from the many loads in our world.

We define a *layer of shelter* as a building component that protects against loads. Thermal insulation in a wall is a layer of shelter that serves to moderate the impact of temperature extremes. The siding or cladding on a building is a layer of shelter that keeps out wind and rain and shields against the effects of ultraviolet radiation and other loads.

Some layers of shelter are intentionally selective, purposefully letting in desired elements while filtering out other loads. For example, windows let in daylight while tempering temperature extremes. Screens let in fresh air, but keep insects out.

A principle of green design is to use multiple layers of shelter to improve the effectiveness of protection from loads. For example, air infiltration is recognized to be a major contributor to heating and cooling loads in buildings. Air barriers and weatherstripping are better able to resist wind-induced infiltration if the wind has first been slowed by trees or other wind breaks. In other words, trees can serve effectively as a layer of shelter. Likewise, if a wall is well sealed with caulked window frames and gasketed electrical receptacles, infiltrating air is less likely to find paths into the building, as each layer of the wall assembly sequentially contributes to resisting the infiltration.

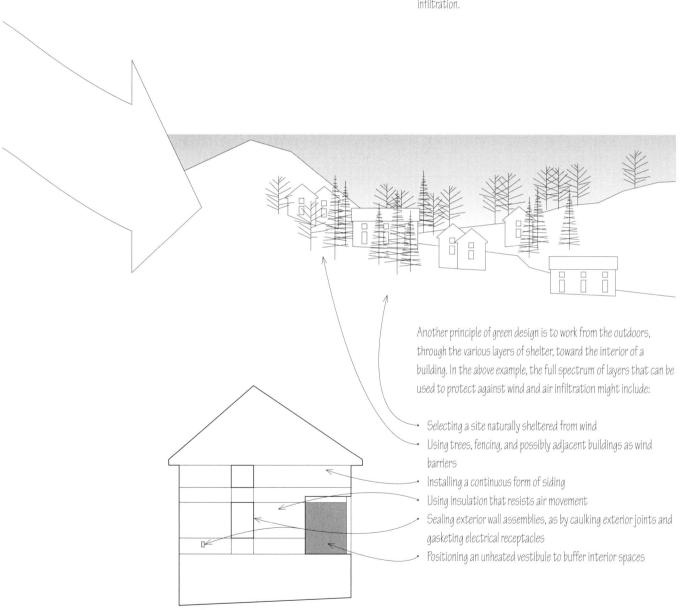

Another principle of green design is to work from the outdoors, through the various layers of shelter, toward the interior of a building. In the above example, the full spectrum of layers that can be used to protect against wind and air infiltration might include:

- Selecting a site naturally sheltered from wind
- Using trees, fencing, and possibly adjacent buildings as wind barriers
- Installing a continuous form of siding
- Using insulation that resists air movement
- Sealing exterior wall assemblies, as by caulking exterior joints and gasketing electrical receptacles
- Positioning an unheated vestibule to buffer interior spaces

2.05 Sheltering against wind and air infiltration.

Starting far from the building and working inward is akin to solving the problem at its source, rather than trying to solve the symptom. If the symptom is a cold, drafty building, solving the symptom would be adding heat, which is simple but inefficient. Solving the problem at its source is reducing wind loads and preventing infiltration through a structured approach with multiple layers of shelter. Working from the outside in is analogous to the medical approach of "prevention instead of pills" when dealing with health issues.

An ordered prioritization of the layers of shelter that can be used to protect a building against loads, working from the outside in, includes:

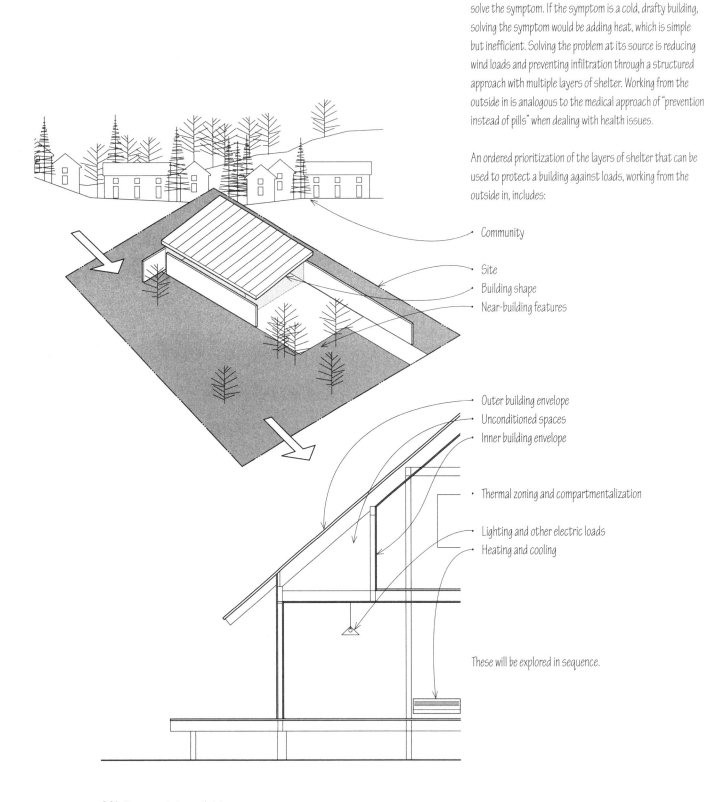

Community

Site
Building shape
Near-building features

Outer building envelope
Unconditioned spaces
Inner building envelope

· Thermal zoning and compartmentalization

· Lighting and other electric loads
· Heating and cooling

These will be explored in sequence.

2.06 Prioritizing the layers of shelter.

Continuity

Another principle of green design is to not only design strong and robust layers but also ensure the continuity of each layer of shelter. The importance of continuity for the thermal boundary of buildings has been widely recognized in recent years. Such layers are weakened when they are broken or are discontinuous. Most conventional buildings have many such discontinuities. For example, attic floors of pitched-roof buildings have been found to have such discontinuities as uncapped wall chases; unsealed gaps around light fixtures, exhaust fans, plumbing vents, and chimneys; and leaky attic hatches.

Physical voids are not the only kind of disruptions a thermal boundary can suffer. Discontinuities can also be created by thermal bridges, which are conductive materials that penetrate or interrupt the thermal insulation layer in a wall, floor, or roof assembly. For example, the wood or metal studs in a framed wall can act as thermal bridges, allowing heat to move through the wall.

Physical gaps in construction assembly

Thermal bridges

2.07 A weak layer of shelter is one that has many discontinuities, whether they be physical gaps or thermal bridges.

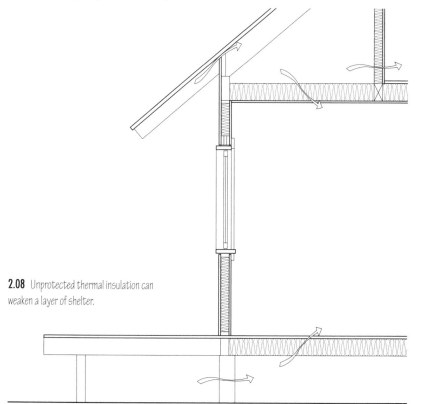

Walls, floors, and roofs having unprotected insulation only on one side are typically weak layers of shelter. For example, the ceilings of basements or crawlspaces often have insulation that is detached. Knee walls in attics are often insulated only on one side, with the insulation at risk of damage or removal. Even if the insulation stays in place, air can move readily around the insulation to the cold side of the interior wall finish, increasing heat loss in the space.

2.08 Unprotected thermal insulation can weaken a layer of shelter.

Weak layers are weak from the start. They are intrinsically weak. We define a nonrobust layer as one that may be strong to start, but weakens over time. A well-insulated door, with good weatherstripping, a door sweep, and a storm door, may well start out as a strong layer of shelter. However, over time, the door frame may shift and settle, the door sweep may move out of position, the caulking around the door frame may shrink and crack, the weatherstripping may compress or fall off, and the storm door may not close fully due to a failed spring. A door assembly is intrinsically nonrobust, its wear and tear over time weakening its function as a layer of shelter.

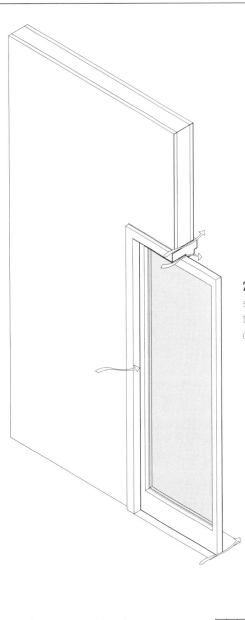

2.09 While walls normally are robust layers, the sheltering layer of doors can weaken over time as their frames shift or settle, caulking shrinks or cracks, or weatherstripping fails.

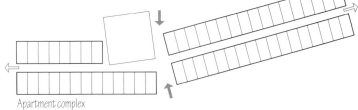

Apartment complex

2.10 Comparison of an apartment complex with interior corridors providing access to units and a layout of townhouses, each with its own set of exterior doors.

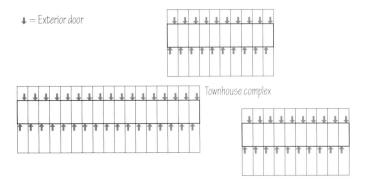

↓ = Exterior door

Townhouse complex

A rigid wall is always more robust than a door assembly, serving as a stronger layer of shelter for a longer period of time. Buildings obviously cannot be built without doors, but if the number of exterior doors are in question, the fewer the better. For example, an apartment building with two exterior doors and an interior corridor for access to each unit has fewer exterior doors than townhouses that have one or two exterior doors for each apartment.

Holistic Design

Another principle of green design is to plan holistically, to view the building and its environment as a whole and to examine all components when designing from the outside in. Energy is used and wasted in many ways. Energy for heating, for example, is required because of conductive and infiltration losses through the building envelope, distribution losses, and heating equipment losses. In order to significantly reduce such energy losses, the building must be treated as a whole and all losses must be minimized.

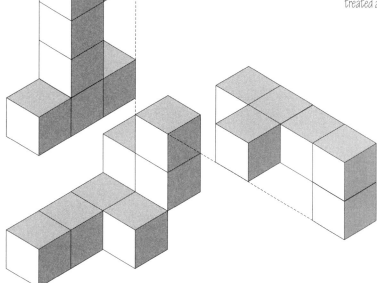

A holistically treated building is one in which many small improvements are made, all of which add up to a significant whole. A 12-inch- (305-mm) thick super-insulated wall cannot itself make a building energy efficient if the windows in it have poor thermal resistance, if there is extensive air leakage through attic fixtures and elements, or if the heating system has an inefficient distribution system. Too often, green buildings have a single highly visible green component, but still use too much energy because insufficient attention was paid to the building as a whole.

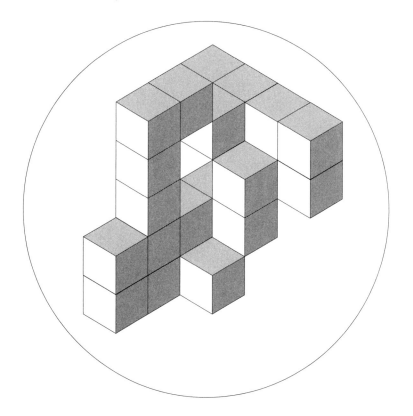

2.11 Like solving a three-dimensional puzzle, effective green design involves a large collection of small steps, all done with the owner's interests fully recognized, to address the complex challenge of making a building both green and affordable.

Integrated Design

An increasingly common practice in the green building field is referred to as integrated design, sometimes alternatively referred to as integrative design. With integrated design, participants in a project, including the owner, architect, engineers, consultants, tenants, and contractors, work together as a team from the early initial stages of a project. This collaborative approach is intended to ensure that all stakeholders contribute to the greening of the building and that important viewpoints and needs are considered early on in the design process. Integrated design has made an invaluable contribution to green building design, most significantly by promoting the early evaluation of energy tradeoffs.

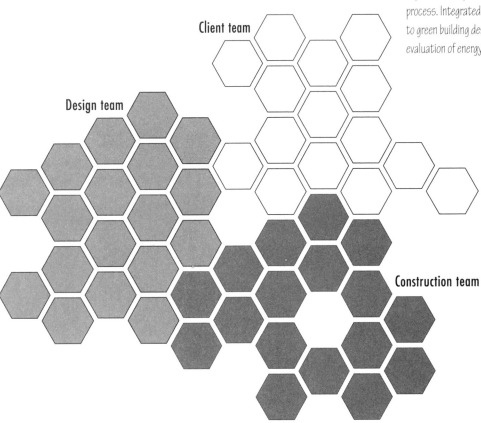

2.12 The integrated design process involves and engages diverse stakeholders and emphasizes connections and communication among the client, design, and construction teams.

In designing from the outside in, we do not seek to relegate later-stage design steps, such as the layout and specification of lighting, heating, and cooling systems, to a lower priority. Early and integrated discussions are essential. We merely suggest that these design issues should not be finalized until later in the process.

We will address how the owner's goals need to be clearly identified early in the process, in as much detail as possible, including which spaces should have temperature control, how many people are expected to be in the building and when, and much more. These early decisions will broadly influence other decisions, such as the type of heating and cooling system to be used, which in turn will influence such decisions as the building height and whether mechanical spaces are needed. Integrated design makes common sense. It allows for all the building's components to work together, rather than as isolated pieces of the design puzzle.

Affordability

Affordability has always played a central role in building design and construction. Buildings are one of the largest capital costs in society. Affordable housing speaks to a society's ability to provide shelter for the poor. Home ownership has become synonymous with the realization of a dream. So significant are the capital costs for construction that these costs can rarely be afforded out of pocket and so are usually borrowed and repaid over decades through that very particular type of loan, the mortgage.

For green design and construction, cost has implications as both an obstacle and an opportunity. A common perception is that building green will cost more and, as a result, can only be done by those who can afford the added cost. This perception is one of the largest obstacles to green buildings.

An emerging view is that costs need to be analyzed on a life-cycle basis, taking into account the lower operating costs of a green building over its anticipated life. The energy costs of a green building are typically lower than those of a traditionally constructed building. Some green improvements, such as geothermal heating and cooling, have also been observed to reduce maintenance costs relative to traditional approaches. A case has also been made that human productivity is higher in green buildings due to improved indoor air quality and thermal and visual comfort, resulting in a cost benefit over time that offsets higher capital costs.

A scrutiny of green strategies reveals a variety of improvements that in fact can lower both energy costs and construction costs. For example, if ceiling heights are not unusually high, material and construction costs can be reduced, fewer light fixtures are required for illumination, and less heating and cooling equipment is needed.

Green design and construction is not cost-neutral and it is imperative to honestly assess both added construction costs as well as cost savings, added operational costs as well as cost savings, and finally to recognize both real and perceived cost impacts. If green buildings are to penetrate beyond innovators and early adopters and reach those people for whom cost will otherwise prevent building green, affordability is best addressed head-on in design discussions.

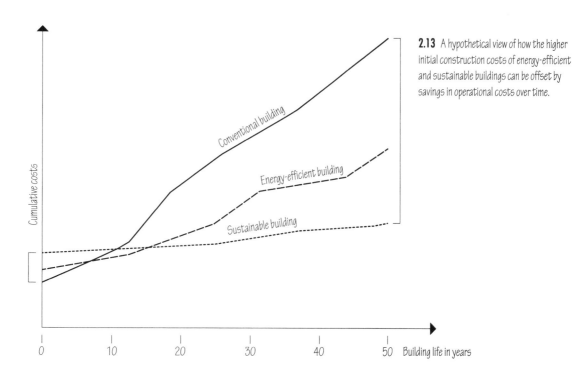

2.13 A hypothetical view of how the higher initial construction costs of energy-efficient and sustainable buildings can be offset by savings in operational costs over time.

Energy Modeling

As building designs are refined, it is relatively easy to examine trade-offs using energy models of proposed buildings. Tradeoffs of wall design, window design, building shape, heating system selection, and other schematic design parameters are readily prepared in less than a day. More advanced energy models, which can examine detailed tradeoffs of such systems as daylighting or energy controls, take longer to prepare and interpret, but are still often worthwhile when compared to the future costs of energy use over a building's life. There is no longer the need for speculation in refining building designs to achieve energy efficiency. Energy modeling should be regarded as essential for green building design.

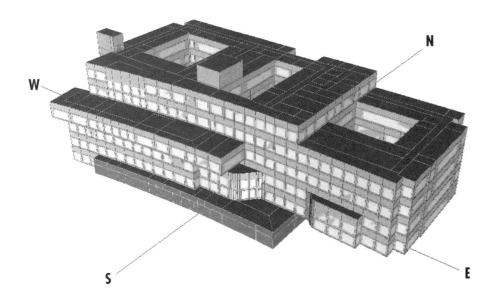

2.14 VA Mental Health and Research Complex, Seattle, Washington, Stantec Architecture and Consulting. Energy modeling uses computer software to analyze a building's numerous thermal components, including the materials of the walls and the rest of the building envelope; the size, shape, and orientation of the building; how the building is occupied and operated; the local climate; system performance; and energy use over time.

3
Codes, Standards, and Guidelines

A variety of green building codes, standards, and guidelines have been developed in recent years. Each of these reflects an invaluable commitment to protecting the environment and human health. Each reflects slightly differing views and values. Each has nudged the green building endeavor forward. And each, like all of we humans, is probably in some ways imperfect.

Green building codes, standards, and guidelines typically include provisions for site selection, water conservation, energy conservation, material selection, and indoor environmental quality. Provisions that are included in some but not all approaches include acoustics, safety and security, historical and cultural significance, and beauty.

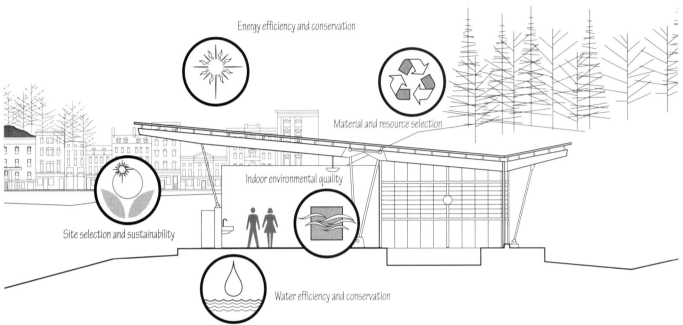

Energy efficiency and conservation

Material and resource selection

Indoor environmental quality

Site selection and sustainability

Water efficiency and conservation

3.01 Typical categories of green building provisions.

Many of these systems lay out a set of absolute requirements (prerequisites) as well as a separate set of best practices that may be traded in order to reach a threshold target of compliance. The metric for compliance is either a credit-based system or, in the case of energy conservation, a target energy-related metric. Implicit in this approach is a recognition that there are mandatory requirements for a green building as well as a set of optional requirements. The mandatory requirements represent the threshold that must be crossed to call a building green. To allow flexibility and balance while recognizing building uniqueness, the optional requirements are typically provided as a menu from which additional building improvements are chosen. The credits assigned to these items can be aggregated such that achieving enough of them enables the building to achieve green certification, or to rise to higher levels of green certification.

These credit systems have widely been found to motivate green building design. Perhaps appealing to some combination of the human tendency to self-regulate, to seek organized systems, to desire recognition, to document, and to enjoy competition, credit systems have become a major focus of green building design activity.

Energy and Atmosphere (33 Possible Points)

[ ] Prerequisite 1 Fundamental Commissioning & Verification (Required)

[ ] Prerequisite 2 Minimum Energy Performance (Required)

[ ] Prerequisite 3 Building-Level Energy Metering (Required)

[ ] Prerequisite 4 Fundamental Refrigerant Management (Required)

[ ] Credit 1 Enhanced Commissioning 6

[ ] Credit 2 Optimize Energy Performance 18

[ ] Credit 3 Advanced Energy Metering 1

[ ] Credit 4 Demand Response 2

[ ] Credit 5 Renewable Energy Production 3

[ ] Credit 6 Enhanced Refrigerant Management 1

[ ] Credit 7 Green Power & Carbon Offsets 2

3.02 Energy and Atmosphere, one of the environmental impact categories that the LEED 4 rating system addresses, has four prerequisites that are mandatory for participation but receive no points, as well as seven credits, which if satisfied, contribute toward the points necessary to achieve LEED certification.

This book recognizes the power of credit systems to advance the discussion, science, and art of green buildings. Rather than focus on credit system compliance, however, this book seeks instead to address strategies for designing green buildings, and on exploring some of the more vexing questions of what designing green buildings really means. We also seek to probe vulnerabilities in the credit systems and to suggest some ways in which buildings might be designed greener regardless of their value in the credits of green building codes, standards, and guidelines.

Codes

We start with what is perhaps a surprising inclusion among green codes, the *International Building Code* (IBC) and its associated codes, which form the basis for most construction code requirements in the United States. The IBC includes a broad number of green provisions, including requirements for energy conservation in the *International Energy Conservation Code*, requirements for ventilation in the *International Mechanical Code*, and requirements for water conservation. These various components, developed over the past two decades and informed perhaps initially by California's *Title 24* in 1978 and the *Model Energy Code* in 1983, form the predecessors of today's green building standards.

These building code requirements remain helpful references because, in many instances, they serve as the baseline for green building codes, standards, and guidelines. And, likely alone among green building requirements, the *International Building Code* happens to be the law in many jurisdictions. Any green building effort might at a minimum take advantage of the requirements of the building code and advocate for enforcement of its green provisions. The *International Building Code* and its ancillary codes are developed and maintained by the International Code Council.

More recently, the International Code Council released the *International Green Construction Code* in collaboration with the American Institute of Architects (AIA), the United States Green Building Council (USGBC), the American Society of Heating, Refrigerating and Air-Conditioning Engineers (ASHRAE), the Illuminating Engineering Society (IES), and ASTM International. This development captures a broad spectrum of green building requirements, is compatible with ICC's full series of building codes, and provides an enforceable code, ready for local adoption.

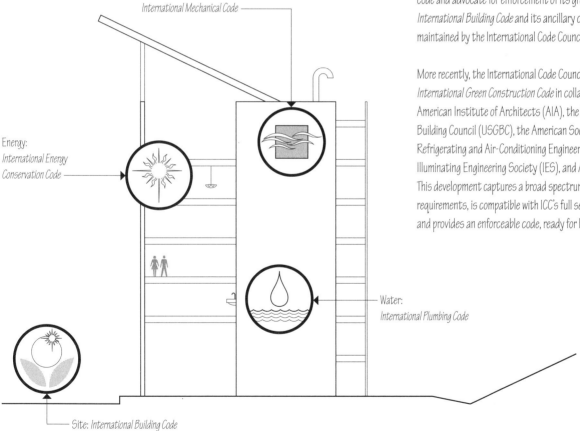

Indoor environmental quality:
International Mechanical Code

Energy:
International Energy Conservation Code

Water:
International Plumbing Code

Site: *International Building Code*

3.03 The *International Building Code* as a Green Building Code.

Standards

The Leadership in Energy and Environmental Design (LEED®) green building certification program, has taken a prominent position among green building standards, first in the United States and increasingly around the world. Its five main credit areas—sustainable sites, water efficiency, energy and atmosphere, materials and resources, and indoor environmental quality—have become part of the lexicon of green building design. The U.S. Green Building Council (USGBC) developed the rating system as a consensus among its members—federal/state/local agencies, suppliers, architects, engineers, contractors, and building owners—and is continually being evaluated and refined in response to new information and feedback. In July 2003 Canada obtained a license from the USGBC to adapt the LEED rating system to Canadian circumstances.

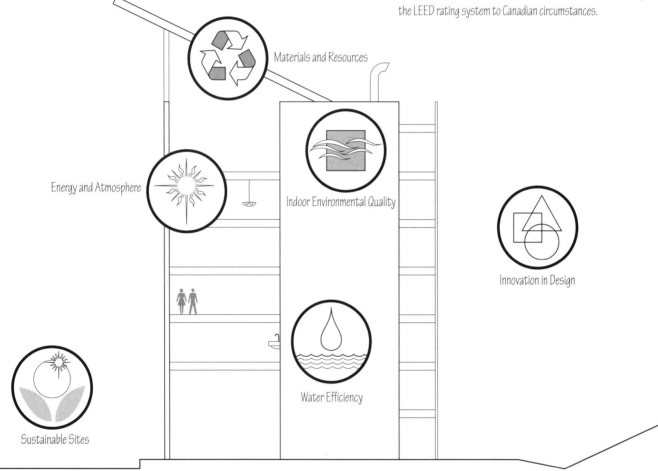

Materials and Resources

Energy and Atmosphere

Indoor Environmental Quality

Innovation in Design

Water Efficiency

Sustainable Sites

3.04 Core requirement areas of the LEED Green Building Certification Program.

LEED's expansion from a program for new construction to programs for existing buildings, neighborhoods, developer-driven core-and-shell buildings, tenant-driven interiors, and such sector-specific programs as homes, schools, healthcare, and retail, give the program unusual breadth and reach.

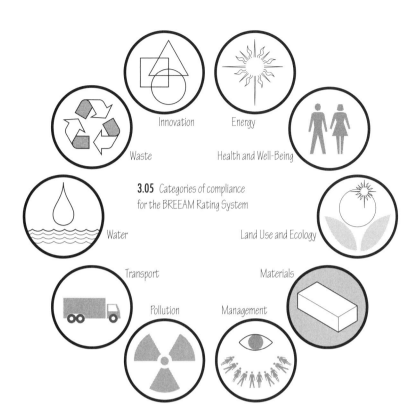

3.05 Categories of compliance for the BREEAM Rating System

The Building Research Environmental Assessment Method (BREEAM) is a system established in the United Kingdom by the Building Research Establishment (BRE) for measuring and rating the sustainability and environmental performance of nondomestic buildings in the following areas: management, health and well-being, energy, transport, water, material and waste, land use and ecology, and pollution. The rating scale for BREEAM buildings includes certifications of Pass, Good, Very Good, Excellent, and Outstanding. Launched in 1990, it is one of the oldest and most widely adopted green rating systems. Extensively used in Europe, BREEAM has also been implemented in construction around the world. Several BREEAM approaches are referenced in the LEED rating system and in other codes, guidelines, and standards.

Another green standard is the *Standard for the Design of High-Performance Green Buildings Except Low-Rise Residential Buildings*, developed by ASHRAE in conjunction with the USGBC and the Illuminating Engineering Society (IES) and formally referenced as ANSI/ASHRAE/USGBC/IES Standard 189.1. The standard provides simple compliance options and more flexible performance options, developed in model code language so that it can be readily adopted by federal, state, and local authorities. The standard itself is not a design guide and is intended to complement rather than compete with current green building rating systems. Although the standard has a particular focus on energy conservation, it also sets minimum requirements for sustainable sites; water use efficiency; indoor environmental quality; impact on the atmosphere, materials and resources; and construction and operations plans.

Green Globes is an online environmental rating and certification system for commercial buildings that is promoted as an affordable and streamlined alternative to the LEED rating system. The Green Globes system focuses on the life-cycle assessment of building design, operation, and management in seven areas: project management; site; energy; water; resources, building materials, and waste; emissions and effluents; and indoor environment. Green Globes originated from the BREEAM system but is now developed in Canada by the Building Owners and Managers Association (BOMA) of Canada and in the United States by the Green Building Initiative (GBI).

3.06 Trademarked logo of the Green Globes online environmental rating and certification system.

Passivhaus (Passive House) is a standard developed in Europe to maximize a building's energy efficiency and reduce its ecological footprint. While its name implies application primarily in the residential sector, the principles of the Passivhaus standard can also be applied to commercial, industrial, and public buildings. The strength of the Passivhaus standard lies in the simplicity of its approach: Produce ultra-low-energy buildings by combining excellent thermal performance and airtightness with a heat-recovery ventilation system that supplies fresh air for indoor environmental quality. Its bold goal of extremely low energy use places the Passivhaus standard squarely within the current urgency to reduce greenhouse gas emissions. The standard contains both a predictive design goal—a maximum energy demand of 120 kWh per square meter (11.1 kWh per square foot)—and an actual performance goal of an infiltration rate no greater than 0.60 air changes per hour @ 50 Pascals. The latter translates into a requirement that construction be meticulously detailed to limit infiltration, recognizing the unique position of infiltration in energy use and the vulnerability of construction to infiltration.

The Passivhaus standard requires very low levels of air leakage, very high levels of thermal insulation with minimal thermal bridges, and windows having a very low U-factor. To meet the standard, a building must have:

- A maximum annual cooling energy use of 15 kWh per square meter (1.39 kWh per square foot);
- A maximum annual heating energy use of 15 kWh per square meter (1.39 kWh per square foot);
- A maximum energy use for all purposes of 120 kWh per square meter (11.1 kWh per square foot); and
- An infiltration rate no greater than 0.60 air changes per hour @ 50 Pascals.

Thermal comfort is achieved through the use of the following measures:

- High levels of insulation with minimal thermal bridges
- Passive solar gains and internal heat sources
- Excellent level of airtightness
- Good indoor air quality, as provided by a whole-house mechanical ventilation system with highly efficient heat recovery

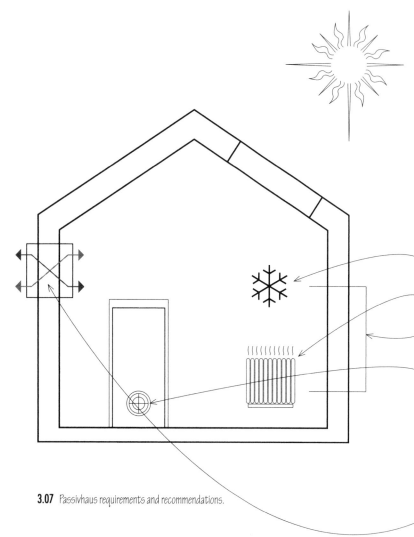

3.07 Passivhaus requirements and recommendations.

A standard used widely for the design of homes is the Mortgage Industry National Home Energy Rating Systems Standard, developed by the Residential Energy Services Network (RESNET) and the National Association of State Energy Officials. Most commonly referred to as the HERS rating system, the standard has gained widespread adoption and use in the United States. The HERS rating system has a focus on energy conservation, but retains a variety of requirements for indoor environmental quality, specifically in the areas of humidity control, ventilation, and combustion appliance safety. The HERS rating system also directs significant attention to quality assurance by including extensive requirements for third-party involvement, accreditation of third-party professionals, energy prediction validation, and inspection and testing of the as-built home. HERS is used as a reference standard for the energy requirements of the LEED for Homes rating system.

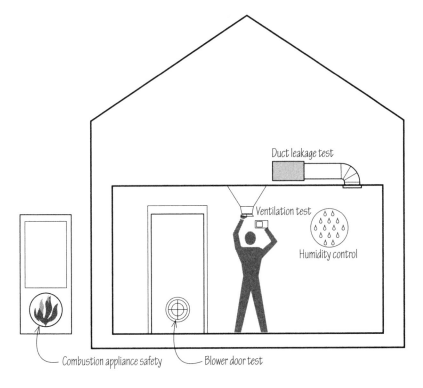

Duct leakage test

Ventilation test

Humidity control

Accredited rater using certified software and test methods

Combustion appliance safety

Blower door test

3.08 HERS rating system requirements.

A newer standard for sustainable planning, design, and construction is the Living Building Challenge, created and maintained by the International Living Future Institute for development at all scales, from buildings to infrastructure, landscapes, and neighborhoods. The *Living Building Challenge* differentiates itself by advocating for net-zero energy use, net-zero water use, and fully onsite waste processing over a minimum of 12 months of continuous occupancy. The standard also contains bold requirements in other green building areas, such as site selection and preservation, material selection, and health. Of note is the inclusion of beauty and equity as major areas of green building design.

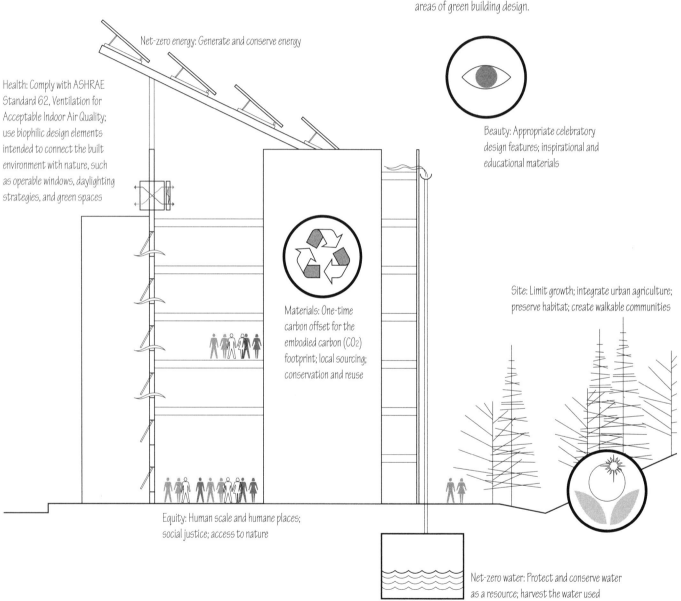

Net-zero energy: Generate and conserve energy

Health: Comply with ASHRAE Standard 62, Ventilation for Acceptable Indoor Air Quality; use biophilic design elements intended to connect the built environment with nature, such as operable windows, daylighting strategies, and green spaces

Beauty: Appropriate celebratory design features; inspirational and educational materials

Materials: One-time carbon offset for the embodied carbon (CO_2) footprint; local sourcing; conservation and reuse

Site: Limit growth; integrate urban agriculture; preserve habitat; create walkable communities

Equity: Human scale and humane places; social justice; access to nature

Net-zero water: Protect and conserve water as a resource; harvest the water used

3.09 *Goals of the Living Building Challenge.*

Guidelines

A number of green building guidelines have been developed by federal and state agencies, universities, nongovernmental organizations, private companies, and even local municipalities.

An example of a green guideline is the *Residential Environmental Guidelines*, developed by the Hugh L. Carey Battery Park City Authority in New York City, written in 1999 and first published in 2000. Like the LEED certification program, the guidelines address energy efficiency, enhanced indoor environmental quality, conserving materials and resources, water conservation, and site management. A section on education, operations, and maintenance is also included.

Some guidelines are limited to a specific area of green design. An example is the Sustainable Sites Initiative, developed by the American Society of Landscape Architects (ASLA), the Lady Bird Johnson Wildflower Center at The University of Texas at Austin, and the United States Botanic Garden. Modeled on the LEED certification program, these guidelines more deeply explore environmentally sensitive sites, addressing the benefits of various ecosystem services such as pollination, articulating a strong host of principles for green sites, and then laying out an extensive set of best practices through the usual set of prerequisites and credits in a scoring system.

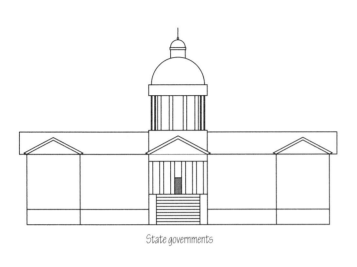
State governments

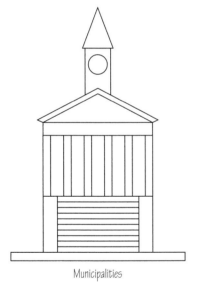
Municipalities

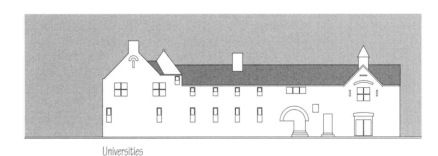
Universities

Developments

3.10 Entities using customized green building guidelines.

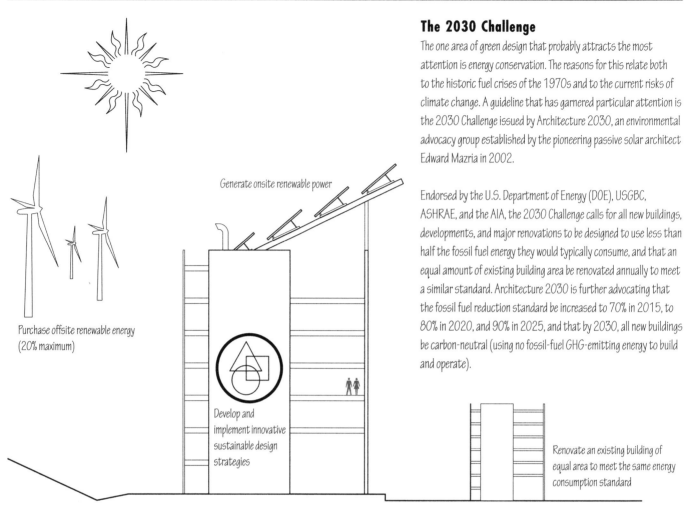

The 2030 Challenge

The one area of green design that probably attracts the most attention is energy conservation. The reasons for this relate both to the historic fuel crises of the 1970s and to the current risks of climate change. A guideline that has garnered particular attention is the 2030 Challenge issued by Architecture 2030, an environmental advocacy group established by the pioneering passive solar architect Edward Mazria in 2002.

Endorsed by the U.S. Department of Energy (DOE), USGBC, ASHRAE, and the AIA, the 2030 Challenge calls for all new buildings, developments, and major renovations to be designed to use less than half the fossil fuel energy they would typically consume, and that an equal amount of existing building area be renovated annually to meet a similar standard. Architecture 2030 is further advocating that the fossil fuel reduction standard be increased to 70% in 2015, to 80% in 2020, and 90% in 2025, and that by 2030, all new buildings be carbon-neutral (using no fossil-fuel GHG-emitting energy to build and operate).

Generate onsite renewable power

Purchase offsite renewable energy (20% maximum)

Develop and implement innovative sustainable design strategies

Renovate an existing building of equal area to meet the same energy consumption standard

Design new buildings and developments that use less than half the fossil fuel energy they would typically consume

3.11 Strategies for slowing and eventually reversing the growth rate of greenhouse gas emissions from the burning of fossil fuels.

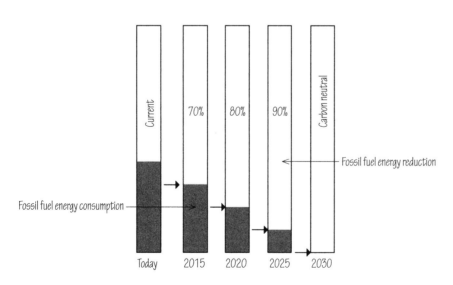

Fossil fuel energy reduction

Fossil fuel energy consumption

Current   70%   80%   90%   Carbon neutral

Today   2015   2020   2025   2030

3.12 Targets set by the 2030 Challenge.

4
Community and Site

The community in which we build, and the site on which we build, can inform and influence every aspect of the building we choose to build.

Primary goals in community and site selection for green buildings include protecting sensitive sites, preserving undeveloped sites, restoring and reusing previously developed sites, reducing impact on flora and fauna, promoting connection to community, and minimizing transportation impacts both on the environment and energy use.

Implicit in these goals is a deep reverence for the natural and the wild and the search for a balance between developed and undeveloped areas, rather than viewing natural areas merely as resources for human settlement. At the same time, we have to pay attention to reducing light pollution, minimizing construction waste, managing storm water, and curtailing site water use.

Interestingly, at this early phase of a project, options are available to substantially reduce energy and water use, as well as improve indoor environmental quality inside the future building itself. These options, which have an impact on what happens inside a building by what is done outside, will be explored in some detail and form the beginning of a theme that will run throughout this book.

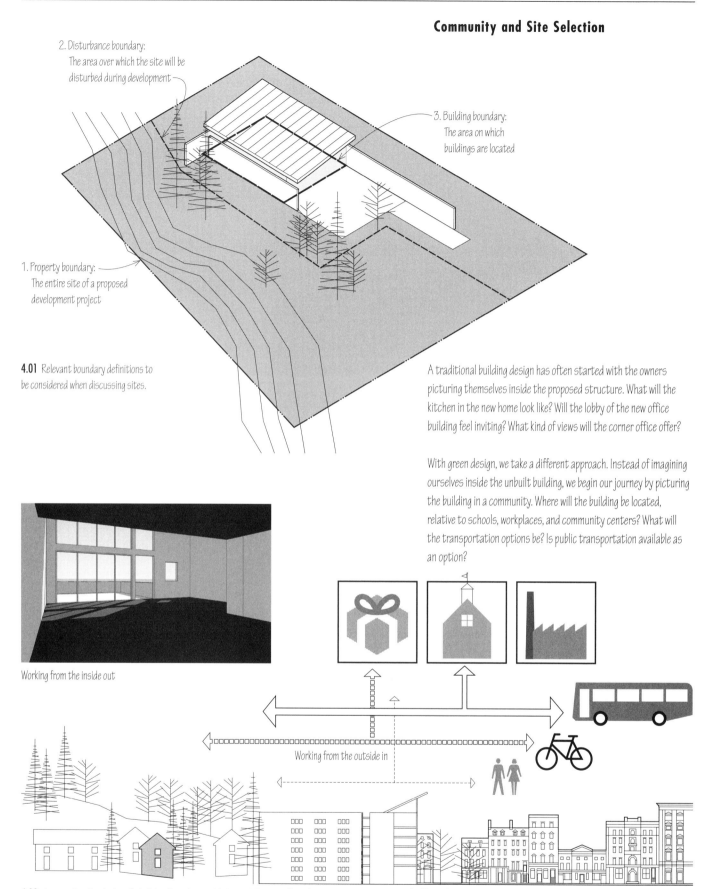

2. Disturbance boundary:
The area over which the site will be disturbed during development

3. Building boundary:
The area on which buildings are located

1. Property boundary:
The entire site of a proposed development project

4.01 Relevant boundary definitions to be considered when discussing sites.

A traditional building design has often started with the owners picturing themselves inside the proposed structure. What will the kitchen in the new home look like? Will the lobby of the new office building feel inviting? What kind of views will the corner office offer?

With green design, we take a different approach. Instead of imagining ourselves inside the unbuilt building, we begin our journey by picturing the building in a community. Where will the building be located, relative to schools, workplaces, and community centers? What will the transportation options be? Is public transportation available as an option?

Working from the inside out

Working from the outside in

4.02 Approaching the design of a building from the outside in—with a view of its place in a community—instead of from the inside out

As we seek to picture the building in a community, we ask whether renovating a derelict building downtown might be a better option than building on an undeveloped rural site. We ask whether an infill site is available in an urban setting. Or we ask whether a site is available that is close to public transportation, even if in a suburban or rural location. We might check with our local planning department to learn whether any community developments are under way that might mitigate the environmental impact of the new construction. Instead of thinking as individuals, we try to think as a community.

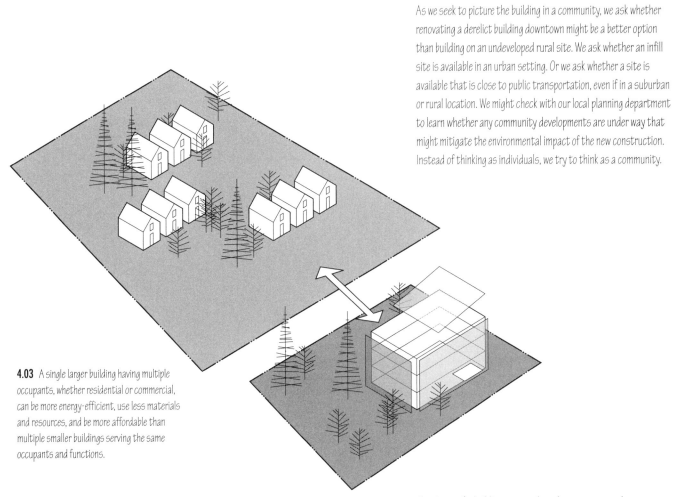

4.03 A single larger building having multiple occupants, whether residential or commercial, can be more energy-efficient, use less materials and resources, and be more affordable than multiple smaller buildings serving the same occupants and functions.

Residents of a building are not the only energy users whose consumption depends on the building's location. The energy use of people providing delivery and other services also varies, depending on the distance of a building from community and work centers. Also, the energy requirements for both pumping water and transporting electricity increase with buildings located farther from a centralized community.

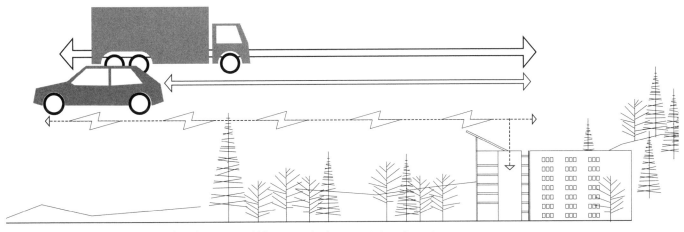

4.04 Energy is expended for transportation—for both commuting and deliveries—and utilities transmission to distant sites.

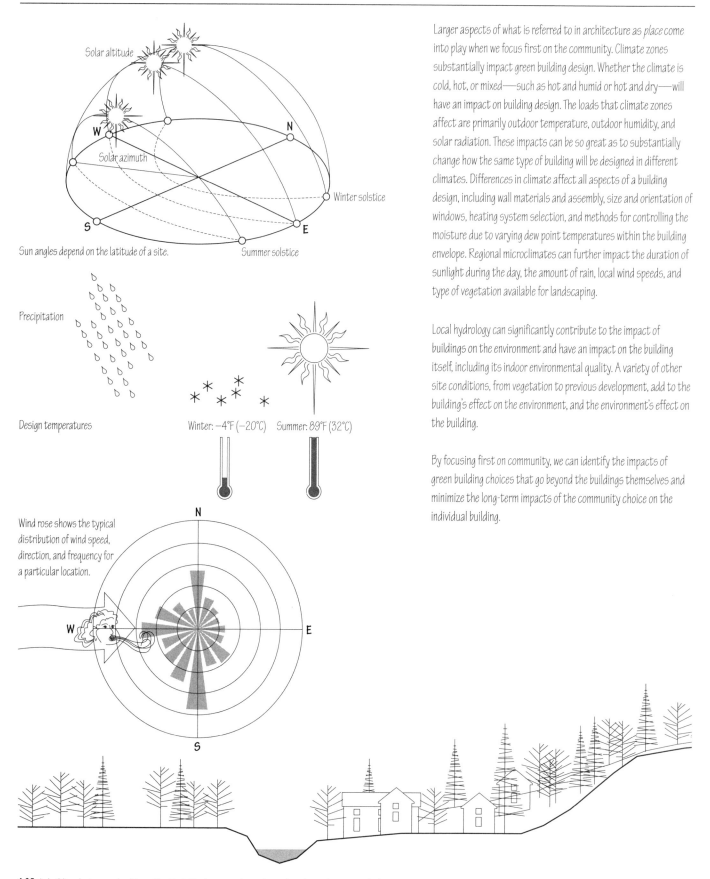

Solar altitude

Solar azimuth

W

N

Winter solstice

S

E

Summer solstice

Sun angles depend on the latitude of a site.

Precipitation

Design temperatures

Winter: −4°F (−20°C)   Summer: 89°F (32°C)

N

Wind rose shows the typical distribution of wind speed, direction, and frequency for a particular location.

W

E

S

Larger aspects of what is referred to in architecture as *place* come into play when we focus first on the community. Climate zones substantially impact green building design. Whether the climate is cold, hot, or mixed—such as hot and humid or hot and dry—will have an impact on building design. The loads that climate zones affect are primarily outdoor temperature, outdoor humidity, and solar radiation. These impacts can be so great as to substantially change how the same type of building will be designed in different climates. Differences in climate affect all aspects of a building design, including wall materials and assembly, size and orientation of windows, heating system selection, and methods for controlling the moisture due to varying dew point temperatures within the building envelope. Regional microclimates can further impact the duration of sunlight during the day, the amount of rain, local wind speeds, and type of vegetation available for landscaping.

Local hydrology can significantly contribute to the impact of buildings on the environment and have an impact on the building itself, including its indoor environmental quality. A variety of other site conditions, from vegetation to previous development, add to the building's effect on the environment, and the environment's effect on the building.

By focusing first on community, we can identify the impacts of green building choices that go beyond the buildings themselves and minimize the long-term impacts of the community choice on the individual building.

4.05 In building design, we should consider the latitude, geography, and prevailing climate for a particular location and site.

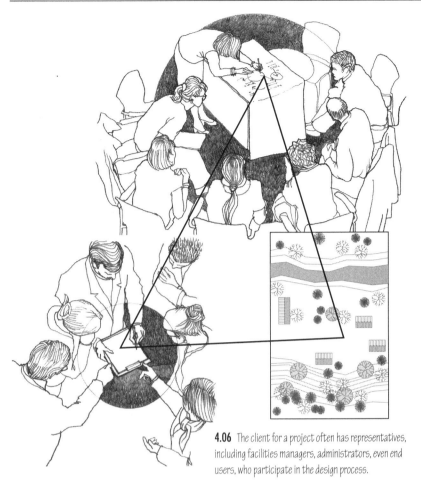

At this early juncture, the owner's goals are established. The Owner's Project Requirements document, described in more detail in Chapter 18, Quality in Green Design and Construction, is written and agreed upon by all involved. Substantial gains in green design can be made by clearly identifying the owner's requirements in the initial phase of the design process. Developing a building is often a new experience for many owners and the process becomes a learning experience that many owners will never forget, as well as a teaching opportunity for design professionals and builders. This is all the more so with green buildings, for which choices and tradeoffs abound and for which clarifying the owner's project requirements may well be an exercise in clarifying the owner's values. There is no better time to perform this clarification than during the first discussions of community and site selection.

4.06 The client for a project often has representatives, including facilities managers, administrators, even end users, who participate in the design process.

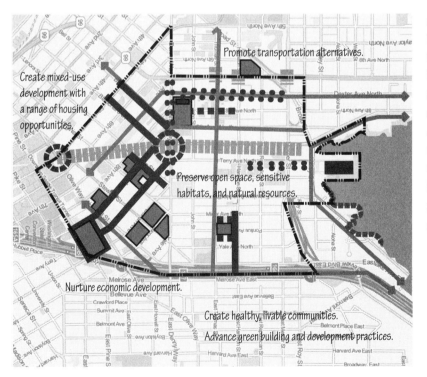

A larger discussion extends the assessment of community and site to neighborhoods and towns, and green approaches to enhancing these connections. These topics are beyond the scope of this book, but are highly relevant to the choice of a building-specific site. The theory of smart growth focuses on community-centered development with a strong sustainable underpinning. LEED has developed a green rating system for neighborhoods, addressing a variety of green features, such as compactness, connectivity, and walkable streets. Many of these issues relate closely to a specific building's choices, needs, and potential impacts around community and site, and have great value in informing the choices of any specific green building project.

4.07 The LEED Rating System for Neighborhood Development integrates principles of smart growth, urbanism, and green building.

Old growth forests and parklands

Habitats of endangered species

Wetlands and water bodies

4.08 Areas that qualify as sensitive sites.

Protection of Sensitive Sites

Green building projects give priority to protecting sensitive sites. Definitions of sensitive sites are generally governed by federal statute or regulation and typically include such areas as prime farmland, parkland, flood hazard areas, habitat for endangered or threatened species, primary dunes, old-growth forests, wetlands, other water bodies, and conservation areas.

The protection of sensitive sites starts with an inventory of the site prior to site selection and continues with documentation of sensitive site characteristics prior to starting work on a site. Protection means not developing in these areas as well as within buffer zones that provide an additional layer of protection. Development includes the construction not only of buildings but also roads, parking, and other infrastructure.

Exceptions are often made for construction that specifically supports or relates to the subject area. For example, in a conservation area, a building might be allowed for a purpose that relates to the conservation area as determined by the body or agency that so designated the area. Sometimes this allowance is for teaching or interpretive activities; at other times, the exception is limited to buildings that actively support the protection of the area. In the case of parkland, development is occasionally allowable if the developed area is replaced with equal or greater parkland, which typically must be adjacent to the property boundary.

In the United States, resources for identifying sensitive sites include surveys of prime farmland by the U.S. Department of Agriculture (USDA), flood plain information maintained by the Federal Emergency Management Agency (FEMA), habitat inventories for threatened and endangered species provided by the Fish and Wildlife Service (FWS), and guidelines for identifying wetlands by the U.S. Army Corps of Engineers.

4.09 Exceptions may allow the housing of teaching, interpretive, or conservation activities in protected areas.

Preservation and Restoration

Greenfields are defined as previously undeveloped areas. *Brownfields* are abandoned or underused industrial and commercial facilities that have actual or perceived levels of environmental contamination. *Greyfields* are previously developed areas that are not contaminated, do not require remediation, but have a visible residue of development and infrastructure, such as vacant buildings, utilities, and asphalt. Sites that have been previously developed but are neither known greyfields nor brownfields are loosely referred to as previously developed sites. It is important to note that previously cleared, farmed, or forested lands are typically regarded as greenfields.

In green building development, restoration and reuse of brownfield sites is regarded positively because it accomplishes two distinct goals. First, it prevents development of greenfields or otherwise sensitive areas; secondly, the development process includes remediation of any environmental contamination. Similarly, development on greyfield sites and other previously developed sites is encouraged.

To preserve undeveloped areas, development of greenfields is discouraged. The degree to which greenfield development is discouraged varies in different codes and standards and goes to the heart of the green building discussion. LEED discourages greenfield development indirectly, by conversely encouraging brownfield redevelopment, promoting urban density, and limiting development on greenfields to areas close to driveways, parking, and the building itself. The International Green Construction Code provides for any adopting jurisdiction to simply ban any development on greenfields. The Living Building Challenge does not allow any greenfield development.

The suggestion that greenfield development is something that we might not only discourage but even disallow raises maybe the largest site question of all: Going forward, are we going to build anywhere other than where we have built before?

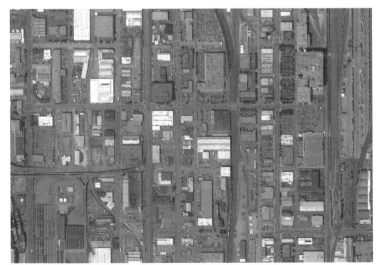

Greenfield

Greyfield

Brownfield

4.10 *Classification of development sites.*

Protection of Natural Features

Where development is allowed on greenfield sites, site disturbance should be minimized. Consensus seems to be emerging to limit such disturbance to within 40 feet (12 meters) of buildings and 15 feet (4.5 meters) of walkways and roads, although various codes and standards vary or supplement these requirements.

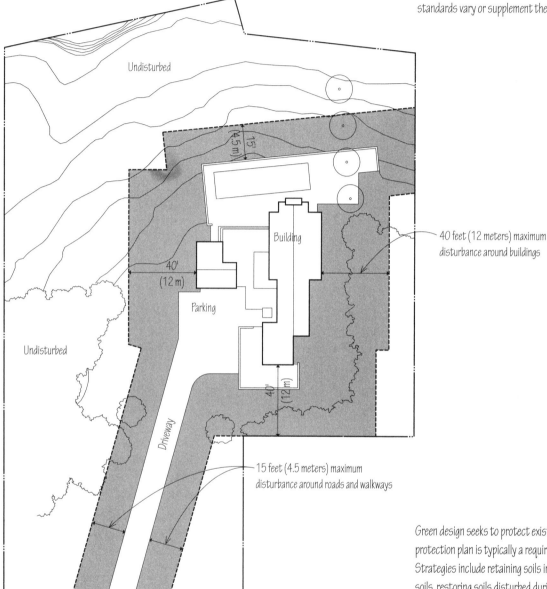

Undisturbed

15' (4.5 m)

Building

40' (12 m)

Parking

Undisturbed

40' (12 m)

Driveway

40 feet (12 meters) maximum disturbance around buildings

15 feet (4.5 meters) maximum disturbance around roads and walkways

4.11 Limiting site disturbances on greenfield sites.

Green design seeks to protect existing soil conditions. A written soil protection plan is typically a requirement for green building projects. Strategies include retaining soils in place, stockpiling and reusing soils, restoring soils disturbed during construction, revegetation of disturbed and restored soils, careful planning of construction staging and parking areas, and measures to prevent soil runoff or wind erosion during construction. Topsoil that is required to be brought onto a site should not originate in sensitive areas.

Protection of vegetation and the re-introduction of plant life are also desirable on the basis of their carbon-absorbing characteristics.

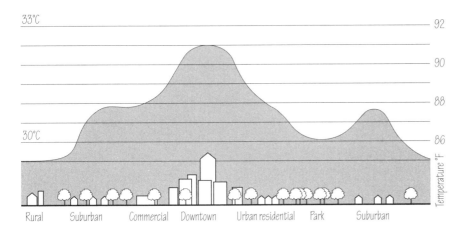

4.12 Heat islands are created by the elevated temperatures from buildings and hardscape, particularly in urban areas. Source: EPA.

The *heat island effect* refers to the absorption and retention of incoming solar radiation by the buildings and hardscape of urban areas. When this heat is released into the surrounding atmosphere, relatively distinct *heat islands* can be formed, having higher temperatures than their rural surroundings. The heat island effect can be exacerbated by the energy use of buildings and their interfering with the ability of the wind to carry away heat.

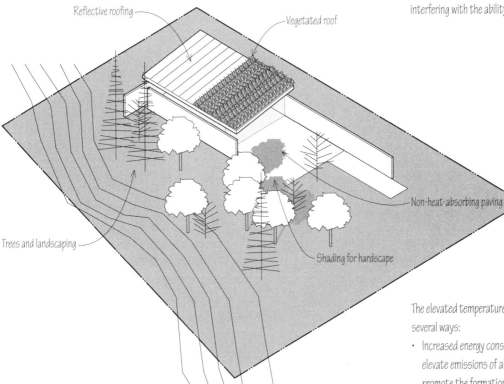

4.13 Some ways to mitigate the heat island effect include using light-colored roofing having a high solar reflectance and installing green roofs. Nonroof options include paving with non-heat-absorbing materials, and planting trees and vegetation to shade parking surfaces and other hardscape.

The elevated temperatures of heat islands can affect a community in several ways:

· Increased energy consumption for cooling during the summer can elevate emissions of air pollutants and greenhouse gases, and promote the formation of ground-level ozone.

· Elevated temperatures can contribute to heat exhaustion and heat-related mortality.

· The heated runoff from storm sewers can raise the water temperatures of streams, rivers, ponds, and lakes, stressing aquatic ecosystems.

Site Waste Management

In preparing a site for construction, much waste is generated, often before construction materials have even been brought onsite. Site waste includes debris such as rocks, soil, and vegetation. Green building projects should prevent such debris from being transported to landfills or to sensitive sites. Strategies include reusing materials onsite and recycling debris offsite. Similarly, hazardous debris needs to be handled in an environmentally sensitive manner. A green building project should have a plan for managing building site waste, preferably one that is integrated with the construction materials waste management plan, to be discussed later.

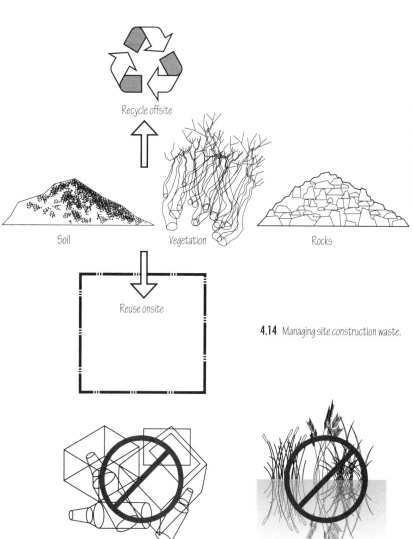

Recycle offsite

Soil   Vegetation   Rocks

Reuse onsite

4.14 Managing site construction waste.

Avoid: Moving debris to landfills

Moving debris to sensitive sites such as wetlands

Average Carbon Emissions in the United States

Mode of Transportation	Pounds of CO_2 per Passenger Mile
Cars (single occupancy)	0.96
Bus	0.65
Commuter rail	0.35
Bicycle, walking	0.00

4.15 Different forms of transportation emit varying levels of carbon emissions.

Transportation Issues

Beyond site selection, which impacts available forms of transportation and ultimately transportation energy use and pollution, further decisions can be made to promote greener forms of transportation.

Careful site planning incorporates facilities that encourage less-polluting modes of transportation. Examples include installing bicycle racks, incorporating facilities for storing and covering bicycles, and providing pedestrian paths for access. Because the safety of pedestrians and bicyclists fosters walking and biking, providing sidewalks, dedicated bicycle lanes, and onsite traffic signs are highly desirable.

LEED's encouragement of bicycling, through its credit for bicycle racks, includes what may be a quintessential green standard requirement: The credit is only given if the building includes showers and changing facilities to allow commuting bicyclists a chance to wash and freshen up after biking.

Efficient motor-vehicle transportation can be promoted by providing preferred parking for high-efficiency vehicles, vehicles serving carpools, low-emitting vehicles, or small vehicles. Electric charging stations can support the use of electric vehicles.

Proximity to public transportation also promotes efficient transportation, as does limiting the number of parking spaces, which has the additional benefit of reducing the amount of paving on the site.

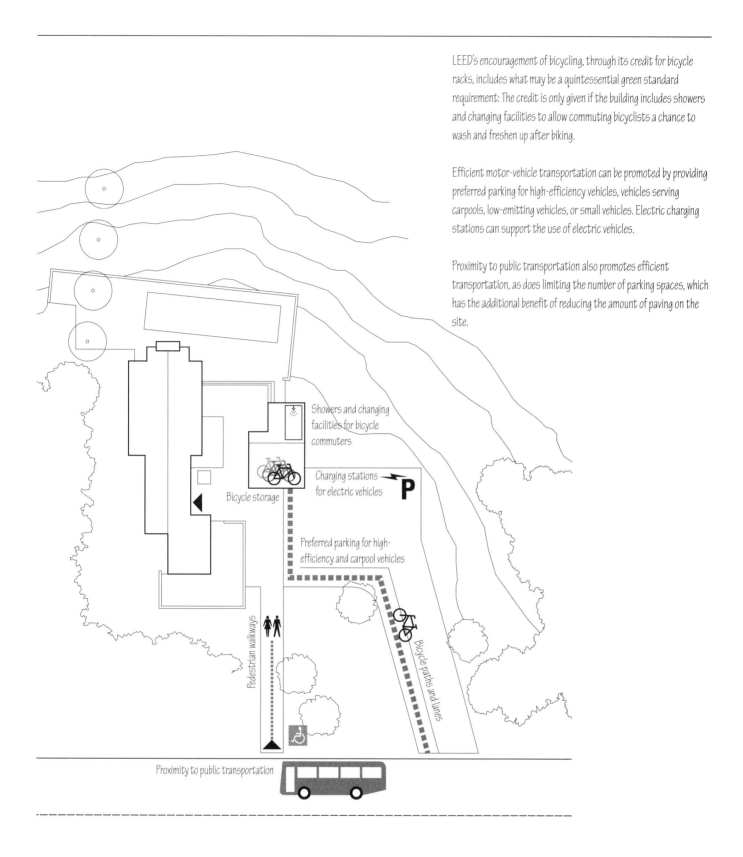

Showers and changing facilities for bicycle commuters

Charging stations for electric vehicles

P

Bicycle storage

Preferred parking for high-efficiency and carpool vehicles

Pedestrian walkways

Bicycle paths and lanes

Proximity to public transportation

4.16 Means of encouraging less-polluting modes of transportation.

Minimizing Light Pollution

Light pollution is the introduction of artificial light into the outdoor environment. Its impacts are many. Light pollution disrupts natural diurnal patterns of light and dark and the rhythms of life to which plants, animals, and humans have adapted, interrupting circadian sleep cycles, interfering with normal plant growth, and disturbing the habitat of nocturnal wildlife.

Light pollution interferes with the ability to view and observe the night sky, stars, and planets. It causes light trespass, which is the nuisance spillage of light from one property onto another, risking conflict between neighbors. It can cause safety hazards, such as glare and temporary blindness, for drivers. Light pollution wastes energy, causing associated adverse environmental and economic impacts.

Night lighting for surveillance can actually increase security risks. Although exterior lighting can create a perception of safety, research has shown that night lighting might not lower crime levels. Lights left on all night provide no signal of illegal activity, whereas lighting turned on by motion sensors can serve as just such a signal, and can possibly deter intruders. Exterior lights can also cause glare in some areas and shadows in others, which can mask intruder access.

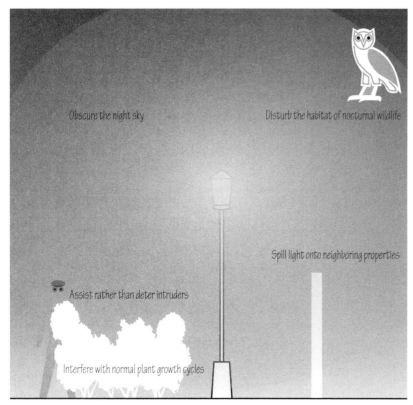

Obscure the night sky

Disturb the habitat of nocturnal wildlife

Spill light onto neighboring properties

Assist rather than deter intruders

Interfere with normal plant growth cycles

4.17 Night lighting can impact the outdoor environment in several ways.

Strategies to reduce or eliminate light pollution include selecting light fixtures that minimize spillage and focus light downward rather than outward and upward into the sky. A variety of other design choices can also reduce light pollution, such as specifying pathway lighting instead of higher pole-mounted area lighting; using pole-mounted lighting instead of wall-mounted lighting; locating outdoor amenities, such as parking and outbuildings, closer together and nearer to the main buildings they serve; designing lower levels of lighting and eliminating uplighting; and specifying such controls as motion sensors that keep exterior lights off most of the time. Installation strategies include aiming light fixtures downward and commissioning outdoor lighting controls, such as delay settings for motion sensors and timer schedules. Another option is to eliminate exterior lighting wherever possible.

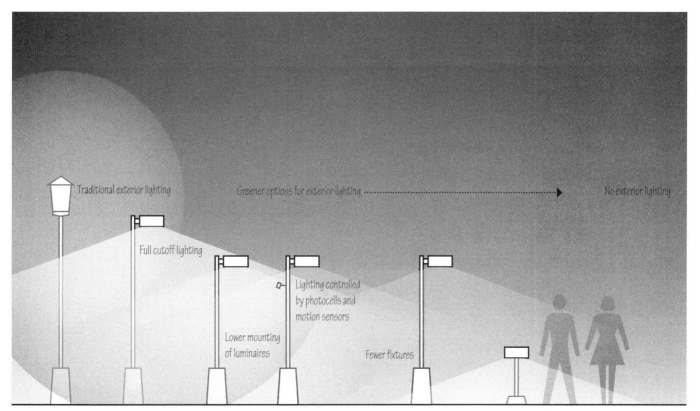

4.18 Design options for mitigating the effects of night lighting.

Traditional exterior lighting

Greener options for exterior lighting ····················▶

No exterior lighting

Full cutoff lighting

Lighting controlled by photocells and motion sensors

Lower mounting of luminaires

Fewer fixtures

Accent lighting of pathways

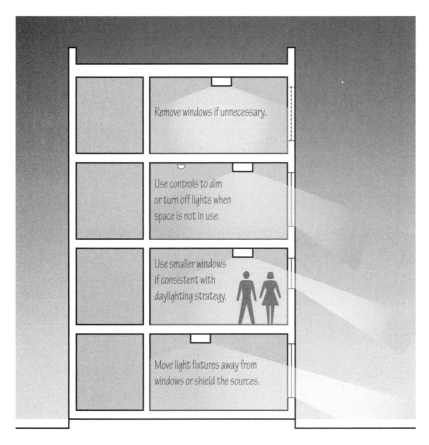

Remove windows if unnecessary.

Use controls to dim or turn off lights when space is not in use.

Use smaller windows if consistent with daylighting strategy.

Move light fixtures away from windows or shield the sources.

A related issue is spillage of light from the indoors to the outdoors. Solutions to this problem include installing lighting controls to turn lights off when not needed at night; reducing light levels indoors during late night hours; eliminating windows in spaces not requiring them, such as stairwells and utility areas; reducing window size in areas where larger windows are not needed; adjusting the relative location of lights and windows; reducing lighting near windows; shielding light fixtures; and avoiding orienting lights toward the outdoors.

4.19 Ways to reduce the spillage of light from the interior spaces of a building to the outdoors

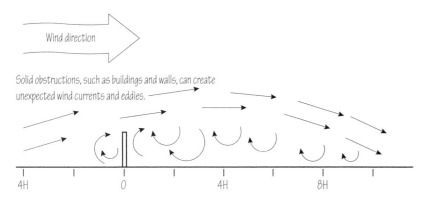

Wind direction

Solid obstructions, such as buildings and walls, can create unexpected wind currents and eddies.

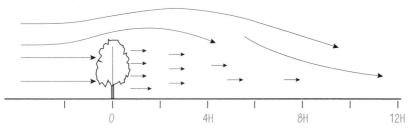

4H   0   4H   8H

Porous obstructions, such as trees and some fencing, can create less pressure differential, resulting in a large wind shadow on the leeward side of the screen.

0   4H   8H   12H

4.20 Trees, structures, fencing, and other forms of shielding help reduce wind velocity downwind of the barriers. Maximum wind reduction occurs in a range of 5 to 8 times the height of the screen. H = height of barrier.

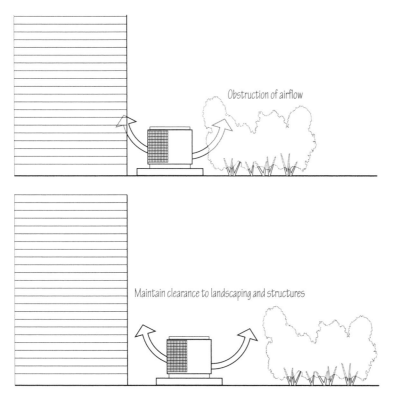

Obstruction of airflow

Maintain clearance to landscaping and structures

4.21 Vegetation, walls, and other obstructions to airflow around heat pumps and air-conditioner condensing units increase energy use.

Site Strategies and Energy Use

Site selection can have a significant effect on energy use. An unprotected building on an exposed hilltop will use more energy than a building sheltered by trees or adjacent buildings. This is because wind carries heat away from a building in the winter and forces hot outside air into the building in the summer. A computer simulation of an exposed building compared to a well-shielded building showed a 12% reduction in energy use. A study of the use of trees to shield office buildings in Scotland showed over 4% annual savings in heating energy.

In addition to trees, shielding from the wind can be accomplished with strategic placement relative to adjacent buildings, garages, sheds, fencing, retaining walls, grading, bushes, and shrubbery.

Likewise, shielding buildings from the sun with deciduous trees reduces solar gain in the summer while allowing solar gain in the winter. A variety of studies have estimated cooling savings as high as 18%, depending on how many trees are planted and where, with additional savings in heating due to protection from the wind.

Site planning does not only relate to landscaping and natural features. Buildings often require exterior equipment on the site, such as air-conditioning condensers, cooling towers, and pad-mounted transformers.

Unlike buildings, exterior air-conditioning and heat pump units, cooling towers, and transformers operate more efficiently when not blocked by vegetation or structures.

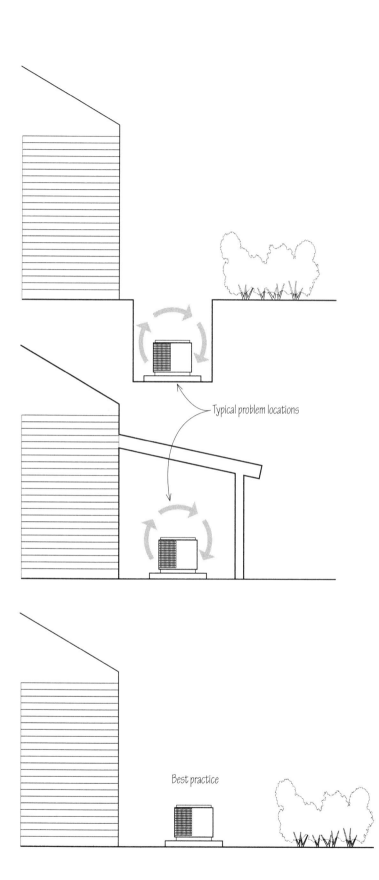

Typical problem locations

Best practice

The issue is critical for air-conditioners and even more so if the systems are also heat pumps that provide heating to the building as well. There are three distinct risks, any one of which can cause the system's energy use to rise by 20% or more:

· Air blockage by vegetation or other obstructions
· Contamination of the heat exchangers by dust or pollen
· Recirculation of exhausted air

The first two risks reduce airflow and therefore reduce heat transfer. This reduced airflow increases the refrigerant pressure against which the compressor must work, thereby increasing the electricity used. In well-intentioned attempts to conceal outdoor units, the units are often located too close to buildings or are surrounded by shrubbery. The bushes grow, and the heat exchangers, over time, are covered in leaves, resulting in a substantial increase in electricity consumption. Clearance between these units and buildings or vegetation prevents these problems. Locating a hose bib close to these units facilitates cleaning.

The third risk is different, but the result is the same. As an air-conditioning condenser rejects indoor heat to the outside air stream, the air leaving the condenser is hot. When operating in heating mode, the opposite happens with a heat pump—as the outdoor unit draws heat from the outside air to deliver the heat indoors, the air leaving the outdoor unit is cold. If this air recirculates and re-enters the condenser, while either cooling or heating, the power consumption rises significantly. Locating an outdoor unit in an enclosed or partially enclosed location, such as below a porch, in a stairwell, or on an enclosed patio, will cause this air recirculation and its associated high energy use.

4.22 Heat pumps and air-conditioner condensing units should not be located where outgoing air can recirculate back into the units, which can substantially increase energy use.

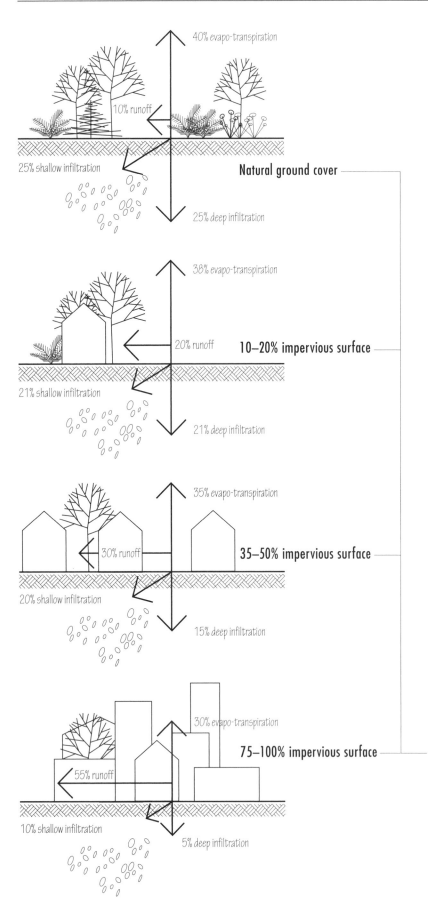

40% evapo-transpiration

10% runoff

25% shallow infiltration

25% deep infiltration

Natural ground cover

38% evapo-transpiration

20% runoff

21% shallow infiltration

21% deep infiltration

10–20% impervious surface

35% evapo-transpiration

30% runoff

20% shallow infiltration

15% deep infiltration

35–50% impervious surface

30% evapo-transpiration

55% runoff

10% shallow infiltration

5% deep infiltration

75–100% impervious surface

Site Water Conservation, Management, and Quality Enhancement

In addition to protecting bodies of water and wetlands by creating a buffer separating them from the project site, green projects have the goals of mitigating the negative environmental effects of storm water runoff and reducing the outdoor use of potable water on the site.

Impervious surfaces, buildings, and conventional storm drainage systems form a high-velocity bypass route around the natural hydrology cycle, preventing rainwater from percolating down into the soil. This causes a host of problems, including soil erosion, habitat damage, flooding, water pollution, aquifer depletion, and physical and chemical degradation of receiving water bodies. Meanwhile, the use of water that has been transported to the site, typically treated potable water for such purposes as irrigation and fountains, only increases the quantity of runoff and exacerbates the associated problems.

4.23 Changes in water cycle associated with urbanization.
Source: Environmental Protection Agency

Quantity of Storm Water Runoff

Runoff describes the flow of storm water from paved surfaces that increases the load on the storm sewer system and raises the risk of flooding and erosion in the path of the flow. Runoff can dislodge and transport surface contaminants along the same path. Runoff also decreases the circulation of storm water through the natural hydrology cycle. The reduced water flow into and through the soil depletes groundwater aquifers and reduces the filtration that happens when storm water percolates through the topsoil and subsoil.

By working from the outside in, site selection seeks to reduce the need for parking hardscape by maximizing the use of public and non-motor-vehicle transportation and minimizing the need for onsite parking through community connectivity and compact development.

Another strategy to reduce runoff is the promotion of onsite percolation by replacing impervious surfaces with permeable options, such as pervious pavers, porous asphalt, pervious concrete, and vegetated landscapes.

Other ways to reduce runoff include onsite harvesting of rainwater and the reuse of storm water for such nonpotable purposes as irrigation and flushing of toilets.

Ultimately, the goal is for postdevelopment hydrology to mimic predevelopment hydrology, retaining as much water onsite as possible.

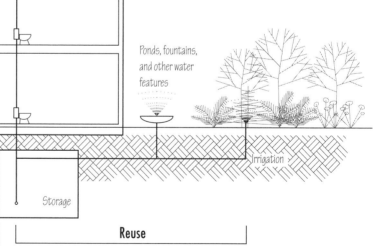

4.24 Reducing the quantity of storm water runoff through harvesting and reuse.

Quality of Storm Water Runoff

We not only seek to reduce the quantity of runoff, we also seek to improve its quality. Benefits include improved onsite water quality for reuse and improved offsite water quality in downstream rivers, lakes, and seas. This improved water quality benefits fauna and flora in natural habitats as well as our own consumption and uses of water.

Water quality has already been partially improved by the management of water quantity. Decreasing the quantity and velocity of storm water runoff reduces the entrainment of contaminants, such as pesticides, heavy metals, oil and grease, biological waste, garbage, and sediments.

The next step is to minimize sources of pollutants. Again, a significant step has already been taken through site selection, before site design has begun. Specifically, locating the site within or close to a community center with convenient access to public transportation minimizes the need for motor-vehicle transportation and the associated tracking of contaminants, such as grease and oil, carried by tires onto the site.

Green building sites should also minimize onsite sources of pollution. Pollution sources generated within a building will be addressed in Chapter 13, Indoor Environmental Quality. Onsite pollution sources outside the building include pesticides, herbicides, fungicides, fertilizers, animal waste, and finishes for outdoor structures and amenities. There are established approaches to address each of these pollution sources, such as integrated pest management and organic gardening methods.

The green building challenge becomes: How can the building design best support these practices during construction and after the building is completed? We can specify outdoor structures, amenities, and materials that do not require high-toxicity treatment or finishes. We can encourage landscaping with hardy and native plants, minimizing the need for pesticides, herbicides, fungicides, and fertilizers. In general, less is more when it comes to reducing pollutant sources. Fewer outdoor structures and reduced artificial landscaping mean less need for chemicals of all kinds.

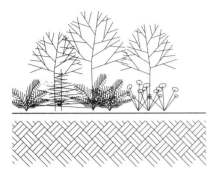

Plant native or hardy vegetation to minimize herbicide use.

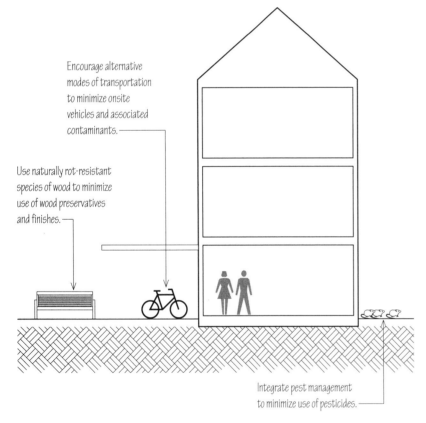

Encourage alternative modes of transportation to minimize onsite vehicles and associated contaminants.

Use naturally rot-resistant species of wood to minimize use of wood preservatives and finishes.

Integrate pest management to minimize use of pesticides.

4.25 Strategies to improve the quality of storm water runoff.

When pollution entrainment cannot be avoided, we should encourage the filtration of storm water by percolating its flow through the topsoil and into the subsoil.

Special attention should be directed to reducing the generation and entrainment of sediment and other contaminants during construction. The construction process is intrinsically so disruptive that the volume of pollution it can generate is large, and, even though temporary, can cause significant, lasting environmental damage. Sources of contamination include washout of concrete from trucks and other equipment. Concrete washout is preferably done offsite. If washout is done onsite, it should be done away from bodies of water or storm sewers, into a protected temporary pit, where it can set, be broken up, and removed from the site for disposal. Provisions for concrete washout and waste disposal should be made within construction specifications. Sediment traps can be used to prevent sediment from being transported offsite or to sensitive areas.

Transported Water

Transported water refers to water that is brought to the building site, either the potable water supplied by a municipal water system or well water pumped from an underground aquifer that typically extends beyond the site and is often treated.

A major goal when transporting water is to minimize the use of potable water for nonpotable applications. This is to reduce depletion of potable water sources, lower the power requirements of pumps, decrease the use of water treatment chemicals, and lessen the volume of runoff. Strategies to reduce the use of transported water include employing water efficiency measures and using nonpotable water for appropriate applications whenever possible.

Potable water use may be reduced on a site by landscaping with hardy and native plant species that require little or no irrigation. More efficient irrigation methods, such as drip irrigation, and irrigation systems adjusted to weather conditions can also significantly reduce consumption. Decorative fountains can also be designed to reduce water use, such as by selecting fountains with lower flow rates and smaller pool surface areas over which evaporation can occur. Programmed or timed operation of fountains will also reduce water use, as would the elimination of fountains altogether. Metering of fountain water use can also help us monitor the quantity of water use.

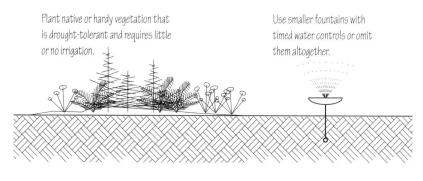

Install a drip irrigation system.

Plant native or hardy vegetation that is drought-tolerant and requires little or no irrigation.

Use smaller fountains with timed water controls or omit them altogether.

4.26 Ways to reduce transported water for site use.

Impact of Outdoor Water on Indoor Environmental Quality

Unmanaged surface water can have a negative impact on indoor environmental quality. Serious indoor environmental quality problems, such as mold, are attributable to high humidity, which is often traced to the intrusion of water into buildings. This water intrusion is not only from the rainwater falling on roofs and walls. It can also be the surface water that finds its way into areas such as basements. These problems are difficult to solve after the fact, when the building's occupants may be suffering from allergies, detecting offensive odors, and experiencing other adverse reactions to mold. The problems are more easily solved before they happen, by preventing the flow of surface water toward and into buildings.

Providing pervious surfaces allows water to percolate into the soil rather than flow toward a building. We form a layer of shelter by grading the site to encourage surface water to flow away from a building. Installing a foundation drainage system serves as another layer of shelter, using crushed gravel, drainage mats, and perforated drainage pipe to collect and divert groundwater away from a building before it can penetrate. Exterior waterproofing is another layer of shelter. Interior waterproofing and drainage are final options, but we do not want to rely on these; we want to work from the outside in. It is more effective to prevent the problem at its source rather than to solve the problem after it has developed, from within the completed building.

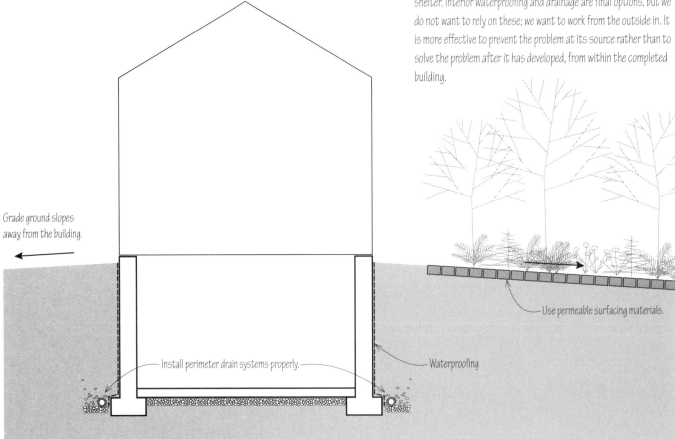

Grade ground slopes away from the building.

Use permeable surfacing materials.

Install perimeter drain systems properly.

Waterproofing

4.27 Strategies to prevent the intrusion of water into buildings.

Other Site Issues

Interestingly, trees and other vegetation, which can be so helpful for shading and protecting a building from the energy effects of sun and wind exposure, can adversely contribute to high humidity and other indoor environmental problems if located too close to buildings. Trees and vegetation can also threaten a building's structure with their roots and branches. Vines can penetrate storm windows, separate windows from their frames, and do extensive damage to siding and roofs on buildings. Buildings need a buffer zone to protect them from such vegetation and this buffer zone serves as a layer of shelter. The one exception may be purposefully vegetated roofs, which provides protection in the form of reducing heat island effects, lessening storm water runoff, and absorbing carbon dioxide in the air. The subject of green roofs is covered in Chapter 7, Outer Envelope.

Green site design can also promote indoor environmental quality by protecting a building from the dirt and moisture that can be tracked in on the footwear of its occupants.

Developing an effective barrier system begins with the approaches to the building itself and includes the appropriate selection of landscaping materials and plants, using textured paving materials instead of gravel, and installing effective dirt track-off or walk-off mats or grating at all entranceways. We might even consider placing a permanent boot and shoe brush outside the main entrance. Each of these measures progressively reduces the risk of dirt reaching the building and each serves as a layer of shelter to keep tracked-in dirt and moisture out.

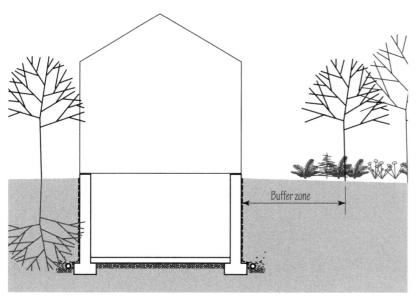

4.28 A buffer zone between a building and the surrounding vegetation is advisable when the root and branch systems of trees and brush can damage and penetrate the building envelope.

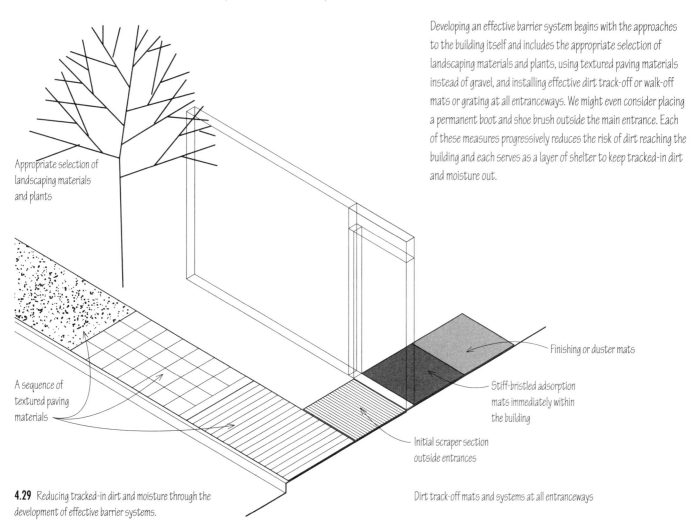

Appropriate selection of landscaping materials and plants

A sequence of textured paving materials

4.29 Reducing tracked-in dirt and moisture through the development of effective barrier systems.

Finishing or duster mats

Stiff-bristled adsorption mats immediately within the building

Initial scraper section outside entrances

Dirt track-off mats and systems at all entranceways

If closed-loop geothermal heat pumps are under consideration, early evaluation of soil conditions should be undertaken to fully evaluate the efficacy of such heat pumps. For example, if soil heat transfer characteristics are poor, a larger well field would be required and the cost of a closed-loop geothermal heat pump system will be higher.

The question arises whether traditional lawns are appropriate for green building sites. Lawns are often maintained with fertilizers, pesticides, and other chemicals. Lawns require irrigation in dryer climates and require energy-intensive mowing. Rock gardens, native vegetation, and permeable paving provide alternatives to traditional lawns.

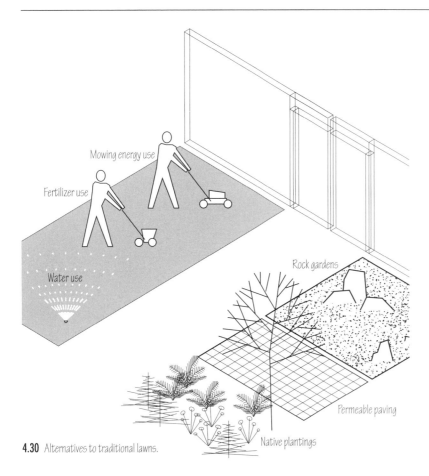

4.30 Alternatives to traditional lawns.

Site and Renewable Energy

A final note regarding sites relates to renewable energy. For a variety of reasons, the best location for solar panels is on roofs. If, however, a roof cannot accommodate solar panels, one option is to locate ground-mounted panels on the site. Site planning for solar panels must include shading studies, including anticipation of potential shading by trees and adjacent buildings. If we plan on shielding a building from wind with tree plantings, they can be located at a sufficient distance from buildings so as to not shade solar panels.

Similarly, if wind turbines are being considered, the best time for a feasibility study is during the site selection and planning phase. Locating ground-mounted solar panels and wind turbines must also take into account their distance from the building to keep trenching and wiring costs reasonable. Finally, the aesthetics of ground-mounted renewable energy components can be sensitive and should be weighed through renderings early in the site design process.

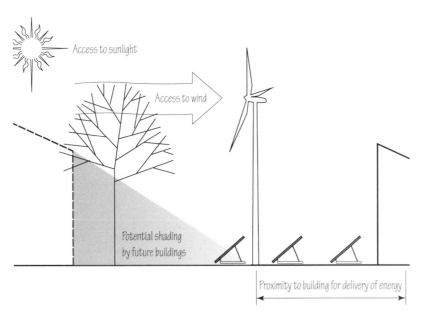

4.31 Site considerations for wind turbines and ground-mounted solar panels.

5
Building Shape

By building shape, we mean its footprint—the projected area on which the building is located—and additionally, the size of the building, its height, the number of floors, and the overall configuration of the building. Traditionally, the focus of such discussions has been on a building's orientation—how the building faces the sun, or the street, or its views. We will examine orientation, but we also examine two geometric characteristics, floor area and surface area. These two characteristics can have significant impacts on the energy efficiency, material conservation, and affordability of buildings.

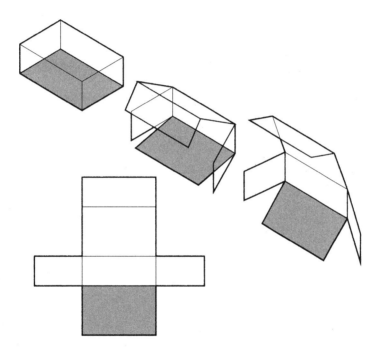

Floor Area

The floor area of a building, simply put, impacts material and energy use because the larger the building, not only is more material needed to build the structure, but more energy is needed for heating and cooling, lighting, ventilation, and for other energy loads that scale with size.

The question as to how large a building might be or should be is relevant to green building design. For example, in the United States the average house grew over 50% from 1,660 square feet (154 square meters) in 1973 to a peak of 2,520 square feet (234 square meters) in 2008. The typical house in the United States is almost twice as large as the typical Dutch house, more than twice as large as the typical Japanese house, and almost three times as large as the typical British house, despite the size of the American household being about the same as in all these countries—about 2.5 people on average. Even modest reductions in the size of buildings, while fully maintaining their functionality, deliver substantial reductions in energy, material use, and construction cost.

LEED's residential rating system, LEED for Homes, acknowledges the relationship between building floor area and energy use, and adjusts its credits to reward smaller homes. However, most other green building rating systems do not credit modest floor areas.

This short discussion of floor area is concluded by emphasizing again what may seem self-evident but bears repeating: A smaller building uses less energy and fewer materials than a larger building. Reduced room size and increased occupant density offer one way to do this, but other options include creative use of storage and moving unconditioned spaces outside the thermal envelope.

U.S. house in 2008: 2,520 SF (234 m²)

U.S. house in 1973: 1,660 SF (154 m²)

Dutch house: 1,200 SF (112 m²)

Japanese house: 1,000 SF (93 m²)

British house: 800 SF (74 m²)

5.01 Average home sizes.

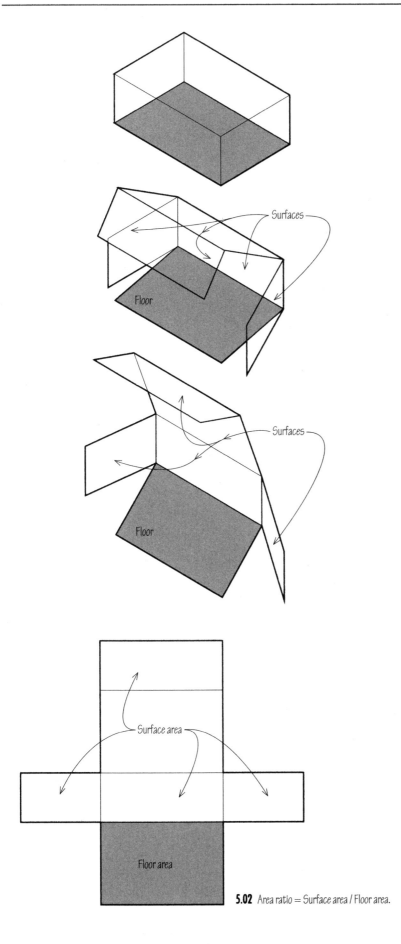

Surface Area

A second geometric characteristic of buildings, surface area, can also be determined to reduce energy use. By surface area, we mean specifically the exterior surfaces that meet the outdoors. Heat is lost from a building in winter in direct proportion to the building's surface area. In summer, the surface area also strongly impacts cooling requirements. Because energy use in most buildings is dominated by heating and cooling, surface area becomes a critical characteristic of a building's energy efficiency.

Similarly, reducing the surface area of a building significantly reduces material use and construction cost because the exterior walls and roof of a building are material-intensive.

The impact of surface area on energy use is seen in the heat transfer equation that governs heat loss from a building:

$$\text{Heat loss} = (A/R) \times (T_{indoor} - T_{outdoor})$$
where:
A is the exterior surface area of the building,
R is its thermal resistance (R-value),
T_{indoor} and $T_{outdoor}$ are the indoor and outdoor air temperatures, respectively.

Historically, the focus of green building design has been to increase the thermal resistance or R-value of exterior assemblies in order to reduce heat loss. This makes sense and it works. In the process, the surface area (A) has perhaps not received the attention it deserves, even though it has an equally important role to play. Furthermore, unlike increasing thermal resistance, which increases material use and construction cost, reducing the surface area not only reduces heat loss, it also reduces material use and construction cost.

The importance of floor area was previously discussed. Now, if one assumes that a building's floor area is finalized and fixed to serve the given purpose of a specific building, an interesting metric is the ratio of the building's surface area to its floor area. This allows the comparison of different building shapes with a single metric. Let us define this ratio of surface area to floor area as the *area ratio*. The larger the area ratio, the more energy the building will use for heating and cooling per unit of floor area.

5.02 Area ratio = Surface area / Floor area.

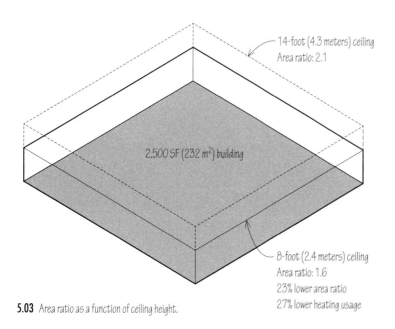

For example, for a single-story, square-shaped building with a flat roof and 2,500 square feet (232 square meters) of floor area, we can examine the impact of reducing the height from 14 feet to 8 feet (4.3 to 2.4 meters). The area ratio for the height of 14 feet is about 2.1. The area ratio for an 8-foot (2.4 meters) height is just over 1.6. What is the impact of the lower ceiling height and smaller area ratio on energy use? The 23% decrease in area ratio results in a 27% decrease in heating energy use. The area ratio significantly impacts energy use and the energy savings are not that different from the change in area ratio. In fact, the savings are slightly higher than the percent reduction in area ratio. Opportunities to examine and select from a range of space heights are not unusual in building design. For example, a typical supermarket has ceilings that vary from 12 feet to 18 feet (3.7 to 5.5 meters) high; however, none of the space above 8 feet is typically used because this is higher than people can reach. Green building design does not necessarily call for low ceiling heights but the need for overly tall ceilings is worth examining. Tall ceilings are frequently inefficient spatially, and lowering them could provide a significant potential reduction in energy use, material use, and construction cost without a sacrifice in building function.

5.03 Area ratio as a function of ceiling height.

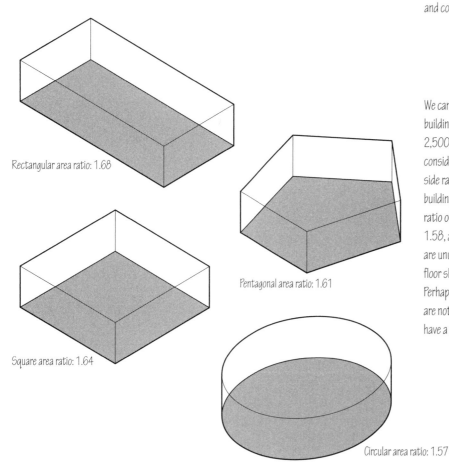

Rectangular area ratio: 1.68

Pentagonal area ratio: 1.61

Square area ratio: 1.64

Circular area ratio: 1.57

We can examine different building footprints for a single-story building with a constant 8-foot (2.4 meters) ceiling height and 2,500 square feet (232 square meters) of floor area. Specifically, consider the following building floor shapes: squares, rectangles with side ratios of 1:2, pentagons, octagons, and circles. A rectangular building has an area ratio of 1.68 while a square building has an area ratio of 1.64. The pentagon has an area ratio of 1.61, the octagon 1.58, and the circle 1.57. Recognizing that the latter three shapes are unusual, we nevertheless observe that a building with a circular floor shape and a cylindrical form has the most efficient area ratio. Perhaps of more significance, the differences between the area ratios are not large. We have flexibility with these footprints; they do not have a major impact on area ratio.

5.04 Area ratio as a function of footprint shapes.

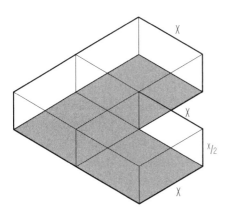

More complex footprints have a greater effect on area ratio and energy use. An L-shaped plan is common for homes and is not unusual in commercial buildings. For example, consider a footprint of three adjacent squares that form an L-shaped plan for a single-story building. If the building height is one-half the dimension of one side of the squares, a proportion fitting a small L-shaped building, the area ratio is 2.33. For the same floor area in the shape of a simple square, the area ratio is 2.15. The reduction in area ratio from an L-shaped plan is about 8%. There are measurable gains in energy efficiency by using a simpler building shape rather than an L-shape.

5.05 Area ratio for an L-shaped building.

Floor area = $3X^2$
Surface area = $7X^2$
Area ratio = $7/3 = 2.33$

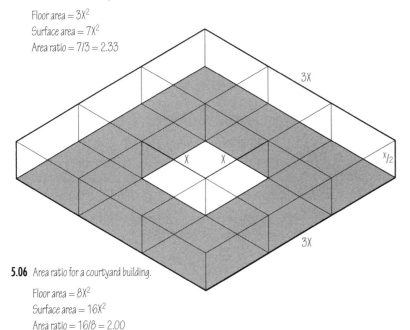

A courtyard plan is another common building shape. Consider a square building with each side equal to three times the length of one side of a square-shaped courtyard in the middle. Assume again a single-story building having a height one-half the dimension of the courtyard side. The courtyard building has an area ratio that turns out to be exactly 2. In comparison, a square building without a courtyard but with the same floor area has an area ratio of 1.71, a substantial reduction of 14% from the building with a courtyard.

5.06 Area ratio for a courtyard building.

Floor area = $8X^2$
Surface area = $16X^2$
Area ratio = $16/8 = 2.00$

If a building having a C-shaped footprint is designed instead as a simple square, the area ratio is, like the courtyard example, also 14% less. Buildings with complex shapes also cost more than simpler-shaped buildings. C-shaped buildings are reported to cost over 3.5% more than a simple square or rectangle to build.

5.07 Area ratio for a C-shaped building.

Floor area = $5X^2$
Surface area = $11X^2$
Area ratio = $11/5 = 2.20$

Next, consider the benefits of what for residential buildings is called row housing—laying out building units side-by-side in a row in a single building. Starting with a single two-story rectangular building that is 1,600 square feet (149 square meters) in area, 20 feet (6.1 meters) wide, 40 feet (12.2 meters) deep and 9 feet (2.7 meters) high per story, we find that its area ratio is 1.85. Turning it into a side-by-side building, such as a duplex, its area ratio is significantly reduced by 24%, to 1.40. The party wall has substantially reduced the exposed surface area of the combined building. Adding a third unit reduces the area ratio to 1.25, a fourth makes it 1.18, a fifth 1.13, and a sixth 1.10. The six-unit building has had its area ratio reduced by a substantial 41% from the single-unit building. We also note the largest drop in area ratio is from one to two units.

Even if we do not expand to a six-unit building, a two-unit building is much more efficient than a single-unit building. However, the difference between a two-unit building (24% less than a single-unit building) and a six-unit building (41% less than a single-unit building) is still significant. Row buildings save substantial amounts of materials and energy and reduce construction cost. We do recognize that the party walls in row housing cuts off potential views and daylight, and this may or may not be acceptable for a specific project. However, the approach may be applied to many types of buildings, such as retail uses, for which the only required glazing is the storefront, and window-free party walls are actually required for merchandise shelving.

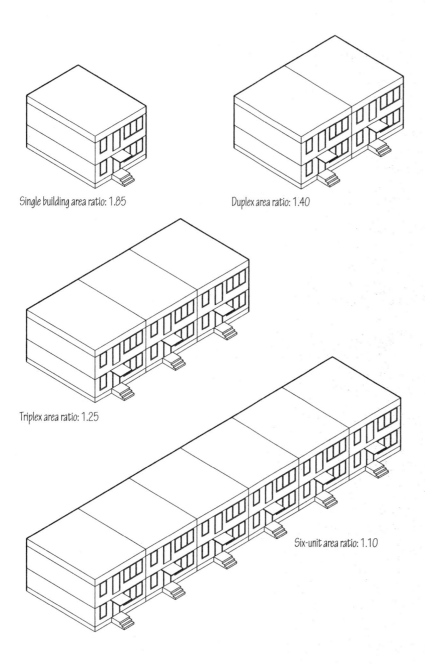

Single building area ratio: 1.85

Duplex area ratio: 1.40

Triplex area ratio: 1.25

Six-unit area ratio: 1.10

5.08 Area ratios for row buildings.

What are the area ratios of real buildings today? Typical small buildings, such as homes, often have area ratios in the 2.0–3.0 range. Real buildings substantially add to the area ratio of simple shapes by adding protrusions, jogs, cantilevers, dormers, exposed floor and ceiling areas, and other complexities, all of which add to the area ratio. Area ratios below 1.5 are readily attainable for the same floor areas by reducing the complexity of a building shape. Simpler building shapes simply use less energy. Given that simpler shapes also use fewer materials and cost less to construct, we start to see a case in favor of simplicity, for both green design and for affordability. Simple building shapes may not be desirable for some buildings, but for buildings for which such simplicity is acceptable, the potential energy and cost reduction can be significant.

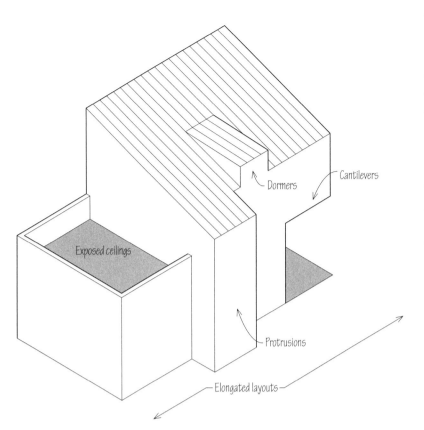

5.09 Building elements that increase the area ratio.

Sloped ceilings also impact the area ratio. For example, a 20-foot (6.1-meter) square standalone building with a flat 9-foot (2.7 meters) ceiling has an area ratio that is increased by 36% if one end of the ceiling is raised an additional 9 feet. If instead the ceiling is vaulted by an additional 9 feet in the middle, its area ratio is 17% higher than the building with a flat ceiling.

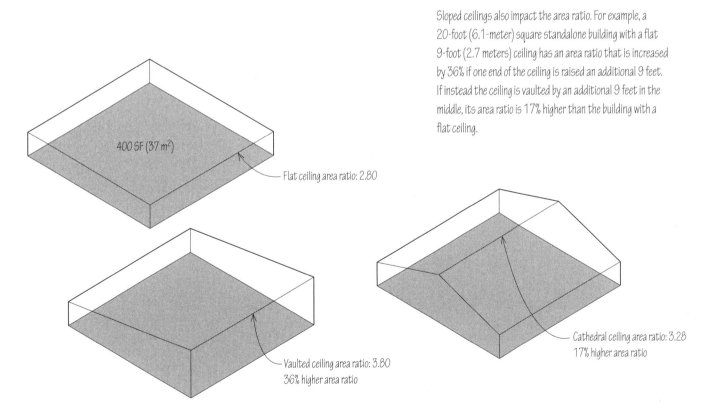

5.10 Area ratios for ceiling types.

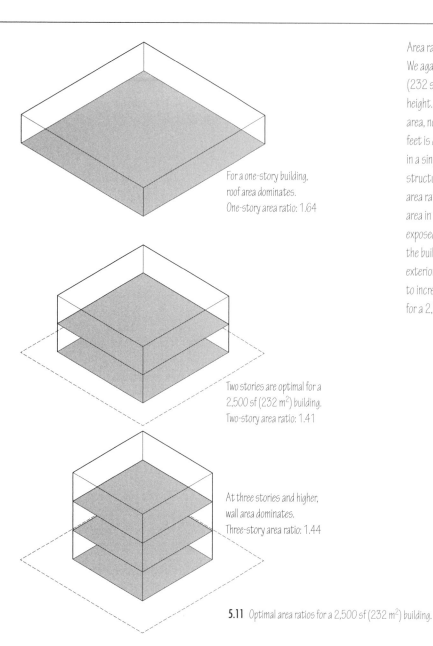

For a one-story building, roof area dominates.
One-story area ratio: 1.64

Two stories are optimal for a 2,500 sf (232 m²) building.
Two-story area ratio: 1.41

At three stories and higher, wall area dominates.
Three-story area ratio: 1.44

5.11 Optimal area ratios for a 2,500 sf (232 m²) building.

Area ratios are also affected by the number of stories of a building. We again examine a simple square building having 2,500 square feet (232 square meters) of floor area and an 8-foot (2.4-meter) ceiling height. Here, the 2,500 square feet refers to the total building floor area, not the area of the footprint. In this example, the 2,500 square feet is divided equally among each of the building's stories. Laid out in a single story, the building's area ratio is 1.64. As a two-story structure, its area ratio is 1.41 and as a three-story structure, its area ratio is 1.44. There is clearly a benefit to housing the same floor area in two smaller stories rather than a single larger story, as the exposed roof area for the two-story structure is reduced. But as the building rises to three stories, becoming taller and thinner, the exterior wall exposure begins to dominate and the area ratio starts to increase again. This indicates that the optimum number of stories for a 2,500 square foot building is two.

5.12 Optimal Number of Stories as a Function of Floor Area

Floor Area in sf (m²)	Optimum No. of Stories
< 1,000 (93)	1
1,000–5,000 (93–465)	2
5,000–10,000 (465–929)	3
10,000–30,000 (929–2,787)	4
30,000–60,000 (2,787–5,574)	5
60,000–100,000 (5,574–9,290)	6
100,000–150,000 (9,290–13,935)	7
150,000–240,000 (13,935–22,297)	8

The optimum number of stories varies slightly depending on the floor-to-floor dimension. This table is for a 10-foot floor-to-floor height.

A single story provides the lowest area ratio for buildings up to 1,000 square feet (93 square meters) in area and a 10-foot (3-meter) story height. From approximately 1,000 to 5,000 square feet (93 to 465 square meters) of floor area the optimum number of stories is two; from 5,000 to 10,000 square feet (465 to 929 square meters) the optimum number is three stories; from 10,000 to 30,000 square feet (929 to 2,787 square meters) the optimum is four stories, and so forth. At 200,000 square feet (18,580 square meters) the optimum is eight stories. It should also be noted that as the optimum number of stories to produce the lowest area ratio increases with floor area, the buildings will likely have a core of interior space.

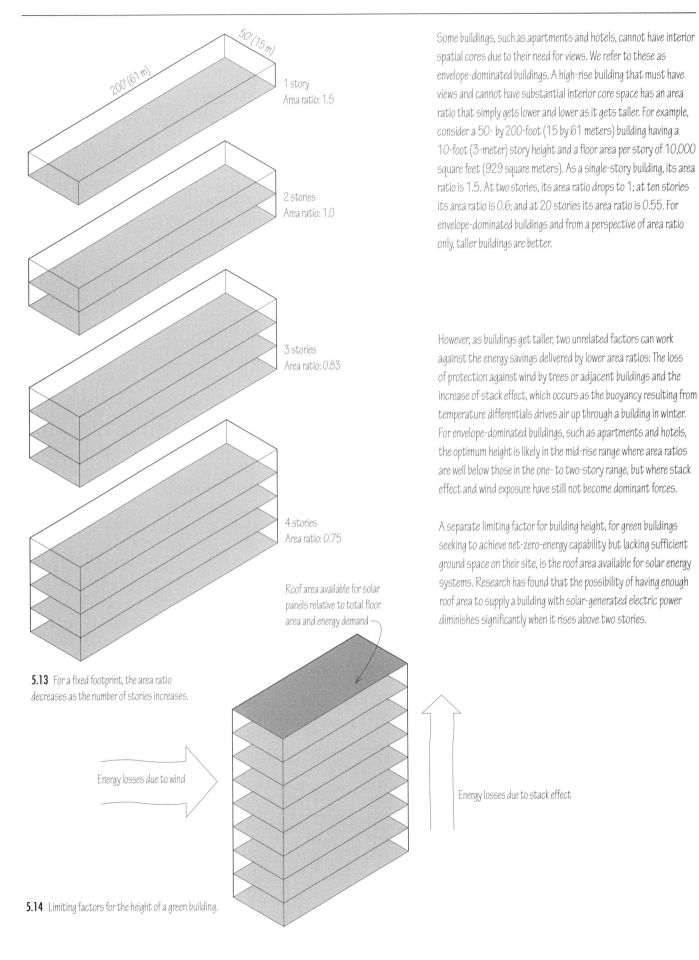

5.13 For a fixed footprint, the area ratio decreases as the number of stories increases.

50' (15 m)

200' (61 m)

1 story
Area ratio: 1.5

2 stories
Area ratio: 1.0

3 stories
Area ratio: 0.83

4 stories
Area ratio: 0.75

Roof area available for solar panels relative to total floor area and energy demand

Energy losses due to wind

Energy losses due to stack effect

5.14 Limiting factors for the height of a green building.

Some buildings, such as apartments and hotels, cannot have interior spatial cores due to their need for views. We refer to these as envelope-dominated buildings. A high-rise building that must have views and cannot have substantial interior core space has an area ratio that simply gets lower and lower as it gets taller. For example, consider a 50- by 200-foot (15 by 61 meters) building having a 10-foot (3-meter) story height and a floor area per story of 10,000 square feet (929 square meters). As a single-story building, its area ratio is 1.5. At two stories, its area ratio drops to 1; at ten stories its area ratio is 0.6; and at 20 stories its area ratio is 0.55. For envelope-dominated buildings and from a perspective of area ratio only, taller buildings are better.

However, as buildings get taller, two unrelated factors can work against the energy savings delivered by lower area ratios: The loss of protection against wind by trees or adjacent buildings and the increase of stack effect, which occurs as the buoyancy resulting from temperature differentials drives air up through a building in winter. For envelope-dominated buildings, such as apartments and hotels, the optimum height is likely in the mid-rise range where area ratios are well below those in the one- to two-story range, but where stack effect and wind exposure have still not become dominant forces.

A separate limiting factor for building height, for green buildings seeking to achieve net-zero-energy capability but lacking sufficient ground space on their site, is the roof area available for solar energy systems. Research has found that the possibility of having enough roof area to supply a building with solar-generated electric power diminishes significantly when it rises above two stories.

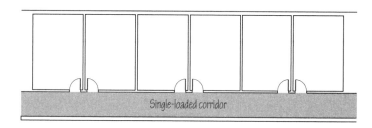

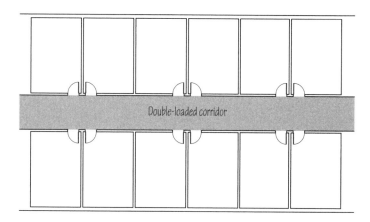

5.15 Buildings with double-loaded corridors have a lower area ratio than similar buildings having a single-loaded corridor.

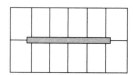

Further improvement in energy efficiency can be gained by not extending the corridor to the ends of the building.

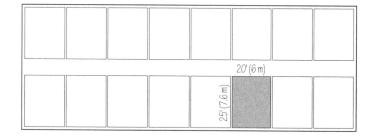

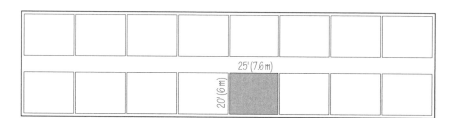

5.16 By using a greater perimeter depth, a building has a lower area ratio, is more energy efficient, and has a lower construction cost, even though the useful floor area remains unchanged.

For envelope-dominated buildings requiring views, such as apartments and hotels, a common question is: Which is preferable, a double-loaded or a single-loaded corridor? The answer is that a building with a double-loaded corridor will always have a significantly lower area ratio. Assume an apartment building is 200 feet (61 meters) long and is five stories high and has 20-foot- (6.1-meter) deep apartments, a 5-foot- (1.5-meter) wide corridor, and 10-foot (3-meter) story heights. If the building has a single-loaded corridor, its area ratio is 1.1, but if converted to a double-loaded corridor, the area ratio is 32% less at 0.74. The benefit of the double-loaded scheme can be extended by not running the corridor to the ends of the building.

Another strategy for such envelope-dominated buildings is to reduce the occupied space exposed to the exterior wall. This means designing deeper perimeter spaces with room lengths perpendicular to the exterior wall.

Taking the above example, the area ratio of the five-story building with a double-loaded corridor was 0.74. Assume that it was initially designed with eight apartments on each side of the corridor, each 20 by 25 feet (6.1 by 7.6 meters), with the 25-foot dimension along the outer wall. If we were to change the orientation of each apartment so that their 20-foot dimension is on the exterior wall but keep the room areas unchanged, their perimeter depth is now 25 feet. The building becomes a little wider and a little shorter, but the apartment areas remain the same at 500 square feet (46 square meters) each. The reduced wall exposure reduces the area ratio by 7.5%, to 0.69. This is the result of a minor change in building dimensions and a small loss of wall exposure for views, although ostensibly the total window area could even be maintained. But it produces a substantial savings in heating and cooling due to reduced building surface area without any loss in apartment floor area. We note that as the corridor becomes a little shorter, which will produce savings in lighting, the overall building floor area and exterior wall area also decrease, resulting in additional savings in construction costs.

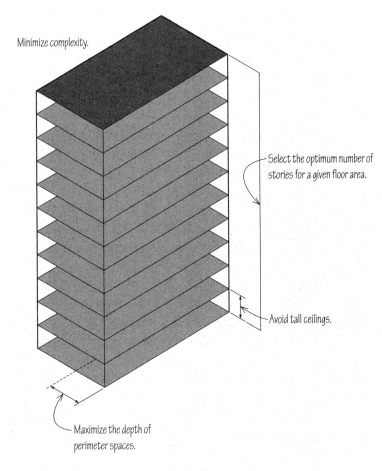

Minimize complexity.

Select the optimum number of
stories for a given floor area.

Avoid tall ceilings.

Maximize the depth of
perimeter spaces.

5.17 Ways to minimize the area ratio of a building.

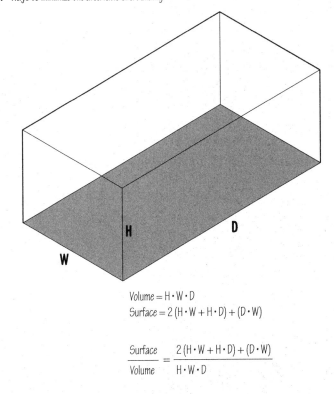

$$\text{Volume} = H \cdot W \cdot D$$
$$\text{Surface} = 2(H \cdot W + H \cdot D) + (D \cdot W)$$

$$\frac{\text{Surface}}{\text{Volume}} = \frac{2(H \cdot W + H \cdot D) + (D \cdot W)}{H \cdot W \cdot D}$$

5.18 Surface-to-volume ratio.

We have seen how powerfully the ratio of a building's surface area to its floor area impacts energy use. A variety of strategies can be used to minimize this area ratio, including reducing floor-to-floor heights and avoiding high ceilings; using row-building arrangements or combining multiple smaller buildings into a single larger building; using the optimum number of stories for a particular total floor area; using deeper spaces relative to outside walls; and minimizing surface complexity.

Maintaining low area ratios gives rise to a variety of secondary benefits. Avoiding tall ceilings reduces the power required for artificial lighting. Comfort is also improved, as temperature stratification is lower, which further reduces energy use. Simpler building lines at the roof also assist in providing locations for solar panels.

Area ratios are best applied when comparing design options for buildings of the same floor area or the same occupant density. Comparing area ratios for buildings with different floor areas or occupant densities can be misleading. For example, a four-bedroom house that is 3,000 square feet (279 square meters) in area may well have a lower area ratio than a four-bedroom house that has only 1,500 square feet (139 square meters) of floor space, but the larger home's smaller area ratio does not necessarily mean that it is more energy efficient. Reducing the floor area of a building should happen first, before examining the area ratio. Reducing the area ratio is best done once the floor area and occupant density is determined.

For some building shapes, lower area ratios can reduce the wall area required for views and the potential for daylighting. Views should be provided when and where they are required. However, options frequently exist to reduce area ratio while still providing the required views and allowing energy savings from daylighting. The use of reduced area ratios should be treated as a useful added tool in the green building designer's toolbox and not as an inflexible requirement to minimize area ratios regardless of impact on the building design.

Some building design professionals have alternatively used surface-to-volume ratio as a metric that should be minimized, rather than the surface-to-floor area ratio. The surface-to-floor area ratio has the benefit of being nondimensional and therefore identical in both common systems of units (the International System and the English System), whereas the surface-to-volume ratio will vary depending on the unit of length measurement used. The surface-to-volume ratio also decreases for any increase in ceiling height, perhaps artificially implying a greater efficiency for tall ceilings. However, both metrics—surface-to-floor area ratio and surface-to-volume ratio—recognize the importance of the exterior surface area and the importance of minimizing it.

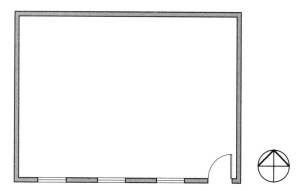

5.19 Buildings having windows on only one wall should have them facing south.

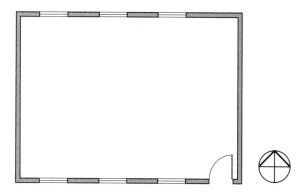

5.20 Buildings having similar-sized windows on opposing sides should orient them north and south.

Orientation

Now that we have examined the powerful influence of both floor area and building shape on energy use, we can return to orientation, the way a building faces. Orientation affects how much solar gain is captured for useful heat in winter, and conversely how much cooling is required due to unwanted solar gains in summer. Orientation will also affect how much air flows through a building due to differentials in wind pressure.

We focus our attention here on buildings without passive solar characteristics, such as thermal mass and other forms of energy storage, or without passive solar controls, such as night insulation of windows. We also focus on heating and cooling; a discussion of daylighting is addressed separately.

To optimize building orientation, decisions are best made if based on computer simulations. Computer simulations can be done fairly rapidly and many simulation programs even allow a building to be rotated so that different orientations can be examined quickly. First, it may seem self-evident, but we note that a square building that has equal windows on all four sides will not have an optimum orientation. For example, if the main entrance is oriented toward any of the four cardinal directions, the building will in each case use about the same amount of energy. So the focus of any discussion of optimum building orientation, relative to solar gains and thermal losses, is on those buildings that do not have equal window areas on all sides of the building.

For a building with windows on only one of four sides, in the northern hemisphere, the orientation requiring the least energy is typically when the windows face south. This is true whether the building is located in cold regions (heating-dominated) or in hot regions (cooling-dominated). Note that the conclusion is not "Place as many windows on the south wall as possible . . ." but rather, "If windows are placed on one wall only, the best wall on which to place these windows is the south wall."

For a configuration in which windows are located only on two opposite walls, having windows on the north and south walls results in the lower energy use than when the windows are on the east and west walls. The energy savings are more pronounced in warmer climates.

When locating windows on two adjacent walls, the least amount of energy is required when windows face east and south, in both warm and cold climates. A close second, in fact almost as low in energy use, are when the windows face west and south. If windows are on two adjacent walls, they should preferably not face north and east or north and west. The energy savings can be pronounced for both warm and cold climates.

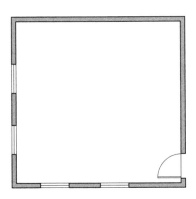
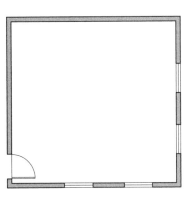

5.21 Buildings having windows on adjacent sides should orient them south and west or south and east.

The above examples focused on a square building. For a rectangular building having an equal window-to-wall ratio on all sides and therefore more window area on the two longer sides, the result is the same as for the square building with windows on opposing sides: The lowest energy use occurs in buildings that are oriented east-west along their long axis with more windows facing north and south than east and west. To be clear, the conclusion is not "Place as many windows as possible facing north and south . . ." but rather, "If windows are distributed evenly in terms of window-to-wall ratio around a rectangular building, the building is best oriented with its long axis running east-west." The gains are again more pronounced in the cooling-dominated south than in the heating-dominated north.

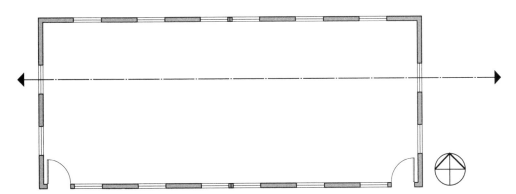

5.22 Rectangular buildings having windows evenly distributed on all four sides should be oriented along an east-west axis.

This discussion does not account for any orientation benefits relating to wind direction, as when breezes are desirable for cross-ventilation. It is possible that the best orientation for cross-ventilation might be different than the best orientation for solar gains and thermal losses.

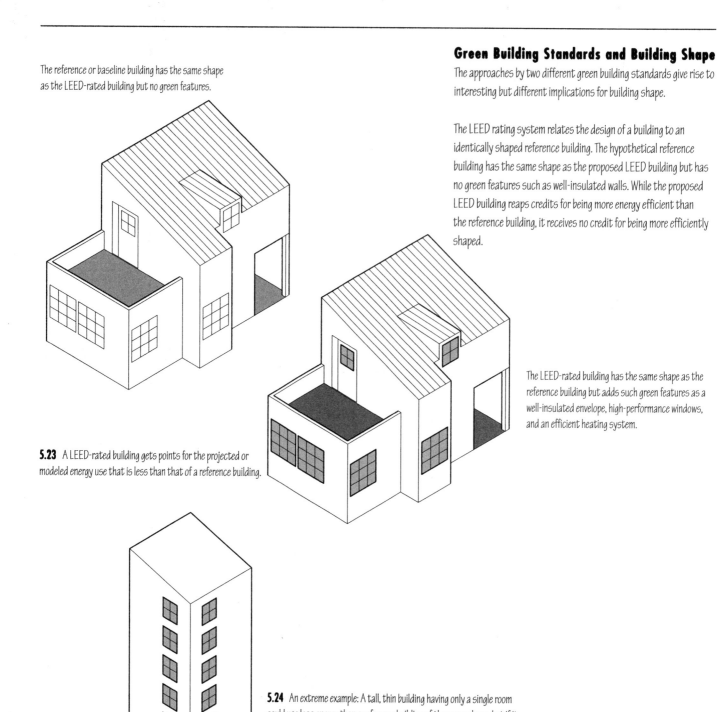

The reference or baseline building has the same shape as the LEED-rated building but no green features.

Green Building Standards and Building Shape

The approaches by two different green building standards give rise to interesting but different implications for building shape.

The LEED rating system relates the design of a building to an identically shaped reference building. The hypothetical reference building has the same shape as the proposed LEED building but has no green features such as well-insulated walls. While the proposed LEED building reaps credits for being more energy efficient than the reference building, it receives no credit for being more efficiently shaped.

5.23 A LEED-rated building gets points for the projected or modeled energy use that is less than that of a reference building.

The LEED-rated building has the same shape as the reference building but adds such green features as a well-insulated envelope, high-performance windows, and an efficient heating system.

5.24 An extreme example: A tall, thin building having only a single room could use less energy than a reference building of the same shape, but if it did not need to be as tall, it might use even less energy.

Let us consider an extreme example, a single-story office building with 1,000 square feet (93 square meters) of floor area in a single room with a ceiling that is 100 feet (30 meters) high. This building, if well-insulated, could well gain significant LEED energy points, might even score a top-level LEED Platinum rating, even though its energy use per unit of floor area will be high.

In contrast to the LEED Rating System, Passivhaus places emphasis on energy use per unit of floor area. For this rating system, the above example will not score well, and in fact would likely not achieve certification due to its high energy use per unit floor area. But its focus on floor area makes Passivhaus vulnerable to the opposite problem.

Consider another extreme example, a single-story building with a large floor area, such as a single-family home that has 100,000 square feet (9,290 square meters) of floor area. If this large house has well-insulated walls and a well-insulated ceiling, low infiltration, and small windows, it could well meet Passivhaus's energy performance criteria, which again, is based on energy use per unit of floor area. However, if the house were inhabited by a family of four, the energy bills would be extremely high when compared to a typical house.

From the two preceding examples, we can see that both the LEED Rating System and Passivhaus have vulnerabilities relative to building size and shape. Interestingly, a tall thin building can meet the LEED criteria and still be highly inefficient, and a large, low, flat building can meet Passivhaus requirements and also be highly inefficient. In fact, a large, low, flat building could also score well in the LEED Rating System and also be highly inefficient, although LEED for Homes does correct for home size, penalizing homes with large floor areas but not those with high ceilings. Other rating systems have similar issues. HERS, like LEED, bases its ratings on a reference building while ENERGY STAR®, like Passivhaus, bases its ratings on floor area.

Building shape can have a greater influence on energy use than the R-value of walls, the U-factor of windows, or other thermal characteristics. This is why building shape should be examined early and scrutinized closely. It can dominate building energy use, no matter how much insulation is in the walls, no matter how efficient the heating system is, and no matter what other energy-efficiency improvements are designed into the building.

The power lies in asking the right question. Instead of asking, "How can we choose a building shape that meets our needs and then incrementally green its structure?" we might consider asking, "How can we meet our needs with an intrinsically greener building shape?"

If we look closely at many certified green buildings, there may even be an opposite tendency. Possibly in an attempt to make the statement "We can be green and still be distinctive," the shapes of certified green buildings are often complex or thin and tall, with a high area ratio. With efficient individual components, such as high wall R-values and low window U-factors, the buildings are able to declare that they did not engage in *greenwashing*, a term describing the use of artificial or superficial claims of being green. But the underlying building shapes are often intrinsically inefficient. And so we come to a different risk than greenwashing, which we might refer to as *greensplashing*, the design of conspicuously green buildings that nominally are green or that are even certified to be green, but that are inefficient because of their complex or otherwise-inefficient shapes.

5.25 An extreme example: A large, low, flat building with a low energy use per unit of floor area could still use more energy than if the building did not need to be of this shape.

Core Spaces versus Perimeter Spaces

Larger buildings, such as sizable office buildings and indoor malls, can have core spaces that do not have exterior walls or roofs. These interior spaces typically only need cooling year-round, even if the buildings are in cold climates.

Some of this cooling can be done by bringing in cool outdoor air when the outdoor air temperature is below the indoor air temperature. Some heat pump systems also allow heat to be moved from the core to the perimeter zone, significantly increasing overall energy efficiency when there is a simultaneous need for cooling the core and heating the perimeter. These characteristics of buildings that are core-dominated raise a series of questions: Is there an energy benefit to buildings having large core spaces that do not require heating? Is there an optimum ratio of core floor area to perimeter floor area? Is there a benefit in affordability?

One issue arises, for example, when core heat is not always being generated at the same time that the perimeter needs it. Perimeter zones typically need heat only in winter whereas core zones generate heat year-round. Perimeter zones need more heat at night when there is no sunlight and possibly less use of lighting and equipment whereas the core zones of many buildings, such as offices, typically produce more heat during daytime working hours. Nonetheless, there are still significant potential gains for core-generated heat to be used for perimeter heating. For a definitive analysis of core versus perimeter tradeoffs for a particular building, an energy model is required.

If it is acceptable for any particular green building to have a core of interior space—in other words, if it is acceptable for a core space to not have windows for views or daylighting and if heat pumps are used to move core heat to the perimeter—it can be efficient to have such a core. Note that it is also lower in construction cost per square foot to have interior core zones. Core zones do not need the costly exterior assemblies, whether of walls or a roof, with their requirements for insulation, weather resistance, cladding, windows, and exterior doors.

Does it make sense to keep adding area to a core of interior space? The answer is probably not. As the core floor area grows to two or more times the area of the perimeter zone, several things occur. First, the core generates more heat than can be used by the perimeter zone, and so the efficiency gain of dual-purpose simultaneous heating and cooling is lost. Second, when outdoor temperatures are low, the distance increases over which free cooling from the outdoors is needed to provide cooling to the core. As a result, the parasitic power of fan motors and/or pump motors increases. Lastly, the core may become so large that the majority of occupants in the building have no connection to the outdoors through views or daylighting, and so indoor environmental quality suffers. However, if large core areas are acceptable, the energy question is most definitively answered by computer simulation. Under some conditions, there may well be significant gains in both energy and affordability by increasing the core area.

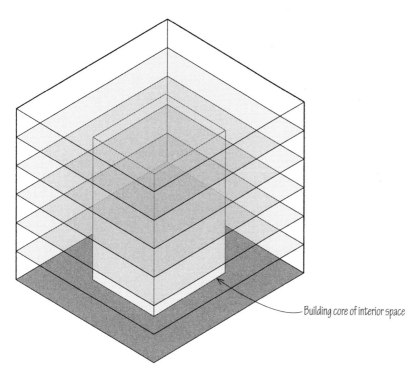

Building core of interior space

5.26 Large buildings often have a core of interior space that has no exterior walls, floors, or ceilings.

6
Near-Building Features

Near-building features include such structures and devices as overhangs, awnings, solar panels, balconies, and shutters. Many of these features can be usefully applied as added layers of shelter. If misapplied, however, some near-building features can inadvertently increase energy use in buildings

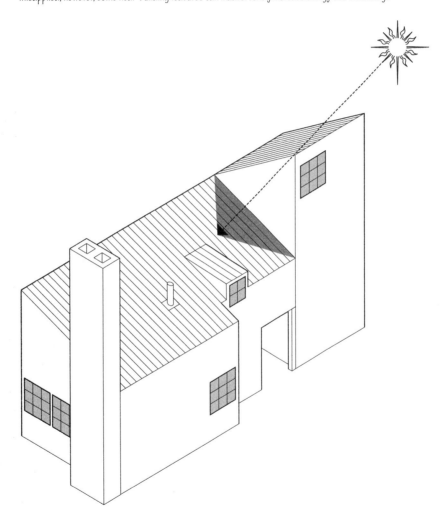

Overhangs and Awnings

Overhangs and awnings that face east, south, or west reduce solar gains in summer, and so reduce the energy required for air-conditioning. If sized correctly, they allow solar gains in winter when the sun's heat is useful. Overhangs also shield walls and windows from water intrusion and protect building materials, such as wood and some types of caulk, from deterioration caused by exposure to the sun's ultraviolet rays. Exterior shutters can serve similar purposes. There is far greater value in blocking the sun before it reaches a building rather than trying to shield its rays with blinds or shades indoors, after they have passed through windows and carried heat into the building.

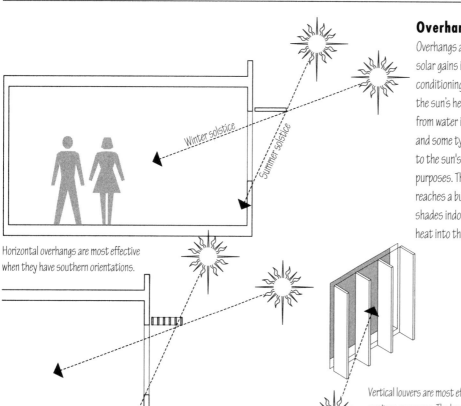

Horizontal overhangs are most effective when they have southern orientations.

Horizontal louvers parallel to a wall permit air circulation near the wall and reduce conductive heat gain. The louvers may be operated manually or controlled automatically with time or photoelectric controls to adapt to the solar angle.

Vertical louvers are most effective for eastern or western exposures. The louvers may be operated manually or controlled automatically with time or photoelectric controls to adapt to the solar angle. Separation from the wall reduces conductive heat gain.

6.01 Shading devices shield windows and other glazed areas from direct sunlight to reduce glare and excessive solar heat gain in warm weather.

Overhangs can be sized in a variety of ways, including numerical calculation, building models, and computer simulation. The following table shows overhang depths required for 48-inch (1,220) tall, south-facing windows at noon on August 22 to provide full shade along the height of the window at various latitudes. Fortunately, where they are needed most, in warmer climates, the required overhang is shorter.

°Latitude	Depth in Inches (mm)
24	11 (280)
32	16 (405)
40	26 (660)
48	36 (915)

Required east and west overhang depths are much greater and, at 6 feet (1,830) or more, can quickly become more extended than is feasible. An alternative are vertical louvers or fins, which offer more effective shading protection for eastern and western exposures. Trellises, other exterior structures, and even vegetation are other options for external shading.

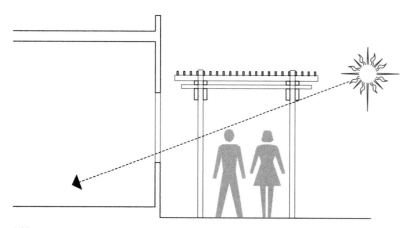

6.02 Trellises and other exterior structures can provide shade depending on their proximity, height, and orientation, especially for east and west exposures requiring greater overhang depths.

Solar Panels

Solar panels consist of an array of either solar thermal collectors or photovoltaic modules. As we design from the outside in, it is important to direct attention to potential locations for solar panels before finalizing the roof design for a building.

Roofs are a logical location for solar panels. The inherent structure of a building makes roof-mounted installations more affordable than ground-mounted installations, which require their own foundation. The elevation of a roof reduces the risk of shading by the building itself, by adjacent buildings and structures, or by vegetation. Limited access to roofs also lessens the risk of theft, vandalism, and other damage to the solar panels.

However, roofs are often not designed or built to host solar panels. Roof orientation relative to the sun is frequently not optimal. Furthermore, roof-mounted building components, such as chimneys, plumbing and mechanical vents, dormers, stairwell penthouses, and satellite dishes, often interfere with the most effective locations for solar panels. These components can obstruct otherwise large contiguous roof areas, breaking them into sections and making the installation of continuous solar arrays more difficult. Some sections of roof may be too small to host even a single panel. Portions of roofs are sometimes shaded by higher sections of the same building, reducing their effectiveness as locations for solar panels.

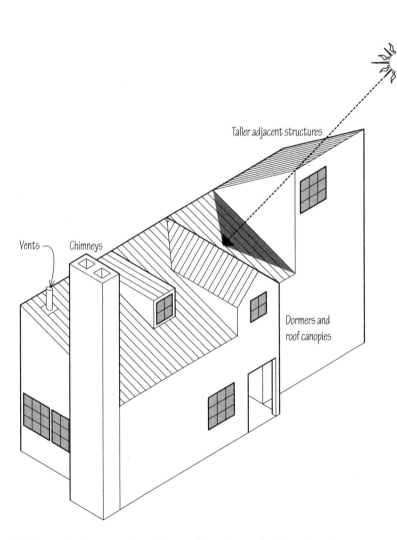

Taller adjacent structures

Vents

Chimneys

Dormers and roof canopies

6.03 Obstructions that may interfere with the most effective locations for solar panels.

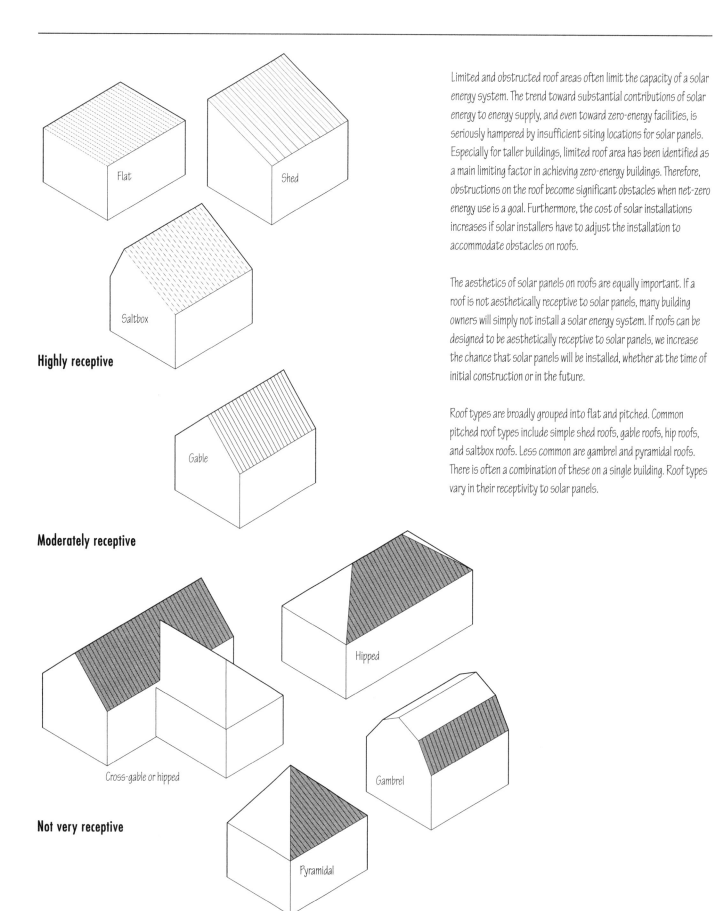

Highly receptive

Flat

Shed

Saltbox

Moderately receptive

Gable

Not very receptive

Cross-gable or hipped

Hipped

Gambrel

Pyramidal

Limited and obstructed roof areas often limit the capacity of a solar energy system. The trend toward substantial contributions of solar energy to energy supply, and even toward zero-energy facilities, is seriously hampered by insufficient siting locations for solar panels. Especially for taller buildings, limited roof area has been identified as a main limiting factor in achieving zero-energy buildings. Therefore, obstructions on the roof become significant obstacles when net-zero energy use is a goal. Furthermore, the cost of solar installations increases if solar installers have to adjust the installation to accommodate obstacles on roofs.

The aesthetics of solar panels on roofs are equally important. If a roof is not aesthetically receptive to solar panels, many building owners will simply not install a solar energy system. If roofs can be designed to be aesthetically receptive to solar panels, we increase the chance that solar panels will be installed, whether at the time of initial construction or in the future.

Roof types are broadly grouped into flat and pitched. Common pitched roof types include simple shed roofs, gable roofs, hip roofs, and saltbox roofs. Less common are gambrel and pyramidal roofs. There is often a combination of these on a single building. Roof types vary in their receptivity to solar panels.

6.04 Relative receptivity of various roof forms to solar panels.

Flat roofs accept solar panels easily, whether at the time of construction or at some point in the future, and provide flexibility in orientation for the solar array. In the northern hemisphere, south-facing shed roofs or saltbox roofs with a main south-facing slope also are highly receptive to solar panels.

Accordingly, best practices to make roofs receptive to solar panels include:

- Choosing a receptive roof design. In order of preference from high to low receptivity:
    - Flat roof
    - Shed roof
    - Saltbox roof
    - Gable roof
    - Hip roof

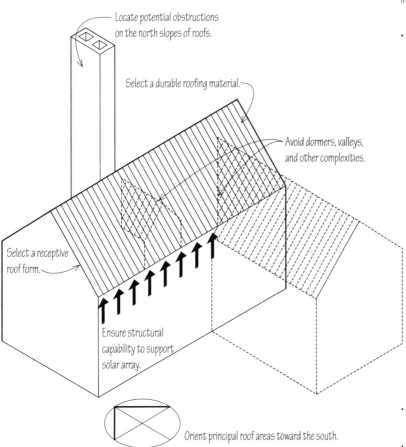

Locate potential obstructions on the north slopes of roofs.

Select a durable roofing material.

Avoid dormers, valleys, and other complexities.

Select a receptive roof form.

Ensure structural capability to support solar array.

Orient principal roof areas toward the south.

6.05 Making roofs receptive to solar panels.

- Orienting the main slope of a roof toward the equator (true south in the northern hemisphere).
- Locating roof penetrations, such as plumbing vents and exhaust fans, on the north slope of a roof or on walls where possible.
- Providing large, contiguous roof areas for solar panels by clustering roof penetrations and minimizing the use of dormers and other projections.
- Keeping roof lines simple and rectangular where possible and avoiding complex roof designs that include features such as valleys.
- Avoiding roof designs where one portion of the roof shades another.
- Designing a structurally sound roof that is able to bear the added weight of solar panels.
- Choosing a durable roofing material to avoid the need to remove the solar panels for reroofing.

The tilt or slope of solar panels affects their energy output. Computer simulation will readily identify the optimal tilt and azimuth angle of solar panels for maximum annual output of solar energy for a given geographic location. Sometimes, the tilt is selected to maximize either summer or winter output to better match the building-specific monthly load profile.

The requirements for both the tilt and orientation of a solar array are somewhat forgiving. Reasonable energy output is still possible for panels at nonoptimal tilts and orientations. For example, within plus/minus 10 degrees tilt from optimal, the sacrifice in capacity of solar photovoltaic systems is typically less than 2%. However, more significant variations from the optimal tilt will more measurably reduce output. Vertically oriented panels have approximately 30% less annual output capacity than optimally tilted systems in northern United States locations, and approximately 50% less in southern locations. Horizontally oriented panels have approximately 20% less capacity than optimally tilted systems in northern locations, and approximately 10% less capacity in southern locations.

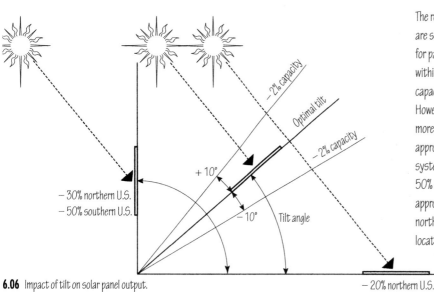

6.06 Impact of tilt on solar panel output.

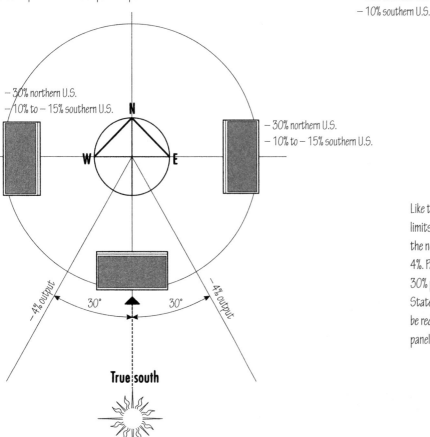

Like tilt, the orientation of a solar array is also forgiving, within limits. Orientations within plus/minus 30 degrees from true south in the northern hemisphere result in a production sacrifice of less than 4%. Panels oriented due east or west will sacrifice approximately 30% production in the northern reaches of the continental United States and approximately 10% to 15% in the south. This loss can be reduced by lowering the tilt from the optimal tilt for south-facing panels.

6.07 Impact of orientation on solar panel output.

For flat roofs where space is more than sufficient for a required solar system, the panels should be tilted for optimum efficiency to minimize material use and maximize cost-effectiveness. Rows of tilted panels need to be spaced such that each row does not shade an adjacent row. This is typically done by evaluating shading at 3 pm on December 21 for a given location. For flat roofs where space is limited and as many panels as possible are sought to maximize capacity—for example, to achieve zero-energy use in a building— the maximum capacity is obtained by using a single set of panels stacked above each other, resulting in the appearance of a shed roof. This may not be practical due to the height of the assembly. For rows of tilted panels, orienting rectangular panels with their long edge parallel to the roof may provide slightly more capacity than if the panels were to have their shorter edge parallel to the roof. To maintain a lower profile with panels not rising above the roof, one option is even to lay the panels horizontally on the roof.

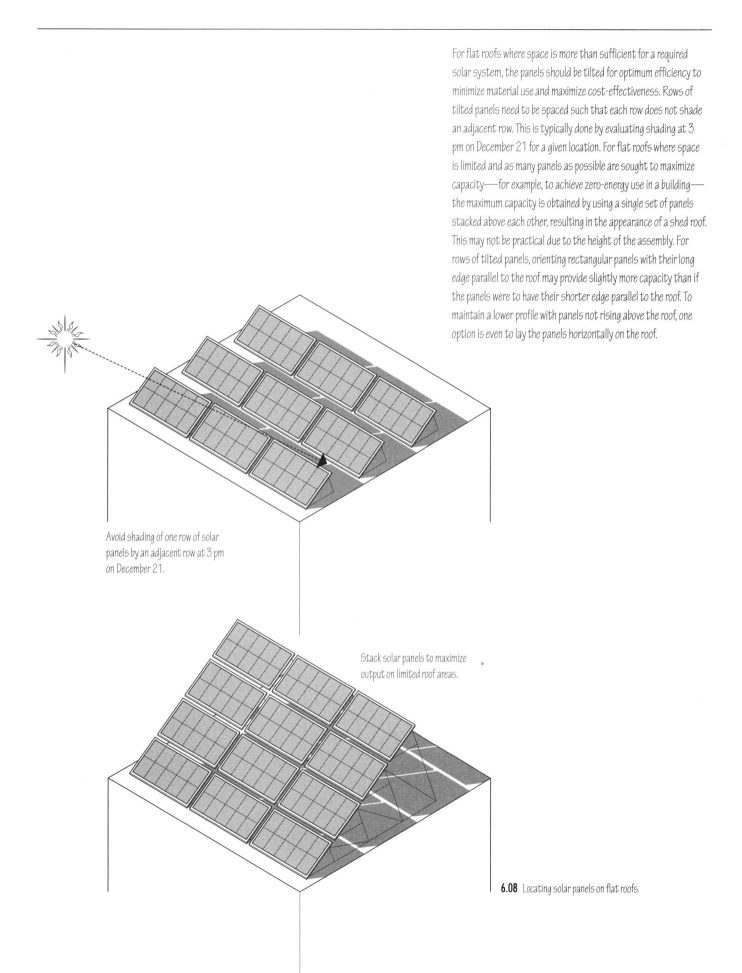

Avoid shading of one row of solar panels by an adjacent row at 3 pm on December 21.

Stack solar panels to maximize output on limited roof areas.

6.08 Locating solar panels on flat roofs.

Balconies

Before the design of a structure is finalized, the role of balconies should be considered. In the field of heat transfer, balconies can be considered to be extended surfaces that increase the rate of heat transfer, similar to the role of fins on radiators in cars or heat exchangers in heating and cooling equipment. There is evidence that balconies can cause significant energy losses by wicking heat away from buildings in winter. In essence, they increase the surface area of a building over which heat can be lost.

Conductive heat flow

Thermally or structurally isolate the balcony from the main structure.

6.09 Balconies can wick heat out of buildings.

We can consider a couple of approaches to thermally isolate balcony structures from a building, so that heat from inside the building is not conducted outdoors by the floors and walls of balconies. Thermal isolation can be achieved by using nonconductive spacers between the balcony structure and the main building structure, or by supporting the balconies with a structure that is external to the main building structure.

Balconies also usually have large glass doors, which themselves are a point of vulnerability for buildings. Large sliding glass doors, typically metal-framed, not only leak air around their long perimeters but they also have relatively low R-values and high U-factors, which can lead to undesirable heat gain or loss through the glazing itself. Smaller insulated doors might be considered for access to balconies where possible.

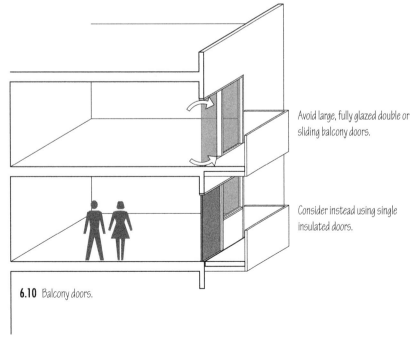

Avoid large, fully glazed double or sliding balcony doors.

Consider instead using single insulated doors.

6.10 Balcony doors.

The Building Facade

Proceeding from the outside in, a building's facade plays a central role in green building design. Windows, window-to-wall ratio, doors, decorative features, floor-to-floor height, roof lines, the entrance and lobby, exterior lighting, and interior lighting seen from outdoors—these all contribute to the critical view of a building from the outside. Many of these elements also contribute substantially to a building's energy use. The place of the facade in the development of a building's appearance relates strongly to its sequence in design, typically developed as one of the first elements of the building's conceptualization. Importantly, early renderings often are developed before energy design occurs. These renderings can receive owner approvals as well as other authorizations, such as from local zoning boards, and subsequently can establish expectations before energy tradeoffs have been evaluated, thereby preventing energy optimization.

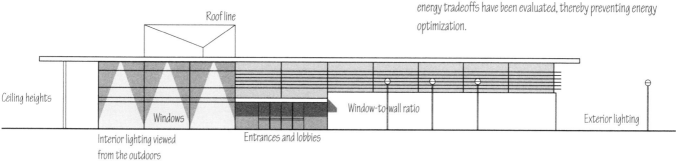

6.11 Elements of a building facade that can contribute to or reduce energy efficiency.

For green buildings, the integrated design process can prevent an early commitment to the building's facade and final appearance before energy tradeoffs have been evaluated. This allows approvals to affirm an intrinsically green design approach early on. Early assessment of the energy tradeoffs of the facade elements is truly designing from the outside in and likely represents one of the most significant impacts that can be made in greening a building.

Rainwater Harvesting

Aspects of rainwater harvesting should be developed during the consideration of near-building features. For example, drains and downspouts need to be coordinated to route rainwater to a single point, preferably to maximize storage for future use, rather than simply away from the building and to the storm drainage system. If this storage is outside a building, its location should be carefully evaluated. Further details of rainwater harvesting will be addressed in Chapter 12, Hot and Cold Water.

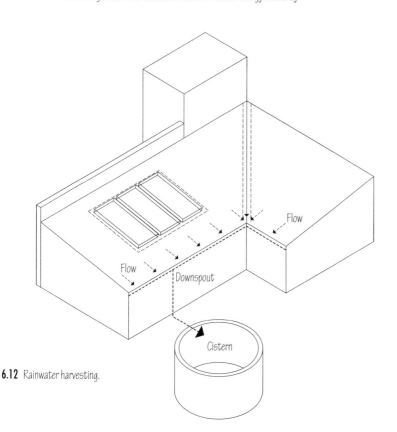

6.12 Rainwater harvesting.

Use of the Roof

Green buildings have many features that require roof space. In addition to conventional roof-mounted components, such as heating and cooling equipment and exhaust fans, and other roof uses, such as patios and penthouses, a variety of green features may compete for roof space:

· Solar photovoltaic modules
· Solar thermal collectors and possibly storage components
· Skylights or monitors for daylighting
· Vegetation for green roofs
· Heat-recovery ventilators

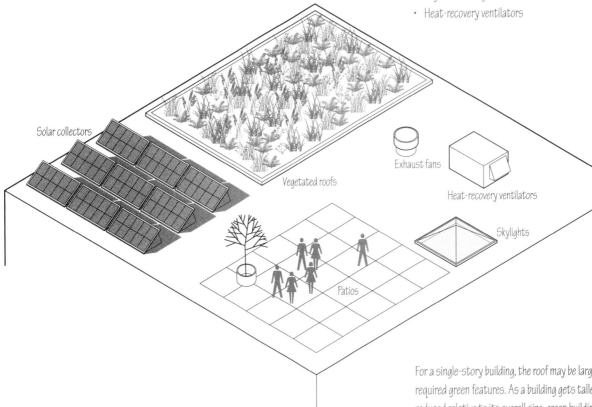

Solar collectors

Vegetated roofs

Exhaust fans

Heat-recovery ventilators

Skylights

Patios

6.13 Green and nongreen elements that compete for space on a roof.

For a single-story building, the roof may be large enough to host all required green features. As a building gets taller and its roof area is reduced relative to its overall size, green building features may need to be prioritized. Prioritization can be based on a life-cycle analysis or on the potential reduction in energy use or carbon emissions. For example, on a building having limited available space on its roof and for which zero energy is sought, priority might be given to solar energy for its higher contribution to energy savings, before considering skylights or a vegetated roof, both of which would offer less savings.

Nongreen elements, such as penthouses, patios, and heating and cooling equipment, deserve scrutiny to possibly locate them elsewhere than on the roof if they risk displacing features on the roof that are needed to deliver the building's green goals.

7
Outer Envelope

The term "envelope" refers to the outer shell of a building. This envelope includes such building components as the walls, windows, doors, roof, and foundation. The term "enclosure" is also seeing increased use when referring to the envelope of a building.

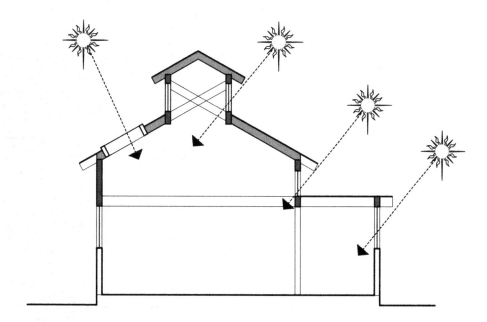

Inner and Outer Envelopes

We distinguish between an outer envelope and an inner envelope because frequently a building has essentially two envelopes. For example, for a building having a pitched roof with an attic below, the outer envelope is the layer of the roof construction assembly while the floor of the attic space serves as the inner envelope. The outer envelope includes components that come into contact with outdoor air or with the ground. The inner envelope consists of components that are in contact with conditioned spaces. Often, as in the case of many walls, the outer and inner envelopes are integrated into the same construction assembly.

The outer envelope is often the most important layer of shelter in a building. As we design from the outside in, we continuously seek to add layers of shelter so that the outer envelope does not need to stand alone in protecting the building occupants from external loads, such as wind and temperature extremes. At the same time, we recognize its paramount importance in the making of a building and seek to strengthen this critical layer so that the shelter it provides and its protection against energy losses will both endure.

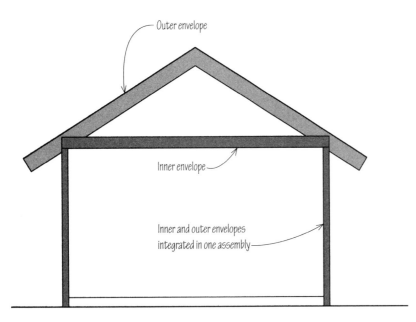

7.01 Inner and outer envelopes.

Parallel to the concepts of outer and inner envelopes, we also consider the concept of the thermal boundary. The thermal boundary, which consists of the surfaces along which insulation is wrapped around a building, can be routed along the outer envelope, as in the case of a roof that is insulated at the roof line, or it can be routed along the inner envelope, as in the case of insulation that is installed in the attic floor assembly, or it can be routed between the two.

The very presence of both outer and inner envelopes can give rise to confusion, especially when the thermal boundary is inadequately defined. We will explore several common scenarios that result in an unclearly defined thermal boundary or even no thermal boundary at all. If we define the thermal boundary clearly and strongly, we can put outer and inner envelopes to work for us in creating the multiple layers of shelter that can serve to effectively resist exterior loads.

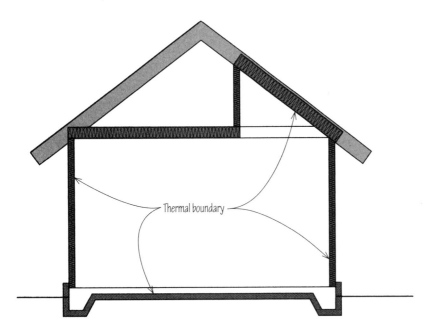

7.02 Thermal boundary of a building.

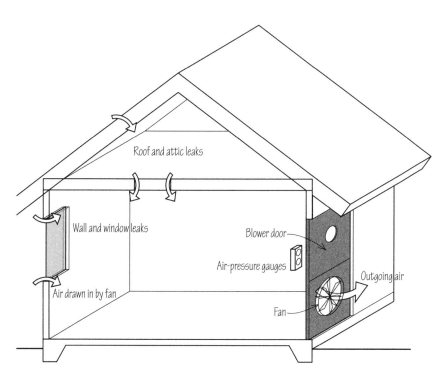

7.03 Blower door test.

Labels in figure: Roof and attic leaks; Wall and window leaks; Blower door; Air-pressure gauges; Outgoing air; Fan; Air drawn in by fan

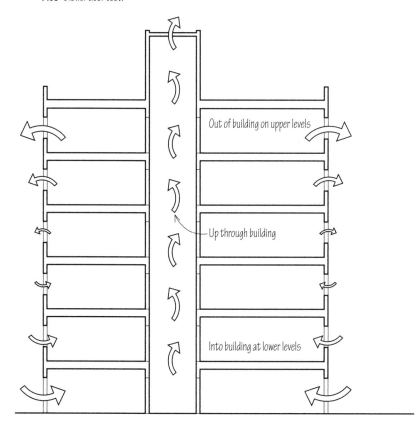

7.04 Airflow from the stack effect in winter.

Labels in figure: Out of building on upper levels; Up through building; Into building at lower levels

Infiltration

The impact of infiltration on energy use in buildings is substantial. "Infiltration" is the term commonly used to describe the exchange of air between a building and the outdoors. Although the pure definition of infiltration is air entering a building—as opposed to exfiltration, which is air leaving a building—the term is more commonly used to represent air that enters and leaves a building, either simultaneously or in alternating cycles. Recent years have given a deeper understanding into the mechanisms of infiltration and its effect on energy use. The advent of the blower door test, which pressurizes or depressurizes a building, has allowed both the quantification of infiltration and understanding where it happens. The blower door has most commonly been applied to single-family homes, but it has also been used occasionally for larger buildings, and the insights that have been gained apply well to all building types.

The information provided by a blower door test is readily perceived during the assessment procedure. In a building depressurized with a blower door, outdoor air can be felt rushing in throughout the building—around door and window frames; through electrical outlets; around air grilles and light fixtures; through wall panel seams; through exhausts and flues; and through piping and wiring penetrations.

In recent years, much understanding has been gained about the stack effect, which is a significant driving force of infiltration, drawing air into the lower stories of buildings in winter and forcing it out of the upper stories. The stack effect can also occur in the reverse, downward direction in an air-conditioned building. Most pronounced in tall buildings, the stack effect is nonetheless active and evident in buildings as low as two stories, or even in single-story buildings with basements. It can be observed by slightly opening a basement or first-floor window in winter and feeling the inrush of cold air.

Stack effect is not the only driver of infiltration. Wind pressure is also a substantial contributor. Furthermore, without either wind or stack effects, a building can still experience infiltration through its many cracks and openings, driven by a variety of air pressure changes within buildings, such as those induced by exhaust fans, ventilation intake systems, ducted heating and cooling systems, and even the opening and closing of doors and windows.

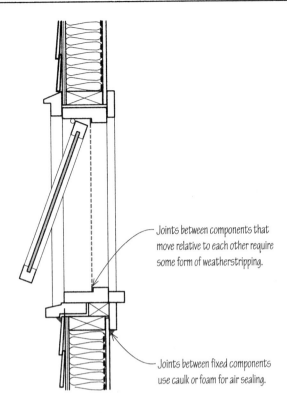

Joints between components that move relative to each other require some form of weatherstripping.

Joints between fixed components use caulk or foam for air sealing.

7.05 Types of joints that require air sealing.

There are numerous locations of infiltration, even in buildings that appear well-designed and well-built. Substantial sources are windows and doors, which exhibit two distinct modes of infiltration. The first mode is air flowing past components that have the ability to be moved, such as a swinging door or a window sash in a double-hung window. The requirement of a door or window sash to be movable in its frame establishes a natural site for infiltration. The second mode of infiltration is air moving through the gaps between a door or window frame and the wall itself, which are often concealed by moldings. This second mode of infiltration is between components that are fixed in place.

The methods for countering infiltration are different for the two different modes of infiltration. On the one hand, preventing infiltration at components that have relative motion requires seals that allow this movement to occur. These are typically referred to as weatherstripping. Weatherstripping comes in many forms, including spring metal, V-strips, and a variety of foam strips that compress on the closure of a window or door. On the other hand, the infiltration between fixed surfaces, such as between a window frame and a wall, can be prevented with materials, such as caulk or foam, which do not need to allow motion of the building components.

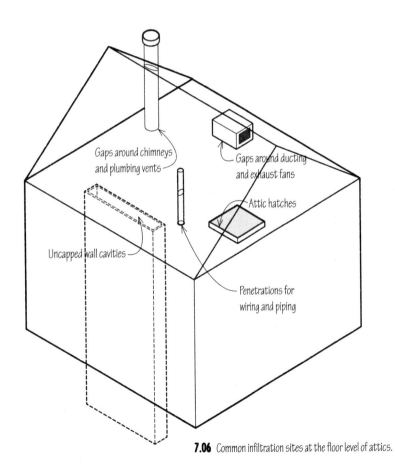

Gaps around chimneys and plumbing vents

Gaps around ducting and exhaust fans

Attic hatches

Uncapped wall cavities

Penetrations for wiring and piping

7.06 Common infiltration sites at the floor level of attics.

Another common group of infiltration sites can be found at the floor level of attics. These include attic hatches and uncapped wall cavities; gaps or cracks around recessed light fixtures, chimneys, plumbing vents, ducts, and exhaust fans; and penetrations of wiring and fire sprinkler piping.

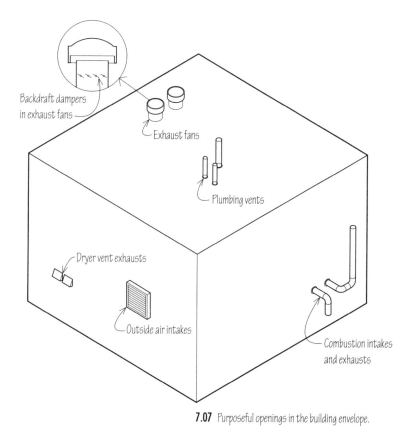

Backdraft dampers
in exhaust fans

Exhaust fans

Plumbing vents

Dryer vent exhausts

Outside air intakes

Combustion intakes
and exhausts

7.07 Purposeful openings in the building envelope.

Infiltration at pipe and
wiring penetrations
and at sheet-metal
joints within the air-
conditioning unit

Heat conduction
through both sleeve and
air-conditioning unit

Infiltration at sleeve—air-
conditioning unit junction

Infiltration at sleeve—
wall junction

Indoors

Outdoors

Typical Problems

Best Practices

To eliminate losses through wall-
mounted or window-mounted
air-conditioning or heat pump units,
use split systems and seal all piping
and wiring penetrations with caulk
or foam.

7.08 Heat loss and infiltration through room air-conditioners.

Purposeful openings in a building's envelope through which air
or other gases are intended to flow represent another class of
infiltration sites. These openings include fireplace and wood stove
chimneys, other combustion vents, clothes dryer vents, exhaust fan
vents, and ventilation air intakes. When not in use, these openings
become sites for infiltration and should be controlled.

Some of these openings have dampers that are intended to reduce
infiltration, but they typically seal inadequately. These backdraft
dampers usually prevent flow in one direction only and allow the
intentional flow of air or other gases in the other direction. The
direction in which these dampers allow flow is usually the direction
in which the air pressure from the stack effect is exerting its force,
and so these dampers can inadvertently open to let air flow out of a
building, even when they are supposed to be closed.

A more subtle yet common set of infiltration sites is in and around
walls. Air can enter through cracks in the siding material, then move
through seams in inadequately sealed air barriers, through cracks in
the sheathing, through porous insulation between framing members,
and into a building through electrical receptacles and switches or
other cracks and holes in the interior finish wall. Air can infiltrate
around top plates of walls and at the sill plate where the wall framing
rests on a foundation wall. Air can infiltrate where the piping for a
split-system air conditioner or heat pump penetrates an exterior
wall, which can be hidden by pipe insulation or by the equipment itself.
Through-wall and window-mounted air-conditioners, in particular,
are sites for significant air leakage. A study of such air-conditioners
found that a typical unit has leakage equivalent to that of a
6-square-inch (3,871 mm^2) hole.

The final class of infiltration sites might be called catastrophic
sites. These are unusual openings in a building envelope, such as
windows that are open in winter due to a building being overheated;
broken windows or damaged door frames; and damaged ductwork in
locations such as in attics or the outdoors.

Thermal Bridging

An area of building construction that has received increasing attention in recent years is thermal bridging. Thermal bridging refers to the penetration of the insulation layer by solid, noninsulating building materials, through which heat can be transferred between the interior, conditioned space of a building to the exterior environment. The most common example of thermal bridging occurs through the wood or metal studs in a frame wall or roof. Thermal bridging has been shown to reduce the effective thermal resistance (R-value) of wood-frame walls by 10% and of steel-frame walls by as much as 55%.

Other examples of thermal bridging include the lintels, sill plates, and top plates of frame walls; structural beams and concrete slabs that support exterior walls; shelf angles; bearing walls that rise up to form parapets; balconies and porches; and various details of foundation floors and walls.

As we move into a discussion of the outer envelope, we will keep in mind the issues of infiltration and thermal bridging, and consider ways in which to minimize their effects.

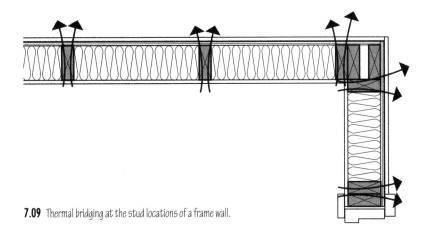

7.09 Thermal bridging at the stud locations of a frame wall.

Continuity and Discontinuities

The heat transfer caused by infiltration and thermal bridging highlights the necessity for continuity in the thermal envelope. There are many obstacles to achieving continuity in the thermal envelope. Buildings are made of many components that are fastened together. Each joint between these components has the potential to be a discontinuity. The envelope of the building also needs to be penetrated by windows, doors, piping, and wires, and each such penetration has the potential to be a discontinuity.

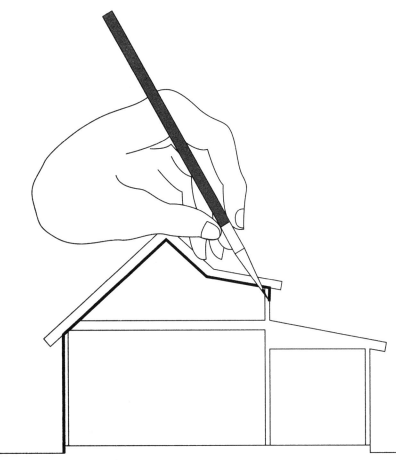

7.10 If we imagine a section through a building, drawn on a piece of paper, we should be able to trace a continuous path around the building that is not interrupted either by the gaps enabling infiltration or by thermal bridging, without lifting the pencil.

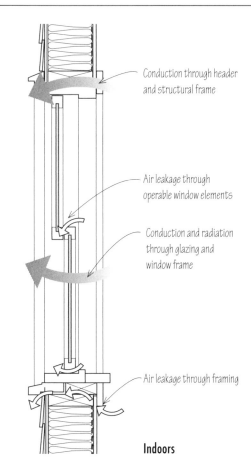

Conduction through header and structural frame

Air leakage through operable window elements

Conduction and radiation through glazing and window frame

Air leakage through framing

Outdoors   **Indoors**

7.11 Heat loss and infiltration paths through a window.

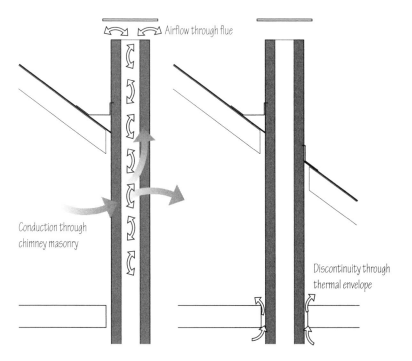

Airflow through flue

Conduction through chimney masonry

Discontinuity through thermal envelope

7.12 Potential locations of discontinuities at chimney locations.

Furthermore, any single penetration in a building, whether it be a window, a door, an attic hatch, a recessed light fixture, or any other discontinuity, can provide multiple paths for energy loss. For example, a window loses energy not only by thermal conduction through the glass panes but also by thermal convection up and down the glass surfaces; by thermal conduction through the window frame; by thermal conduction through the wall framing and header around the window; by the leakage of air between the sash and the frame; by air leakage between the frame and the building; by air leakage in or out of the frame into the wall cavity; and by radiant heat loss between the indoors and outdoors. Additional, inadvertent energy losses can occur if a window is left open by mistake, if it is broken or cracked, or if its storm window is left open or is broken.

Another common set of discontinuities can be created by the traditional masonry chimney. If the chimney is located on an outside wall, the masonry allows heat to be conducted from the indoors to the outdoors, both laterally out through the chimney walls and vertically up toward the roof. The flue also serves as a discontinuity, allowing warm indoor air to flow up and out the building in winter and cold outdoor air to flow in and down. If the chimney is located on the interior of a building, it will often have required clearances to combustible materials around its perimeter as it rises through upper floor and ceiling structures, forming another discontinuity in the thermal envelope.

Many of the energy losses from these discontinuities increase over time. We can refer again to the example of windows, which are intrinsically nonrobust. Energy losses increase as window frames settle and shift; window caulking dries and cracks; weatherstripping is detached through the repeated opening and closing of windows; as the gas in double- or triple-glazed windows leaks; and as thermal seals break. Similar deterioration happens in doors and other openings having movable surfaces, such as attic hatches, which are often bent and broken. Some deterioration likely even occurs for discontinuities that do not have intentionally moving parts, such as cracks in walls and attic penetrations. Once a crack or hole exists in a building, it likely only gets larger as the structure settles and shifts.

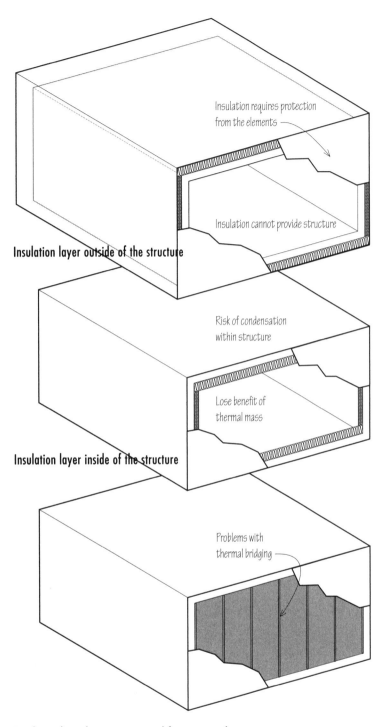

Insulation layer outside of the structure

Insulation requires protection from the elements

Insulation cannot provide structure

Insulation layer inside of the structure

Risk of condensation within structure

Lose benefit of thermal mass

Insulation layer between structural framing members

Problems with thermal bridging

7.13 A topology of challenges in providing continuity of the thermal envelope.

In many areas of the outer envelope, providing continuity of the thermal envelope presents a spatial challenge. It is almost a problem of topology, the mathematical study of surfaces in space and their connections. Insulation is typically not a structural material. It cannot provide the structural properties necessary to bear loads, resist shear, or brace against the wind. We also prefer insulation to be on the outside of the building structure for a variety of reasons, including the need to control moisture and to locate thermal mass inside the thermal envelope. But when located on the outside of a building, the insulation itself is not protected from the elements and must follow a tortuous path to fully enclose a building that has a foundation, walls, a roof, and a variety of projecting elements, such as parapets and porches.

We can move the insulation to the building interior but then we lose the benefits of having the thermal mass inside the thermal envelope. We must also be mindful of moisture problems resulting from the possible condensation of water vapor within the wall or roof structure. We can route the insulation along the interior in some locations (for example, the roof), and exterior in other locations (for example, the walls) but then we are faced with challenges at the interface between the various surfaces. We can locate the insulation between structural members, as has been common practice in light-wood or light-gauge metal frame construction, but then we lose energy through thermal bridging.

Finally, we can wrap the insulation continuously between the cladding or siding and the main structural frame of the building, and this solution appears to be gaining acceptance in both low-rise and high-rise construction. But attention still needs to be directed toward maintaining continuity, which is a challenge at a variety of structural penetrations, and at wall-roof, wall-floor, and wall-foundation interfaces.

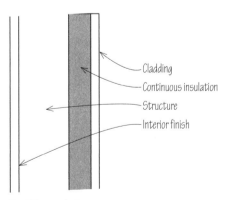

Cladding
Continuous insulation
Structure
Interior finish

Possible resolution

Using insulated spacers, or spaced steel standoffs, between shelf angles and masonry wall

Continuing insulation layer up and over the top of a parapet wall to meet the roof insulation

Installing thermal breaks where balcony structure extends from the main structure

7.14 Ways to reduce or eliminate thermal bridging in masonry walls.

Walls

Masonry Walls

Masonry walls often use concrete masonry units (CMU) as the main structural material for both low-rise and high-rise construction. A wide variety of claddings serve to finish and protect the outside of the building, including brick, stone, stucco, terra cotta, and metal siding. Similarly, on the interior, a variety of finishes can be used, including gypsum board over metal or wood studs and furring strips. In some cases, the CMU can be left exposed on the interior.

High-performance concrete masonry units are available, which are typically 40% lighter than traditional CMU and, having R-values between R-2.5 and R-3.0, offer over 30% better thermal resistance. If insulated with Perlite or similar insulation fillers, high-performance CMU has R-values between R-7 and R-10.

Thermal bridging occurs in masonry walls in several ways, each of which may be reduced or eliminated:

- Shelf angles used to support wall cladding, such as brick, offer paths for thermal conductance. A thermal improvement is to use insulated spacers between the shelf angles and the main CMU wall, or to use spaced steel standoffs between the shelf angles and the CMU.
- Where a masonry wall rises above the roof line to form a parapet, the wall itself can act as a thermal bridge as it rises between the layer of exterior rigid insulation and the roof insulation that terminates at the wall. A thermal improvement is to continue the wall insulation up over the top of the parapet and down to meet the roof insulation. The top of the parapet is still protected by a coping over the top of the continuous insulation.
- Any structural steel that penetrates the thermal barrier acts as a thermal bridge. One option is to use stainless steel instead of plain carbon steel for these penetrating components because stainless steel has lower thermal conductivity. Another option is to insulate around the exterior of any penetrating structural steel.
- External structures, such as balconies, can break the continuity of the thermal insulation layer. A thermal improvement for balconies is to support them externally rather than connect them both structurally and thermally to the main building. Another option is to use nonconductive spacers between the balcony structure and the main building structure.

Masonry walls are best insulated on the outer face of the main wall, on the inside of the cladding or siding. This location allows the thermal mass to be inside the thermal layer, where it can moderate temperature swings and serve as a form of thermal storage. This location also lowers the risk of condensation in cold climates. If the insulation is located on the interior of the main wall, there is a risk in cold climates that the interior face of the main wall will become cold and come into contact with warm moist air that finds its way past the insulation layer, causing moisture in the air to condense on the cold surface.

The insulation between a masonry bearing wall and cladding is usually rigid. The type and thickness of insulation are first established by the energy code and then can be incrementally increased to lower energy use as an added investment.

A secondary thermal layer can be added by insulating the interior cavity formed by the fastening of gypsum board to stud framing on the interior of the masonry wall. With the exterior of the masonry wall insulated, thus warming the interior of the wall in cold climates, this secondary layer of insulation can be added without risk of condensation. Light-gauge metal studs or Z-channels are commonly used for the stud framing, but wood studs with its lower thermal conductance can also be considered. Because the interior cavity is often available for the application of interior finishes and routing of electrical wiring, a good case can be made for adding this insulation, either as batts or as rigid insulation. Another secondary layer of insulation can be placed in the cores of the concrete masonry units.

Because rigid insulation is the primary form of insulation for masonry walls, taping of the rigid insulation seams takes on importance. Taping helps to reduce air movement through the walls and also serves to shed any water that might have penetrated the exterior cladding.

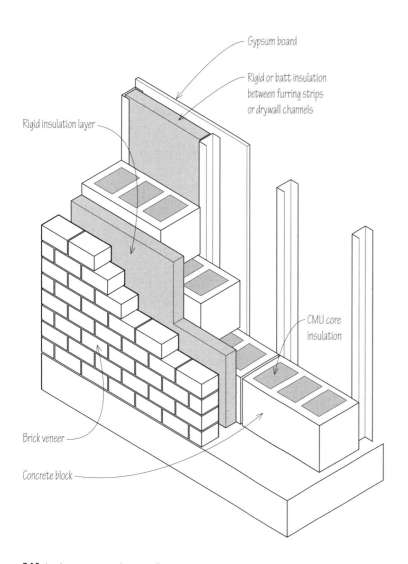

Gypsum board

Rigid or batt insulation between furring strips or drywall channels

Rigid insulation layer

CMU core insulation

Brick veneer

Concrete block

7.15 Insulating a masonry bearing wall.

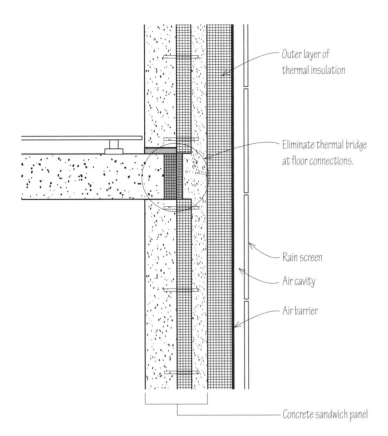

- Outer layer of thermal insulation
- Eliminate thermal bridge at floor connections.
- Rain screen
- Air cavity
- Air barrier
- Concrete sandwich panel

7.16 Improving the thermal insulation of concrete sandwich panel buildings.

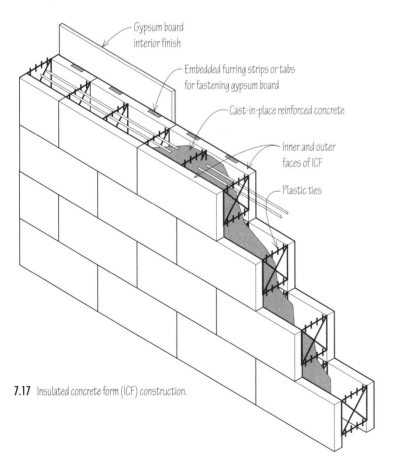

- Gypsum board interior finish
- Embedded furring strips or tabs for fastening gypsum board
- Cast-in-place reinforced concrete
- Inner and outer faces of ICF
- Plastic ties

7.17 Insulated concrete form (ICF) construction.

Poured Concrete Walls

Poured concrete walls can take several forms. They can be precast, or cast horizontally on a construction site and then tilted up, or poured in place. As with masonry walls, a variety of interior finishes and exterior cladding systems are available, including leaving either face exposed as a structural finish.

A green option is the loadbearing concrete sandwich panel, which is fabricated by fastening a thin layer of reinforced concrete to either side of a layer of rigid insulation with a series of nonthermally conducting connectors or fasteners. The resulting assembly is relatively lightweight, durable, and fire-resistant. To maintain continuity of the thermal layer and prevent thermal bridges from forming, the edges of the insulation layer must remain in contact along their entire length.

It should be noted that concrete sandwich panels are similar to insulated masonry cavity walls in that the two layers of concrete are analogous to the two wythes of a masonry wall and the captured layer of rigid insulation serves the same role as the rigid insulation in the cavity of the masonry wall. In some installations, an added layer of insulation is installed on the exterior of the sandwich panels and covered by cladding.

Another form of poured concrete wall is known as insulated concrete forms (ICF). ICFs are the opposite of concrete sandwich panels. Instead of a layer of insulation being sandwiched between two layers of concrete, ICF walls have a layer of concrete sandwiched between two layers of insulation, such as expanded polystyrene foam (EPS), which serve as forms into which the concrete is poured in place. Again, the interior can be finished and the exterior clad in a variety of ways. A typical interior finish is gypsum board, which can be fastened to tabs embedded in the interior insulation form. A benefit of the ICF wall is that the interior layer of insulation does not have the thermal bridging associated with furring or studs. The continuous poured-in-place wall also supports continuity of the thermal envelope.

Wood-Frame Walls

Conventional light-wood framing uses wood studs typically spaced at 16 inches (405) on center with insulation filling the cavities between the studs. Gypsum board is the most common interior finish while the exterior cladding is usually a combination of sheathing and wood, vinyl, or one of a variety of composite sidings. The studs in conventional wood-framed walls form thermal bridges and the many joints in the framing make the walls vulnerable to air infiltration.

"Advanced framing" is an umbrella term used to cover a variety of conventional framing design details that reduce thermal bridging. Examples include spacing the studs at 24-inch (610) centers rather than at 16-inch (405) centers; using single top plates, single studs at window and door openings, and single headers or no headers in nonloadbearing walls; and simplifying corner framing. Frequently, rigid insulation is added to the exterior of the stud frame, on top of the sheathing and beneath the siding.

Several energy-efficient variations are possible for wood-frame walls. These include using double-stud framing in which each row of studs is offset or separated from the other to reduce thermal bridging; substituting prefabricated structural insulating panels (SIP) for the normal stud framing; and employing various infiltration-resistant insulation materials, such as dense-packed cellulose, spray-foam, and rigid foam panels.

Wood-frame walls are common, are low in embodied energy*, use a renewable structural material, can be assembled with strong thermal resistance if thermal bridging is minimized, and can be constructed to prevent infiltration if attention is directed to air-sealing details.

* See Chapter 16, Materials, for a discussion of embodied energy.

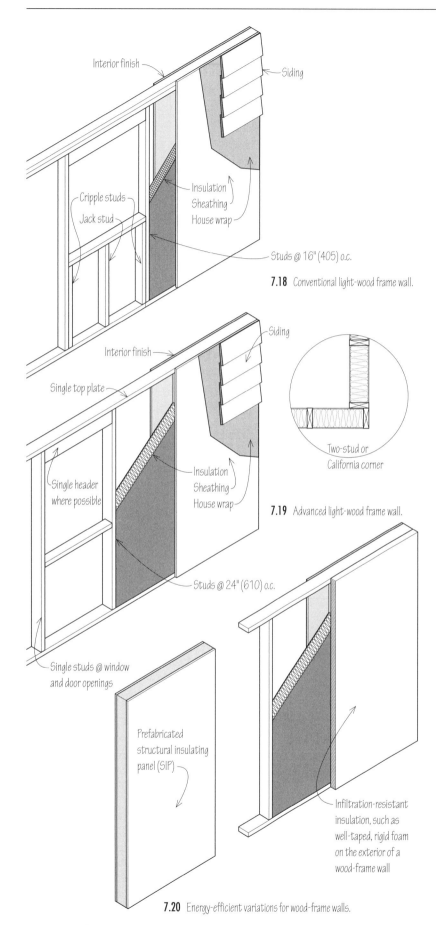

Interior finish
Siding
Cripple studs
Jack stud
Insulation
Sheathing
House wrap
Studs @ 16" (405) o.c.

7.18 Conventional light-wood frame wall.

Siding
Interior finish
Single top plate
Single header where possible
Insulation
Sheathing
House wrap
Single studs @ window and door openings
Studs @ 24" (610) o.c.

7.19 Advanced light-wood frame wall.

Two-stud or California corner

Prefabricated structural insulating panel (SIP)

Infiltration-resistant insulation, such as well-taped, rigid foam on the exterior of a wood-frame wall

7.20 Energy-efficient variations for wood-frame walls.

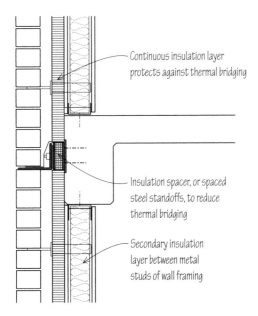

Continuous insulation layer protects against thermal bridging

Insulation spacer, or spaced steel standoffs, to reduce thermal bridging

Secondary insulation layer between metal studs of wall framing

7.21 Metal-frame wall detail.

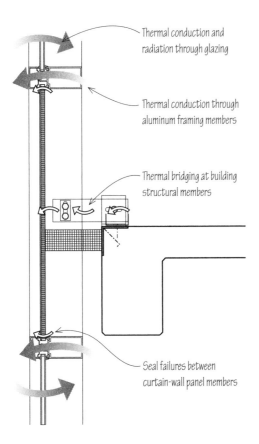

Thermal conduction and radiation through glazing

Thermal conduction through aluminum framing members

Thermal bridging at building structural members

Seal failures between curtain-wall panel members

7.22 Energy losses through curtain walls.

Metal-Frame Walls

Metal-frame walls have many similarities to wood-frame walls. It is a common framing type with which designers and builders have much experience.

Its embodied energy is similar to wood-frame walls and is among the lowest available for wall assemblies. Limitations of metal-frame walls for green construction are also similar to those of wood-frame walls. Studs form thermal bridges and the many joints in the framing offer many sites for infiltration. The high thermal conductivity of steel results in thermal bridging that is even higher than for wood studs. The means of overcoming these limitations are also similar to wood-frame walls. Advanced framing should be considered, such as 24-inch (610) metal stud spacing to reduce material use and thermal bridging. Well-taped rigid insulation can be placed on the exterior of the framing to add thermal resistance while reducing the effects of thermal bridging and reduce infiltration. Attention should be directed to air-sealing the joints and other infiltration sites, such as at wall penetrations.

Curtain Walls

Curtain walls are common in high-rise buildings. They are nonloadbearing assemblies that typically consist of a combination of vision glass and opaque spandrel panels supported by metal, usually aluminum, framing. They are called curtain walls because they literally hang from the structural frame of the building. While curtain walls provide no loadbearing function, they must be able to resist lateral wind and seismic loads and transmit these loads to the building structure. Curtain walls can be prefabricated or field-fabricated. If prefabricated, the discrete sections are referred to as unitized panels.

Curtain walls are vulnerable to a variety of energy losses, including thermal conduction and radiation through the glazing, thermal conduction through the aluminum framing members, thermal bridging at the building structural members, and seal failures between the curtain-wall panel members.

Even with high-performance glazing, insulated spandrel panels, and thermally broken framing, curtain walls are low-performance energy assemblies. Typical curtain walls have low thermal resistance, with R-values between R-2 and R-3. Higher-performance curtain walls have R-values around R-4 and the best available curtain walls only have R-values between R-6 and R-9.

7.23 Embodied energy of exterior walls in the U.S.

Exterior Wall Type	Embodied Energy (MMBtu/SF)	
	U.S. North	U.S. South
2x4 Steel Stud Wall		
16" (405) o.c. with brick cladding	0.10	0.10
24" (610) o.c. with brick cladding	0.10	0.09
16" (405) o.c. with wood cladding	0.07	0.07
24" (610) o.c. with wood cladding	0.06	0.06
16" (405) o.c. with steel cladding	0.24	0.24
2x6 Wood Stud Wall		
16" (405) o.c. with brick cladding	0.09	0.09
16" (405) o.c. with steel cladding	0.23	0.23
24" (610) o.c. with stucco cladding	0.07	0.07
24" (610) o.c. with wood cladding	0.05	0.05 ←
Structural Insulated Panel (SIP)		
with brick cladding	0.15	0.14
with steel cladding	0.30	0.29
with stucco cladding	0.14	0.13
with wood cladding	0.12	0.11
8" Concrete Block		
Brick Cladding	0.26	0.26
Stucco Cladding	0.25	0.25
Steel Cladding	0.41	0.41 ←
2x4 Steel Stud Wall [16" (405) o.c.]	0.24	0.24
6" Cast-in-Place Concrete		
Brick Cladding	0.13	0.13
Stucco Cladding	0.11	0.11
Steel Cladding	0.28	0.28
2x4 Steel Stud Wall [16" (405) o.c.]	0.11	0.11
8" Concrete Tilt-Up		
Brick Cladding	0.14	0.14
Stucco Cladding	0.12	0.12
Steel Cladding	0.29	0.29
2x4 Steel Stud Wall [16" (405) o.c.]	0.12	0.12
Insulated Concrete Forms		
Brick Cladding	0.16	0.16
Stucco Cladding	0.14	0.14
Steel Cladding	0.30	0.30

Source: U.S. Department of Energy

Choosing Between Wall Systems

Traditionally, the choice of a structural system for building walls has involved tradeoffs among cost, structural requirements, required fire ratings, available materials, and the experience of the design professionals and local contractors. Building aesthetics, including the facade or cladding, also influences the selection of structural systems. Green buildings add other considerations, such as thermal characteristics—both thermal resistance and thermal mass, infiltration control, moisture control, and embodied energy.

Wood-frame walls have the lowest embodied energy (0.07 MMBtu/SF), followed closely by steel-frame walls (0.08 MMBtu/SF) having equivalent overall thermal resistance and assuming the same stucco cladding. Various concrete walls, such as cast-in-place construction, tilt-up panels, and ICF panels, have embodied energy in the 0.11–0.14 MMBtu/SF range. Structural insulated panels (SIP) have an embodied energy of 0.14 MMBtu/SF. Walls of 8-inch (205) concrete block have an embodied energy of 0.25 MMBtu/SF. See Chapter 16, Materials, for more information on embodied energy.

Wood cladding has the lowest embodied energy, followed by stucco and brick. At the highest level of embodied energy is steel cladding.

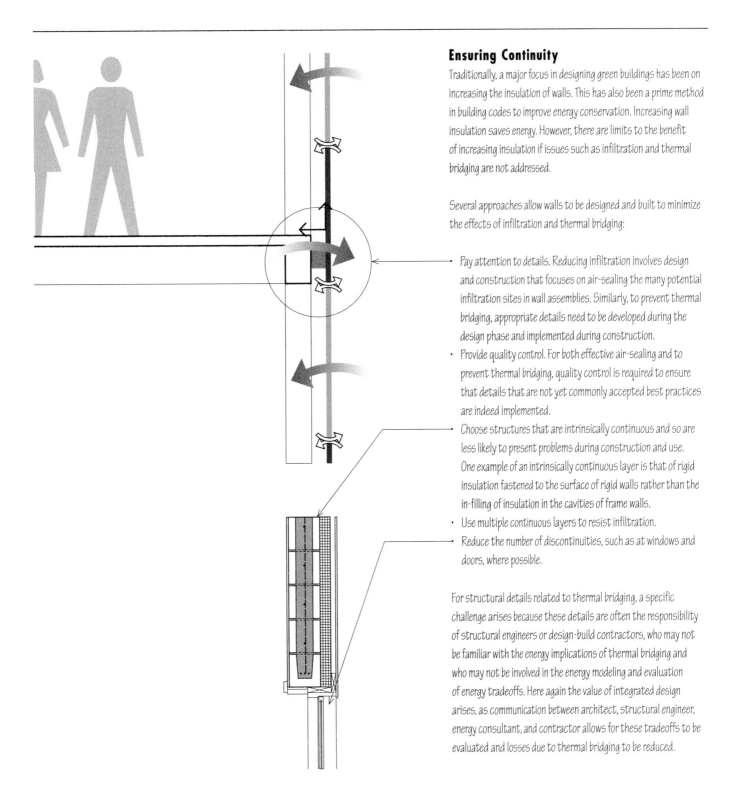

Ensuring Continuity

Traditionally, a major focus in designing green buildings has been on increasing the insulation of walls. This has also been a prime method in building codes to improve energy conservation. Increasing wall insulation saves energy. However, there are limits to the benefit of increasing insulation if issues such as infiltration and thermal bridging are not addressed.

Several approaches allow walls to be designed and built to minimize the effects of infiltration and thermal bridging:

- Pay attention to details. Reducing infiltration involves design and construction that focuses on air-sealing the many potential infiltration sites in wall assemblies. Similarly, to prevent thermal bridging, appropriate details need to be developed during the design phase and implemented during construction.
- Provide quality control. For both effective air-sealing and to prevent thermal bridging, quality control is required to ensure that details that are not yet commonly accepted best practices are indeed implemented.
- Choose structures that are intrinsically continuous and so are less likely to present problems during construction and use. One example of an intrinsically continuous layer is that of rigid insulation fastened to the surface of rigid walls rather than the in-filling of insulation in the cavities of frame walls.
- Use multiple continuous layers to resist infiltration.
- Reduce the number of discontinuities, such as at windows and doors, where possible.

For structural details related to thermal bridging, a specific challenge arises because these details are often the responsibility of structural engineers or design-build contractors, who may not be familiar with the energy implications of thermal bridging and who may not be involved in the energy modeling and evaluation of energy tradeoffs. Here again the value of integrated design arises, as communication between architect, structural engineer, energy consultant, and contractor allows for these tradeoffs to be evaluated and losses due to thermal bridging to be reduced.

7.24 Ways to minimize the effects of infiltration and thermal bridging.

Windows

Considering the many parts of a building, windows present one of the largest conundrums. Windows welcome natural light into buildings, offer building occupants views and connections to the outdoors and to the community beyond, and for many people bestow on buildings a natural beauty. However, windows are significant contributors to energy losses in a building and can also contribute to such discomfort as drafts, glare, convective air currents, and thermal and radiation losses.

High-Performance Windows

The first option for green buildings is to consider the use of high-performance windows. The evolution of high-performance windows may be traced through history, beginning with the origination of glass blowing in Babylon in about 250 BCE and the development of polished plate glass in France in the late 17th century.

Around 1950, storm windows were developed to add a second pane of glass, albeit separate from the main window. The original purpose of storm windows, as their name suggests, was not for energy efficiency but rather to protect the main window and the building from the impact of storms. Also known as hurricane windows, these added panes trap air between the main window and the storm window. This trapped air turns out to be a good insulator. This was an effective improvement, approximately doubling the thermal resistance of a single-pane window. A single-pane window has a U-factor of 1.1 in a wood-frame wall and 1.3 in a metal-frame wall. A storm window reduces the U-factor to approximately 0.5.

The double-pane window, invented in the 1930s, became commercially available in the 1950s as a factory-made assembly in a wood frame, complete with window hardware. The double-pane window offers similar efficiency gains to the storm window, but with the advantage of reliability; storm windows are often inadvertently left open.

As a result of the energy crisis of the early 1970s, low-emissivity technology was developed and introduced in the early 1980s. Low-emissivity (low-e) windows are manufactured by typically coating the inside surface of the outer pane with a thin metal or metallic oxide film so that visible light is transmitted but longer wavelengths of radiant heat are reflected. In winter, this means that more indoor heat is retained indoors, and in summer more outdoor heat is retained outdoors. Today, double-pane, low-e windows have U-factors of approximately 0.40.

In the 1980s, window manufacturers introduced vinyl and wood-vinyl composite frames, which reduced heat loss through the frame. Subsequently, insulation was added inside the hollow window frames. Around the same time, nonmetallic spacers holding the windows apart were introduced to reduce conductive heat loss at the frame.

Gas-filled windows, introduced in the late 1980s, use one or a combination of inert, colorless gases to fill the space between the panes of multipaned windows. Being more dense than the atmosphere, these gases minimize the convection currents within the space between the panes and reduce the overall heat transfer across the glazing assembly. Argon is the gas most often used. Krypton is denser, more effective, but also more expensive than argon. Argon-filled, double-pane windows with low-e coatings achieve U-factors of approximately 0.30. Triple-pane windows with low-e coatings and an inert-gas fill have U-factors in the 0.20 to 0.25 range.

High-performance windows offer increased R-values and lower U-factors, reduce energy use, and lessen the possibility of condensation and frost. They also improve comfort in buildings in winter by raising the temperature of the inner glazing surfaces closer to the air temperature within a space, thus reducing convective drafts and radiant heat loss. In summer, windows with low solar heat gain coefficients reduce solar radiation and the discomfort associated with overheating of a space.

Indoors   Outdoors

Surface numbering starts with surface #1 as the outer face of the outer pane.

Low-e coating is on surface #2.

Double-pane window

Low-e coating on surfaces #2 and #5.

Triple-pane window

7.25 Numbering of surfaces in multipaned windows.

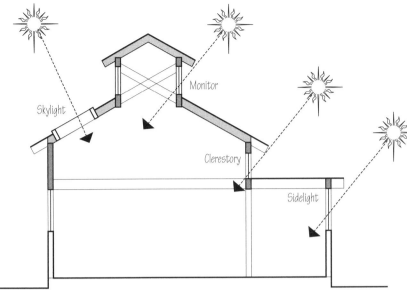

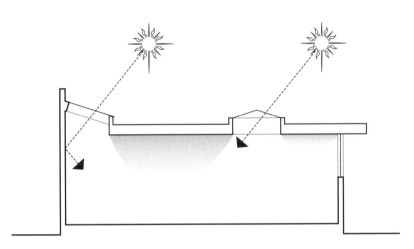

7.26 Daylighting options.

Daylighting

For green buildings, windows offer the potential for energy savings through daylighting. Daylighting can be provided by sidelighting and or by toplighting. Sidelighting is supplied by windows in walls while toplighting may be provided by a variety of roof-mounted windows, including skylights and roof monitors.

Optimum glazing for daylighting is different from the glazing for views. The best daylighting approach is evenly spaced toplighting on the flat roof of a building, casting light evenly over a space. This is limited to single-story buildings, to the top floor of multistory buildings, or to those floors that can be readily reached through the use of light tubes. For sidelighting, windows are ideally located high on a wall, close to the ceiling, to cast light as deeply as possible into a space without introducing glare.

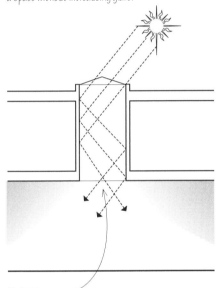

7.27 Toplighting is largely limited to single-story buildings or the top floors of multistory buildings, although a variety of light tube products have been introduced that allow extending light penetration through attics and top floors to reach the floors below.

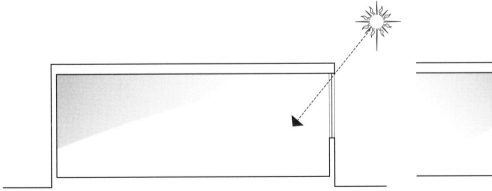

7.28 Sidelighting windows should be located high enough on a wall to cast light as deeply into a space as possible.

7.29 Example of a global illumination technique that uses sophisticated algorithms to more accurately simulate the illumination of a space or scene. These algorithms take into account not only the light rays that are emitted directly from one or more sources. They also track the light rays as they are reflected or refracted from one surface to another, especially the diffuse inter-reflections that occur among the surfaces in a space or scene.

Daylighting is a complex topic, best handled with models of illuminance, optimized for energy efficiency by trading off lighting gains against window heating and cooling losses, with the risk of glare evaluated and prevented, and implemented with careful attention to daylighting controls. Daylighting is best addressed at exactly this phase of the design, during consideration of the outer envelope, when it can be optimized, and before the design of artificial lighting begins.

Daylighting involves more than just adding windows to buildings. There is a significant tradeoff between the energy savings gained through daylighting and the heating and cooling losses resulting from larger window areas. The savings in electricity increase along with the expansion of window areas for daylighting, but window thermal losses also increase. For smaller window areas, the reduction in electric lighting requirements resulting from daylighting is typically greater than the negative impact of window thermal losses on heating and cooling loads, and so there are net savings. However, the savings in electricity from daylighting reach a maximum as window areas increase, whereas the negative impact of window thermal losses continues to increase with increased window area. So, there is an optimum window size, above which thermal losses reduce the net savings from daylighting.

The potential energy savings from daylighting has decreased in recent years because of greater efficiencies in artificial lighting technologies and the increasing use of controls for reducing the duration of use of artificial lighting. There is a further decrease in potential savings if the reflectance of interior surfaces is increased. With these changes, the optimum window-to-wall ratio or window-to-roof ratio has also decreased.

For many types of buildings and occupancies, if the recommended glazing sizes for daylighting are applied indiscriminately, without regard to window thermal losses, building energy use may increase instead of decrease.

7.30 Example of optimizing window sizes for daylighting.

7.31 Reflectance values of a room's surface affect the daylighting strategy for the space.

The success of a daylighting strategy is strongly dependent on the reflectance of interior surfaces, such as ceilings, walls, floors, and furnishings. For example, by increasing the average interior reflectance from 50% to 75%, the required glazing area for daylighting in a 12 x 15 foot (3.7 x 4.6 meter) office is reduced by over 50%, from 25 square feet (2.3 m²) to 12 square feet (1.1 m²). Choosing reflective finishes for ceilings, walls, floors, window coverings, and furnishings becomes a potentially important and affordable green improvement. But to take advantage of the benefits of higher reflectances for daylighting, the increased reflectances are best combined with reducing the daylight-window sizes or quantities, thereby reducing thermal losses.

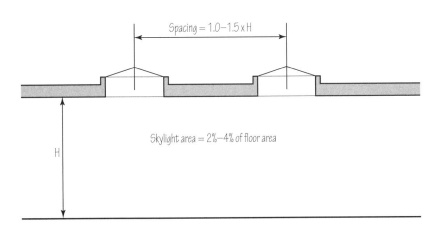

7.32 Rules of thumb for skylight daylighting.

It is helpful to differentiate between daylighting that is designed purposefully to reduce the use of electricity for artificial lighting, and daylighting that is obtained as a result of vision glazing that cannot be eliminated for aesthetic purposes. The latter might be called incidental daylighting, which is not simply an added benefit of required vision glazing but rather a means of avoiding a double energy penalty—the increase in energy use from both artificial lighting and window thermal losses.

There are several advantages to toplighting through skylights and monitors, including greater uniformity of illumination, simpler controls, greater space coverage, and fewer problems with glare. Just as with sidelighting, the glazing for toplighting should not be oversized. Otherwise thermal losses would outweigh daylighting gains. Optimal glazing sizes for toplighting should be calculated by computer simulation. Rule-of-thumb sizing suggests the area of toplighting skylights should be only 2%–4% of the floor area with the units being spaced at 1 to 1.5 times the ceiling height. Because the majority of commercial buildings in the United States are two stories or less, 60% of the floor area below U.S. roofs can be toplit. Of the various choices for toplighting, skylights provide more uniform lighting and provide more daylight for more hours of the year than roof monitors.

The benefits of daylighting can only be achieved with associated control of indoor artificial lighting. Without this control, instead of saving energy, daylighting would add to a building's energy use by adding to its thermal load without saving on its lighting load. There are two primary types of lighting controls: stepped switching and continuous dimming. Both reduce energy consumption by using photosensors to detect daylighting levels and automatically adjusting the output level of electric lighting to create the desired or recommended level of illumination for a space. If the daylighting from windows is sufficient to meet the user's needs, the lighting control system can automatically turn off all or a portion of the electric lighting or dim the lighting, and immediately reactivate the lighting if the daylighting falls below a preset level. These daylight harvesting controls can be integrated with occupancy sensors for automated on/off control to further increase energy savings as well as with manual override controls to allow for adjustment of lighting levels by occupants. Some control systems can also adjust the color balance of the light by varying the intensity of individual LED lamps of different colors installed in the overhead fixtures.

Automatic lighting controls need to have their switching points carefully set to deliver energy savings without causing nuisance operation of the lights. For example, an office with a single light fixture controlled by a stepped lighting control may have a light-level requirement of 30 foot-candles. In the morning, when passing clouds dim the space to a light level of 10 foot-candles, the automatic lighting control turns on the electric light. When the sun comes out, rapidly increasing the lighting level from 10 foot-candles to well above 30 foot-candles, the electric light is turned off. If the control is set to turn the light off when the light level in the space rises above 31 foot-candles and to turn the light on when the light level falls below 30 foot-candles, there is a risk that with each passing cloud the light will rapidly turn on and off, which soon becomes a nuisance.

If instead the control is set to turn on the electric light when the light level falls below 30 foot-candles and to turn off the light when the light level rises above 50 foot-candles, the light no longer cycles on and off as rapidly with each passing cloud, but now the office light level rises and falls, which may result in a different kind of nuisance. Also the light may well be on for longer than it needs to be, reducing some of the energy savings. Finding the right balance between nuisance cycling and nuisance light-level fluctuations can be a challenge. Automatic dimming controls can solve this problem to some degree, but the controls still need to be carefully set. The daylighting sensor must also be carefully located and oriented to avoid being activated by other artificial lighting.

In summary, daylighting can offer energy savings for those buildings for which the duration of lighting in hours per day is high, and where possible variations in light level over time and across space are acceptable. To be energy efficient, the glazing should not be over-sized so as to increase window thermal losses and the automatic lighting controls must be properly designed, installed, commissioned, operated, and maintained.

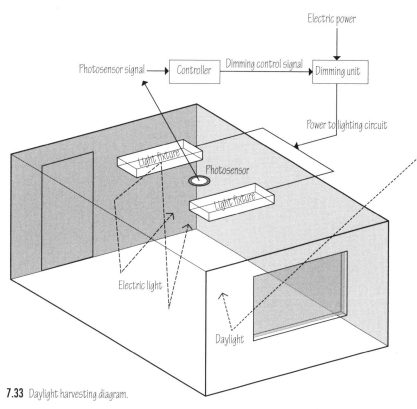

7.33 Daylight harvesting diagram.

Views

Views through windows offer a vital connection to the outdoors, give occupants an indication of outdoor weather conditions, and contribute to human mental health and productivity. Vision glazing is defined in the LEED Rating System as being between 30 inches (760) and 90 inches (2,285) above the floor. BREEAM defines a view as being able to see the sky from a desk height of 28 inches (710), as well as states that a view out exists when the window-to-wall ratio is 20% or higher.

As with daylighting, the size of windows required for views should be carefully evaluated in order to avoid the introduction of undue window thermal losses. For example, the lower edge of a window can be higher than 30 inches (760) and still typically afford good views. Window head heights also do not need to be as high as 90 inches (2,285) to afford good views. LEED's definition of vision glazing rising to 90 inches is intended to define the zone above which daylighting glazing starts, rather than the zone at which vision glazing needs to end. Further, windows need not stretch the length of a wall to afford good views. BREEAM defines a view as being able to see out within 23 feet (7 m) of an exterior wall by providing a minimum 20% window-to-wall ratio.

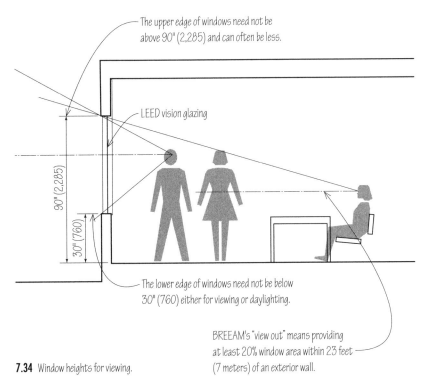

The upper edge of windows need not be above 90" (2,285) and can often be less.

LEED vision glazing

90" (2,285)

30" (760)

The lower edge of windows need not be below 30" (760) either for viewing or daylighting.

BREEAM's "view out" means providing at least 20% window area within 23 feet (7 meters) of an exterior wall.

7.34 Window heights for viewing.

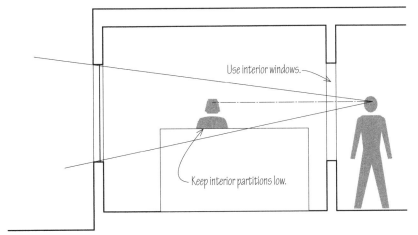

Use interior windows.

Keep interior partitions low.

LEED suggests that windows are needed for views only in regularly occupied spaces. They are not needed in spaces that are predominantly unoccupied. Each step of the way, we need to recall the large thermal energy losses that windows introduce and to consider ways in which to reduce these losses.

LEED suggests further strategies for views that include using interior windows, allowing occupants of interior spaces to see outdoors through perimeter spaces, and using lower interior partitions to prevent obstructing views.

7.35 Additional strategies for enhancing viewing from within rooms.

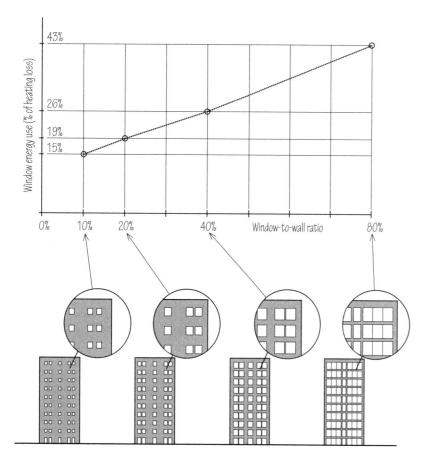

7.36 Energy loss through windows.

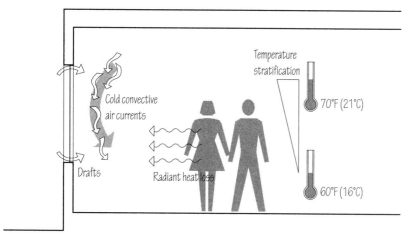

7.37 Comfort issues related to windows.

Window Losses

In contrast with the benefits of daylighting and views, windows represent multiple and significant energy inefficiencies. Windows lose heat in the winter by thermal conduction, air infiltration, and radiation, and conversely are a substantial source of heat gain in summer and the associated need for air-conditioning. Windows also typically carry a higher construction cost for both low-rise and high-rise buildings, relative to the wall area that they displace.

To put the significant energy losses of windows in perspective, a typical wall has a thermal resistance (R-value) in the range of between R-10 and R-30 with an average around R-20, whereas a typical double-pane window has an R-value of about R-2, ten times more inefficient than an average wall. Even high-performance windows have an R-value of only between R-3 and R-5. And this does not account for infiltration losses, radiation losses, and losses through the thermal bridging of the wall framing around windows. There are more subtle losses as well, as a window at night reflects little light back into the room and so can require more artificial lighting inside the room. Accounting for all these window losses, it is likely that windows often account for well over ten times more energy use than the walls they displace. For this reason, a typical building loses 25% of its energy through its windows, and energy losses are even greater in buildings with a high window-to-wall ratio.

The impact of windows is not only felt in higher energy and construction costs but also in discomfort. Signs of this discomfort can be seen in the common practice of providing heat below windows in order to counter the cold from windows, or in the need to move furniture away from windows to avoid drafts. Furthermore, placing a heat source below windows only exacerbates window losses in winter, as the interior of the window surfaces meet a warmer temperature than the average indoor air temperature. The human body also loses heat in winter by radiant heat transfer to the window and through the window to cold surfaces outdoors. Even fixed windows cause discomfort. It is not unusual to find significant temperature stratification in rooms with large or full-height windows, with air temperature variations of 10°F (5.6°C) or more between the heads and feet of occupants. Finally, windows often cause glare, resulting in windows that need tinting or interior blinds or curtains to be drawn closed, eliminating the views and daylighting for which the windows were originally designed.

For windows having exposure to the sun, window losses are partially offset by solar gains in winter.

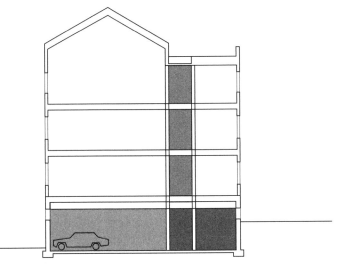

7.38 Minimize or eliminate windows in utility and service spaces.

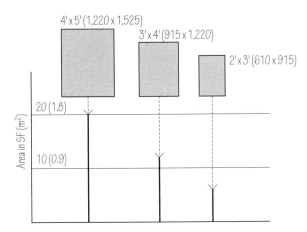

7.39 A comparison of window sizes and areas.

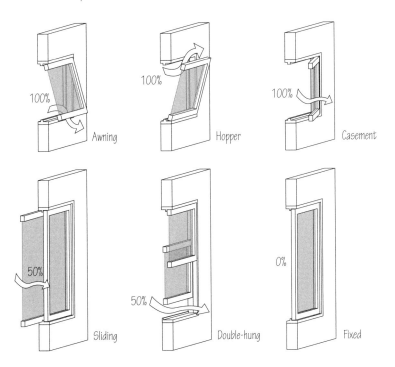

7.40 Relative effectiveness of window types for ventilation.

Reducing Window Losses

How can window losses be reduced in green buildings? First, avoid or reduce the number of windows in spaces in which they are not needed, such as garages, stairwells and stair landings, corridors, closets, basements, laundry rooms, entries and vestibules, and other utility spaces where the duration of occupancy is short.

Secondly, where possible, allocate one or two windows in common room types, such as small offices and residential bedrooms, instead of the three or more that are common. The size of windows can also be judiciously selected. A 3 x 4-foot (915 x 1,220) window is almost half the area of a 4 x 5-foot (1,220 x 1,525) window. A 2 x 3-foot (610 x 915) window is half again the area of the 3 x 4-foot (915 x 1,220) window.

A third strategy is to use fixed windows wherever operable windows are not needed. Fixed windows reduce infiltration, although attention still needs to be directed to preventing air leakage between the windows and the wall structure. For example, a single-hung window offers less potential infiltration than a double-hung window, while sacrificing no operable area.

If windows are sized for natural ventilation, casement or awning windows offer more open area than sliding or double-hung windows, which are intrinsically limited to opening only one-half of their total area. Casement and awning windows generally are tighter, with lower air leakage than vertical or horizontal sliding windows. So if the full size of a window is not needed for light or views, a casement or awning window offers a way to provide more ventilation in a smaller, energy-efficient, and affordable way.

For a given desired window area, a smaller number of larger windows is more efficient than a larger number of smaller windows. A major weak link for energy losses is the window frame, along which infiltration occurs both through the operable portion of the window and through the wall framing or structure around the window, and along which conduction losses are also higher than at the center of the glazing. A 4 x 6-foot (1,220 x 1,830) window has 20 feet (6,095) of window perimeter. Two 3 x 4-foot (915 x 1,220) windows that provide the same 24 square feet (2.2 m^2) of window area have a total of 28 feet (8,535) of window perimeter, a 40% increase. Four 2 x 3-foot (610 x 915) windows, again providing 24 square feet (2.2 m^2) of window area, have a total perimeter of 40 feet (12,190), 100% more than a single 4 x 6-foot (1,220 x 1,830) window. And eight 1 x 3-foot (305 x 915) windows more than triple the total perimeter. Note that proportion is also important. A single thin ribbon window that measures 1 x 24 feet (305 x 7,315) for the same 24-square-foot area, has a 50-foot perimeter. So squarer is better than long and thin, although the differences between perfectly square and slightly rectangular are small.

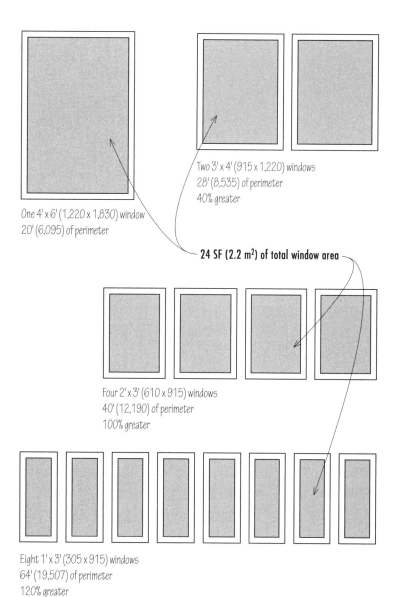

One 4' x 6' (1,220 x 1,830) window
20' (6,095) of perimeter

Two 3' x 4' (915 x 1,220) windows
28' (8,535) of perimeter
40% greater

24 SF (2.2 m^2) of total window area

Four 2' x 3' (610 x 915) windows
40' (12,190) of perimeter
100% greater

Eight 1' x 3' (305 x 915) windows
64' (19,507) of perimeter
120% greater

7.41 The larger a window, the lower its perimeter infiltration and conduction per unit area.

A smaller number of larger windows also reduces construction cost when compared to a larger number of smaller windows having the same total window area. For example, one 3 x 4-foot (915 x 1,220) double-hung window costs approximately 25% less fully installed than two 2 x 3-foot (610 x 915) windows.

Other characteristics of windows, such as their visual massing and the quality of the views and daylighting they afford, should also be weighed in conjunction with the energy tradeoffs of size and quantity. In any such evaluations, attention is well directed to maintaining views and providing the daylight that people so deeply value in frequently occupied spaces.

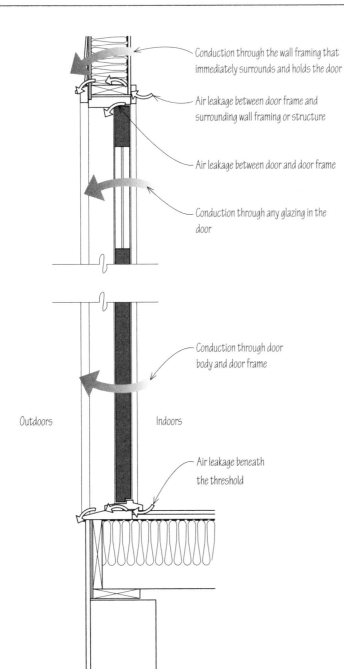

Conduction through the wall framing that immediately surrounds and holds the door

Air leakage between door frame and surrounding wall framing or structure

Air leakage between door and door frame

Conduction through any glazing in the door

Outdoors   Indoors

Conduction through door body and door frame

Air leakage beneath the threshold

7.42 Heat loss and infiltration paths through a door.

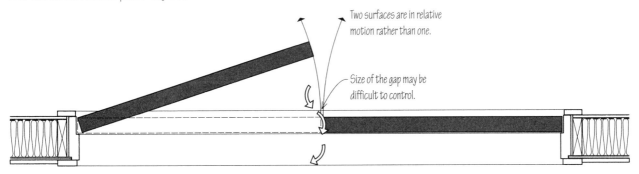

Two surfaces are in relative motion rather than one.

Size of the gap may be difficult to control.

7.43 Two challenges in sealing double doors.

Doors

Doors are in many ways similar to windows. Exterior doors also penetrate the building envelope or thermal boundary. Each door presents several paths for air to infiltrate: Between the door and door frame; between the door frame and the surrounding wall framing or structure; and beneath the threshold. Each door also presents several paths for heat loss and heat gain to occur by conduction: Through the door body, through glazing in the door, through the door frame, and through the surrounding wall structure.

However, exterior doors are in some ways different than windows with regard to energy losses. Solid doors allow lower heat loss and heat gain than windows, and insulated doors allow even less. There are also typically fewer doors in a building than there are windows, although some building types do have many doors, such as townhouses and hotels with exterior entries.

A common mistake with doors is to inadvertently use an uninsulated interior door as an exterior door, especially between heated spaces and attached unconditioned spaces, such as garages or attics.

Even if there are fewer exterior doors than windows in buildings, they are opened and closed more often than windows. This operation results in the components that guard against air leakage but are subject to relative motion, such as weatherstripping and door sweeps, to experience more wear and tear than do the moving components on windows.

Double doors are more challenging to seal tightly because there is not just one moving component and one fixed component; instead, there are two moving components that need to seal against each other. There is often no weatherstripping between the doors, or there may be a gap that is too large for the weatherstripping to bridge.

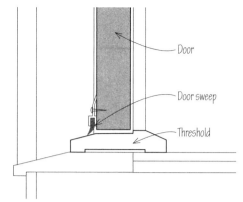

Door

Door sweep

Threshold

7.44 Weatherstripping the bottom edge of an exterior door.

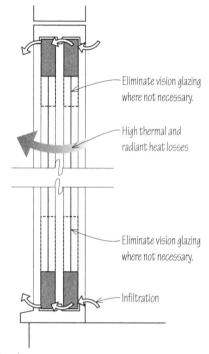

Eliminate vision glazing where not necessary.

High thermal and radiant heat losses

Eliminate vision glazing where not necessary.

Infiltration

7.45 Sliding glass doors.

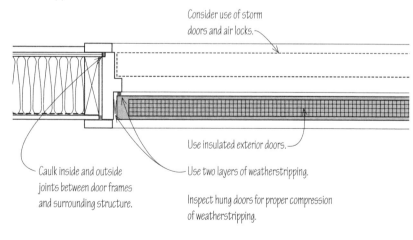

Consider use of storm doors and air locks.

Use insulated exterior doors.

Caulk inside and outside joints between door frames and surrounding structure.

Use two layers of weatherstripping.

Inspect hung doors for proper compression of weatherstripping.

Avoid excessive glazing and use of double doors and sliding doors where possible.

7.46 Best practices for doors.

Because exterior doors are typically located on the bottom floors of buildings and on the top floors for roof access, they can also be more subject to stack effect pressures than are windows.

The bottom edge of an exterior door is unique in that weatherstripping on the fixed surface, the threshold, is not as viable because it is subject to foot traffic. What has been developed to deal with this challenge is the door sweep. The flexible portion of the sweep is typically a brush or a vinyl or rubber strip. Door sweeps may not fit well and can be damaged over time. Because the door sweep is a vulnerable location, there is a need for another layer of shelter, which a storm door can provide. However, for a storm door to be effective, it needs to itself have a good sweep, weatherstripping, and frame caulking.

Sliding exterior doors, which typically are fully glazed, are particularly susceptible to misalignment and air infiltration.

Any glazing in doors replicates the high thermal losses of windows. Therefore, glazing should be limited to those instances where it is required for views or for safety vision. Limit the use of fully glazed doors, such as sliding patio or balcony doors, if their high-loss vision glazing is not fully needed. Lobby doors in commercial buildings as well as side and rear-entry doors are other examples where full glazing is not always necessary.

Best practices for doors in green buildings include:
· Minimize the number of exterior doors in a building.
· Avoid sliding doors where possible.
· Avoid double doors where possible.
· Avoid doors with excessive glazing where possible.
· Use insulated exterior doors and insulated doors between conditioned and unconditioned spaces.
· Use storm doors, where possible. They offer an additional layer of shelter, not only for increased thermal resistance but also added protection against infiltration.
· Caulk door frames and beneath door threshold, both inside and out. Also caulk the frame of storm doors.
· Consider incorporating air locks into building entries.
· Insulate around door frames.
· Weatherstrip doors and ensure proper compression by requiring testing.

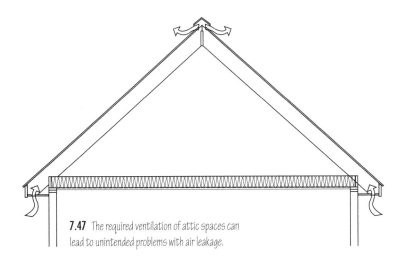

7.47 The required ventilation of attic spaces can lead to unintended problems with air leakage.

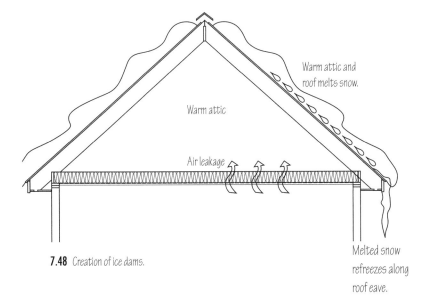

Warm attic and roof melts snow.

Warm attic

Air leakage

7.48 Creation of ice dams.

Melted snow refreezes along roof eave.

Roofs

Energy codes and high-performance standards such as ASHRAE 189 provide requirements for roof insulation, which are typically optimized for specific geographic locations. Like walls, roofs can have losses due to thermal bridging but a continuous layer of insulation can prevent this. Roofs typically do not allow air infiltration because they are built to prevent water infiltration. However, roof vents, such as ridge vents, are part of a strategy to purposefully introduce air into attics, and this can be an unintended cause of problems, especially in buildings with pitched roofs.

Pitched Roofs

From an energy perspective, the most significant development relating to roofs has been the discovery of how seriously air leaks from buildings into attic spaces and then out through the attic vents of pitched roofs. The number and variety of types of air leakage at the attic floor is significant. Air can leak through attic hatches and the top of wall cavities; around chimneys and vents; through uncapped chases; around electrical and other wiring penetrations; around exhaust fans and recessed light fixtures; and along the edges of party walls.

Another negative impact of this air leakage is the formation of ice dams on roofs in cold climates, caused when leaking air melts the snow on roofs and the melted water runs down the roof and refreezes in roof valleys and at the roof edge and on gutters.

Why do pitched roofs and attics have so many infiltration problems? The answer lies possibly in the confusion that arises between the role of the roof and the role of the top-story ceiling or, in other words, the floor of the attic. The function of the pitched roof is primarily to stop rain from entering a building. The role of the attic floor has been primarily to serve as the thermal boundary. However, this division of roles has allowed the attic floor to be sealed inadequately. If the attic floor needed to be impervious to water, as is the case with walls or flat roofs, it likely would not allow air to escape.

A case might even be made that flat roofs are greener than pitched roofs for two reasons: They avoid the substantial air leakage to which pitched roofs and vented attic spaces are susceptible, and they are more receptive to the installation of green components, such as solar panels and vegetated roofs.

Flat roofs are also more affordable than pitched roofs. Pitched roofs essentially require the cost of two separate roof structures, one at the roof line, and one at the attic floor, whereas flat roofs require only one structure. One estimate puts the cost of flat roofs as 22% less than that of pitched roofs. We recognize the various vulnerabilities of flat roofs in terms of aesthetics, a tendency for water to puddle, and their inability to shed snow. If a pitched roof is determined to be vital to a building's aesthetic design or for other reasons, attention must be directed to providing a strong and continuous thermal boundary, either along the pitched roof line or at the attic floor.

A separate discussion can be had about green or vegetated roofs themselves. There are debates about the high cost of vegetated roofs and the magnitude of their thermal energy benefits. Nevertheless, there are some benefits in terms of reducing heat island effects, controlling runoff, and providing green space on top of buildings. Should vegetated roofs prove cost-effective and reliable over time, flat roofs are more receptive to them than are pitched roofs.

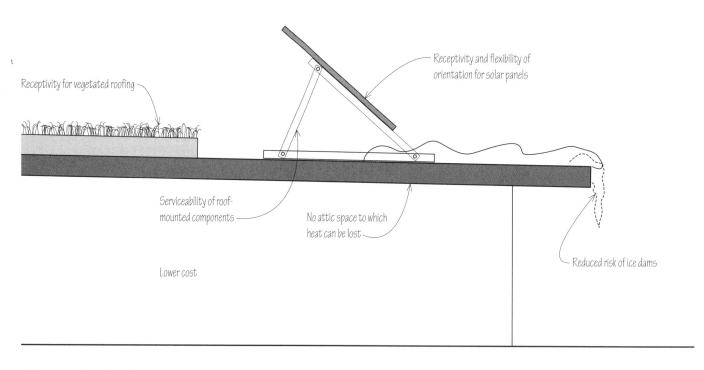

Receptivity for vegetated roofing

Receptivity and flexibility of orientation for solar panels

Serviceability of roof-mounted components

No attic space to which heat can be lost

Reduced risk of ice dams

Lower cost

7.49 Green benefits of flat roofs.

Floors

We conclude our examination of the outer envelope with a discussion of floors, specifically slab-on-grade floors, as basements and crawlspaces are addressed in Chapter 8, Unconditioned Spaces.

Buildings lose heat through slab-on-grade floors to the ground below. The ground is usually colder than the air in buildings, in the 30°F to 60°F (−1.1°C to 5.5°C) range in the shallow earth in winter, depending on the geographic location. However, the air in buildings is approximately 70°F (21.1°C) in winter, so the ground below will draw heat down from a building above. One study of 33 energy-efficient homes found ground losses to be 24% of total heat losses, with speculation that losses are even higher in nonefficient homes. Edge insulation is especially important, as heat can move through the floor edge, through the ground, to the cold air above in winter. Infrared scans show this heat loss. The edge of building slabs typically show up as warm in infrared scans, as the heat is conducted outward.

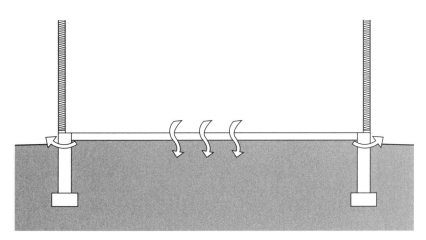

7.50 Heat loss through slab-on-grade floors.

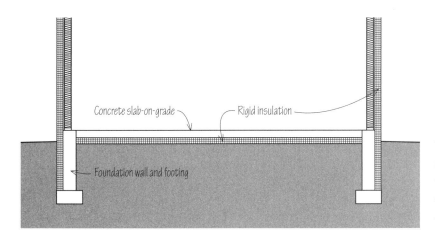

Thermal continuity is a challenge here. An insulated wall typically rests on a solid concrete slab, which is a conductor of heat. If the floor is insulated on its top surface, the slab is moved outside of the thermal envelope, with thermal bridging via the exterior and interior wall structures down to the slab. If the slab is insulated on its underside, there is a thermal bridge at the edge of the slab, unless the edge is insulated. For continuity, it is likely more effective to insulate the exterior of the slab, both at the perimeter and below it.

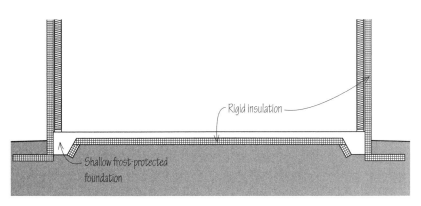

7.51 Providing thermal continuity for slab-on-grade floors.

There is a trend toward in-floor radiant systems to heat buildings for the comfort and temperature uniformity they provide. There is also potential for energy conservation because indoor air temperatures can be reduced as a result of the higher comfort that radiant heat systems provide. However, for floors on grade, there is a risk of losing heat to the earth below, even if the slab has insulation below it. If considering radiant in-floor heat in a slab-on-grade foundation, an evaluation of energy losses to the ground below should be performed, even if the slab is fully insulated.

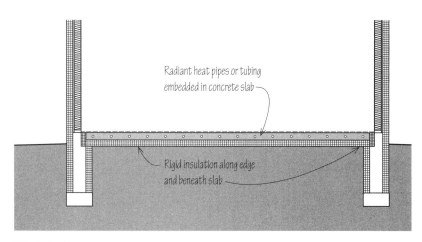

Radiant heat pipes or tubing embedded in concrete slab

Rigid insulation along edge and beneath slab

7.52 Radiant heat system.

Insulating the floor is important not only for energy reasons but also for comfort. A cold floor is uncomfortable for the feet and is also a heat sink for radiant losses from the body, making the body feel cold.

Preventing moisture migration up through a slab-on-grade floor is also critical. Otherwise, materials in contact with the floor will become wet and the space will become humid. A full set of protective layers is needed to prevent such problems: Grading to direct surface water away from a building; perimeter drainage to direct away any water that does get close to the building; subslab gravel to minimize the contact of wet soil with the slab; and a strong and continuous subslab vapor barrier.

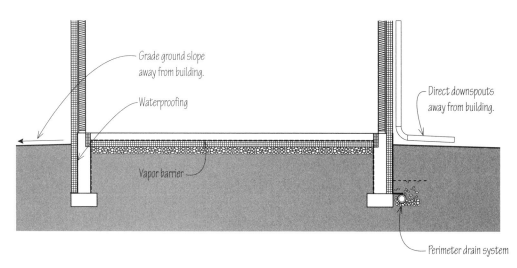

Grade ground slope away from building.

Waterproofing

Direct downspouts away from building.

Vapor barrier

Perimeter drain system

7.53 Ways to prevent migration of moisture through slab-on-grade floors.

8
Unconditioned Spaces

Unconditioned spaces are spaces that are neither heated nor cooled. There can be a variety of unconditioned spaces between the outer envelope and the inner envelope of a building. These spaces include attics, basements, crawl spaces, attached garages, mud rooms, vestibules, mechanical rooms, and storage rooms.

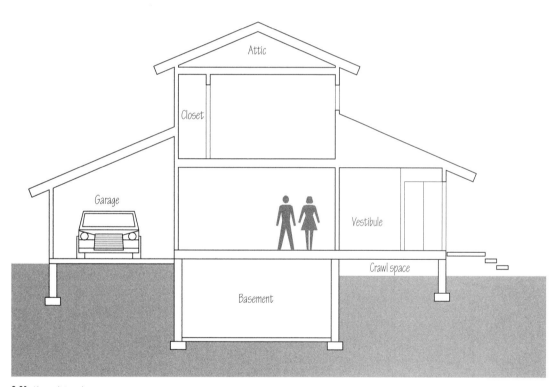

8.01 Unconditioned spaces.

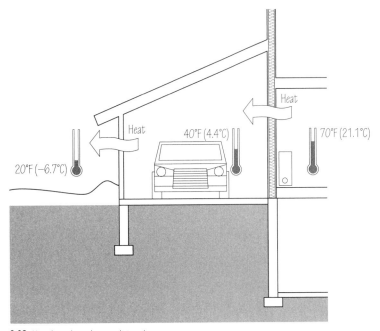

8.02 Heat loss through unconditioned spaces.

20°F (−6.7°C)   Heat   Heat   40°F (4.4°C)   70°F (21.1°C)

Unconditioned spaces receive some heating or cooling passively. In winter, heat travels across shared walls, from heated spaces into unconditioned spaces, and then from the unconditioned spaces to the outdoors. The opposite is true in summer, with heat flowing into the building. Unconditioned spaces typically are at an equilibrium temperature somewhere between the temperature of the conditioned spaces and the outdoors. As a result, even though the unconditioned spaces receive heating or cooling passively, this heat transfer must ultimately be made up in the conditioned spaces, and so the heat loss through the unconditioned spaces uses energy.

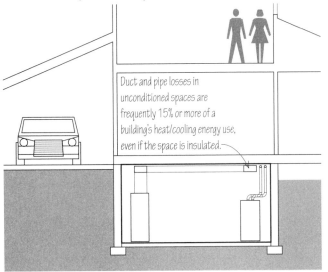

Duct and pipe losses in unconditioned spaces are frequently 15% or more of a building's heat/cooling energy use, even if the space is insulated.

8.03 Distribution system losses.

Unconditioned spaces have a second energy-related vulnerability. They are often spaces through which heating and cooling distribution systems are routed. These distribution systems comprise ductwork or piping, or both. Because the unconditioned spaces, by definition, do not need to be conditioned, heat loss to and from these distribution systems in any unconditioned space results in wasted energy.

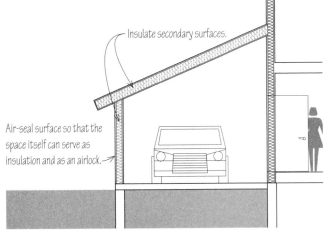

Insulate secondary surfaces.

Air-seal surface so that the space itself can serve as insulation and as an airlock.

8.04 Putting unconditioned spaces to use to reduce energy consumption.

These energy vulnerabilities of unconditioned spaces need attention. We can go beyond just solving these problems and instead take advantage of unconditioned spaces by putting them to use as another layer of shelter. Unconditioned spaces are, essentially, trapped air that can be used as a form of insulation. Furthermore, unconditioned spaces usually have at least one uninsulated surface, either between the unconditioned space and the outdoors or between the unconditioned space and an adjacent conditioned space. This allows insulation to be added, often affordably, to firm up an additional layer of shelter. Finally, unconditioned spaces can serve as an airlock and reduce infiltration as people enter and leave a building.

Later in this chapter, we will examine a variety of common types of spaces to see which ones might be changed from being typically conditioned to being unconditioned. This can further reduce energy use as well as reduce construction costs.

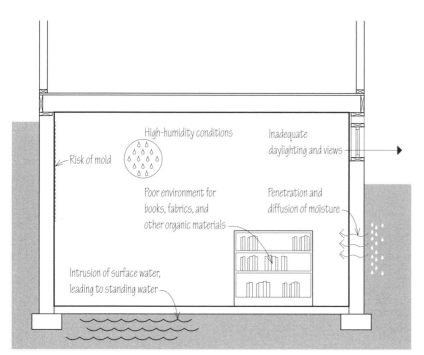

8.05 Environmental quality issues in basement spaces.

High-humidity conditions

Inadequate daylighting and views

Risk of mold

Poor environment for books, fabrics, and other organic materials

Penetration and diffusion of moisture

Intrusion of surface water, leading to standing water

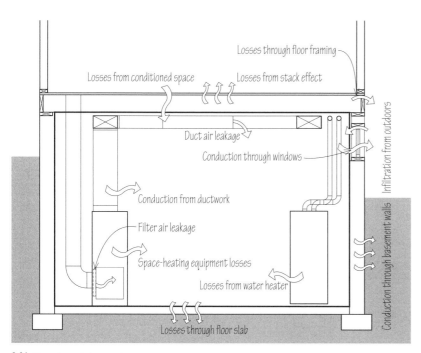

8.06 Energy losses in basement spaces.

Losses through floor framing

Losses from conditioned space

Losses from stack effect

Duct air leakage

Conduction through windows

Infiltration from outdoors

Conduction from ductwork

Conduction through basement walls

Filter air leakage

Space-heating equipment losses

Losses from water heater

Losses through floor slab

Basements

Basements are common in homes and are also found in many commercial buildings. These partially or wholly underground spaces are convenient for providing storage and work areas, locating mechanical equipment, and concealing various utilities, such as piping, ductwork, and electrical distribution systems. Basements are sometimes occupied and used as TV rooms, dens, and, with proper daylighting and ventilation, as offices, bedrooms, even full apartments. From a heating and cooling point of view, basements are spaces that are mostly earth-bermed and so have lower heat losses and gains than spaces that are fully exposed to outdoor air. Basements can, nevertheless, lose or gain a significant amounts of heat.

On the negative side, basements can suffer from high humidity if moisture is transported through concrete foundation walls and slabs into the space. Surface water can also find its way by gravity into basements. As unconditioned spaces having a utilitarian function, basements are relatively expensive due to the excavation and foundation work required for their construction. Basements offer little or no daylight, little or no views, and can be unwelcoming as occupied spaces.

Basements are not always recognized to be either conditioned or unconditioned spaces, which can lead to indecisiveness as to whether to actually condition or not condition these spaces. Basement ceilings are sometimes insulated, but often are not, and so they serve as a path for heat loss from the heated space above down to the basement.

Basements are sites where a large amount of energy is lost in heating and cooling distribution systems. Recent studies have confirmed the substantial effect of such losses. Energy is lost by conduction from the equipment and distribution system, including boilers, furnaces, ductwork, pipes, valves, and pumps. Energy is also lost by air leakage into and out of forced-air systems along ductwork seams, at duct connections, from the air handlers themselves, and at filters. For buildings in which the heating and cooling equipment and distribution are located in a basement, 15% or more of the heating and cooling energy used in the building can be lost in such basement distribution systems. Distribution systems in basements are also vulnerable to deterioration over time. Duct and pipe insulation can detach or be removed and not be replaced; duct blanket insulation can compress, reducing its thermal resistance; duct air leaks can develop and get worse over time; and duct grilles that are intended to be shut can inadvertently be left open.

Another energy penalty attributable to basements relates to the stack effect. Basements add another story to buildings, which amplifies the stack effect, even in buildings that have only one main floor. Basements are typically leaky and cold air in winter can be readily drawn into the basement from such locations as sill plates, ill-fitting windows, and basement doors. Basements are rarely well-sealed relative to the heated spaces upstairs, so stack-effect air can rise readily from the basement up to the first floor of the building through doorways; pipe, duct, and electrical penetrations; and between floorboards or joints in subflooring. As soon as this air enters a heated space, it becomes an added load on the building's energy use. The heated air then leaves the building through the windows and walls of upper floors, and through the attic.

Basements can be made more energy efficient by air-sealing walls, windows, and basement ceilings, and ensuring that basement doors to the upstairs are weatherstripped. Ducts, pipes, and pipe fittings can also be insulated and ducts air-sealed. Conduction losses can be reduced by insulating walls and basement ceilings and improving the thermal performance of windows.

A common misconception is that insulating basement walls brings them into the thermal envelope, negating any basement heat losses. As long as a basement is unconditioned, losses in the basement are still losses and can be significant. For example, ASHRAE's Method of Test for Determining the Design and Seasonal Efficiencies of Residential Thermal Distribution Systems only estimates a small reduction in distribution losses, from 19.1% to 17.6% for a typical house, when basement walls are insulated.

Another option is to not include basements in green buildings. The potential energy savings can be significant when we consider the elimination of heating and cooling distribution losses; the reduced stack effect and infiltration losses to heated spaces above; and the removal of conduction heat losses from the upstairs down to the basement and out through the foundation walls and slab.

Unconditioned basements historically were large mechanical rooms. Although large mechanical rooms might have been needed 100 years ago, when boilers and furnaces were much larger than they are today, basements now are larger than necessary to serve only as mechanical rooms.

Basements with high humidity are not ideal for storing materials such as paper, books, clothing, and other organic materials. Humid conditions and any collected water can also present indoor air quality problems. Being partly or wholly underground, it is also a challenge for basement spaces to have access to natural light and views.

When the sum total of energy problems, air quality problems, and the absence of views and natural light are examined, we are left with the question as to whether basements can be considered healthy spaces for green buildings, unless substantial measures are taken to prevent the full gamut of problems.

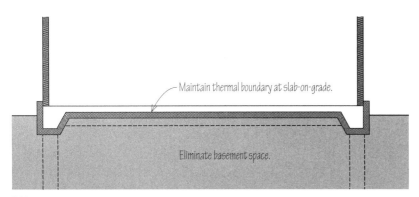

Air-seal pipe and wiring penetrations.

Insulate walls.

Seal duct joints.

Insulate ducts.

Insulate pipes.

Gasket filter housing.

8.07 Reducing energy losses in basement spaces.

Maintain thermal boundary at slab-on-grade.

Eliminate basement space.

8.08 Eliminating basement losses.

Attics

Attics, like basements, substantially contribute to the stack effect in buildings. This is due primarily to how attics allow air to leak out in winter. Conductive heat loss is also an issue, exacerbated by the large surface area of attics. Heating distribution systems are not located in attics as frequently as they are in basements, but when they are, the losses can be even more pronounced. Unlike basements, attics are purposefully vented, and so their temperatures are closer to the temperature outdoors in winter, and even hotter than outdoors in the summer, due to the heat trapped in the space. The temperature difference between conditioned air inside ductwork and the ambient air around the ductwork is more pronounced in attics and, therefore, losses are higher when ductwork is routed through attics.

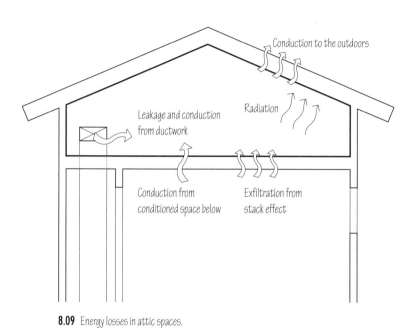

Conduction to the outdoors

Radiation

Leakage and conduction from ductwork

Conduction from conditioned space below

Exfiltration from stack effect

8.09 Energy losses in attic spaces.

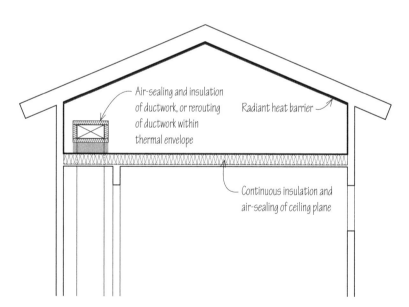

Air-sealing and insulation of ductwork, or rerouting of ductwork within thermal envelope

Radiant heat barrier

Continuous insulation and air-sealing of ceiling plane

8.10 Reducing energy losses in attic spaces.

Like basements, attics can be made more efficient through air-sealing; adding insulation to either the attic floor or the roof plane, or both; and insulating and sealing any distribution systems. Distribution systems are preferably not located in attics. Bringing the attic into the thermal envelope by insulating along the roof planes is another possibility. A third option is to avoid attics entirely.

Crawlspaces

Crawlspaces are essentially low basements, typically located above grade. Primarily developed after World War II, crawlspaces have historically been vented spaces. They are also common below mobile homes.

Recent research has found that the traditional approach of venting crawlspaces has many problems. Crawlspaces suffer from many of the same problems as basements: high humidity; conductive losses, distribution losses, and energy losses due to infiltration from the stack effect; and unsuitability for use as an inhabited space. There is often the risk of pipes in crawlspaces freezing in winter as well as the possibility that the insulation installed along the underside of the floor above a crawlspace can become detached.

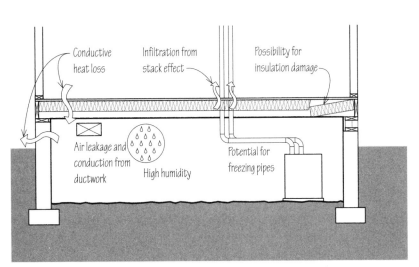

8.11 Problems with crawlspaces.

A consensus is gathering that crawlspaces should be brought within the thermal envelope by eliminating their vents, insulating the enclosing walls, and placing a robust vapor barrier on the crawlspace floor in order to retard moisture migration into the space. This treatment makes the crawlspace more energy efficient, eliminates the risk of pipes freezing, and reduces the presence of moisture and associated indoor air quality problems. Additionally, insulating the crawlspace ceiling offers yet another layer of shelter.

As with attics and basements, another solution is to not include crawlspaces in green building design, an approach that would eliminate rather than simply lessen all of the problems associated with crawlspaces.

8.12 Reducing losses in crawlspaces.

Garages

Garages may be freestanding or attached to a building, and can be open or enclosed.

Enclosed attached garages have many energy-related problems similar to those of attics, basements, and other unconditioned spaces: Conductive heat losses, infiltration losses, and losses due to distribution systems passing through them. The problems associated with an unclearly defined thermal boundary in garages have previously been discussed. Another vulnerability of garages is the reduction in air quality due to car fumes and chemicals stored in the garage. Freezing pipes are occasionally also a problem.

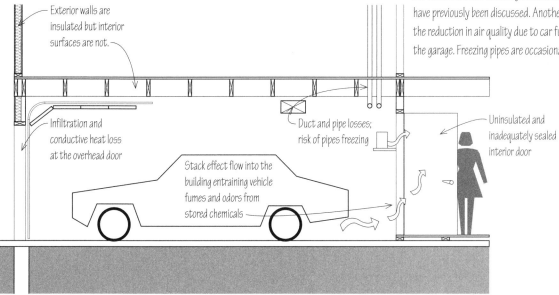

Exterior walls are insulated but interior surfaces are not.

Duct and pipe losses; risk of pipes freezing

Uninsulated and inadequately sealed interior door

Infiltration and conductive heat loss at the overhead door

Stack effect flow into the building entraining vehicle fumes and odors from stored chemicals

8.13 Problems with garages.

Garages can be used productively as a thermal buffer between heated spaces and the outdoors. Care should be given to the definition, design, and execution of the thermal boundary. The exterior walls of a garage can be improved through air-sealing, thermal insulation, and the use of insulated overhead doors. These all strengthen the outer envelope and transform the garage into an additional layer of shelter.

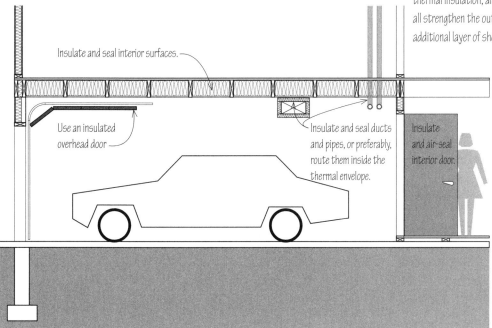

Insulate and seal interior surfaces.

Use an insulated overhead door

Insulate and seal ducts and pipes, or preferably, route them inside the thermal envelope.

Insulate and air-seal interior door.

8.14 Reducing losses in garages.

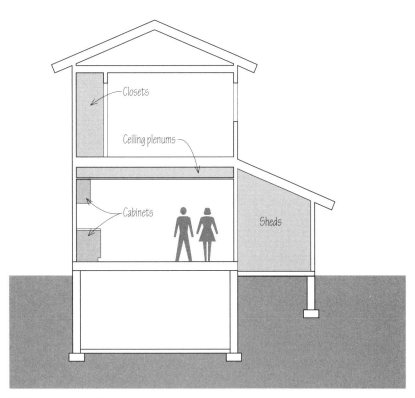

8.15 Unrecognized unheated spaces.

Unrecognized Unconditioned Spaces

There is a class of spaces that might be called "unrecognized unconditioned spaces." These include attached sheds, closets, and the spaces above ceilings. These spaces can be used productively as added layers of shelter. To effectively do so:

- Locate these spaces so that they have at least one surface adjacent to an outside wall or the roof.
- Take additional measures to reduce air exchange between these spaces and the indoors (if inside the thermal envelope) or outdoors (if outside the thermal envelope, like attached sheds).
- Consider adding thermal insulation to form yet another layer of shelter.

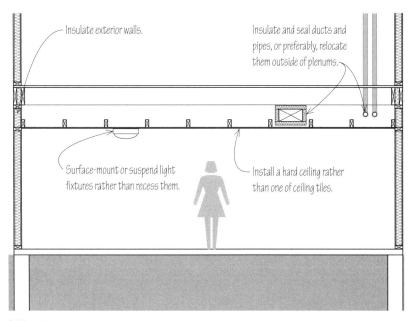

8.16 Reducing losses in ceiling plenums.

A widely used space is the plenum above ceilings. In commercial buildings, this space is a common location for heating and cooling distribution systems and other utilities. Traditionally, energy codes have not required that the piping and ductwork be insulated in a plenum because the space is formally within the thermal envelope. However, any energy losses in a plenum can heat or cool the space unnecessarily and change its equilibrium temperature, thus increasing losses to and from the outdoors through exterior walls around the edge of the plenum space, and through the roof if the space is on a top floor. Ceiling tiles allow a fairly free exchange of air between the space above ceilings and the conditioned space below. Greener approaches to constructing the space above ceilings include not locating distribution systems above ceilings and insulating and sealing those that are; avoiding the use of recessed light fixtures; and using hard, solid ceilings rather than porous ceiling tiles. These improvements turn the space above ceilings into a more robust unconditioned space, which can be used as a buffer between the indoors and the outdoors.

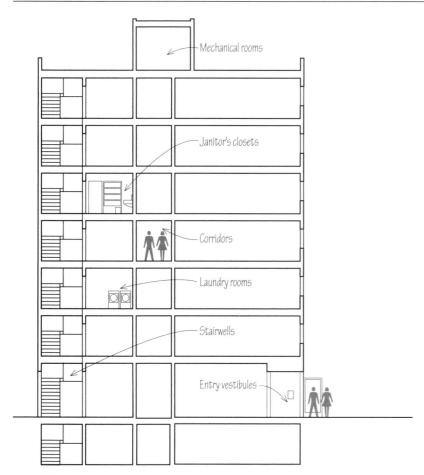

Mechanical rooms

Janitor's closets

Corridors

Laundry rooms

Stairwells

Entry vestibules

8.17 Spaces that are sometimes conditioned but may not need to be.

Corridors, Stairwells, and Other Spaces

A number of spaces in a building are sometimes conditioned but may not need to be. These include corridors, stairwells, mechanical rooms, laundry rooms, janitor's closets, entries, vestibules, and mud rooms. There are energy savings from not conditioning any spaces that do not need to be conditioned.

For example, corridors and stairwells do not always need to be conditioned. People entering or leaving a building in winter typically wear coats as they move between the front entrance and the occupied spaces. Having the entry heated, along with the corridors and stairwells, typically means that these spaces feel uncomfortably warm. The only reason to heat such spaces as corridors and stairwells is if these spaces are actively used as interior spaces during the day, which might be the case in such buildings as senior housing or nursing homes.

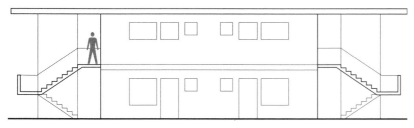

8.18 Exterior stairways can sometimes be a viable option.

A case can even be made to place some stairways outdoors. Many buildings have only two stories and need only a single flight of stairs, from the first to the second floor. If only outdoor access is needed to the second floor—in other words, if the first and second floors do not need interior access to each other and the stairway can be moved outdoors—a variety of benefits accrue: reduced conditioned floor area; reduced stack effect; and potentially reduced construction cost. Locating stairways outdoors was common in old brownstone buildings and is still common internationally for many types of buildings. For a 2,000-square-foot (186 m^2), two-story building, placing the stairs outdoors delivers a 2% to 3% reduction in building surface area and associated savings in heating and cooling. For multiple-story buildings, exterior stairs are obviously less feasible, although a case can still be made for not heating stairwells and possibly moving them outside the thermal envelope, even if they are still enclosed.

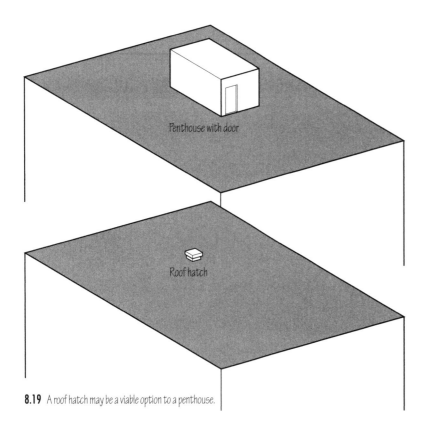

Penthouse with door

Roof hatch

8.19 A roof hatch may be a viable option to a penthouse.

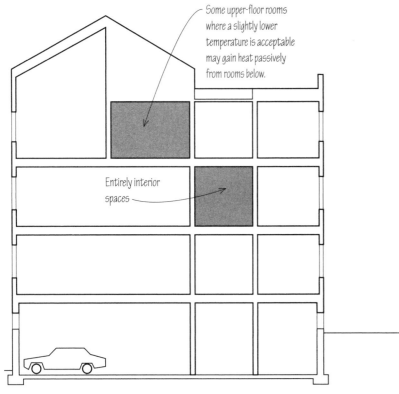

Some upper-floor rooms where a slightly lower temperature is acceptable may gain heat passively from rooms below.

Entirely interior spaces

8.20 Other rooms that may not need to be heated.

Separately, an interesting discussion can be had about whether stairwells are needed to reach the roof level of buildings with flat roofs. In high-rise buildings, one or more stairwells often rise to a small penthouse landing with a door that offers convenient walkout access to the roof level. However, the penthouse takes up room on the flat roof that could be used for solar panels or other green features. The penthouse space adds to the surface area and accompanying heat loss of the building. The penthouse also adds to the cost of the building and creates a larger penetration of the thermal envelope. A simpler hatchway would mitigate the energy issues and reduce costs, although the ease of access of a stairwell would be lost.

Entry vestibules are often heated, even overheated, as well as cooled. Conditioned vestibules only add to a building's energy use, especially because of the foot traffic through the vestibule and the associated high rate of local infiltration as the entry doors open and close. Clearly, if the vestibule or entry area is to be occupied continuously by building staff, it must be conditioned. Otherwise, heating and cooling of the space are optional and can be considered for elimination.

By not conditioning spaces that do not need to be conditioned, construction cost is reduced, heating and cooling energy and costs are lessened, and environmental comfort is often improved.

Further Removing Conditioning from Rooms

A case can be made that, specifically in green buildings, a portion of the heating and cooling load can be removed from even more rooms than just unconditioned or occasionally occupied spaces. A well-designed and constructed thermal envelope significantly moderates air temperature variations within a building, curtails drafts, and reduces cold interior window and wall surfaces in winter, allowing heating and cooling to be provided at fewer locations in a building.

For example, rooms that are entirely interior to a building may not need to be heated. It is plausible that even some rooms having outdoor exposure on the perimeter or top floor of a green building can do without the supply of heat. Some evidence exists that heating and cooling can be provided only to the living rooms of apartments without the need for supplying the same to some or all of the bedrooms. Decisions to not supply heat to comfort-critical rooms are best based on computer simulation. Many computer programs can predict the minimum equilibrium air temperature in unconditioned rooms that would ensure that room temperatures will remain within the range of target comfort requirements.

Locating Storage

If we consider eliminating such spaces as attics, basements, and crawlspaces, storage spaces may need to be augmented as the potentially eliminated spaces have traditionally been used for storage. There are energy and environmental benefits of eliminating some of these problematic spaces, but meeting the resulting need for additional storage becomes a key to green building design.

Where easy access to storage from the indoors is not needed and where lower temperatures are acceptable, attached storage spaces, like sheds, can be considered. By attaching the storage spaces to the main building, they can serve as an added layer of shelter. Access from indoors might even be possible, in which case the integrity of the thermal envelope should be maintained. Exterior-only access is preferable, along with a tightly fitting door and air-sealing of both the wall shared with the heated building as well as the exterior wall.

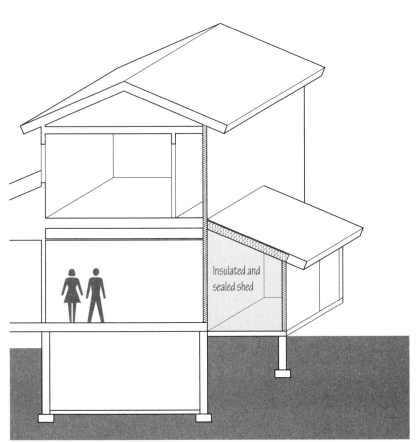

Insulated and sealed shed

8.21 An attached shed, if insulated and sealed, can act as an additional layer of shelter.

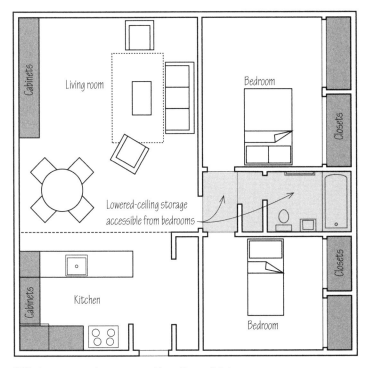

Cabinets
Living room
Bedroom
Closets
Lowered-ceiling storage accessible from bedrooms
Cabinets
Kitchen
Closets
Bedroom

8.22 Storage spaces that can act as additional layers of shelter.

When access to storage from the indoors is important or where warmer temperatures are required, additional closet space can be considered, preferably located adjacent to an exterior wall to serve as an added layer of shelter. Lowered ceilings in such areas as bathrooms and hallways can provide above-ceiling storage.

Controlling Temperatures in Unconditioned Spaces

Although temperatures in unconditioned spaces cannot be precisely controlled, we can bring a measure of temperature control by the design of the spaces.

To raise the temperature of an unconditioned space in winter so as to prevent pipes or stored liquids from freezing, we can insulate the exterior surfaces between the unconditioned space and the outdoors and not insulate between the unconditioned space and adjacent conditioned spaces. To maintain the temperature of the unconditioned space roughly halfway between that of the indoors and outdoors, we can insulate all of its surfaces equally. Air movement between the unconditioned space and the indoors and outdoors also impacts the temperature of the space. If more accurate predictions of air temperatures in unconditioned spaces are needed, computer simulation may need to be used.

Unconditioned Spaces — Summary

In summary, several details of unconditioned spaces need attention in order to avoid substantial energy losses in buildings and, in many cases, to turn these spaces into opportunities for energy conservation.

- Provide at least one well-defined and strong thermal boundary, both for insulation and to minimize air leakage.
- Consider adding a second thermal boundary so that the unconditioned space provides a significant added layer of shelter. For example, an attached garage that already has insulation between it and the heated building can also have its exterior walls insulated and air sealed.
- Avoid locating heating, cooling, and distribution systems in unconditioned spaces.
- Locate unconditioned spaces so that they serve as an added layer of shelter and a buffer between the indoors and outdoors.
- Consider not heating such spaces as corridors, stairwells, mechanical rooms, and storage rooms to turn them from conditioned spaces into unconditioned spaces.

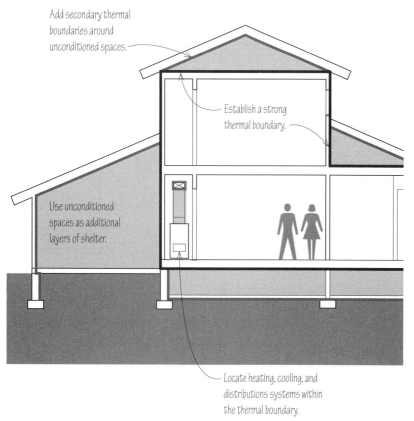

Add secondary thermal boundaries around unconditioned spaces.

Establish a strong thermal boundary.

Use unconditioned spaces as additional layers of shelter.

Locate heating, cooling, and distributions systems within the thermal boundary.

8.23 Avoiding losses through unconditioned spaces.

9
Inner Envelope

In Chapter 7, we distinguished between the outer and inner envelopes, the outer envelope being in contact with the outdoors and the inner envelope in contact with the conditioned spaces indoors.

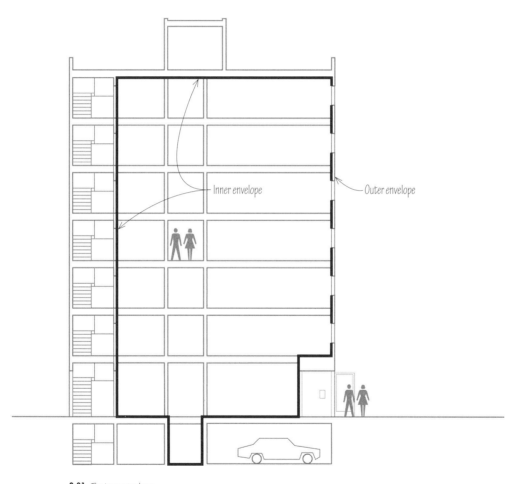

9.01 The inner envelope.

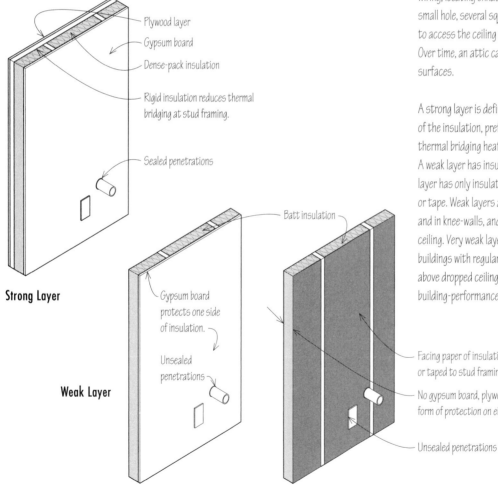

9.02 Inner envelope in a low-rise building.

Attic

Inner envelope

Garage

Basement

Plywood layer

Gypsum board

Dense-pack insulation

Rigid insulation reduces thermal bridging at stud framing.

Sealed penetrations

Strong Layer

Batt insulation

Gypsum board protects one side of insulation.

Unsealed penetrations

Weak Layer

Facing paper of insulation stapled or taped to stud framing

No gypsum board, plywood, or other form of protection on either side

Unsealed penetrations

Very Weak Layer

9.03 Layers varying from strong to very weak.

Vulnerabilities

We touched on vulnerabilities of the inner envelope when we discussed attics and other unconditioned spaces in Chapter 8. All too often, the outer envelope, such as a pitched roof or an exterior garage wall, gives the false impression that the inner envelope does not need to have thermal integrity. However, all thermal boundaries need to be strong. Surfaces must not leak significant quantities of air because air leaks are a major cause of energy loss. Also, insulation requires protection on both sides of a wall, floor, or roof assembly. Without two-sided protection, insulation is subject to physical damage, accidental removal, and air leakage through and around the insulation. The important advent of insulations that resist air movement, such as dense-pack cellulose, rigid insulation board, and spray foam, can prevent the latter of these risks—air leakage through and around the insulation. However, physical damage and removal remain risks.

Insulation is often removed or disturbed in attics. In a typical attic, renovation work is common, such as installing and routing data wiring, locating exhaust fans, and placing solar panels. To drill even a small hole, several square feet of insulation may need to be removed to access the ceiling surface. Often, this insulation is not replaced. Over time, an attic can become a patchwork of exposed ceiling surfaces.

A strong layer is defined as one having rigid surfaces on both sides of the insulation, preferably with a layer of rigid insulation to reduce thermal bridging heat losses, and is well-sealed against air leaks. A weak layer has insulation and only one rigid side. A very weak layer has only insulation, typically held in place by a paper facing or tape. Weak layers are common in attics, both on the attic floor and in knee-walls, and in basements, such as along the basement ceiling. Very weak layers are not as common but still show up in new buildings with regularity in locations such as attic knee-walls and above dropped ceilings. Weak and very weak layers cause significant building-performance problems.

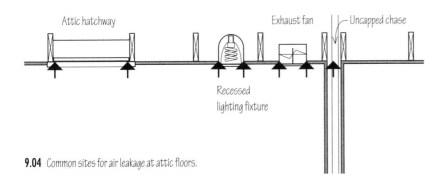

Attic hatchway

Exhaust fan

Uncapped chase

Recessed
lighting fixture

9.04 Common sites for air leakage at attic floors.

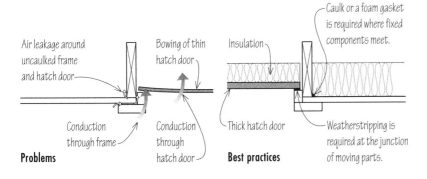

Air leakage around
uncaulked frame
and hatch door

Bowing of thin
hatch door

Insulation

Caulk or a foam gasket
is required where fixed
components meet.

Conduction
through frame

Conduction
through
hatch door

Thick hatch door

Weatherstripping is
required at the junction
of moving parts.

Problems

Best practices

9.05 Hatchway doors.

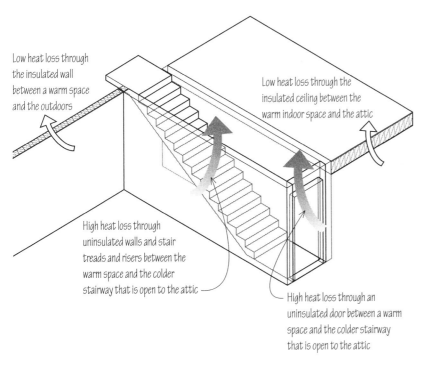

Low heat loss through
the insulated wall
between a warm space
and the outdoors

Low heat loss through the
insulated ceiling between the
warm indoor space and the attic

High heat loss through
uninsulated walls and stair
treads and risers between the
warm space and the colder
stairway that is open to the attic

High heat loss through an
uninsulated door between a warm
space and the colder stairway
that is open to the attic

9.06 Heat losses at stairways leading to attics.

The attic floor is a common weak layer in the inner envelope. There are many penetrations for recessed lights, exhaust fan housings, ducts, and wiring, and access hatches. Chases may be uncapped. Gaps may exist around chimneys and vents. In addition, insulation is frequently unprotected from disturbance and removal.

A particularly vulnerable area of the inner envelope is the point of access to an attic. A recent study showed that a simple attic hatch has several weaknesses. Typically made of a square piece of $1/4$- or $1/2$-inch (6.3- or 12.7-mm) plywood, the hatch door itself ends up bowing over time due to thermal stresses, allowing air to leak past where the door rests on its frame. Only $3/4$-inch- (19) thick plywood was found to have the rigidity necessary to maintain its shape. And even a rigid wood-on-wood seal is not enough to prevent some air leakage. Weatherstripping is necessary to further reduce air leakage at this joint and air leakage is only substantially eliminated if a latch is used to ensure compression of the weatherstripping. Once the door-frame joint is sealed, air leakage may remain between the frame and the ceiling, which requires caulking. Finally, the hatch door must be insulated to reduce conduction losses.

Walk-up stairways leading to attics can have even more weaknesses than attic hatches. The door to an attic, intended for interior use, is often not insulated even though a vented attic is at a temperature close to that of the outdoors. Nor is this door usually weatherstripped, allowing air to exfiltrate by stack effect up into the attic. Nor is the frame around the door typically caulked. Further, it is common to treat the walls between the heated space and the attic stairway as interior walls and to leave them uninsulated and without air-sealing. The walls around the stairwell are often not capped, allowing thermal communication between the attic and the wall cavities in the heated space below. Even the stair treads and risers themselves are not treated as part of the thermal boundary, being neither air-sealed nor insulated, even though they separate the heated space from the unconditioned attic. This lack of insulation is also not unusual in stairways leading from a first floor to a full second floor, where the space above the stairs in the attic above is not capped and the exposed ceiling and walls above the stairs are not insulated.

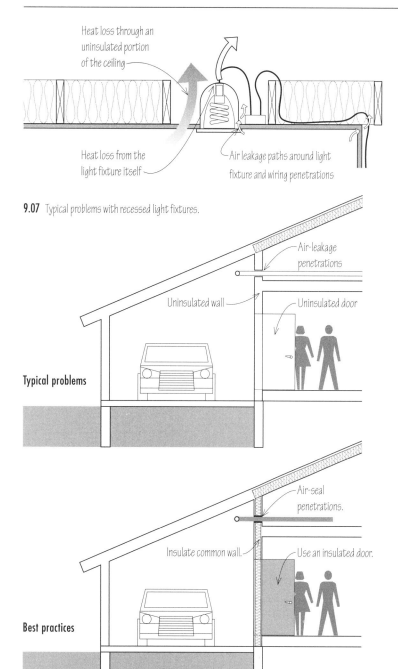

Heat loss through an
uninsulated portion
of the ceiling

Heat loss from the
light fixture itself

Air leakage paths around light
fixture and wiring penetrations

9.07 Typical problems with recessed light fixtures.

Air-leakage
penetrations

Uninsulated wall

Uninsulated door

Typical problems

Air-seal
penetrations.

Insulate common wall.

Use an insulated door.

Best practices

9.08 Maintaining the thermal boundary where an unheated garage is attached to a building.

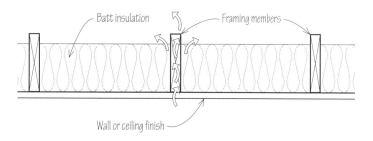

Batt insulation

Framing members

Wall or ceiling finish

9.09 Heat transfer through stud or joist framing members.

Another area of weakness for the inner envelope on the top floor of buildings is where light fixtures are recessed into the ceiling. Again, rather than presenting a single issue, the problems are multiple. Heat from the light fixtures enters the attic and is lost to the building. The fixtures themselves serve as thermal bridges from the heated space to the unconditioned attic space. Air can leak around the edge of the fixtures. The wiring serving the fixtures from the attic above must also originate in the building below and so presents another path for air leakage, separate from that of the fixture itself.

Attached garages, either in low-rise buildings like homes or in larger buildings having integrated parking, often have weak inner-envelope layers at the wall or ceiling between the garage and the conditioned building spaces. Again, weaknesses include a lack of insulation in the wall or ceiling, uninsulated doors, and penetrations which allow air movement.

We have discussed how a section of the inner envelope, such as an attic floor or the wall between an attached garage and a heated space, can form a weakness in the thermal layer because it has one rigid side and insulation but no second rigid side to protect the insulation. Another negative aspect of this kind of weak layer is that the framing, whether they be wall studs or attic joists, serves as thermal bridges to exacerbate the loss from the heated space to the unconditioned space. In this case, unlike thermal bridging in a typical wall cavity, there is no second rigid surface, such as the sheathing and siding in an exterior wall, to act as a minimal form of insulation. And so the wood framing not only forms thermal bridges but acts as a series of heat-transfer fins. Heat losses occur not just in one dimension, through and out the back edge of the framing members, but also in two dimensions, out the sides of the framing members as well.

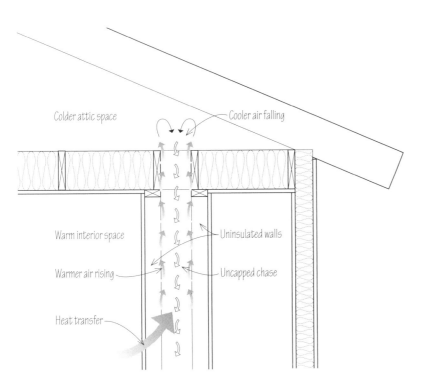

9.10 Heat transfer from warm interior space to colder chase.

Colder attic space

Cooler air falling

Warm interior space

Uninsulated walls

Warmer air rising

Uncapped chase

Heat transfer

Uncapped chases and wall cavities are significant weaknesses in the floors of attics. The seriousness of this problem arises from the size of the openings through which air can flow, combined with the area of interior walls in the chases and wall cavities below, through which heat can flow to warm the rising air. Even if the walls below were airtight, the cavities are large enough to sustain thermo-siphoned air flow in which cold air flows down into the cavities from the attic and the same air, once warmed, rises back up into the attic.

Another area of weakness in attics is party walls, fire-rated walls that separate two occupancies, such as apartments, and rise up from the foundation through the attic to the roof. Infrared photos of these walls in attics show them to be warm relative to the attic space in winter, indicating that heat is being lost. Party walls suffer from three forms of energy losses: air leakage in the cracks between the party wall and the attic floor; thermo-siphoned heat transfer through the cores of the concrete blocks which make up some of these walls as warm air from the heated building rises, is then cooled in the attic space, and falls back down; and conduction up along the structure of the party wall.

In basements and crawlspaces, the weakness in the thermal layer is often the suspended insulation between the spanning members above the basement or crawlspace, which is easily disturbed and commonly found detached. When the facing paper of the insulation is stapled along its edges to the supporting framing, there is little to stop air from flowing freely around these edges. For example, a 1,000-square-foot (93 m^2) basement has over a quarter-mile of stapled insulation edges. The air then flows up through the insulation, which is typically porous fiberglass, to either touch the underside of the subflooring or flow up through holes or cracks in the floor to the heated space above.

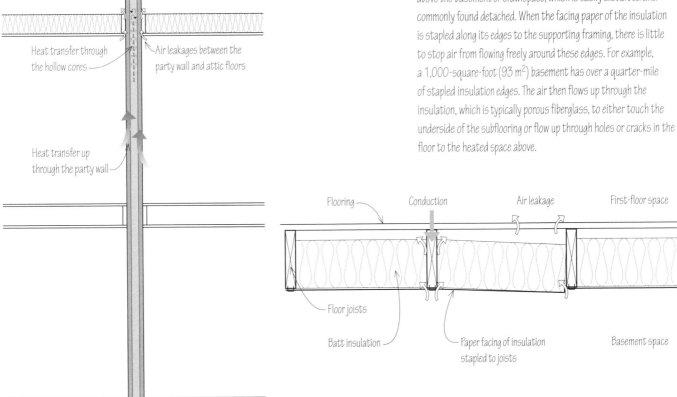

Heat transfer through the hollow cores

Air leakages between the party wall and attic floors

Heat transfer up through the party wall

9.11 Energy losses through hollow masonry party walls.

Flooring

Conduction

Air leakage

First-floor space

Floor joists

Batt insulation

Paper facing of insulation stapled to joists

Basement space

9.12 Energy losses at ceilings of basement spaces.

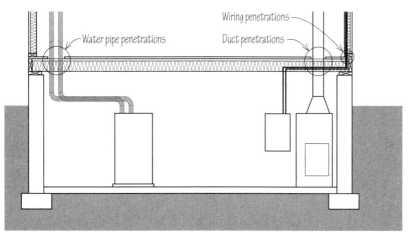

Water pipe penetrations
Wiring penetrations
Duct penetrations

9.13 Sites of air leakage at ceilings of basements and crawlspaces.

The inner envelope at the basement or crawlspace ceiling is a site for many utility penetrations. Cold and hot water pipes, ductwork, electrical wiring, data and cable wiring, plumbing drainage lines, and other utilities all typically pass up through this inner envelope. If these holes are not sealed, air from the basement will rise, drawn up by the stack effect.

Basements and crawlspaces, like attics, also have weaknesses at their doors or hatches. The vulnerability may not be quite as great, simply because the typical basement temperature is not as extreme as in the typical attic. But research has shown that an open basement door can still increase energy losses in a building.

Higher conduction loss
Higher temperature
Higher infiltration
Unconditioned space
Conditioned space

9.14 Reducing infiltration in and out of unconditioned spaces also reduces conductive heat loss.

Lower conduction loss
Lower temperature
Lower infiltration

Plywood layer protects insulation
Attic space
Rigid insulation layer prevents thermal bridging

9.15 Establishing a strong layer at the attic floor.

Solutions

There are several solutions to the weak layers of inner envelopes.

The first priority is to reduce air movement through the inner envelope by eliminating holes in its surfaces. There are reasons for giving priority to air-sealing:

· Airflow in and out of unconditioned spaces adjacent to inner envelopes reduces the potential of these spaces to serve as a form of insulation—as well-tempered buffer spaces.
· Sealing holes in these surfaces must be done before insulating these assemblies. If the insulation is installed first, it would be difficult to find the locations of these holes and to seal them.

Next, a strong layer should have rigid surfaces on both sides of the insulation. Where possible, the insulation should be continuous to prevent thermal bridging from occurring.

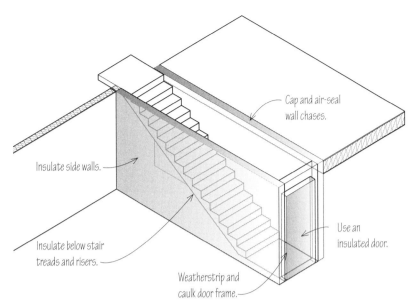

9.16 Preventing heat losses at attic stairways.

Cap and air-seal wall chases.

Insulate side walls.

Insulate below stair treads and risers.

Weatherstrip and caulk door frame.

Use an insulated door.

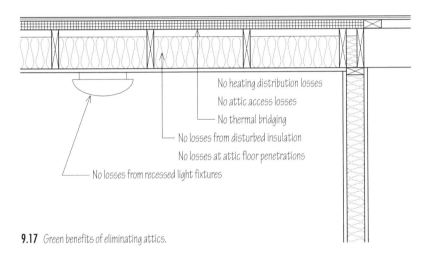

9.17 Green benefits of eliminating attics.

No heating distribution losses
No attic access losses
No thermal bridging
No losses from disturbed insulation
No losses at attic floor penetrations
No losses from recessed light fixtures

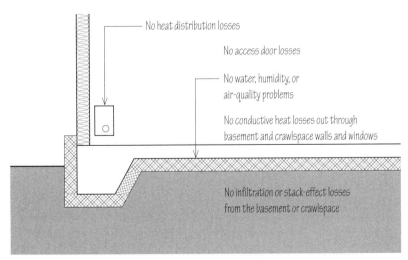

9.18 Green benefits of eliminating basements and crawlspaces.

No heat distribution losses
No access door losses
No water, humidity, or air-quality problems
No conductive heat losses out through basement and crawlspace walls and windows
No infiltration or stack-effect losses from the basement or crawlspace

Wherever possible, other discontinuities, such as recessed light fixtures, should be eliminated. Stairways and hatches providing access from a heated space into an unconditioned space should be treated completely and holistically so that no discontinuities exist in the inner envelope, either in insulation or in air-sealing. The complexity of these access sites requires special attention to detail, not only at the door or hatch itself, but also in the surrounding frames and passageways. Doors and hatches should be insulated; weatherstripped along surfaces where relative motion occurs; and caulked along nonmoving surface joints, such as where a door frame meets the surrounding wall. In attics, chases and wall cavities should be capped, sealed, and insulated.

For attics, complexity brings a high risk of discontinuities and energy problems. Simple roof lines can help lower this risk. As suggested earlier, one possible solution is to avoid attics altogether and to design buildings with flat or gently sloping roofs. Consider the problems that would be eliminated. Without attics, there are no attic floor penetrations; no surfaces weakened by unprotected insulation; no vulnerabilities at attic access hatchways or doors; no problems associated with recessed light fixtures; no distribution heat losses in the attic; no thermal bridging issues; and a reduced risk of ice dams in cold climates.

Similarly, consider the benefits of eliminating basements and crawlspaces and instead building on slab foundations. With a slab foundation, utility services, such as plumbing piping and electrical and data wiring, could rise well-sealed from the concrete slab. There are no longer the large heating distribution losses which can be common in basements; no longer the stack-effect contributions from a basement or crawlspace; no longer door-related or hatch-related energy losses; and no longer conductive heat losses from heated spaces above down into the basement or crawlspace and out through its walls and windows. As an added benefit, indoor air-quality problems associated with humid basement spaces and crawlspaces are eliminated.

In summary, the inner envelope turns out to be a generally weak layer of shelter, which needs attention and strengthening. What are the economic costs of strengthening the inner envelope? In general, strengthening the inner envelope does require added cost. Providing rigid surfaces on both sides of insulation adds to the construction cost, as does ensuring thermal continuity at attic stairways and hatches, along attic floors, and across basement ceilings. However, other improvements can reduce construction costs, such as not recessing light fixtures. And if we consider the option of omitting basements and attics, eliminating these areas of weakness would further reduce construction costs, although the storage functions of these spaces may need to be provided elsewhere.

Thermal Mass

Thermal mass refers to construction elements that have the capacity to absorb and store heat. Thermal mass is most effective if it is located on the inside of the thermal boundary. In winter, thermal mass serves to absorb and store the sun's heat when solar radiation is available and to release this heat slowly into the interior of a building when sunlight is not available. Thermal mass can also be used with nighttime ventilation in summer as a form of passive cooling, releasing absorbed heat to the cooler night air and then cooling a space during the day. Thermal mass is preferably located in the space which it serves, typically a south-facing space when used in the winter. If this is not possible, the thermal mass must be thermally connected to the served space by air-circulating ducts or water-circulating pipes.

Thermal mass can take a variety of forms but typically consists of high-mass walls, floors, and ceilings. For passive heating or cooling, thermal mass is usually part of an integrated strategy that uses an appropriate collection system and such controls as movable window insulation or thermal shades to avoid nighttime heat losses or to enable nighttime ventilation for cooling.

Thermal mass should only be included in a building if energy modeling predicts a reduction in energy use. If used indiscriminately, thermal mass can increase building energy use. Various studies show energy savings that range from a high of over 10% to negative savings (increases in energy use).

Because thermal mass usually means higher embodied energy, the tradeoffs of employing thermal mass should be carefully examined. For example, a 6-inch- (150) thick concrete wall with 4 inches (100) of rigid foam insulation has an R-value of 17 but an equivalent thermal resistance of an R-27 wood frame wall due to the benefits of thermal mass. However, the additional R-10 in equivalent insulation provided by the 6 inches of concrete represents an increase in embodied energy that is more than twice that of using an additional 2.5 inches (63.5) of rigid foam insulation on the wood-frame wall to reach the equivalent thermal resistance of R-27.

Thermal mass can also be provided by floors and ceilings. For ceilings to be effective as thermal mass, they need to be exposed, not hidden behind a finished ceiling.

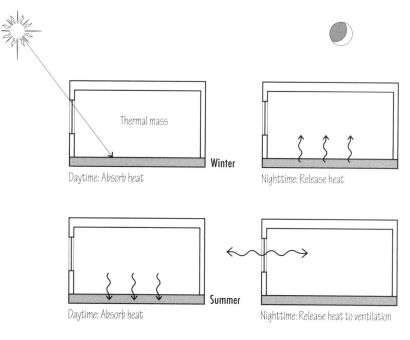

Thermal mass

Daytime: Absorb heat — **Winter** — Nighttime: Release heat

Daytime: Absorb heat — **Summer** — Nighttime: Release heat to ventilation

9.19 Thermal mass schematics.

Insulation is placed on the exterior of the thermal mass.

Exposed on ceiling

Walls

Floor

9.20 Options for locating thermal mass.

Finishes

Having moved from the community and the site through the outer envelope, through unconditioned spaces, and through the inner envelope, we find ourselves squarely inside a conditioned building. But there are yet more layers of shelter that we can put to use. For example, interior finishes can be used productively to save energy or, if misapplied, can inadvertently work against energy efficiency.

Thermal and Radiant Properties of Finishes

Carpeting has modest thermal resistance, in the range of R-0.5 to R-2.5. When a carpet pad is added to the layer, an additional thermal resistance of R-0.6 to R-2.1 can be expected. Beyond these conductive gains, the reduced radiant losses afforded by carpeting may allow the indoor air temperature to be lowered. Carpeting also reduces noise transmission in a building. The use of wall-to-wall carpeting makes sense here to be consistent with the position that insulation should be maintained continuously across layers of shelter. Carpeting, however, is not a substitute for a subslab rigid insulation or surface insulation in general.

On the negative side, many carpets contain chemicals, although some with lower chemical content are now available. Carpets also need vacuuming along with the associated use of energy. Carpeting can reduce the benefits of thermal mass in a concrete floor. And, most significantly, carpeting has low light reflectance and so requires more artificial lighting and increased window area for daylighting.

For windows, insulated shades are a beneficial added finish. Adding approximately R-5 in insulating value, insulated shades can double or triple the thermal resistance of windows. Further, insulated shades can include a radiant barrier to reduce radiant losses, as well as provide modest air-sealing benefits to reduce infiltration if properly sealed to the window frame.

Other finishes can provide a variety of thermal and solar radiation benefits. Tinted glazing can be used to reduce unwanted solar gain in warm climates. Radiant shields can be placed behind heaters to reflect heat loss away from walls. Blinds can reduce glare, provide minor protection against solar gains in the summertime, and reduce radiant losses from a space to the outdoors. Recall, however, that exterior shading is far more effective at reducing solar gain. Blinds also have the ability to provide high lighting reflectance, thus reducing the required amount of artificial lighting.

9.21 Finishes as a layer of shelter.

Insulating shades

Wall-to-wall carpeting

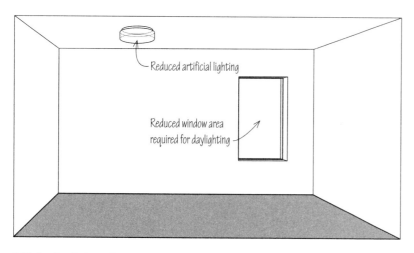

9.22 Benefits of reflective finishes.

Lighting Reflectance

Whereas the thermal and radiant properties of finishes offer modest gains, their lighting reflectance can have a significant impact on a building's energy use. Two distinct savings result from the use of reflective interior surfaces:

1. A reduced need for artificial lighting, thus saving electricity.
2. A reduced need for daylighting to achieve the same level of illumination, thus requiring fewer windows and/or a smaller window area and saving on associated heating and cooling costs. Other cascading benefits accrue, such as reducing lighting fixture costs and lessening air-conditioning requirements and associated energy use.

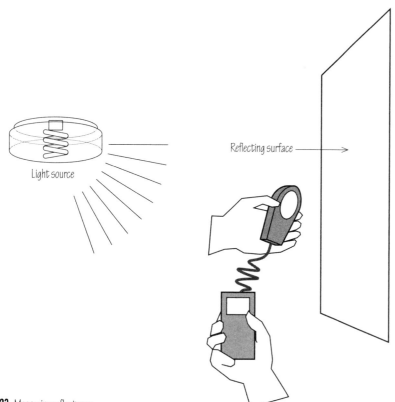

9.23 Measuring reflectance.

Reflectance can be measured by placing a light meter close to a surface, directing it toward a light source, measuring how much light is reaching the surface, and then turning the light meter toward the surface to see what fraction of the incoming light is reflected.

Example:
Point light meter to light source: 100 foot-candles
Point light meter to reflecting surface: 45 foot-candles
Reflectance = 45/100 = 45%

Paints

Highly reflective white	90
Typical white	70–80
Light cream	70–80
Light yellow	55–65
Light green*	53
Kelly green*	49
Medium blue*	49
Medium yellow*	47
Medium orange*	42
Medium green*	41
Medium red*	20
Medium brown*	16
Dark blue-gray*	16
Dark brown*	12

* Estimated for flat paints. For gloss paints, add 5%–10%.

Woods

Maple	54
Poplar	52
White pine	51
Red pine	49
Oregon pine	38
Birch	35
Beech	26
Oak	23
Cherry	20

Carpet

Low maintenance, dark	2–5
Moderate maintenance	5–9
Higher maintenance	9–13
Very high maintenance	13+

Linoleum

White	54–59
Black	0–9

Concrete

Black polished concrete	0
Gray polished concrete	20
Light polished concrete	60
Reflective concrete floor coatings	66–93

Walls

Dark paneling	10
Burlap	10
Plywood	30

Furnishings

Gray plastic-coated steel desk	63
Bulletin boards	10
Gray fabric partitions	51
Countertops	4–85

Ceiling Tiles

Typical ceiling tiles	76–80
High-reflectance tiles	90

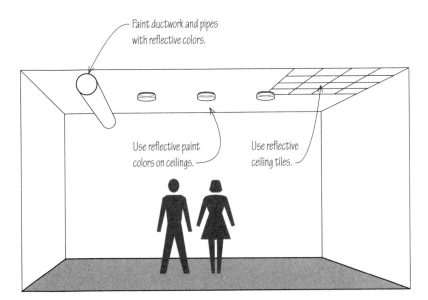

Paint ductwork and pipes with reflective colors.

Use reflective paint colors on ceilings.

Use reflective ceiling tiles.

9.25 Ceiling reflectance strategies.

For walls and ceilings, priority should be given to reflective surfaces that minimize the need for artificial lighting. Reflective flooring and furnishing can also contribute to this end. While flooring is typically assumed to have a default reflectance of 20%, this does not need to be accepted as a given. Some hardwood floorings have a reflectance value of over 50%, a variety of commercial flooring products are as high as 75% reflective, and some concrete floor coatings have been reported to be 93% reflective. Countertops, too, have widely ranging reflectance values, from below 10% to as high as 85%. By establishing the design of finishes at an early stage, the final lighting design can be optimized to take advantage of reflective interior surfaces.

Although white surfaces are indeed highly reflective, they are not the only option. Research has shown that a variety of paint colors can be highly reflective, as can a variety of other surfaces, such as certain metals and wood finishes, reflective blinds, and reflective concrete coatings.

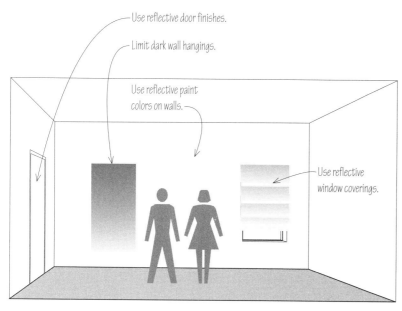

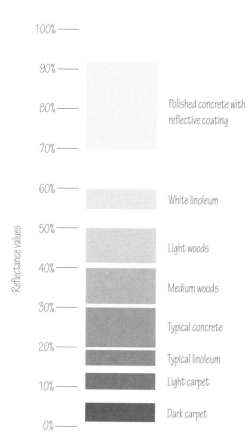

For example, a building with reflective interior surfaces, such as 90% for the ceilings, 60% for the walls, and 30% for the floors, requires 11% less artificial lighting than a building having more typical surface reflectances of 80% for the ceilings, 50% for the walls, and 20% for the floors. Higher reflectance values save even more. Surface reflectances of 90% for ceilings, 70% for walls, and 40% for floors saves a substantial 28% in lighting energy use. Note also that the higher surface reflectances mean proportionally fewer light fixtures and lower construction costs.

Since walls are typically assumed in lighting design to have a reflectance value of 50%, there is clearly room for improvement. The key is to not only choose reflective wall finishes, but also to avoid nonreflective wall coverings, such as fabric, and to consider more reflective finishes for doors and wall-mounted furnishings, such as countertops and cupboards. Likewise, reflective window coverings are better than nonreflective coverings like most curtains. Note that uncovered windows at night, when artificial lighting is most needed, are highly unreflective, and so will require more lighting unless covered by reflective blinds or shades.

The relatively low reflectance of carpeting deserves particular mention. Carpeting with a reflectance above 9% is reported to require a higher level of maintenance. When its reflectance is above 13%, carpeting requires very high maintenance. Assuming that carpeting has a typical reflectance of 10%, using a lighter wood finish or tile that has, for example, a 50% reflectance reduces the lighting power and number of light fixtures by a significant 36%, and also has the potential to maximize daylighting.

To reap the savings of using surfaces that have higher reflectance values, a concerted effort needs to be made to:
· Select these finishes early in the design process;
· Convey these values to the lighting designers so that the lighting design can be optimized;
· Ensure the finishes are installed in construction; and
· Document the finishes for future repainting and other upgrades of finishes, such as ceiling tile replacement.

The building owner needs to be made aware of the importance and relevance of reflectance values. This is where integrated design helps, as the owner is actively engaged in the design process, as is the lighting designer, and all parties can agree on the use of high-reflectance surfaces to reduce artificial lighting and the fenestration required for daylighting. Historically, lighting has been designed assuming 80% reflectance for ceilings, 50% reflectance for walls, and 20% reflectance for floors. These values are so widely used that they have become defaults in most lighting design software programs. For lighting savings to accrue when using high-reflectance finishes, a specific focus should be directed to not only selecting such finishes but to designing the lighting system accordingly.

9.26 Wall reflectance strategies.

9.27 Floor reflectance strategies. Because lighting is usually designed for a default floor reflectance of 20%, the floor offers a greater opportunity for improving its reflectance value than either the ceiling or walls.

10
Thermal Zoning and Compartmentalization

Thermal zoning and compartmentalization help to reduce energy use by using interior layers of shelter to limit the unwanted flow of heat and air within a building.

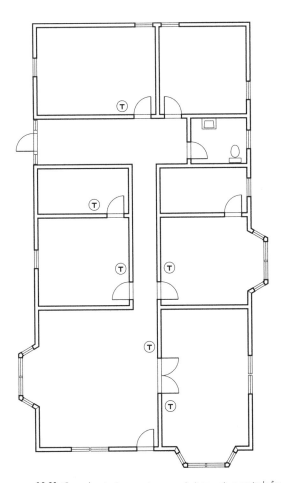

10.01 Thermal zoning incorporates separate temperature controls for different areas of a building.

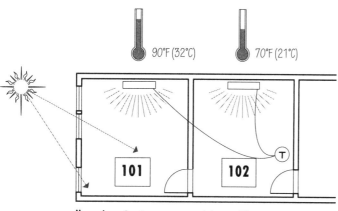

No zoning *One thermostat controls heat in different spaces. Solar gains overheat Room 101.*

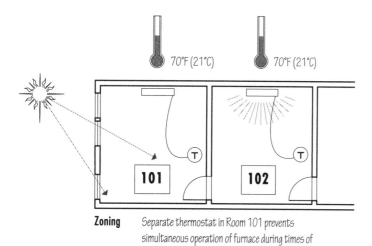

Zoning *Separate thermostat in Room 101 prevents simultaneous operation of furnace during times of solar gain, thereby saving energy.*

▲

10.02 *Preventing overheating of spaces receiving heat from other sources.*

10.03 *Allowing conditioned spaces to be left unconditioned at appropriate times.* ▶

Thermal Zoning

Thermal zoning enables different areas of a building to have separate temperature controls and respond better to individual temperature preferences. It can also save energy, in two primary ways:

- Thermal zoning can prevent overheating in spaces receiving heat from other sources, such as the solar gains on the south side of a building; the unusually high occupancy rates of conference rooms, classrooms, and other assembly spaces; and the unusually high internal gains from machinery or lighting.
- Thermal zoning can allow conditioned spaces to be left unconditioned at appropriate times. Lowering the air temperature in a space in winter or raising the temperature in summer in this manner reduces heating and cooling loads.

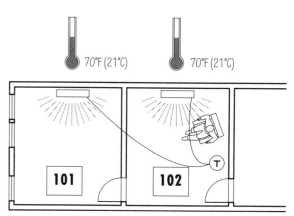

No zoning *One thermostat controls heat in different spaces. Both spaces are heated even though Room 101 is unoccupied.*

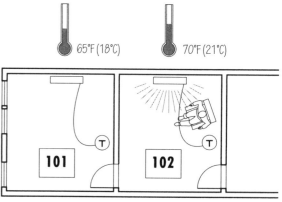

Zoning *Separate thermostat in Room 101 prevents heating when the room is unoccupied, thereby saving energy.*

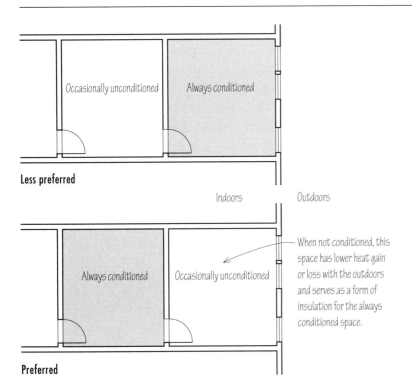

Less preferred

Indoors | Outdoors

Always conditioned | Occasionally unconditioned

When not conditioned, this space has lower heat gain or loss with the outdoors and serves as a form of insulation for the always conditioned space.

Preferred

10.04 Locating occasionally unconditioned spaces.

Because thermal zoning for either of these reasons can save significant energy, it is important to identify spaces that may not always require heating or cooling.

For spaces that can, at times, be left unconditioned, it is constructive to locate them on outside walls where possible. In this way, they can serve to reduce heat loss from heated spaces to the outdoors.

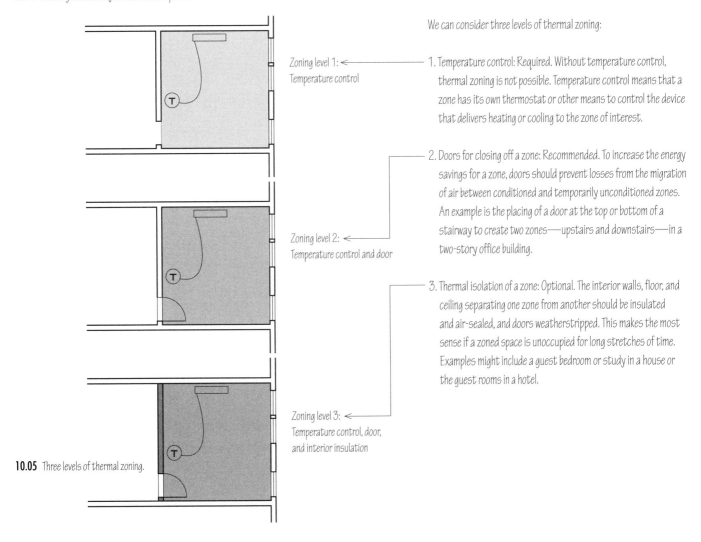

Zoning level 1:
Temperature control

Zoning level 2:
Temperature control and door

Zoning level 3:
Temperature control, door, and interior insulation

10.05 Three levels of thermal zoning.

We can consider three levels of thermal zoning:

1. Temperature control: Required. Without temperature control, thermal zoning is not possible. Temperature control means that a zone has its own thermostat or other means to control the device that delivers heating or cooling to the zone of interest.

2. Doors for closing off a zone: Recommended. To increase the energy savings for a zone, doors should prevent losses from the migration of air between conditioned and temporarily unconditioned zones. An example is the placing of a door at the top or bottom of a stairway to create two zones—upstairs and downstairs—in a two-story office building.

3. Thermal isolation of a zone: Optional. The interior walls, floor, and ceiling separating one zone from another should be insulated and air-sealed, and doors weatherstripped. This makes the most sense if a zoned space is unoccupied for long stretches of time. Examples might include a guest bedroom or study in a house or the guest rooms in a hotel.

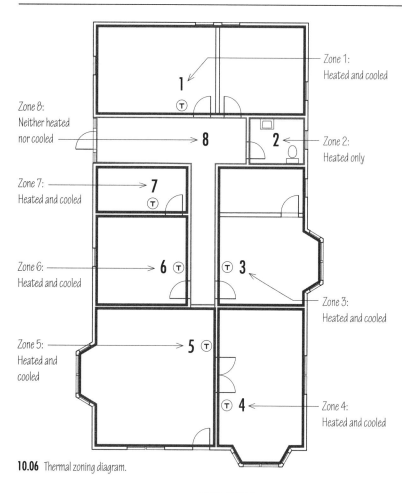

Zone 1:
Heated and cooled

Zone 8:
Neither heated
nor cooled

Zone 7:
Heated and cooled

Zone 2:
Heated only

Zone 6:
Heated and cooled

Zone 3:
Heated and cooled

Zone 5:
Heated and
cooled

Zone 4:
Heated and cooled

10.06 Thermal zoning diagram.

Because some heating and cooling systems cannot support thermal zoning, it is helpful to define the thermal zones first, before selecting an appropriate heating and cooling system that supports thermal zoning.

A thermal zoning diagram might be included in the construction documents to help delineate which zones are controlled by which temperature controls; which spaces are heated but not cooled; and which spaces are altogether unconditioned.

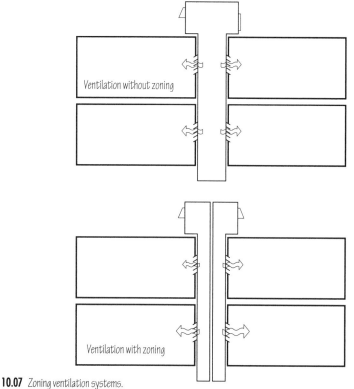

Ventilation without zoning

Ventilation with zoning

10.07 Zoning ventilation systems.

The concept of dividing a building into zones can also be applied to ventilation. A large commercial building often has large air handlers that serve significant portions of a building. Such larger systems are less able to respond to localized ventilation needs, and so they risk either over-ventilating a particular zone, wasting energy in the process, or under-ventilating the zone and placing indoor air quality at risk. By dividing a building into smaller zones, each zone's ventilation system can respond appropriately to its own ventilation needs and deliver acceptable indoor air quality at a lower energy cost.

The impact of thermal zoning on construction costs can be negative or positive. When additional temperature controls, doors, or insulation are necessary, costs go up. However, when heating or cooling can be removed from spaces, cost savings accrue.

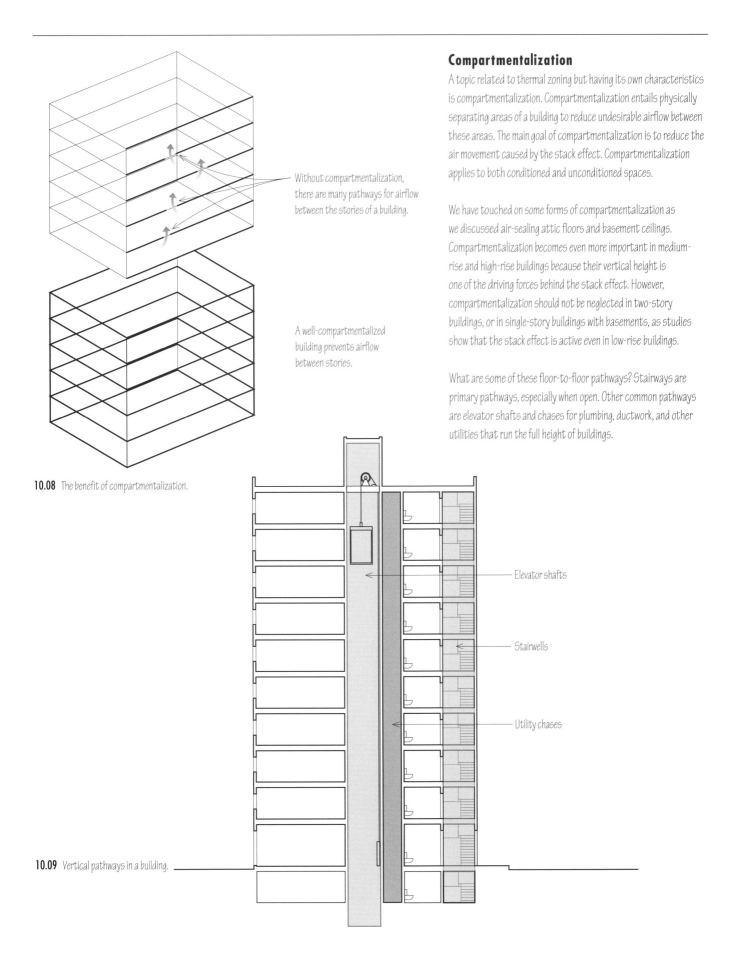

Compartmentalization

A topic related to thermal zoning but having its own characteristics is compartmentalization. Compartmentalization entails physically separating areas of a building to reduce undesirable airflow between these areas. The main goal of compartmentalization is to reduce the air movement caused by the stack effect. Compartmentalization applies to both conditioned and unconditioned spaces.

We have touched on some forms of compartmentalization as we discussed air-sealing attic floors and basement ceilings. Compartmentalization becomes even more important in medium-rise and high-rise buildings because their vertical height is one of the driving forces behind the stack effect. However, compartmentalization should not be neglected in two-story buildings, or in single-story buildings with basements, as studies show that the stack effect is active even in low-rise buildings.

What are some of these floor-to-floor pathways? Stairways are primary pathways, especially when open. Other common pathways are elevator shafts and chases for plumbing, ductwork, and other utilities that run the full height of buildings.

Without compartmentalization, there are many pathways for airflow between the stories of a building.

A well-compartmentalized building prevents airflow between stories.

10.08 The benefit of compartmentalization.

Elevator shafts

Stairwells

Utility chases

10.09 Vertical pathways in a building.

As we seek to limit this airflow, it is instructive to follow the path of the stack effect airflow in wintertime. Consider the air as it flows from the outdoors, into and up through a building, and then outdoors again when it reaches the top of the building. Air enters a building at any point below a neutral pressure plane. At the neutral pressure plane, there is no difference in air pressure between the indoors and outdoors and therefore no infiltration due to stack-effect pressures. We might visualize the neutral pressure plane as typically being halfway up the height of a building, although its exact location varies, depending on the relative locations of infiltration sites along the building's height.

The stack effect pulls more air into a building the farther a location is below the neutral pressure plane because the lower to the ground the location is, the higher the vacuum pressure in the building caused by the stack effect. It is therefore expected that air enters at the lower levels of a building, most significantly at the basement level or the first floor. It might enter through an open front door, a crack around a window frame, or through a utility entrance, such as a loading dock or back door. The basement and first floor have both the strongest negative air pressure from the stack effect and frequently the most openings. So the first defense against the stack effect should be at these large lower-level entrances. For example, an airlock at the front door provides good prevention against stack-effect air movement and should be considered even for other first-floor doors. A wide variety of other openings should also be identified and sealed.

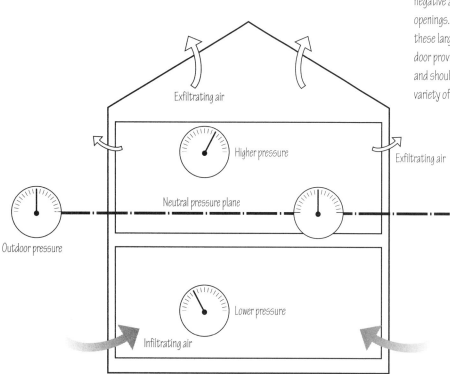

Exfiltrating air

Higher pressure

Exfiltrating air

Neutral pressure plane

Outdoor pressure

Lower pressure

Infiltrating air

10.10 The neutral pressure plane.

Now, to rise up through a building, air needs to make its way horizontally to a stairwell, chase, or elevator shaft. Because this air can move through open doorways, under closed doors, and through rooms and corridors, we can put the doors that are useful for thermal zoning to a second use, preventing this horizontal airflow as it seeks a path to rise. Doors that can close along this path will reduce the airflow. Weatherstripped interior doors will reduce airflow even more. Note the application of layers of shelter, as we seek to stop the airflow from stack effect at multiple points along its path.

Next, the air must enter the vertical shaft of a stairwell, elevator, or mechanical chase. Connections to plumbing and ventilation shafts are often made in kitchens and bathrooms. The air seeks openings where pipes enter shafts from sinks and toilets and where ventilation grilles connect to ductwork. Pipe escutcheons can help reduce airflow but to be more effective, a bead of caulk should be placed around the escutcheons.

In chases, floor-to-floor seals are highly effective to counter the airflow from stack effect and are often required by fire codes. For stairwells, weatherstripping and sweeps on the doors are effective in reducing stack-effect airflow. To prevent air from entering a mechanical shaft from the ductwork and rising due to stack effect, the ductwork must be well-sealed and the connection from the takeoff duct to each grille must be sealed as well. See figure 10.12.

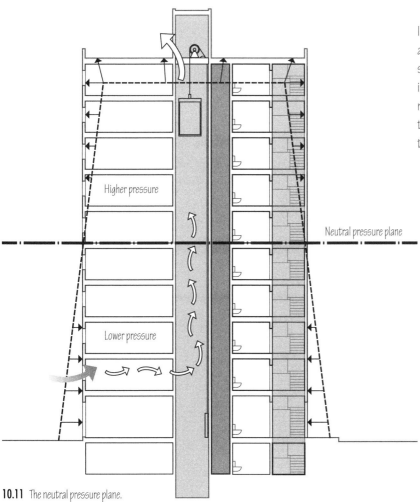

Higher pressure

Lower pressure

Neutral pressure plane

10.11 The neutral pressure plane.

As the air rises to the upper floors, the increasingly positive stack-effect air pressure is now exerted to move the air out of chases and stairwells. Therefore, the same seals used to prevent air from entering these pathways serve also to prevent air on upper floors from leaving them. Likewise, interior doors serve to prevent the outward flow of the air. This is where the need for a robust top ceiling is so critical and why attics are so vulnerable. If a building has a hard cap, such as a rigid flat roof, the stack-effect airflow cannot leave the building through the roof. It is limited to leaving through windows and walls. If the walls are monolithic, the air is limited to leaving through windows. If the windows are smaller, fewer in number, and well-sealed, we have effectively choked the stack-effect airflow. Particular attention must be directed to window frames, where moldings and trim work often conceal unsealed openings.

Because elevator doors are not airtight, we must rely on preventing airflow air from reaching the elevators in a building and that means preventing the air from entering the corridors that lead to elevators. Elevator shaft louvers can be equipped with low-leakage motorized dampers and be kept in the closed position, although provision should be made for the required interconnection with fire control systems.

What is the affordability impact of compartmentalization? In general, it increases construction cost. Air-sealing between the floors of a building adds to construction cost, as does preventing air from entering and leaving the building.

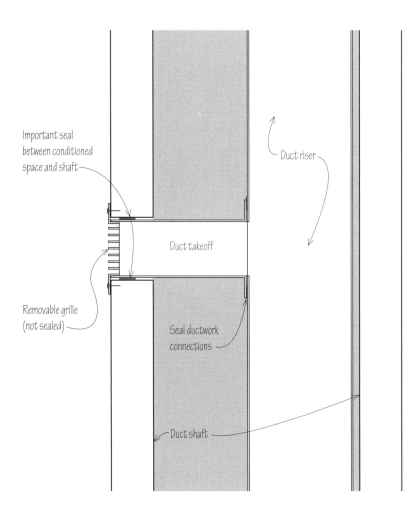

Important seal between conditioned space and shaft

Removable grille (not sealed)

Duct takeoff

Duct riser

Seal ductwork connections

Duct shaft

10.12 Preventing air from entering a mechanical shaft from the ductwork or conditioned space and rising due to stack effect.

11
Lighting and Other Electric Loads

By designing from the outside in, the design professional will have examined daylighting options earlier, as part of the design of the outer envelope, and before beginning the design of artificial lighting. In this chapter, we will examine ways to make artificial lighting more efficient.

Artificial lighting shelters us from the dim and the dark. Until the time arrives when we can get daylight to penetrate and reach all the inner recesses of a building and we are able to store it for use at night, we will continue to rely on artificial lighting, as nonnatural as the term sounds.

Lighting

Lighting is a major energy load in buildings, consuming the second largest share of primary energy use attributed to buildings, after only space heating and cooling. Lighting can readily be designed to use 50% or less of the energy traditionally consumed for the service, and in many cases far less.

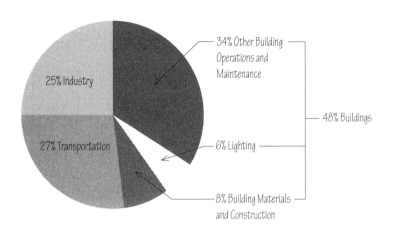

11.01 Percentage of energy use attributable to lighting.

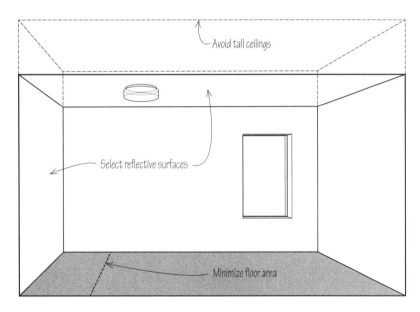

11.02 Space design to minimize artificial lighting.

Space Design to Minimize the Need for Lighting

The need for artificial lighting has also already been minimized by intelligent space design. Referring back to the earlier phases of design, if a specific building can be designed to fit within a smaller floor area, the amount of artificial light needed and, therefore, the amount of energy required to light the building, will be less.

Furthermore, when a building is smaller, harvested daylight penetrates into a larger fraction of the building area than it does for a larger building serving the same purpose.

Gains may also have previously been made by avoiding tall ceilings. For example, a space with 8-foot (2,440) ceilings requires 5% less artificial light to deliver the same light level than the same space with 10-foot (3,050) ceilings.

Reflective finishes may have also already been selected to minimize the need for lighting. Recall the example where only a 10% higher reflectance in the ceiling, wall, and floor finishes resulted in a 13% lighting energy savings while delivering the same amount of light to a space. Savings over 30% are possible by further increasing the ceiling, wall, and floor reflectances.

Optimized Lighting Design

With a space designed to minimize the need for artificial lighting, we can proceed to design the lighting. For green buildings, this calls for the use of photometric calculations or computer software to examine light fixture selection and layout on a space-by-space basis. Historically, much lighting has been designed by rule of thumb, often resulting in more light than is required. Room-by-room lighting design is a best practice for green building design. Without room-by-room design, a building will likely have too much lighting; use more energy with more light fixtures than is required; and use more material with a greater amount of embodied energy than is necessary.

46.2	55.1	40.9	60.3	43.4	55.0	55.1
55.0	53.0	38.3	58.3	42.1	55.0	55.0
51.2	52.0	36.2	55.2	40.6	51.2	52.0
46.2	55.1	40.9	60.3	43.4	55.0	55.1
55.0	55.0	38.3	58.3	42.1	55.0	55.0
51.2	52.0	36.2	55.2	40.6	51.2	52.0
46.2	55.1	40.9	60.3	43.4	55.0	55.1
55.0	55.0	38.3	58.3	42.1	55.0	55.0

11.03 Example of a photometric calculation:

Luminaire quantity	9
Average Illuminance	55.4 foot-candles*
Maximum illuminance	60.3 foot-candles
Minimum illuminance	36.2 foot-candles
Total power	540 watts
Lighting power density	0.82 watts per square foot

* 1 foot-candle = 1 lumen per square foot or 10.764 lux.

11.04 Examples of lighting levels recommended by the Illuminating Engineering Society.

Task area	Foot-candles
Conference rooms	20–50
General offices	50–100
Classrooms	50–75
Gymnasiums	30–50
Merchandising	30–150
Manufacturing	50–500
Corridors and stairways	10–20

When designing lighting, there is a wide range of recommended light levels. For green buildings, consider designing to the lower end of recommended ranges in the Illuminating Engineering Society (IES) handbook. For example, the energy use for a light level of 50 foot-candles is more than twice as high as that required for a light level of 20 foot-candles.

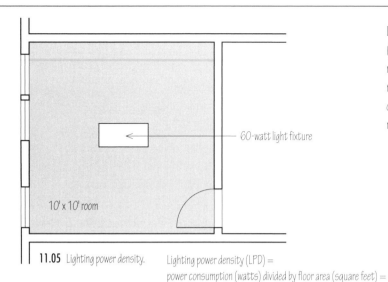

11.05 Lighting power density.

Lighting power density (LPD) =
power consumption (watts) divided by floor area (square feet) =
60 W/10' x 10' = 0.6 W/sf

Lighting power density (LPD) is the power consumption of lighting (watts) divided by the floor area (in square feet). LPD is a useful metric for lighting design. Various energy codes and standards mandate or recommend maximum lighting power densities, either on a whole-building basis or on a space-by-space basis. A maximum required LPD is called a lighting power allowance (LPA).

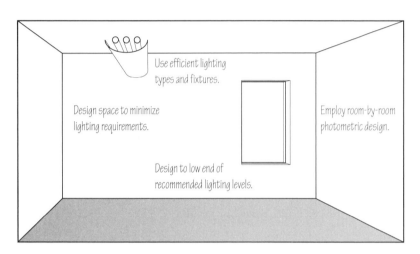

Use efficient lighting types and fixtures.

Design space to minimize lighting requirements.

Employ room-by-room photometric design.

Design to low end of recommended lighting levels.

11.06 Integrated strategies for lighting design.

Because the lighting power allowances cited in codes and standards provide some built-in flexibility for variations in building design, the values required by the codes and standards are typically higher than necessary or achievable. Green buildings can readily achieve lower lighting power densities, even relative to the requirements in high-performance codes and standards. However, reaching lower lighting power densities requires a combination of the aforementioned approaches, including room-by-room photometric design; designing to the lower levels of IES recommendations; using reflective walls, ceilings, and floors; and installing efficient light fixtures.

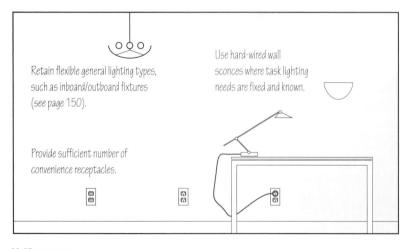

Retain flexible general lighting types, such as inboard/outboard fixtures (see page 150).

Use hard-wired wall sconces where task lighting needs are fixed and known.

Provide sufficient number of convenience receptacles.

11.07 Task lighting strategies.

Task lighting is generally thought to allow a reduced lighting level and lower energy use while still providing individuals with adequate local lighting for certain activities. However, research indicates that successful, low-energy task lighting is difficult to achieve. Since task lighting is still being developed as a strategy, green building design might preferably not rely solely on the potential for task lighting. Rather, flexibly controlled and energy-efficient general lighting is a more prudent approach. To allow for future task lighting, sufficient convenience receptacles at locations needed for task lighting might be considered.

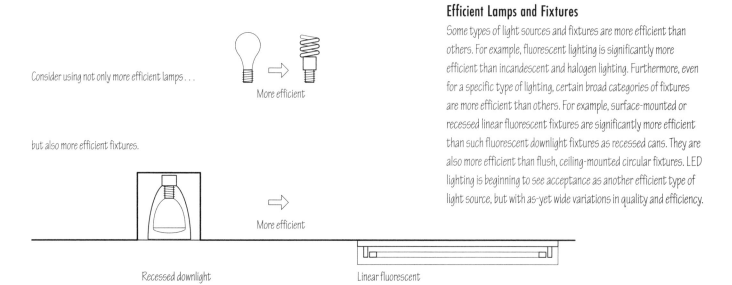

Consider using not only more efficient lamps . . .

More efficient

but also more efficient fixtures.

More efficient

Recessed downlight

Linear fluorescent

11.08 Using more efficient lamps and fixtures.

Efficient Lamps and Fixtures

Some types of light sources and fixtures are more efficient than others. For example, fluorescent lighting is significantly more efficient than incandescent and halogen lighting. Furthermore, even for a specific type of lighting, certain broad categories of fixtures are more efficient than others. For example, surface-mounted or recessed linear fluorescent fixtures are significantly more efficient than such fluorescent downlight fixtures as recessed cans. They are also more efficient than flush, ceiling-mounted circular fixtures. LED lighting is beginning to see acceptance as another efficient type of light source, but with as-yet wide variations in quality and efficiency.

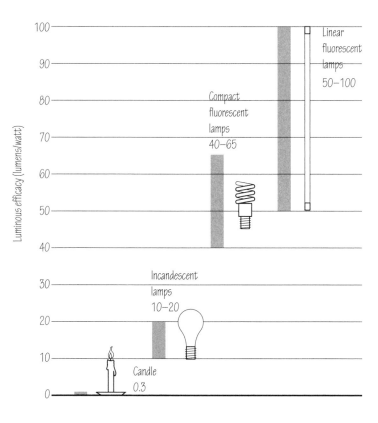

11.09 Table of approximate luminous efficacies.

A useful metric for selecting lighting fixtures is the luminous efficacy, expressed in lumens/watt (lm/w). By way of reference, a candle has a luminous efficacy of 0.3 lm/w. Incandescent lamps have luminous efficacies roughly in the 10 to 20 lm/w range. The higher lighting efficiency of compact fluorescent lamps (CFL) is evident in their higher luminous efficacies, typically in the 40 to 65 lm/w range. Linear fluorescent lamps are even more efficient, with efficacies in the 50 to 100 lm/w range, affirming their advantage over point source fixtures, such as downlights. Emerging LED lighting fixtures have widely varying luminous efficacies, ranging from 20 to 120 lm/w.

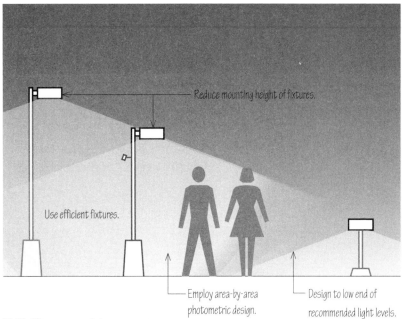

11.10 Efficient exterior lighting strategies.

Labels in figure 11.10:
Reduce mounting height of fixtures.
Use efficient fixtures.
Employ area-by-area photometric design.
Design to low end of recommended light levels.

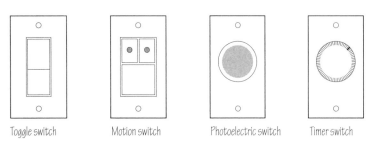

Toggle switch

Motion switch

Photoelectric switch

Timer switch

11.11 Four types of lighting control.

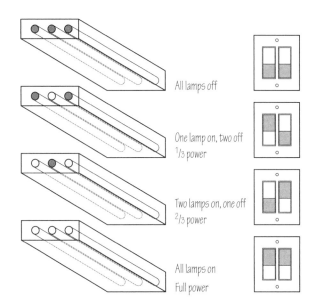

All lamps off

One lamp on, two off
1/3 power

Two lamps on, one off
2/3 power

All lamps on
Full power

11.12 Inboard/outboard control of lighting.

Exterior Lighting

Exterior lighting can be delivered most efficiently by using many of the same tools as interior lighting: high-efficiency lighting fixtures; computerized area-by-area lighting design to provide safe lighting at a level no higher than needed; low light-fixture mounting to bring the illumination closer and more efficiently to where it is needed; and efficient lighting controls. The additional challenge of minimizing light pollution has previously been discussed and harmonizes well with the goal of minimizing energy use.

Active discussions with the owner at an early phase of design and a careful assessment of how much exterior lighting is needed on an area-by-area basis can minimize lighting, cost, energy use, and light pollution. For example, low-level footpath lighting can be achieved with ground-level fixtures rather than pole-mounted fixtures. The Owner's Project Requirements might detail the requirements for various types of outdoor lighting: parking, building access, security, decorative needs, and other purposes, such as evening outdoor recreation or sports. A central question is whether every type of lighting is needed. Each unnecessary light fixture removed from a project will reduce construction cost, material use, and energy demand.

Controls

There are four main types of controls, each of which can be used to reduce lighting energy use, either alone or in combination: manual controls, motion sensors, photosensors, and timers.

Manual control is typically handled through the use of toggle switches or dimmers. Using more than one control in a single space gives more flexibility for lighting levels and for saving energy. This control strategy is referred to as multilevel switching. Even for small rooms, at least two switches are recommended, each controlling some of the light fixtures. The controls can switch or dim either separate light fixtures or different lamps within the same fixture, which is sometimes referred to as inboard/outboard or multilevel switching. For larger rooms, more switches are recommended, and if rooms have two entrances, switches should be considered at each entrance, which is referred to as 3-way switching.

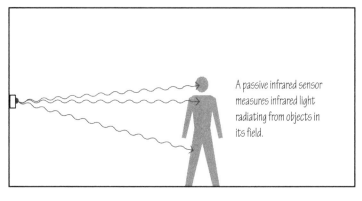

A passive infrared sensor measures infrared light radiating from objects in its field.

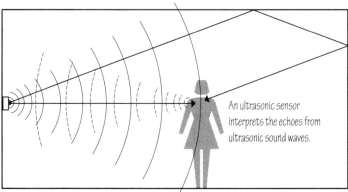

An ultrasonic sensor interprets the echoes from ultrasonic sound waves.

11.13 Passive infrared and ultrasonic sensors.

Selecting the correct motion sensor for a specific application ensures proper operation. Passive infrared sensors work by detecting heat from occupants in a space and are suitable for where the sensors have a direct line of sight to occupants. Ultrasonic sensors work by detecting responses to ultrasonic signals sent out by the sensors, so they do not require a direct line of sight to the occupant. However, ultrasonic sensors can sometimes be mistakenly activated by motion in adjacent spaces. Dual technology motion controls incorporate both passive infrared and ultrasonic sensors.

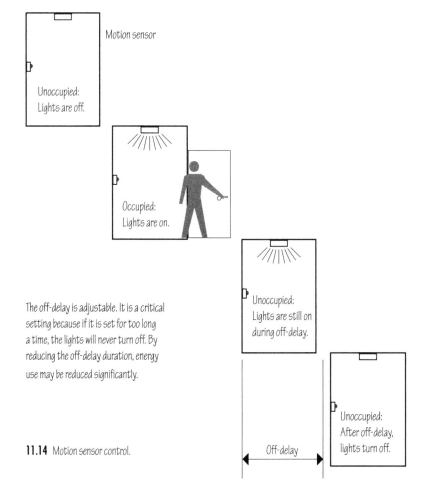

Motion sensor

Unoccupied: Lights are off.

Occupied: Lights are on.

Unoccupied: Lights are still on during off-delay.

Unoccupied: After off-delay, lights turn off.

Off-delay

The off-delay is adjustable. It is a critical setting because if it is set for too long a time, the lights will never turn off. By reducing the off-delay duration, energy use may be reduced significantly.

11.14 Motion sensor control.

Commissioning is important with motion sensors. A motion sensor keeps the light on for a set amount of time after occupancy is no longer detected. This setting is called the off-delay. For example, where ASHRAE Standard 90 requires off-delays to be 30 minutes maximum, it has been found that shortening the off-delay from 30 minutes can almost triple the energy savings, from a 24% energy reduction to 74% energy reduction, in the corridor lighting of high-rise apartment buildings. Apartment corridors may be unoccupied over 97% of the time, but a 30-minute off-delay means that the lights stay on throughout the waking hours of the day, as motion sensors in the corridors see occupants more often than every 30 minutes. A shorter off-delay allows the motion sensor to truly detect unoccupied periods. Savings from shorter motion sensor off-delays can be expected in other high-occupancy areas, such as lobbies and corridors in schools and office buildings. It should be noted that, for fluorescent lighting, very short off-delay settings may impact lamp life. As with all lighting controls, the best chance for implementing the proper off-delay is for this setting to be specified in the construction documents.

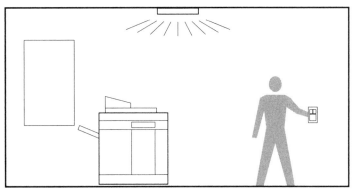

Manual-on motion sensors, also called vacancy sensors, require the occupant to turn on the lights manually. The motion sensor will automatically turn off the lights after motion is no longer detected for a set amount of time (off-delay).

Manual-on motion sensors, also called vacancy sensors, require the occupant to turn on the lights in a space manually; the motion sensor will then automatically turn off the lights after motion is no longer detected. This type of control is applicable for spaces where artificial lighting might not always be needed, such as offices where there may be adequate daylight or laundry rooms where a brief occupancy may not require the lights to be turned on. Manual-on motion sensors are especially effective in avoiding false-on switching of the lights in a space. On the other hand, auto-on motion sensors are more appropriate for spaces where the occupants might not be familiar with, or have easy access to, the light-switch location, such as public restrooms, garages, and corridors.

Lights stay off during transient occupancy, such as for a brief walk-through, if the manual-on sensor is not turned on.

11.15 Manual-on motion sensors.

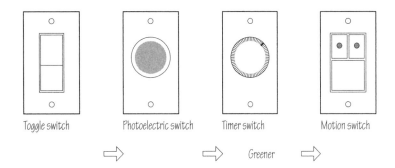

Toggle switch   Photoelectric switch   Timer switch   Motion switch

Greener

11.16 Greener options for controlling exterior lights.

The most energy-efficient control of **exterior** lighting is obtained by asking two questions:

1. Of the various outdoor lighting needs, which lights could be controlled by motion sensors? Well-applied motion sensors typically result in the least lighting-energy use and reduced light pollution. Like the motion sensors used indoors, exterior motion sensors need to be specified and commissioned to have their off-delay set as short as possible, preferably 5 minutes or less. Motion sensors for exterior lighting control are best used in conjunction with a photosensor control to prevent lights from inadvertently coming on due to motion during the day. Note the hierarchy of this type of control: the exterior lights will not turn on unless there is both motion and an absence of ambient light.

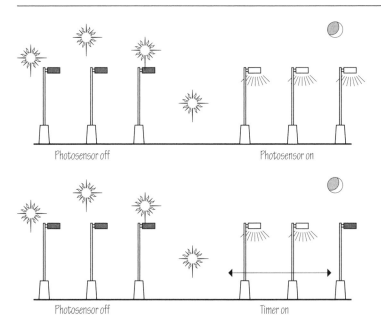

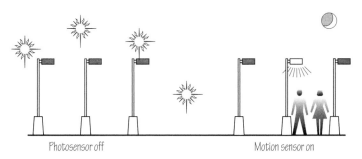

11.17 Greener options for controlling exterior lighting.

11.18 Typical outdoor light levels.

Phase	Foot-candles	Lux
Direct sunlight	10,000	100,000
Full daylight	1,000	10,000
Overcast day	100	1000
Dusk	10	100
Twilight	1	10
Deep twilight	0.1	1
Full moon	0.01	0.1
Quarter moon	0.001	0.01
Moonless night	0.0001	0.001
Overcast night	0.00001	0.0001

If some outdoor lights must be on continuously at night, then photosensors can be used to turn them on so that the lights are on only when it is dark outside. For energy-efficient design, it is instructive to further ask:

2. Is the lighting needed for security or access for the entire night, or is it needed only for evening access? If the latter, then require a photosensor to turn on the lights but require a timer to turn them off. In this way, perhaps 50% of the energy required to have the light on all night can be saved. Again, the Owner's Project Requirements might specify the requirements for security and evening access for each exterior light, including the time of evening when lights can be shut off so that timers can be commissioned accordingly.

Note how exterior lights typically need two separate controls to avoid lights being on when not necessary, either a combination of photosensor plus motion sensor or a photosensor plus timer. Manual control is another option but it too is best combined with a photosensor to avoid exterior lights inadvertently being left on during the day.

Like motion sensors, exterior photosensors need to be installed properly and commissioned carefully. They should preferably not be aimed where artificial light, such as the headlights from a passing vehicle at night, might unnecessarily trip the sensor and turn off the lights. Maximum savings from exterior lighting photosensors depends on setting the appropriate light level. Photosensors should be set at the level for which artificial light is sought outdoors.

Photosensors are often shipped with settings to turn lights on when the light level falls below 10 foot-candles or higher, which is too high a setting. These high settings can cause outdoor lights to be inadvertently turned on in the middle of overcast days. Various codes and standards recommend light levels of only 0.5 to 2.0 foot-candles for different applications of outdoor lighting, such as the illumination of sidewalks and parking lots. The required level of outdoor lighting should be documented in the construction and commissioning documents and the photocell control should be set to turn on the lights when the ambient light level drops below this level.

Greener

The deadband for photosensors should also be specified. The deadband is the difference between the cut-out set point and the cut-in set point. It should be set at a value sufficiently higher than the cut-in set point to avoid the nuisance cycling of lights. For example, if the design level is 1 foot-candle, the photocell should be set to turn on the lights when the ambient light level drops below 1 foot-candle and to turn off the lights when the ambient light level rises above 3 foot-candles. In this example, the deadband is 3−1 = 2 foot-candles.

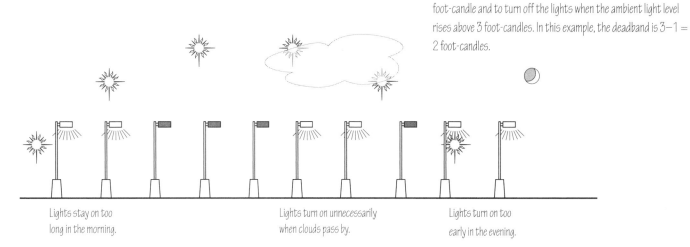

Lights stay on too long in the morning.

Lights turn on unnecessarily when clouds pass by.

Lights turn on too early in the evening.

11.19 Results when the photosensor set points for light level are too high.

The correct setting of exterior lighting controls can be assessed by inspection after construction. If an outdoor light is on when clouds pass by, or is on too late after dawn or too early before dusk, and the lighting does not change the ambient light level near the fixture when it is turned on, then the photocell control set point is too high. Note that proper commissioning can only occur at such times of low light level. Simply covering the photosensor to see if the light comes on does not reveal if the set point is correct.

Decorative Lighting

Decorative lighting merits its own discussion within the context of green buildings. Decorative lighting includes interior lighting intended to draw attention from the outdoors to the building interior; exterior lighting intended to highlight facades or other exterior elements; signage lighting; and lighting to highlight artwork or retail displays. Decorative lighting is often inefficient, although high-efficiency fixtures and lamps are available, which can be controlled with high-efficiency controls.

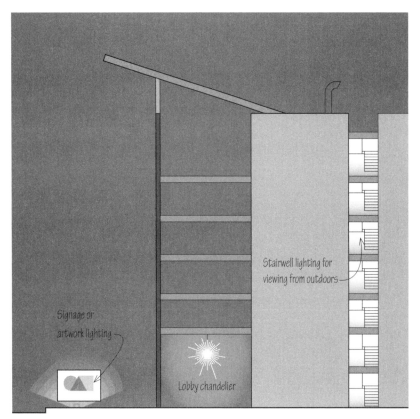

Stairwell lighting for viewing from outdoors

Signage or artwork lighting

Lobby chandelier

11.20 Decorative lighting for buildings.

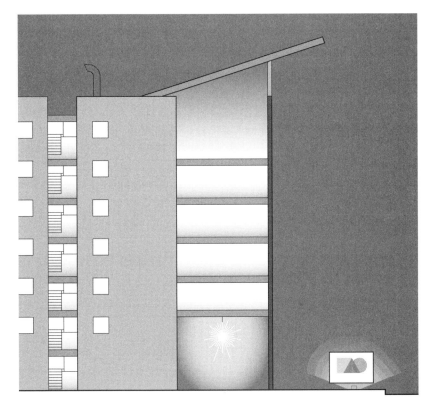

Beyond high-efficiency fixtures and controls, green building design typically warrants the question: Is each decorative light necessary for a specific building? Historically, buildings have been conceptualized during schematic design in renderings depicting windows brightened by interior lighting in an attempt to convey a feeling of warmth. Such renderings can lead to the design of lighting and controls that keep lights on at night and window designs dictated by exterior views rather than by the interior lighting needs of occupants.

Decorative lighting is given latitude or exemptions in some green building codes, standards, and guidelines. However, because decorative lighting is often inefficient, the need for decorative lighting is best examined on a case-by-case basis in green building design.

11.21 Renderings often emphasize the exterior lighting scheme for buildings over interior lighting needs of occupants.

Other Lighting Issues

Lowering lighting energy use provides the added benefit of reducing air-conditioning use. Reducing the lighting in a space increases its heating needs in winter, but because electricity is an inefficient way to provide heat, there is still an energy and cost benefit to reducing lighting requirements. Since heating systems are not sized for when lights are on, there is no penalty in construction cost when lighting is reduced. However, since cooling systems are sized for when lights are on in the summer, there is a construction cost benefit to reducing lighting, specifically in terms of smaller cooling systems being required. However, these savings only accrue if the lighting design is specified before the cooling equipment is sized.

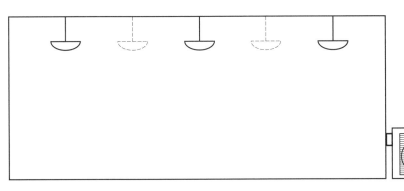

11.22 Reduced lighting often results in reduced loads on air-conditioning systems.

Efficient lighting design often reduces construction cost as the correct amount of lighting rather than excessive lighting is installed. On the other hand, high-efficiency fixtures and more efficient lighting controls typically cost more than conventional-efficiency options.

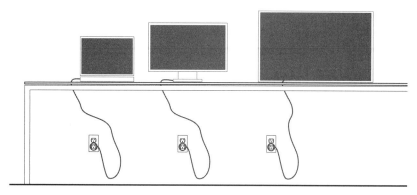

11.23 The growth in plug loads.

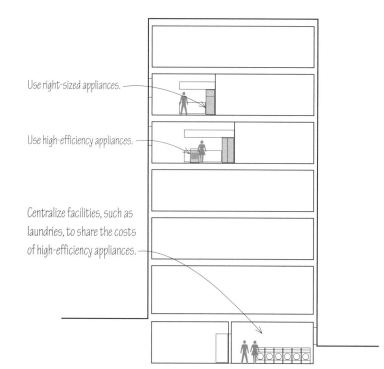

Use right-sized appliances.

Use high-efficiency appliances.

Centralize facilities, such as laundries, to share the costs of high-efficiency appliances.

11.24 Strategies for reducing appliance plug loads.

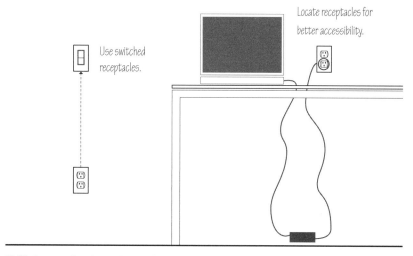

Use switched receptacles.

Locate receptacles for better accessibility.

11.25 Strategies for reducing plug loads from power supplies.

Plug Loads

Plug loads are a rapidly increasing cause of energy use in buildings. Equipment, such as larger television screens, computers, electronic game controllers, extra refrigerators and freezers, and power supplies for electronics are contributing to this growth in plug loads.

Traditional building design leaves the plug loads to the building owner or occupants. However, in some cases appliances are now being chosen by design professionals. And in the future, the energy use of plug loads may also be influenced in design in other ways.

For large appliances like refrigerators, dishwashers, and clothes washers, high-efficiency versions can be specified. In some cases, changing the fuel or type of appliance results in a reduction in energy usage or carbon emissions, as is the case with heat pump clothes dryers.

Centralizing the use of appliances—for example, providing a laundry room in an apartment complex rather than installing an individual machine in each apartment unit—allows the incremental cost of higher-efficiency machines to be distributed or shared among multiple users. In this scenario, higher-efficiency domestic hot water can also be provided more cost effectively. A central laundry also results in fewer building penetrations for water supply, dryer venting, gas piping, and ventilation, resulting in lower infiltration rates than if the machines were installed in individual apartments.

Appliances should also be appropriately sized. For example, a 22-cubic-foot (0.6 m³) refrigerator should not be specified for a studio apartment if a 15-cubic-foot (0.4 m³) model might suffice. Efficient appliances should also be used efficiently. For example, refrigerators should not be located next to stoves, which reduce the efficiency of the refrigerator, or in other warm locations. Refrigeration machinery, such as compressors for walk-in coolers and other commercial refrigeration, should also not be located in warm locations.

Many power supply devices for electronics, such as portable computers and mobile phones, draw power continuously. By designing receptacles at a more accessible height than at floor level, it has been found that people are more likely to unplug or turn off these power supplies when not in use. Alternatively, plug loads are more easily turned off if convenient control is provided for the receptacles, such as by wall-mounted, hand-height toggle switches.

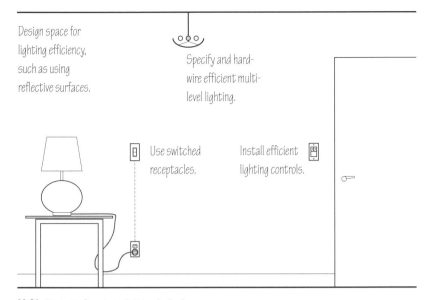

Design space for lighting efficiency, such as using reflective surfaces.

Specify and hard-wire efficient multi-level lighting.

Use switched receptacles.

Install efficient lighting controls.

11.26 Strategies for reducing lighting plug loads.

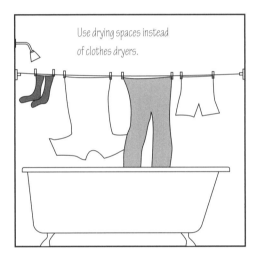

Use drying spaces instead of clothes dryers.

11.27 Strategy for reducing the plug loads of clothes dryers.

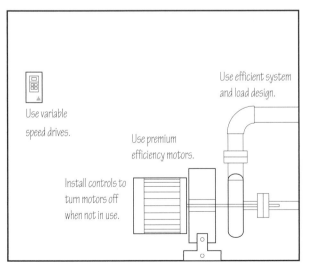

Use variable speed drives.

Use efficient system and load design.

Use premium efficiency motors.

Install controls to turn motors off when not in use.

11.28 Strategies for reducing the energy use of large motors.

In the case of lighting plug loads, building design can potentially reduce plug load energy use by providing high-efficiency, hard-wired light fixtures. This would be in lieu of leaving lighting solely to plug-in lamps, which often use inefficient incandescent or halogen bulbs. Not only can light fixtures be more efficient, but lighting design can also be made more effective through uniformity and spacing of the light fixtures. Lighting control can also be more efficient, whether through the use of motion sensors, photo controls, timers, or accessible wall switches where people more reliably turn lights on and off. Adequate quantities of convenience receptacles should still be provided to allow task lighting as this approach to efficient lighting evolves.

Additional creative approaches exist to reduce plug loads through building design. For example, BREEAM gives credit for the provision of drying space or clothes lines for drying laundry.

The advent of Internet-enabled controls offers further opportunities for controlling plug loads and reducing energy use. The availability and affordability of these controls will likely expand over time.

Large Electric Loads

Large electric loads include the motors that drive elevators, escalators, and the fans and pumps of mechanical equipment. Separately, large transformers are also a common type of electric load.

Attention should be directed to large motors that run for long hours. Green options include using premium efficiency motors, variable speed drives, efficient design, and controls that allow motors to be turned off when not in use.

Elevators are estimated to account for between 3% and 5% of a modern multistory building's energy use. Low-rise buildings often use hydraulic elevators for their low cost and high-rise buildings use variable-voltage, variable-frequency (VVVF) drives with AC motors for their greater energy efficiency and high speed.

The energy consumption of an elevator depends on many factors, including frequency of use, elevator capacity, and elevator efficiency. Energy use may be reduced by using elevators with high-efficiency drives and features such as regenerative braking. Elevators can also save energy by using high-efficiency lights, automatically turning off lights when not in use, and by automatically turning off ventilation fan motors when not in use. Advanced controls can further reduce energy use by optimizing elevator car travel algorithms, which place cars where they will most likely be needed, and also by turning off power to some cars during periods of low use in buildings with multiple elevators. For purposes of estimating energy usage, hydraulic elevators use approximately 0.02–0.03 kwh/start in light-duty, low-rise applications and more for heavier-duty or medium-rise buildings. This use can be reduced to 0.01–0.02 kwh/start with higher-efficiency drives. Elevators with VVVF drives in high-rise buildings use approximately 0.03–0.04 kwh/start, and this usage can be reduced to 0.02–0.03 kwh/start with regenerative braking or DC pulse-width modulated drives.

Traditional escalators typically use between 4,000 and 18,000 kwh of electricity per year per escalator. Variable-speed motors can reduce this energy use by sensing when no passengers are being carried and slowing the motors accordingly, or by stopping some escalators during periods of very low use.

Standard transformers must meet federal standards for minimum efficiencies ranging from 97% for 15 kVA transformers to 98.9% for 1,000 kVA transformers. Premium efficiency transformers are currently defined as 97.9% for 15kVA transformers, rising to 99.23% efficiency for 1,000 kVA transformers. Transformers must be well-ventilated and operate at a higher efficiency when located in lower-temperature environments. Therefore, they should not be located in hot rooms or in enclosed outdoor areas without adequate air circulation.

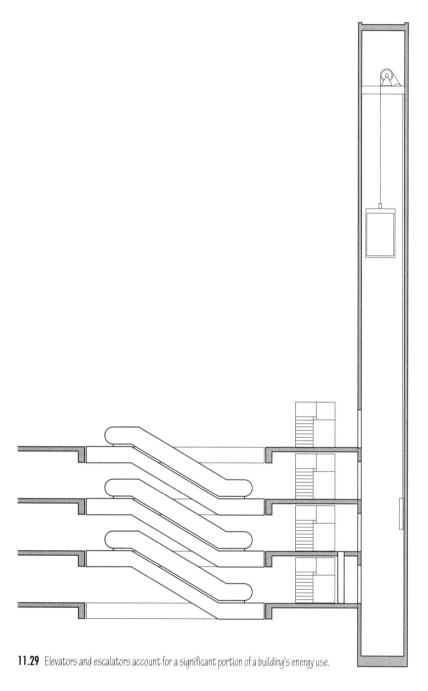

11.29 Elevators and escalators account for a significant portion of a building's energy use.

12
Hot and Cold Water

Water is being increasingly viewed as a finite resource. In evaluating water improvements for green buildings, the delivery and consumption of both cold and hot water should be considered. Reducing the consumption of hot water saves both water and the energy for heating the water.

Site water use was previously addressed in Chapter 4, Community and Site. This chapter will focus on indoor water use.

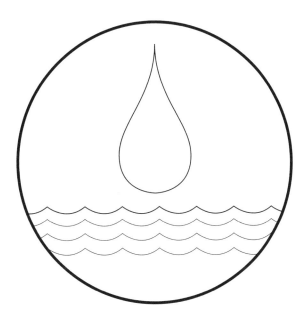

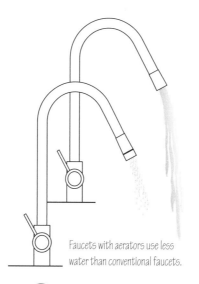

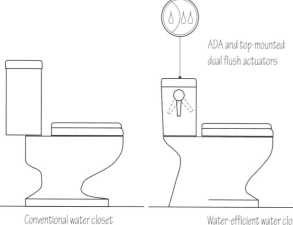

High-efficiency clothes washer is front loading with a high-speed drum on a horizontal axis and uses less water than a conventional washer.

Faucets with aerators use less water than conventional faucets.

ADA and top-mounted dual flush actuators

Conventional water closet

Water-efficient water closets have smaller tanks than conventional water closets.

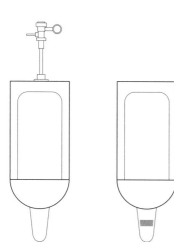

Conventional urinal

Waterless urinals use a liquid sealant that floats on top of the liquid collected in a trap, through which draining liquid can pass while preventing odors from escaping the drain.

12.01 Efficient appliances and fixtures.

Reducing Use

A reduction in water and energy use is most effectively accomplished by first examining water loads. Starting at the point of end use, a first step is to use efficient appliances and fixtures—devices that deliver the same end effect but use less water.

Efficient dishwashers use 20% less water than standard dishwashers. Efficient clothes washers use 50% less water than standard washers. Low-flow shower heads and faucet aerators also reduce water use.

Dual flush toilets use less water to flush liquid waste. Waterless urinals do not use any water at all, using instead an oil-based liquid seal in the drain to prevent odors from migrating back into a building. Composting toilets also do not use water.

12.02 Low-use fixtures listed by EPA's voluntary Water Sense program.

Fixture	Federal Requirement	EPA Water Sense Requirement
Shower heads	2.5 GPM*	2.0 GPM
Urinals	1.0 GPF**	0.5 GPF
Residential toilets	1.6 GPF	1.28 GPF
Commercial faucets		
Private lavatories	2.2 GPM	1.5 GPM
Residential faucets		
Bathrooms	2.2 GPM	1.5 GPM

*GPM: gallons per minute

**GPF: gallons per flush

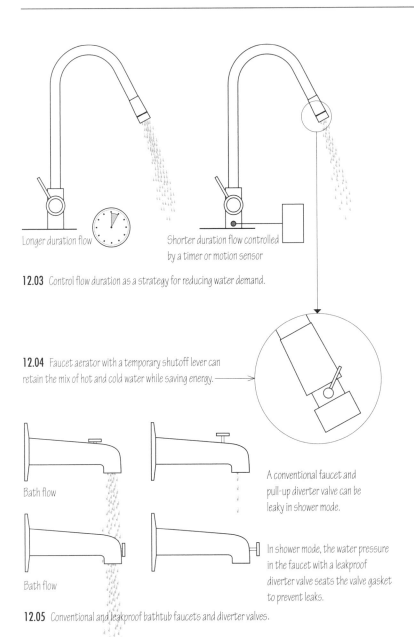

Longer duration flow

Shorter duration flow controlled
by a timer or motion sensor

12.03 Control flow duration as a strategy for reducing water demand.

12.04 Faucet aerator with a temporary shutoff lever can retain the mix of hot and cold water while saving energy.

Bath flow

A conventional faucet and pull-up diverter valve can be leaky in shower mode.

Bath flow

In shower mode, the water pressure in the faucet with a leakproof diverter valve seats the valve gasket to prevent leaks.

12.05 Conventional and leakproof bathtub faucets and diverter valves.

As a load, water does not comprise just flow but also duration. Reducing water use can be done by both lowering the flow rate and shortening the duration of the flow. Flow-duration limiters, such as those in public lavatories that shut off the water automatically, can decrease water use by limiting the duration of flow. Similarly, levers on shower heads and faucets that allow the water to be turned off temporarily but conveniently retain the mix of hot and cold water also save energy by reducing the flow duration.

An important water load is caused by leaks. We might think of leaks as an unusual condition, a failure that cannot be controlled through building design. However, some leaks are widespread because they are intrinsic to certain types of equipment. These can be eliminated simply by avoiding their use by design. For example, bathtub spouts with pull-up handles frequently leak water when the handles are pulled to supply water to a shower. A study found leaks in 34% of these devices at an average rate of 0.8 GPM. By using spouts with diverter valves with a handle at the end of the bath spout, leaks are eliminated. Another example is toilet fill-valves that provide leak detection.

A type of equipment that has intrinsic water leaks are steam boiler systems. While typically thought of as a 19th-century technology, steam boilers are seeing a small resurgence. However, steam boiler systems frequently leak steam, as these systems are open to the atmosphere and steam leaks typically go undetected. These leaks can be prevented in building design by avoiding the use of steam boilers. Separately, the makeup water for boilers, whether steam or hot water boilers, should not be allowed to flow automatically because this automatic supply of water can mask leaks in the system. Makeup water should be shut off with a valve and only used to fill the boiler, not to continually replace leaking water.

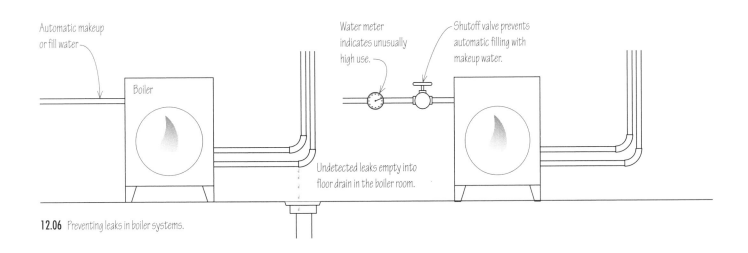

Automatic makeup or fill water

Boiler

Water meter indicates unusually high use.

Shutoff valve prevents automatic filling with makeup water.

Undetected leaks empty into floor drain in the boiler room.

12.06 Preventing leaks in boiler systems.

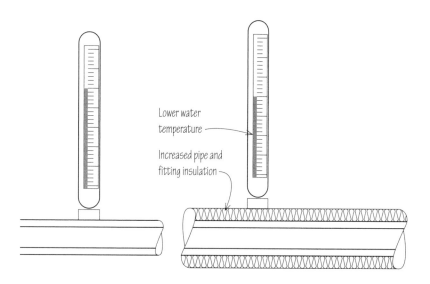

Hot Water

Hot water for kitchens, bathrooms, laundry rooms, and other consumable uses is often a large energy load—the second highest load in residential buildings, over 9% of the primary energy use in all buildings, and the fourth highest load overall after space heating, lighting, and space cooling. Offices are generally low users of hot water whereas other building types, such as hospitals, hotels, apartments, and factories, are high users. This consumable hot water is commonly referred to as domestic hot water or service hot water. It should not be confused with the hot water systems used to heat the spaces in buildings.

The energy load of domestic hot water is not immediately related to exterior forces like temperature, the sun, and the wind, although the load does increase slightly in winter as water temperatures entering the building decrease.

12.07 Lowering the water temperature and increasing the insulation of pipes and fittings can help to reduce hot water losses.

For the supply of heat, it makes sense to keep domestic hot water heaters entirely within the thermal envelope so that standby losses can be productively used for space heating in winter, especially in northern climates. In other words, it is best if hot water heaters are not located in unconditioned spaces with connections to the outdoors, like basements. Likewise, if the distribution piping is kept in heated spaces, distribution losses can be useful for much of the year, although such losses do negatively impact air-conditioning. Therefore, it is important to minimize such losses by insulating pipes.

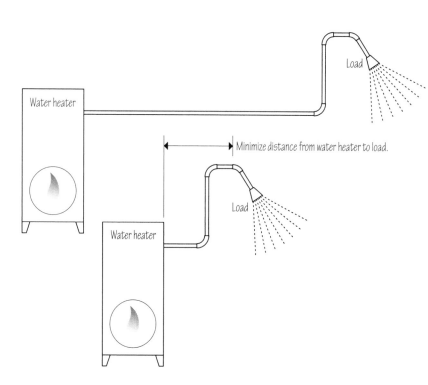

Another strategy to curtailing energy use is to minimize the distance between the hot water heater and the points of use. This can be done by using point-of-use water heaters or by clustering points of use, such as in bathrooms and kitchens.

12.08 Minimizing the distance from the hot water heater to points of use can help to reduce energy use.

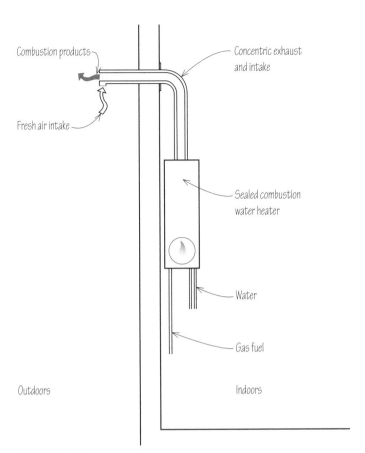

Combustion products

Concentric exhaust
and intake

Fresh air intake

Sealed combustion
water heater

Water

Gas fuel

Outdoors

Indoors

12.09 Higher-efficiency gas water heater.

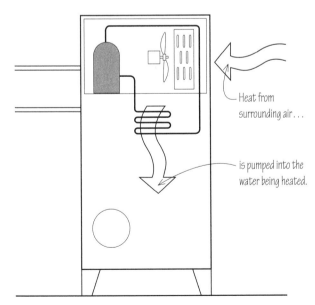

Heat from
surrounding air...

is pumped into the
water being heated.

12.10 Heat pump water heater.

For water heaters that burn fossil fuels like natural gas, sealed combustion systems typically operate at higher efficiency and also eliminate the infiltration that is induced by combustion in systems that are not sealed. Some combustion fuels are also more efficient than others. For example, natural gas and propane heaters are typically available in higher efficiencies than those of oil-fired heaters.

Another emerging type of water heater is the heat-pump water heater. This device uses electricity to power a heat pump that moves the heat from the surrounding air into the hot water. Such systems are generally efficient although the technology is still developing. Since the surrounding air supplies the heat, heat pumps typically cool the space in which the heat pump is located. Sufficient space needs to be available from which to draw this heat; otherwise, the heat pump efficiency will drop and energy use will rise. Also, as the heat pump cools the space it is in, a cool space may not be desirable. This cooling may result in increased heat being needed for the building in winter.

Heat pump water heaters are also limited in the temperature they can generate. At higher temperatures, their efficiency and capacity decreases and they may not provide the high temperatures required for hot water in commercial kitchens. Despite these tradeoffs, heat pump water heaters deserve consideration for green buildings. We anticipate that as geothermal heating and cooling systems gain acceptance, the geothermal loop will increasingly be used as a heat source for domestic hot water heaters, and this will be an efficient system for heating water without the issues of drawing heat or rejecting heat within the building.

In larger buildings, domestic hot water can also be generated as a by-product of combined heating and power (CHP) systems.

For domestic hot water, the heat needed to raise the temperature of the water is typically smaller than the heat that is lost in producing and delivering the hot water. There are many losses, including standby conduction losses out the sides of a water heater storage tank; standby losses up the chimney for combustion water heaters; losses due to standing-pilot igniters that burn continuously; losses due to induced infiltration; distribution piping thermal losses; higher flow than necessary at faucets and shower heads; and leak losses from pipes, leaky faucets, and valves. The focus of improving water heating efficiencies should first be on reducing losses. Sealed-combustion, tankless water heaters, for example, reduce several of the losses: standby losses, chimney losses, and induced-infiltration losses. Tankless water heaters do have some unique characteristics, including requiring a minimum water flow rate to fire; taking time to fire; delivering fluctuating water temperatures under certain conditions; and being susceptible to problems if the water is hard. Point-of-use water heaters further reduce piping losses.

Losses can be eliminated in many cases by simply not providing hot water at all to a particular load location. Consider not piping hot water, for example, to half-bathrooms. These small bathrooms can often do without hot water, which is common practice in many countries. This assessment of whether hot water is necessary can be applied to other water end uses, although plumbing codes should be consulted to confirm whether hot water is required for any particular load.

Domestic hot water production and space-heating systems can be integrated, for example, in combined boiler systems. Historically, this was wasted energy because boilers were run year-round to provide domestic hot water through the nonwinter months. It is possible that there are unacceptable thermal losses even when domestic hot water is provided in a tank as part of a high-efficiency condensing boiler system. Such systems also use power to run a pump that circulates heat from the boiler to the water storage.

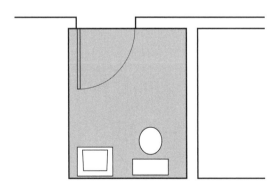

12.11 Consider supplying only cold water to the sink in half-bathrooms.

New Water and Heat Sources

Once point-of-use loads are reduced and leaks and losses are minimized, the demand for water and the heat required for hot water can be further lessened through a variety of recapture approaches.

Water and Heat Recycling

Water recycling allows the same water to be used for different purposes. For example, a toilet-lid sink is a device that allows clean water to be used first to wash hands, before filling a toilet tank. Wastewater can be filtered and reused within a building. Likewise, the heat from waste hot water can be recaptured through gray water heat recovery. This reduces the load of the incoming cold water by raising its temperature.

12.12 Toilet-lid sink.

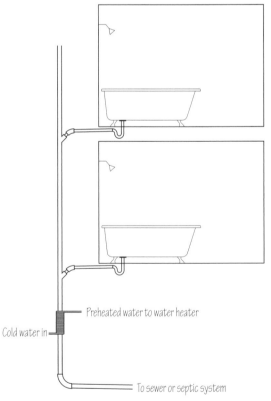

Preheated water to water heater

Cold water in

To sewer or septic system

12.13 Heat recovery from gray water.

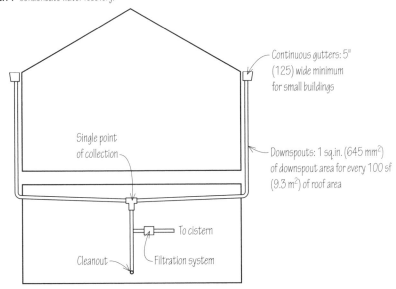

12.14 Condensate water recovery.

Continuous gutters: 5"
(125) wide minimum
for small buildings

Single point
of collection

Downspouts: 1 sq.in. (645 mm²)
of downspout area for every 100 sf
(9.3 m²) of roof area

Cleanout

To cistern

Filtration system

12.15 Rainwater harvesting: Collection and filtration.

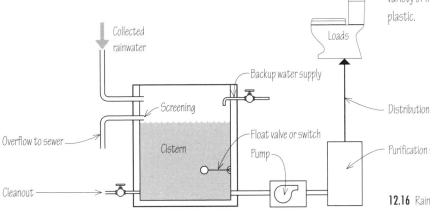

Condensate Recovery

Condensate can be recovered from air-conditioners, which produce water that generally does not contain impurities, although flows are small, intermittent, and drop to zero in the winter. The amount of condensate that will be generated varies, depending on the building and on the climate. One rule of thumb estimates 1 to 2 gallons per square foot (3.8 to 7.5 liters per 0.1 m²) per year but less for buildings that require little cooling in northern climates or dehumidification in dry climates and more for buildings that require more cooling and dehumidification, such as in the southeast United States. The condensate must be collected and supplied to either a storage location, such as a cistern being used for rainwater collection, or for immediate use, such as an open cooling tower sump.

Finally, with loads and losses minimized, attention may be turned to renewable sources of water and sources of heat.

Rainwater Harvesting

Rainwater can be captured for use in a building, reducing the use of municipal or well water. A rainwater harvesting system includes a collection area, typically the building roof; a conveyance system to route the rainwater to storage; a storage tank or cistern; a filtering and possibly a disinfection treatment system; a backup system to provide water for times of low rainwater; provision for overflow; and a distribution system to deliver the water to the water loads.

As mentioned previously, rainwater gutters, downspouts, and drains need to be located and pitched to centrally route and collect the rainwater. A rule of thumb is that gutters should be 5 inches (125) wide for small buildings and downspouts should provide one square inch (645 mm²) of downspout area for every 100 square feet (9.3 m²) of roof area.

In cold climates, the storage must be indoors or underground to prevent freezing of the collected water. Tanks are fabricated from a variety of materials, including steel, concrete, wood, fiberglass, or plastic.

12.16 Rainwater harvesting: Storage and distribution.

The most frequent use of rainwater is for toilet flushing. In this case, the toilets in a building are piped to the rainwater storage rather than to the cold-water distribution system. Typically, these installations use a pump to transport the water to the toilets. However, if the storage is located at an elevation higher than the toilets, a pump may not be needed. Rainwater harvesting systems usually have a float valve, which allows the tank to be supplied with cold water from the building water system during periods of low rain. If the toilets use flush valves, the pump needs to be selected to provide the minimum pressure required by the flush valves, typically 10 psi. Alternatively, flush tanks can be used for water closets in a rainwater-fed system.

While rainwater itself is regarded as clean, it can become contaminated as it falls if the air is polluted and as it is collected and conveyed for storage and use. The best way to prevent contamination is to have the roof free from standing water that can serve as a host to bacteria. Other possible biological contaminants include urine and feces of birds and other small animals. In its flow path from the roof, rainwater may also pick up chemical contaminants from either debris on the roof or the leaching from construction materials. Rainwater may also pick up particulate matter, such as leaves, twigs, and other debris. If the rainwater is to be used for nonpotable applications, such as the flushing of toilets, the main treatment required is a cleanable filter to remove particulate debris. If the rainwater is to be used for potable uses, additional treatment is required to provide disinfection of biological contaminants.

Rainwater harvesting systems are best designed using software based on local rainfall conditions, available roof area, and anticipated water demand.

Solar Energy

Solar energy is a highly suitable application for heating domestic hot water. It makes the most sense for buildings that see a year-round, centralized domestic hot water load, such as apartments, hotels, hospitals, and some factories. It has also found a place around the world in single-family homes, especially in non-freezing climates where exterior water piping is simplified and freeze-protection is not required. Solar energy is covered in more detail in Chapter 15, Renewable Energy.

Cost of Water Improvements

What is the impact on affordability of these various water improvements? High-efficiency, low-water end-use appliances and fixtures generally cost more than standard appliances, although the cost differences are diminishing. Reducing the distances from water heaters to end uses will typically reduce construction cost, as will eliminating the hot water supply from sinks where it is not necessary. High-efficiency water heaters cost more than standard water heaters. Solar water heaters and rainwater harvesting systems will add to a building's construction cost. Overall, expect to pay more for a building that substantially saves water use and seeks to eliminate the use of fossil fuels to heat water.

Water Summary

In summary, approaches for efficient hot water systems include reducing the loads as much as possible, minimizing losses, using high-efficiency water heaters, and placing the water heater and distribution systems entirely within the heated space and as close as possible to the points of use. In the process, the goal is to reduce the demand for heat to within a range that can be served by solar energy. Likewise for cold water, loads and losses should be reduced as much as possible to bring demand within a range where it can be served by captured rainwater.

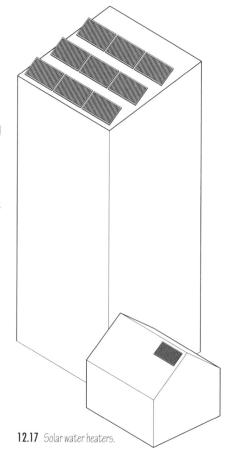

12.17 Solar water heaters.

13
Indoor Environmental Quality

Indoor Air Quality

Indoor air of good quality does not have objectionable concentrations of airborne contaminants, such as dust particles, carbon dioxide, hazardous chemicals, tobacco smoke, odors, humidity, and biological contaminants. Airborne contaminants constitute a load on a building but with the added complication that the load does not only originate outside the building; it can also originate inside the building.

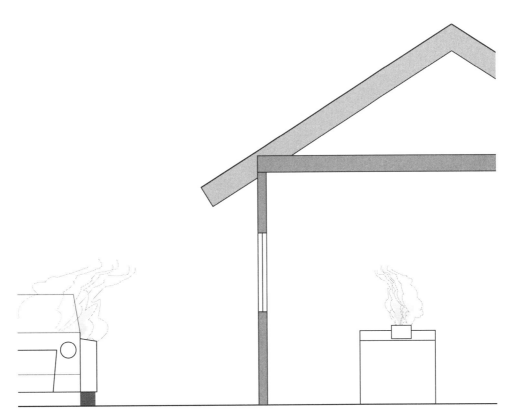

13.01 Airborne contaminants originate not only from outside a building but from the inside as well.

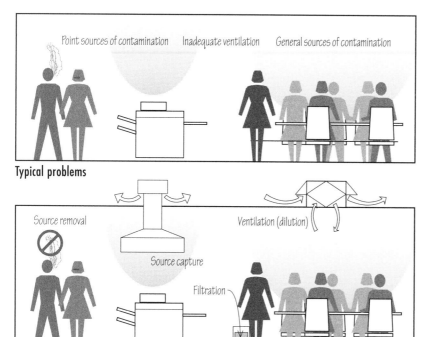

Typical problems

Point sources of contamination   Inadequate ventilation   General sources of contamination

Source removal   Ventilation (dilution)

Source capture

Filtration

Best practices

13.02 Approaches to providing good indoor air quality.

The four main approaches to providing good indoor air quality are contaminant source reduction, contaminant capture, filtration, and dilution. The best approach is to start at the source. We first seek to eliminate indoor sources of contaminants, such as by banning indoor smoking or by using paints and carpeting that emit fewer chemicals. Contaminant capture involves intercepting contaminants before they reach the human breathing zone. This typically means the installation of exhaust fans in kitchens and bathrooms, fume hoods, and the like. Filtration removes contaminants from the air. The first three approaches are all sound but they can miss contaminants that cannot be eliminated, captured, or filtered. Examples include trace chemicals emitted from new products and the carbon dioxide in exhaled air. This is the purpose of the final approach to providing good indoor air quality—dilution with outdoor air, otherwise known as ventilation.

For ventilation, a presumption is made that the air outdoors is clean, but steps are also taken to ensure that it is in fact as clean as possible.

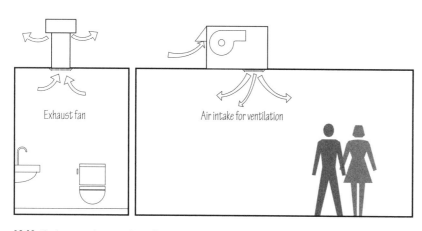

Exhaust fan   Air intake for ventilation

13.03 The distinction between exhaust fans and intakes for ventilation with outdoor air.

There can be confusion between exhaust fans, which are means of contaminant capture, and ventilation with outdoor air, which is the dilution of contaminants. The confusion arises because both are often referred to as ventilation and are analyzed together. The two often also interact, because exhaust causes the intake of outside air into a building.

Confusion also arises because of the interrelationships between ventilation and infiltration. Ventilation is typically fan-induced. However, infiltration can deliver the same effect as ventilation by bringing in outside air to dilute indoor airborne contaminants. Also, as with the interaction between exhaust fans and infiltration, ventilation with outdoor air and infiltration can also interact. If air is brought into a building for ventilation with a fan but without any accompanying fan exhaust, then air will leak out of the building. So discussions of ventilation inevitably include discussions of infiltration as well.

Finally, confusion can arise between ventilation and cooling because ventilation is at times used for cooling.

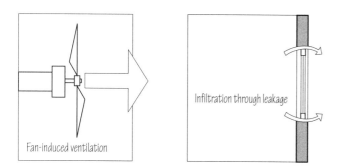

Fan-induced ventilation   Infiltration through leakage

13.04 The distinction between ventilation and infiltration.

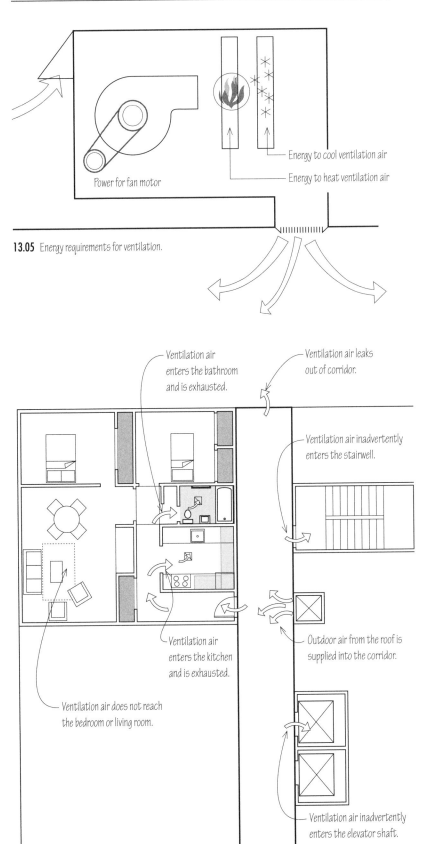

Ventilation Challenges

The traditional approach to improving indoor air quality is through ventilation but ventilation also presents many challenges.

Ventilation uses much energy. Electricity is required to run the motors that turn the fans that move ventilation air. Even more significantly, energy is used to heat and cool the ventilation air that is brought into a building. The rate of energy use in a building is extremely sensitive to ventilation. A measurable increase in ventilation will result in an immediate and significant increase in a building's energy use.

It is a challenge to bring outdoor air into a building without causing discomfort. If it is not heated or cooled, outdoor air enters a building at whatever temperature it happens to be. It is very different to bring 0°F (−18°C) outdoor air into a building than when the outdoors is 32°F (0°C), or 70°F (21°C), or 100°F (38°C). The main challenge is that the energy required to heat or cool the outdoor air keeps changing as the outdoor temperature changes. The problem is especially critical in heating, where the risk of discomfort is high. Documented problems include the overheating of ventilation air and the associated spaces into which it is supplied, failed heaters, and ventilation systems that have been shut off due to inadequate temperature control.

Ventilation often does not reach the people for whom it is intended. For example, in many high-rise apartment buildings and hotels, ventilation air is drawn in from above the roof and supplied to the corridors through grilles in the corridor walls, usually just above head height. The ventilation system is designed to have air flow into the corridor and under the doors of the apartments or hotel rooms. However, a significant portion of this air never reaches the people for whom it was intended. Rather, much of the air moves back out of the building via elevator shafts, stairwells, trash chutes, and corridor windows. Some of the air does flow under the doors into apartments or hotel rooms, but much of this air usually then just flows out of the kitchen or bathroom exhaust. Kitchens and bathrooms are typically located near the entrance to the apartment or hotel room, away from the perimeter of the building. So the fresh air flows out of the building without having reached the people who are in the living rooms or bedrooms.

13.05 Energy requirements for ventilation.

Ventilation air enters the bathroom and is exhausted.

Ventilation air leaks out of corridor.

Ventilation air inadvertently enters the stairwell.

Outdoor air from the roof is supplied into the corridor.

Ventilation air enters the kitchen and is exhausted.

Ventilation air does not reach the bedroom or living room.

Ventilation air inadvertently enters the elevator shaft.

Power for fan motor

Energy to cool ventilation air

Energy to heat ventilation air

13.06 Ventilation air does not always reach the people for whom it is intended.

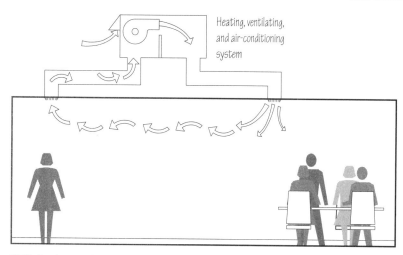

13.07 Ventilation can bypass the breathing zone of occupants.

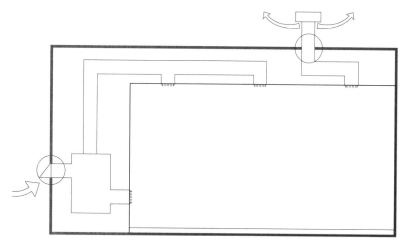

13.08 Ventilation openings break the continuity of the thermal boundary.

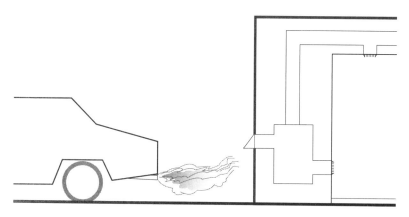

13.09 Ventilation can introduce contaminants into a building if air intake openings are located too close to sources of contaminants.

Similar bypass issues, also termed ineffectiveness, occur in buildings that have ventilation air transported with heating or cooling air. In many such buildings, the air is both supplied at ceiling level and also returned to ductwork at the ceiling level, so that much of the ventilation does not reach the breathing zone of the occupants.

Another problem with ventilation is the unintended consequence of introducing holes into a building and breaking the continuity of the thermal boundary. These holes are supposed to enable the ventilation air to flow. A properly designed ventilation system has ventilation air flowing only when the air is needed. For example, an office building does not need ventilation air at night, when the building is empty. The ventilating holes are typically closed at these times with dampers, which are valve-like devices that can open or close. But air is a fluid, adept at finding its way past dampers—in other words, leaking. And dampers break and stick, either permanently open and leaking more air than necessary or permanently closed and not providing ventilation at all.

Ventilation is difficult to measure and ventilation systems are difficult to inspect and to understand. As a result, building inspectors usually cannot tell if something is wrong with the design or installation. So ventilation systems not only fail after a building is built, they often fail before the building is even occupied. Even when a ventilating system fails, the building occupants or operators typically do not realize that it has failed. Compare ventilation to other things that fail in a building. If the heating or cooling fails, we know within a few hours because the building gets cold or hot. Or if an elevator fails, we usually know immediately. If the hot water heater fails, we also usually know when we open a faucet. But ventilation is different. If the ventilation fails, often it is not noticed, sometimes not for months or years.

Even if the ventilation system is working and can provide enough air to the right locations, it is a challenge to reduce and increase the ventilation in response to occupancy that comes and goes. The closest we have come to achieving this is demand-controlled ventilation, typically using carbon-dioxide sensors that increase ventilation if the concentration of carbon dioxide gets too high. This has been a significant advance. However, demand-controlled ventilation is typically applied only in commercial buildings. It has not reached a variety of other common building types, such as single-family homes, multifamily buildings, or hotels.

Another problem with ventilation is that air intake openings are sometimes located close to the sources of contaminants. So instead of diluting indoor air contaminants with fresh outdoor air, the ventilation introduces contaminants into the building. Evidence of this is seen in the traces of vehicle exhaust fumes, such as the black smudges on air grilles, in buildings that have loading docks or parking lots close to air intakes.

Indoor Air Quality Solutions

Using the outside-in approach, we start far from the building and work inward.

Community

We try to choose a community that does not suffer from intense air pollution, and we try to reduce air pollution in our communities, knowing that our indoor air can only be as good as the outdoor air that we bring in. We avoid point sources of air pollution, especially vehicle exhausts, such as streets with heavy vehicular traffic or street corners where vehicles idle. Industrial sources of air pollution should also be scrutinized and avoided. We either want to keep our buildings away from these sources of pollution or, at the least, keep the ventilation air intake for a building away from pollution sources.

Maintain distance from sources of air pollution.

13.10 Community strategies to prevent indoor air quality problems.

Site

Moving on to the site, as we lay out vehicle traffic patterns and parking, we try to keep vehicles away from the building. We consider prohibiting tobacco smoking near the building, especially near ventilation air intakes, but also near pathways and entries, and possibly even from the entire site. We seek to reduce or eliminate other site-based sources of contaminants, such as combustion machinery, chemical processes, and burning. And, of utmost importance, we direct attention to grading and to site water management. Many of the more serious air quality problems in buildings are due to humidity, and the source of the humidity is often traced back to surface water that finds its way into the building, especially if there is a basement.

Building Shape

In regard to the building shape, some work has already been done by earlier phases of design from the outside in. Specifically, designing a smaller building footprint for a given occupancy and avoiding tall ceilings can combine to significantly reduce ventilation requirements. For example, in residential buildings, including apartment buildings, where the required ventilation rate for many years has been 0.35 air changes per hour (ACH), using smaller floor areas and avoiding tall ceilings where possible substantially reduce the ventilation rate. As an example, the required ventilation rate for a U.S.-average 2,600 sf (242 m^2) home with 10-foot (305) ceilings is 152 cubic feet per minute (CFM), whereas the ventilation rate for a more modest 1973-era size home of 1,660 sf (154 m^2) home with 8-foot (245) ceilings is only 77 CFM, saving almost 50% in the energy required to transport and condition the ventilation air. In many building codes, kitchen exhaust is also dependent on air changes per hour and therefore related to the area and height of a kitchen.

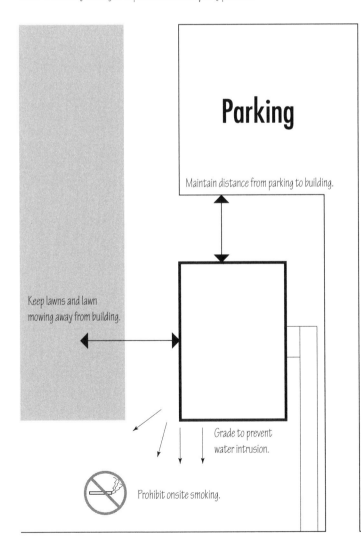

Parking

Maintain distance from parking to building.

Keep lawns and lawn mowing away from building.

Grade to prevent water intrusion.

Prohibit onsite smoking.

13.11 Site strategies to prevent indoor air quality problems.

Near-Building

When it comes to near-building features, loading docks present a risk. They should be located at a substantial distance from ventilation air intakes. In addition, loading docks should have their own exhaust ventilation to avoid entrainment of exhaust fumes into the building by stack effect. Finally, a strong layer of shelter, such as an air lock, should stand between the loading dock and the building itself.

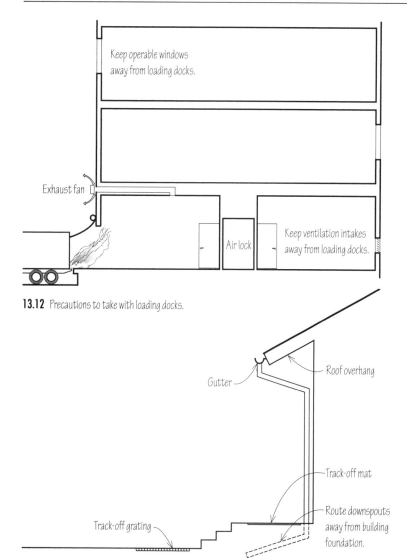

Keep operable windows away from loading docks.

Exhaust fan

Air lock

Keep ventilation intakes away from loading docks.

13.12 Precautions to take with loading docks.

We seek to keep particulates out of buildings by minimizing the entrainment of dust and dirt through devices, such as track-off mats and grates, for people to use as they approach the building. Again, water management is critical, and in the case of near-building features, this means primarily the effective use of gutters. Gutters collect roof rainwater, and, most importantly, gutters need to thoroughly direct this water away from the building if it is not harvested for reuse. Overhangs can also help to protect a building from the effects of rainwater intrusion that lead to indoor humidity problems.

Gutter

Roof overhang

Track-off mat

Route downspouts away from building foundation.

Track-off grating

13.13 Near-building features to prevent indoor air quality problems.

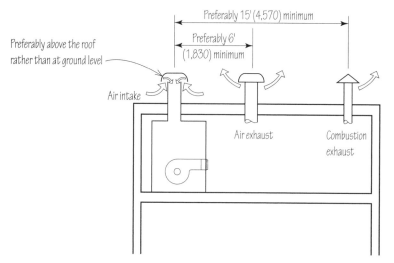

Preferably 15' (4,570) minimum

Preferably 6' (1,830) minimum

Preferably above the roof rather than at ground level

Air intake

Air exhaust

Combustion exhaust

13.14 Preferred location of ventilation air intakes.

Outer Envelope

Outside air should be brought into buildings as high above the ground as possible, preferably at rooftop level, where the air is cleaner and farther away from contaminant sources, such as vehicles, lawnmowers and other small-engine equipment, and tobacco smoke. Air intakes should also be located away from building exhausts, either ventilation exhaust or, more importantly, combustion vents and chimneys.

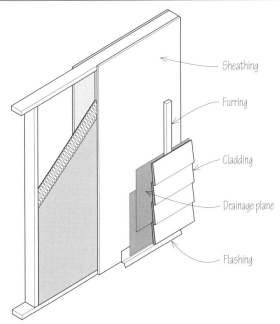

Sheathing

Furring

Cladding

Drainage plane

Flashing

13.15 Strengthening the outer envelope against water intrusion.

The focus on water management continues with efforts to strengthen the outer envelope against rainwater intrusion. Strong layers of shelter help. The first layer is the cladding. Behind the cladding, a well-defined and continuous drainage plane actively sheds water that has penetrated the cladding. The drainage plane may be constructed with building paper, faced and well-taped insulation, or sealed sheathings. Flashings also form part of the drainage plane, protecting discontinuities at windows, doors, and the tops and bottoms of walls. The dual functions of preventing air infiltration and water penetration are often compatible. Walls and roofs that are strongly resistant to air penetration are less likely to allow water intrusion.

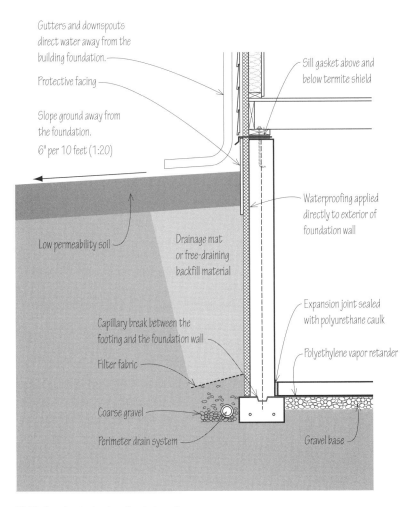

Gutters and downspouts direct water away from the building foundation.

Protective facing

Slope ground away from the foundation.
6" per 10 feet (1:20)

Sill gasket above and below termite shield

Low permeability soil

Drainage mat or free-draining backfill material

Waterproofing applied directly to exterior of foundation wall

Capillary break between the footing and the foundation wall

Filter fabric

Expansion joint sealed with polyurethane caulk

Polyethylene vapor retarder

Coarse gravel

Perimeter drain system

Gravel base

13.16 Vapor barrier details at foundation wall.

Below grade, a vapor barrier is essential. Sections of vapor barrier should be well-overlapped and sealed to prevent discontinuities. The vapor barrier should preferably be at least 10 mil thick. Avoid penetrations of the vapor barrier; even small failures can allow moisture intrusion. Slab edges as well as expansion joints should be caulked. Resistance to moisture at the foundation also means resistance to radon, an odorless carcinogen, the source of which is also the ground.

We want to reduce the discontinuities in the thermal boundary introduced by ventilation requirements. One solution is using automatic (motor-driven) dampers, which can prevent air movement in both directions when ventilation is not needed, rather than gravity dampers, which only prevent air movement in one direction. Tight-sealing, gasketed dampers also help, rather than loose ungasketed dampers that are common on many exhaust fans.

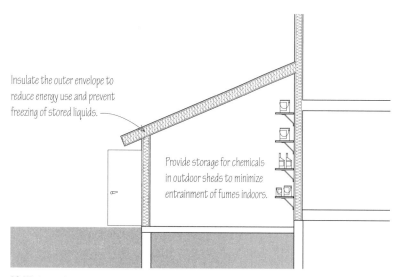

Insulate the outer envelope to reduce energy use and prevent freezing of stored liquids.

Provide storage for chemicals in outdoor sheds to minimize entrainment of fumes indoors.

13.17 Strengthening layers of shelter with attached sheds.

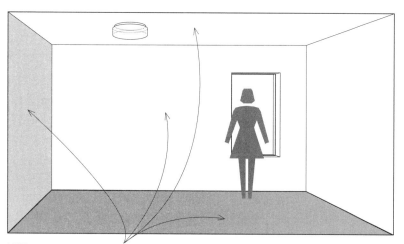

13.18 Minimize use of chemicals in interior finishes and furnishing to promote indoor air quality.

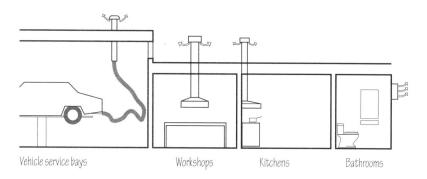

Vehicle service bays   Workshops   Kitchens   Bathrooms

13.19 Use exhaust ventilation to capture sources of contamination.

Unconditioned Spaces

Attached garages present a risk for poor indoor air quality due to the migration of vehicle fumes into a building. As previously indicated, attached garages also present an opportunity to be unconditioned spaces, which can serve as an extra layer of shelter to reduce heat gain and loss. If planning an attached garage, use it as another reason to establish a strong layer of shelter between the garage and the building, not only for thermal insulation but also for air-sealing to prevent the migration of fumes into the building.

Eliminating basements can help to reduce moisture issues substantially. Consider moving the storage of chemicals, such as cleaning fluids, pesticides, and paints, into attached sheds instead of keeping them in inadequately defined unconditioned spaces like basements or attics. A well-constructed attached shed, with strong layers of shelter on both the building side and on the outdoor side, will not have a risk of freezing stored liquid products in most climates. In colder regions, the inner envelope can be left uninsulated (but still air-sealed) to prevent freezing, but in this case the outer envelope must be insulated. The strong layers of shelter, through effective air-sealing, also prevent the inadvertent migration of fumes into the occupied building.

Inner Envelope

Principles of source reduction may be applied to minimize the use of chemicals in construction, specifically in the finishes of the inner envelope, such as paints, carpeting, and wood finishes. This is addressed in more detail in Chapter 16, Materials.

Internal Gains

Where internal gains were previously discussed in the context of energy gains, such as from lighting and appliances, the concept of indoor gains may be applied to airborne contaminants as well. Finishes may be selected that minimize the use of chemicals in cleaning and building operations. Tobacco smoke can be kept out of buildings and in the area around buildings. Beyond source reduction, source capture may be considered, as with exhaust hoods in kitchens that exhaust to the outdoors rather than just recirculating air back into the space. Bathroom exhaust fans are another form of source capture. Source capture principles may be extended to other sources of contaminants, such as workshops; craft areas where gluing and finishing occurs; areas where vehicles are serviced; and areas where chemicals are stored.

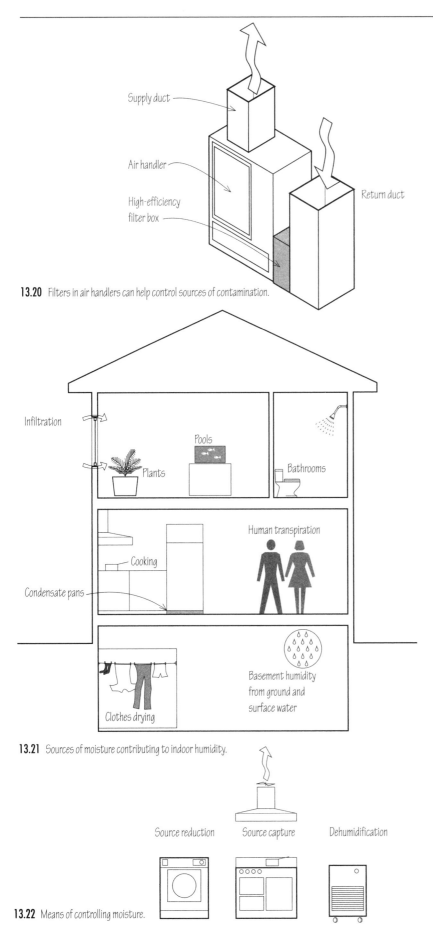

13.20 Filters in air handlers can help control sources of contamination.

13.21 Sources of moisture contributing to indoor humidity.

13.22 Means of controlling moisture.

In addition to source control, filtration may be used. Rather than using low-efficiency filters in air handlers, higher-efficiency particulate filters or even chemical filters may be considered. Filters in air handlers should fit tightly, preventing air bypass that reduces the effectiveness of the filter. Filter housings should also be well-sealed with gaskets to prevent air leakage.

A form of indoor gain that deserves its own distinct priority is humidity control. Humidity is a primary cause of indoor air quality problems, damaging materials as well as supporting the growth of mold. Humidity comes from many indoor sources: cooking, human transpiration, plants, showering and bathing, clothes drying, water stored in swimming pools and aquariums, and water piping leaks. As mentioned previously, humidity also originates from the outdoors as a result of the intrusion of rainwater and groundwater through concrete foundation walls and slabs. Humidity can also be transported by air infiltration when the outdoor humidity is higher than that of the indoors, as is usually the case in summer.

Indoor humidity control is essential for good indoor environmental quality. Relative humidity should preferably be kept below 60% to maintain a level safely below 70%, a key metric above which mold growth is actively supported.

As usual, source reduction is the most effective way to reduce indoor humidity. This can be accomplished by drying clothes outdoors or with well-vented clothes dryers; using high-efficiency clothes washers that wring more moisture from clothes; using low-flow shower heads; limiting the number of plants indoors; and designing to prevent water leaks. For air-conditioners located within finished spaces, condensate pans eventually can clog and overflow. Consideration should be given to a secondary condensate pan under the air-conditioner, equipped with an alarm to alert when there is a risk of overflow. Source capture can also be used with kitchen and bathroom exhaust fans. Finally, dehumidification is extremely effective in serving as a safety net. Dehumidification can be accomplished not only with traditional dehumidifiers but also with air-conditioners, some of which are available with a humidity set point separate from the temperature set point.

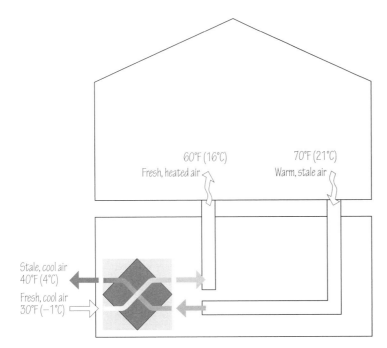

13.23 Heat recovery ventilation.

60°F (16°C)
Fresh, heated air

70°F (21°C)
Warm, stale air

Stale, cool air
40°F (4°C)

Fresh, cool air
30°F (−1°C)

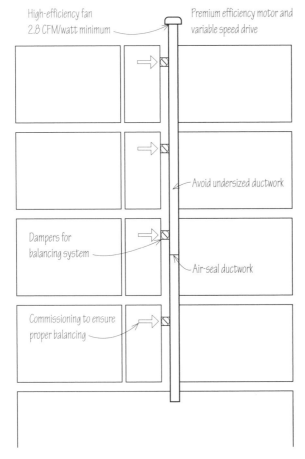

High-efficiency fan
2.8 CFM/watt minimum

Premium efficiency motor and
variable speed drive

Avoid undersized ductwork

Dampers for
balancing system

Air-seal ductwork

Commissioning to ensure
proper balancing

13.24 Best practices for ventilation.

Ventilation

With many potential indoor contaminants reduced or eliminated, attention can be directed to the ventilation system. Heat recovery ventilation can be considered, which reduces the need for heating and cooling the ventilation air and also lessens some of the temperature control challenges. This approach combines true ventilation—the introduction of outdoor air—with source capture, as with a bathroom exhaust, into one system, as long as the exhaust is not so dirty as to foul the heat exchanger, as is sometimes the case with kitchen exhausts. For buildings that are air-conditioned, a form of heat recovery called "energy recovery ventilation" is available, which transfers both heat and moisture. This keeps moisture out of buildings when not needed in summer and keeps moisture within buildings when desirable in winter, further reducing energy use. The moisture control benefits of energy recovery ventilation in summer are only obtained if the building is air-conditioned; if the building is not air-conditioned, energy recovery ventilation risks keeping unwanted moisture indoors in summer. Heat or energy recovery ventilation systems should have their equipment, along with all the ductwork for conditioned air, located within the thermal envelope rather than outdoors. Roof-mounted equipment and ductwork would lose energy to the outdoors by conduction and by air leakage. Heat recovery aligns well with design from the outside in, heating or cooling the outside air before it enters a building and reducing the load on the heating and cooling system.

Ventilation systems come in varying energy efficiencies. For systems covered by ENERGY STAR's program, typically up to 500 CFM, specify a requirement for ENERGY STAR to ensure a minimum efficiency rating for the fan and motor system and also a low level of noise. For larger exhaust fans, options include requiring premium efficiency motors; a minimum fan and motor system efficiency, such as the 2.8 CFM/watt minimum required by ENERGY STAR; and considering variable-speed motor drives where the ventilation rate will be variable. Appropriately sizing ductwork and grilles can also reduce fan power, as long as the ventilation fan and motor are not themselves over-sized. Balancing and air-sealing the system can also contribute to the overall system effectiveness, allowing the lowest possible fan motor power for the required level of ventilation.

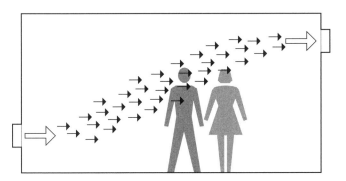

13.25 Achieving effective ventilation through proper placement of supply and exhaust points.

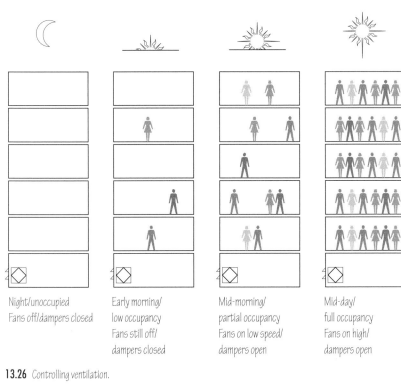

Night/unoccupied
Fans off/dampers closed

Early morning/
low occupancy
Fans still off/
dampers closed

Mid-morning/
partial occupancy
Fans on low speed/
dampers open

Mid-day/
full occupancy
Fans on high/
dampers open

13.26 Controlling ventilation.

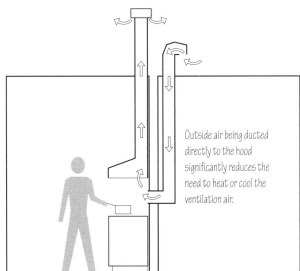

Outside air being ducted directly to the hood significantly reduces the need to heat or cool the ventilation air.

13.27 Hood ventilation.

Attention should be paid to where ventilation is supplied and exhausted. Outside air should be supplied at locations that are unobtrusive and where temperature issues will be minimized. Ventilation air should be supplied in a manner that ensures it will sweep a room and reach people's breathing zones before being exhausted. To achieve a higher level of effectiveness, ventilation might be designed to enter a room at the ceiling level and leave the room at floor level, or vice versa, with openings at opposite ends of a room.

Ventilation controls can also be used to save energy. Consider ventilation apart from the heating or cooling airflow so that it can be controlled independently and heated or cooled if necessary. Allow ventilation to be controlled so that it increases with higher occupancies and decreases or is halted with reduced or zero occupancy. This could mean the use of demand-controlled ventilation, timer-controlled ventilation, the use of multiple fans, or even the use of windows for ventilation.

Commissioning of ventilation systems is important. Measure ventilation at the time a building is built. On an ongoing basis, consider some form of measurement, such as with a carbon dioxide display on the wall next to the temperature control or carbon dioxide sensors that are automatically monitored, with alarms or other indicators to alert when ventilation has failed.

For specialty exhaust ventilation applications, such as commercial kitchen hoods, rooms with refrigeration compressors, and lab fume hoods, energy can be saved by supplying outdoor air directly to the device being exhausted. This allows the required exhaust to occur without having the replacement air needing to be heated or cooled. Attention should be directed to this directly supplied outdoor air not creating comfort problems. For example, the air can be ducted behind a commercial kitchen hood, where it can flow into the hood, entrain the hood's contaminants, and be exhausted without causing discomfort to the people working near the hood.

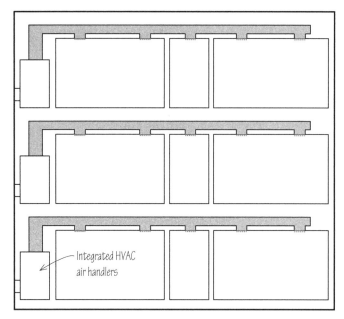

Traditional approach: Ventilation is integrated with the heating and cooling system.

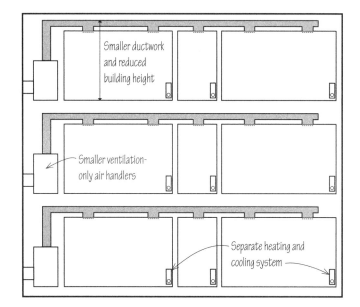

Separate ventilation approach:
Dedicated outside air system is separate from the heating and cooling system.

13.28 Separating the ventilation system from the heating and cooling systems.

A trend is developing in favor of ventilation systems that are separated from heating and cooling systems. Historically, commercial buildings have had the ventilation system integrated with the heating and cooling system. They can be seen on the roofs of typical single-story retail stores: The boxes are the heating and cooling units and the small triangular shaped appendages are the rain hoods for the ventilation intakes. In larger commercial buildings, the air intake is usually a large wall grille, which is ducted to central heating and cooling air handlers. However, separating the ventilation from the heating and cooling systems is desirable in green buildings for several reasons:

- It reduces fan power. Ventilation airflow rates are typically several times smaller than heating and cooling airflow rates. By relying on the large central fan to move the small amount of ventilation air, we are using more power than necessary during times when heating and cooling are not required.
- It allows more customized control of the ventilation airflow rate, separate from the heating and cooling flow rates.
- It allows more customized heating and cooling of the ventilation air.
- It allows the air pressure in the building to be more readily balanced. A typical small rooftop unit, for example, pulls in ventilation air without exhausting any air, and so pressurizes the building, forcing exfiltration, and creating risks such as condensation in the wall assembly.
- It requires smaller ductwork and thus lowers floor-to-floor heights.

Natural ventilation is also an option. Natural ventilation uses openings in buildings, such as operable windows; trickle ventilators, the small openings in walls and below windows; and towers or wind catchers that promote stack effect, buoyancy-driven airflow. Wind-driven, roof-mounted turbine ventilators can be used to induce the flow of air out of buildings while openings in buildings, typically on lower levels, allow air to enter. Natural ventilation can be controlled by occupants, as in the case of operable windows; uncontrolled through the use of fixed openings; or can potentially be automatically controlled.

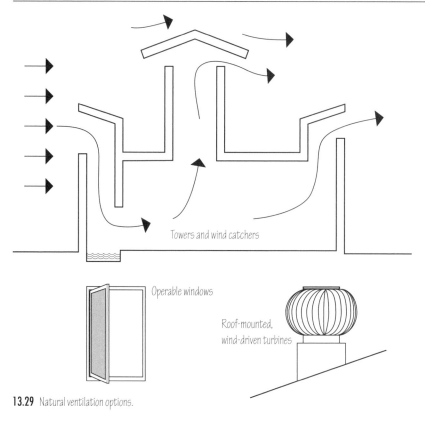

Towers and wind catchers

Operable windows

Roof-mounted,
wind-driven turbines

13.29 Natural ventilation options.

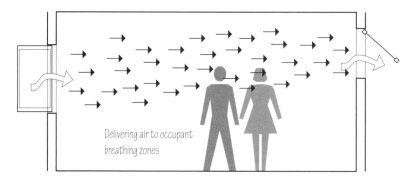

Delivering air to occupant
breathing zones

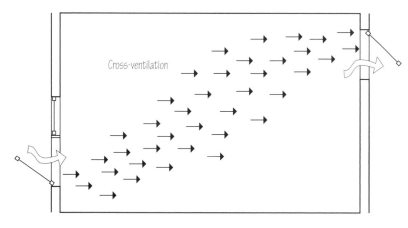

Cross-ventilation

13.30 Effective natural ventilation.

BREEAM includes a widely referenced approach to natural ventilation, requiring two levels of control for natural ventilation: a high level for removal of temporary odors, and a low level for continuous ventilation. Cross-ventilation is an important strategy, where feasible, with openings on opposing sides of spaces. For buoyancy-driven ventilation, attention must be directed to the pathways by which ventilation air flows through the building. To be effective, the fresh air must be delivered to occupant breathing zones.

It should be noted that natural ventilation, requiring pathways for air to move through a building, conflicts with the benefits of compartmentalization. So the tradeoffs of the two approaches, and their relative benefits, should be considered. Cross-ventilation within a room conflicts less with compartmentalization than does building-wide, buoyancy-driven natural ventilation.

The primary forces that drive natural ventilation include buoyancy and wind, neither of which can be well-controlled, and so natural ventilation brings a high level of unpredictability. Benefits include savings in fan power and, in the case of windows, control by occupants. Disadvantages include inadequately controlled ventilation, resulting either in under-ventilation and poor indoor air quality or over-ventilation and excessive energy use to heat or cool the ventilation air. Natural ventilation is sometimes used for temperature control, although its main purpose is to improve indoor air quality through the dilution of contaminants with outdoor air.

How do ventilation improvements affect building affordability? Reduced ventilation resulting from smaller building sizes for a given occupancy reduces construction cost. Avoiding contaminant sources is generally cost-neutral. Tightly controlling ventilation penetrations of the building envelope with low-leakage dampers adds cost. Source reduction through the use of low-toxicity paints, finishes, and carpets is typically a modest cost adder. Heat recovery ventilation is a larger addition to construction cost and should be scrutinized through the lens of life-cycle operating costs. It will typically pay for itself in buildings where the runtime duration is high but may be less attractive where ventilation is required for just a few hours per day. Separating the ventilation system from the heating and cooling system typically adds cost because separate ductwork is required. Ventilation controls, such as carbon dioxide controls, typically add modestly to construction costs.

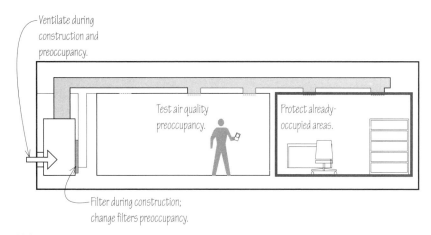

Ventilate during construction and preoccupancy.

Test air quality preoccupancy.

Protect already-occupied areas.

Filter during construction; change filters preoccupancy.

13.31 Means of preventing contamination during construction.

Indoor Air Quality during Construction and Preceding Occupancy

As an adjunct to designing for long-term indoor quality, steps are frequently taken to prevent contamination of the building and building systems during construction itself. These steps can include ventilating during construction, shielding air handlers and ductwork from airborne dust, protecting already-occupied areas in buildings undergoing renovation or addition, and ensuring that odors and off-gassing from finishes have been adequately diluted with fresh air or the passage of time before occupancy, as for example, by performing air quality testing.

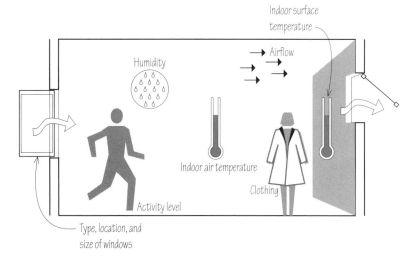

Indoor surface temperature

Airflow

Humidity

Indoor air temperature

Clothing

Activity level

Type, location, and size of windows

13.32 Factors affecting thermal comfort.

Thermal Comfort

Background

Historically, the primary factor that influences comfort has understandably centered on indoor air temperature. Over time, additional factors came to be understood as also contributing to comfort, including humidity; airflow; clothing; activity level; the temperatures of surrounding surfaces, such as walls and floor; the area of windows through which radiant heat transfer occurs; and other physical factors. More recently, the role of outdoor air temperature has gained additional recognition, as well as the role of personal human preferences, sensitivities, and psychological responses to the building environment.

Effects of inadequate comfort include dissatisfaction, low productivity, and stresses on the human immune system. High air temperatures can create the perception of poor indoor air quality. Extreme effects of poor thermal control include sickness, heat exhaustion, hypothermia, and death.

Additional distinct effects relate to inadequate humidity control, which impacts not only thermal comfort but also the materials within a building. High humidity causes such problems as mold growth; expansion of wood in such building components as windows and doors; and condensation on cold surfaces. Low humidity causes drying and cracking not only of human skin but also of materials, such as wood, paper, and films. Humidity fluctuations can cause stress and damage to materials, such as cracking and warping.

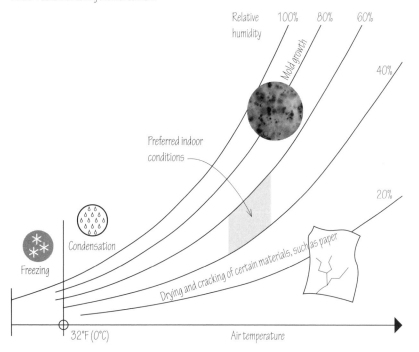

Relative humidity 100% 80% 60%

Mold growth

40%

Preferred indoor conditions

20%

Condensation

Drying and cracking of certain materials, such as paper

Freezing

32°F (0°C)

Air temperature

13.33 Effects of humidity on thermal comfort.

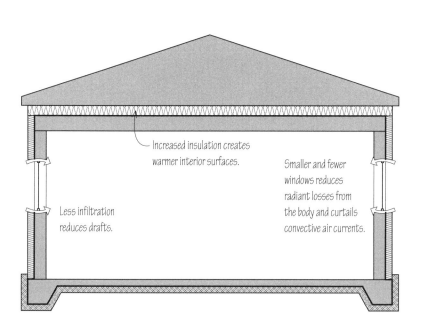

Green buildings generally have fewer comfort problems, even before specific steps are taken to address thermal comfort. More wall and roof insulation warms the temperature of the interior surfaces of these assemblies in winter. Less infiltration reduces drafts and also lessens the impacts of low outdoor humidity in the winter and high outdoor humidity in the summer, with the caveat that low infiltration can raise some risks for high indoor humidity under certain conditions. Smaller and fewer windows reduces radiant losses from the body and curtails convective air currents. Energy recovery ventilation systems keep humidity where it is desirable—indoors in the winter and outdoors in the summer.

Temperature stratification can also be reduced if vaulted ceilings and sunken floors are avoided and if buildings are well-compartmentalized.

Despite the head start already provided by green buildings, we still need to plan for and deliver acceptable thermal comfort.

13.34 Advantages of green buildings in addressing thermal comfort.

Measuring Comfort

Indoor comfort is measured primarily by air temperature and secondarily by humidity. More detailed predictions can use such quantities as air speed, radiant temperature, clothing level, air pressure, and metabolic rate, to determine if a specific space will likely be comfortable for a particular set of occupants.

Occupant surveys form an optional path for measuring whether a building provides good thermal comfort. Most codes, standards, and guidelines define over 80% of occupants being comfortable as a metric of overall thermal comfort in a building.

Recent research has shown that for occupants of buildings with operable windows, who do not have access to air-conditioning, there may be more tolerance for a wider range of temperatures over which they consider themselves comfortable. There appears to be a capacity for these people to adapt to local climate conditions and to make adjustments, such as opening and closing windows or adjusting clothing, which is less often the case for occupants of closed buildings with central air-conditioning. These findings have led to an alternate approach of measuring thermal comfort in naturally ventilated buildings.

13.35 Having operable windows enables occupants to better adjust and adapt to local climate conditions.

Goals/Requirements

The most common goal in achieving thermal comfort is compliance with ASHRAE Standard 55, Thermal Environmental Conditions for Human Comfort, either through documented design or through measurement and verification, or both. ASHRAE Standard 55 establishes a comfort zone, which is based primarily on a combination of temperature and humidity, within which we seek indoor air conditions to lie. Compliance with ASHRAE Standard 55 is established through the use of a psychrometric chart.

Additionally, as previously indicated, an occupant survey may be used to determine satisfaction with thermal comfort.

In establishing goals for a project, before design begins, it may be worthwhile to go beyond simply requiring compliance with a standard, such as ASHRAE 55. Specifically, answers to the following questions will go far in delivering thermal comfort for a building's occupants:

· Which spaces will be cooled?
· Which spaces will be heated?
· Which spaces will have temperature control?

The first two questions may seem self-evident but are worth asking in the event that some spaces, in fact, do not need heating or cooling, or both.

In conjunction with the question—which spaces will be cooled?—is the question whether to cool a building at all. Mechanical air-conditioning comprises two distinct functions relating to thermal comfort: reducing a building's air temperature and reducing its humidity. In many climates and for many people, air-conditioning is not necessary and is even regarded as a luxury. A variety of passive cooling strategies is available and should be explored. We previously addressed some of these, including overhangs to reduce solar gain; reduced infiltration; heat recovery ventilation; increased insulation; smaller building size; simplified building shape; decreased internal gains; and reduced lighting gains. Our need for air-conditioning may in fact have been eliminated, depending on the climate and specific building needs. The previously mentioned recent findings about human ability to adapt to conditions without air-conditioning further support a path to thermal comfort without air-conditioning.

However, in many climates and for many building uses, avoiding air-conditioning is simply not possible if we want to maintain comfortable and healthy indoor environmental conditions. Furthermore, for many people, we have over time created high expectations around air-conditioning. The green building movement will likely strive toward significantly reduced air-conditioning, and in many instances it will achieve buildings that are free from mechanical cooling. However, we will also likely still need to account for many mechanically cooled buildings for the foreseeable future.

The third question is critical: Which spaces will have temperature control? The answer to this question will have significant impact both on thermal comfort and on energy use. There are many ways in which temperature control can be achieved. Therefore, early decisions about these thermal comfort goals will likely affect the type of heating and cooling system chosen, and the degree to which thermal comfort is delivered, both on a measured basis and on an occupant-perception basis.

13.36 An important question: Which spaces will have temperature control?

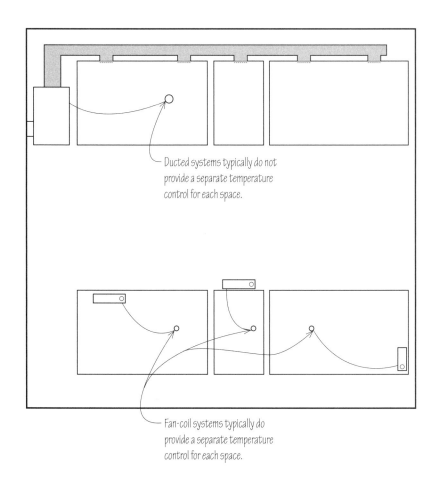

Ducted systems typically do not provide a separate temperature control for each space.

Fan-coil systems typically do provide a separate temperature control for each space.

13.37 A comparison of ducted and fan-coil systems.

Strategies

The first strategy is to define thermal comfort goals and requirements in the project documentation, such as in the Owner's Project Requirements.

Next, a temperature control strategy is chosen. In the early days of central heating, the number of locations in a building where temperature was sensed and controlled were few, possibly even a single temperature for an entire building or one temperature for each building exposure—north, south, east, and west. This is less often the case today. However, perhaps as a result of the simple original whole-building temperature control strategy, we still do not often provide a separate temperature control for each space. And this is where green buildings need to examine available choices carefully, because separate temperature controls in each space will deliver more thermal comfort and result in greater energy efficiency.

Most forced-air, ducted systems, from central air handlers to residential furnaces and ducted heat pumps, do not provide one temperature control per space. Even variable-air-volume (VAV) systems, which use thermostatically controlled terminal units to provide multiple temperature controls per air handler, still typically do not provide one temperature control per space. It is possible, but rare in practice. Forced-air systems are rarely made in sizes small enough to serve a single room and control is rarely applied on a room-by-room basis.

Because these systems do not have a single temperature control per space, they are forced to locate the temperature sensor in one of several spaces served by the control device or to average the temperatures of the various spaces served, resulting in a forced compromise for thermal comfort. When a specific space is served by airflow from a system where the temperature is measured elsewhere, whatever happens in the space will affect its air temperature—whether the lights are turned on or off; machinery is operating or not; occupancy increases or decreases; or solar gain does or does not occur—and will not be responded to appropriately by the system. Discomfort is virtually guaranteed.

Conversely, nonducted systems, such as fan-coil units, typically provide one temperature control per space because each system usually serves one space and each system has its own temperature control.

Here we return to the critical question that was asked during the establishment of thermal comfort requirements for a project: Is room-by-room temperature control required? If the answer to this question is yes, then we are fairly strongly guided to nonducted systems, such as fan-coil units, as the basis for our heating and cooling distribution. Radiant systems are another option.

We will revisit heating and cooling options in more detail in the next chapter, but the critical importance of thermal comfort in guiding the selection of a heating and cooling system cannot be overstated.

Other strategies to fulfill thermal comfort goals include proper sizing of the heating and cooling equipment and the associated distribution system. Enough capacity is required to deliver the needed heating and cooling but if the system is undersized, sufficient heating and cooling will not be delivered and the space will be uncomfortable. There are also comfort risks and energy waste to over-sizing, which is now discouraged in green building standards.

Delivery air speeds and locations also impact thermal comfort and need to be established through space-by-space design. High airflow delivered over building occupants will result in discomfort, even if the temperature in the space is comfortable.

Operable windows have been shown to increase thermal comfort by allowing occupants to adjust ventilation on a space-by-space basis. If a decision is made to provide operable windows, the number of operable windows provided is important. Recall that each operable window is an added potential infiltration site. The number and location of operable windows should be selected to meet the needs for occupant-controlled ventilation and should not simply be assumed to be needed for all windows.

Commissioning of thermal comfort systems is another important strategy. This includes documentation of requirements, measurement and verification of delivered thermal comfort, and corrective action to improve areas where comfort is deficient.

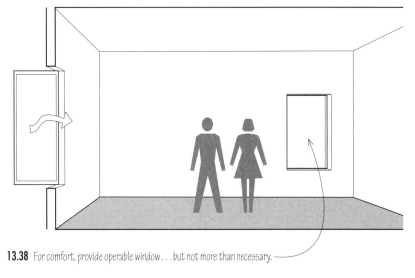

13.38 For comfort, provide operable window . . . but not more than necessary.

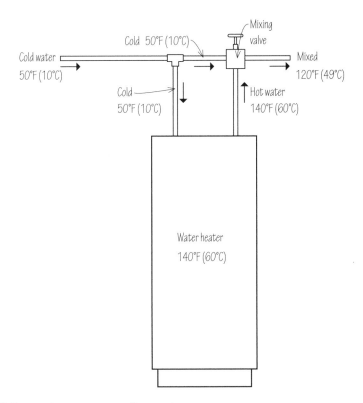

Mixing valve

Cold water 50°F (10°C)

Cold 50°F (10°C)

Mixed 120°F (49°C)

Cold 50°F (10°C)

Hot water 140°F (60°C)

Water heater 140°F (60°C)

13.39 Managing the water temperature of hot water heaters.

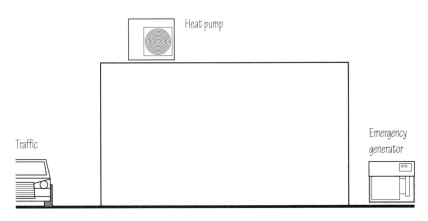

Heat pump

Traffic

Emergency generator

13.40 An inventory of outdoor noise sources.

Water Quality

Water quality is sometimes overlooked in green building codes, standards, and guidelines. Perhaps we take for granted the great strides that have been made in providing good water quality to buildings. However, inadequate water quality can be a significant health hazard.

A green building should provide clean drinking water. If treated municipal water is not the only source of potable water and if, for example, either well water, rainwater, or recycled water is to be used, adequate filtering and treatment is essential.

On a related topic, water in a building should be managed to eliminate the risk of Legionella, an infectious group of bacterium. This means maintaining hot water temperatures high enough to kill Legionella but not so high as to cause energy losses or the risk of scalding. An effective strategy is to generate the water at a high temperature and then to use a mixing valve to lower its temperature before distribution. Standing water, such as in cooling towers, should also be managed to eliminate risk of Legionella.

Acoustics

Design for good acoustics includes prevention of unwanted noise transmission from the outdoors into a building; from loud areas of a building into quieter areas of the building; and into and out of spaces where even low levels of noise are objectionable.

Outdoor noise sources can include heavy machinery, traffic, and even rain on lightweight roofs.

As is the case with thermal comfort, green buildings typically are more soundproof than traditional buildings for two reasons:
1. Lower infiltration means less noise transmission through holes and cracks, which are pathways for noise to travel.
2. More wall and roof insulation means more sound isolation.

Green buildings also often have a head start on preventing noise transmission from loud areas within a building—such as spaces with amplified music or mechanical equipment rooms—to other areas, and on preventing noise transmission into noise-sensitive spaces, such as conference rooms, private meeting rooms, and music performance spaces. This advantage derives from the thermal zoning and compartmentalization that are desirable for energy conservation.

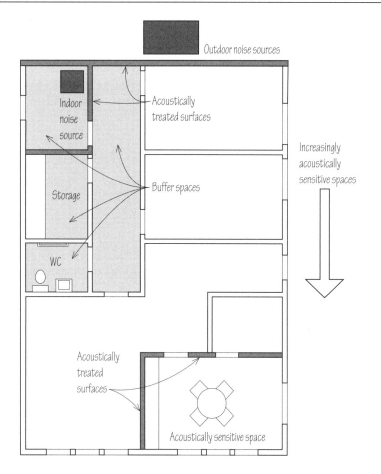

13.41 Isolating acoustically sensitive spaces from noise sources.

Outdoor noise sources

Indoor noise source

Acoustically treated surfaces

Storage

Buffer spaces

WC

Increasingly acoustically sensitive spaces

Acoustically treated surfaces

Acoustically sensitive space

But we should not assume that a green building will prevent all sound problems. It is good practice to inventory potential noise sources, sensitive spaces, and potential sound transmission pathways, and to address them early in design.

Starting from the outside in, the building orientation and shape can be used to minimize the impact of major sources of outdoor sound. Inside the building, work from sound sources and seek to isolate these, then move toward sensitive spaces, treating and isolating these if the noise reaching them is still too high.

Specific attention should be directed to major noise sources within the building, such as HVAC equipment and elevators. These areas should first be isolated physically within the building, by layout and by placing buffer spaces between them and occupied spaces. Then they should be acoustically isolated by appropriate sound transmission class (STC) ratings for walls, ceilings, and floors, as well as by sound-rated acoustic doors with acoustic seals.

Airflow in ducts and out of grilles and diffusers is also a major source of noise and should be designed to appropriately low levels by sizing ducts large enough to reduce air velocity; using elbows and other physical isolators; acoustically lining ducts; and correctly sizing grilles and diffusers. Water flow in pipes can also be an objectionable source of noise if the pipes are undersized and water velocity is too high. Cast iron pipes transmit less noise than plastic pipes. Consider other common noise sources: photocopiers and printers, lunchrooms and break rooms, and kitchens. Avoid overlooking unusual or intermittent noise sources, such as emergency generators that may require brief periodic testing.

Sound level goals should be established for different space types, and best practices followed to deliver targeted goals. Requirements should be documented in project commissioning documents. Projects should include requirements for testing to ensure quality control. If necessary, an acoustical engineer or acoustician can be engaged as part of the project team to provide professional direction in this process.

Size ducts for low air velocity.

Line or insulate ducts.

Duct elbows can reduce the transmission of equipment noise.

Size grilles and diffusers for low air noise.

13.42 Reducing the noise level from airflow through ductwork and out of grilles and diffusers.

14
Heating and Cooling

Heating and cooling systems often cause challenges in building design, construction, and operation. They can be complex, costly, prone to cause comfort problems, noisy, energy-intensive, maintenance-intensive, and physically large, with a significant impact on architectural design. Ultimately, the best heating and cooling systems are the ones not noticed—not seen, not heard, and not causing discomfort.

Heating and cooling constitute the last layer of shelter. However, heating and cooling preferably comes fully from within the building thermal envelope. Traditionally, heating and cooling equipment has been placed in locations where much of its heating and cooling output is lost, near or beyond the outer edges—outdoors, on roofs, in basements, in crawlspaces, in attics, in wall cavities, in floor cavities, and next to windows and exterior walls. There is an emerging consensus that buildings are best heated and cooled from the inner core and not from their outer edges.

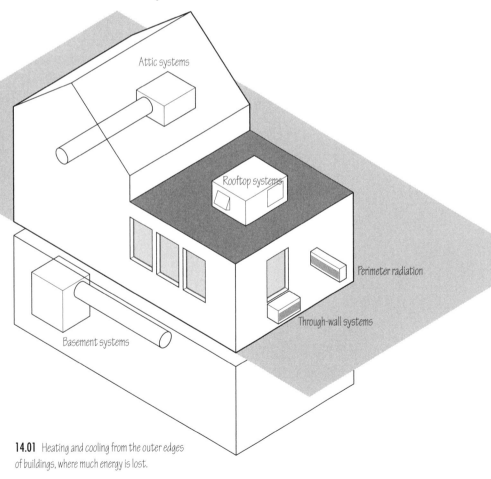

Attic systems

Rooftop systems

Perimeter radiation

Through-wall systems

Basement systems

14.01 Heating and cooling from the outer edges of buildings, where much energy is lost.

Natural gas   Oil   Propane   Electricity   Biomass

Fuel type

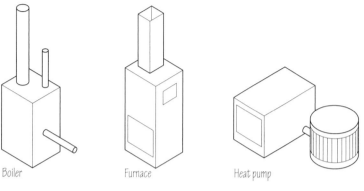

Boiler   Furnace   Heat pump

Heating plant

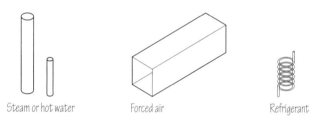

Steam or hot water   Forced air   Refrigerant

Distribution medium

14.02 Classification of heating and cooling systems.

System Types

Heating and cooling systems can be most effectively selected with an understanding of available systems.

Heating and cooling systems may be classified in a number of ways. They may be identified by the type of fuel used: fossil-fuel-fired systems, such as those fired by natural gas, oil, coal, or propane; electric-fired systems, such as heat pumps or electric resistance heaters; or biomass systems, such as those burning firewood, wood pellets, or wood chips. Another way to distinguish heating systems is by the system used to generate the heat. These include furnaces, which heat air; boilers, which heat water or steam; and heat pumps, which heat either air or water. Yet another way to classify heating systems is by the distribution system: steam, hot water, forced air, or refrigerant. It is also possible for heating systems to have no distribution system, such as electric baseboard heaters, cabinet heaters, room heaters, or the infrared heaters that are often found in factories.

There is no best classification system. These classifications attest to the complexity of system choices. However, they can help us to begin to understand system options and stimulate helpful questions early on in choosing a system: What will the fuel be? What will the heating and cooling system be? What will the distribution system be?

Historic trends provide a lens into the development of heating systems. Prior to 1900, wood burned in fireplaces was prevalent. Steam and hot water systems largely took over in the first half of the 20th century, during which time gravity-powered ducted systems saw some use as well. Ducted forced air systems became popular in the second half of the 20th century. More recently we have had the advent of ductless, refrigerant-based systems and geothermal heat pumps, which are also refrigerant-based. It should be noted that older systems remain popular, with hot water systems seeing a resurgence and even antiquated steam heating being included in the design of some new buildings.

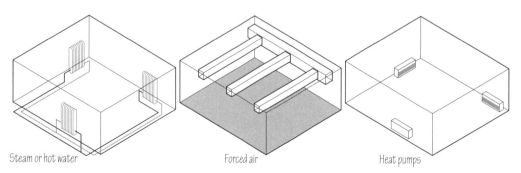

Steam or hot water   Forced air   Heat pumps

14.03 Historic development of heating systems.

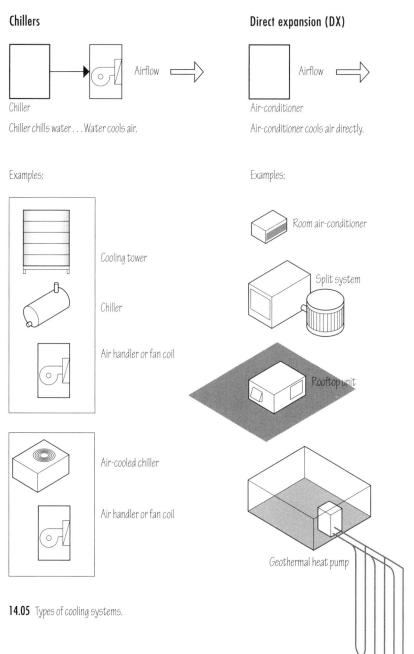

Urban and suburban: Natural gas   Rural: Fuel oil, electricity, propane, and wood

14.04 Urban, suburban, and rural preferences for heating system selection.

Geographic factors play a role in heating system selection, especially for fuel selection. Natural gas is preferred in urban and suburban areas where piped gas is available, whereas propane, fuel oil, wood, kerosene, and electricity dominate in rural areas. In the southern United States, heat pumps have become widespread since the 1980s due to their high efficiency at mild outdoor air temperatures and their integration into the air-conditioning systems required in warmer climates. Overseas, ductless heat pumps predominate in many countries where central heating and cooling was not yet adopted and where there is a shorter history of either fossil-fuel-fired systems or ducted systems.

Cooling systems are broadly divided into two classes: chiller systems, which first chill water before the water chills the air, and direct expansion (DX) systems, in which cold refrigerant in a heat exchanger directly chills the air. However, cooling systems may also be classified in several other ways. If the entire system is in one box, it is called a "packaged system," subcategories of which include rooftop systems, which are common on single-story retail stores; indoor packaged systems, which are less common these days; small through-wall units, which are used in hotels and motels; and window-mounted units, which are the most inexpensive form of cooling equipment. If the system comes in two sections—indoor and outdoor—it is referred to as a split system, subcategories of which are ducted and nonducted or ductless systems. The ducted split system is ubiquitous in the suburbs and is the most common form of air-conditioning today. The ductless split system is the most common system outside of the United States. For large buildings, the chillers themselves are subclassified by compressor type (centrifugal, scroll, screw, reciprocating) and by type of heat rejection (liquid-cooled or air-cooled).

Building type and size can also influence system types. Large buildings tend to have boiler and chiller equipment, using water as a distribution medium. Small buildings tend to have furnace heating and direct-expansion cooling, without using water as an intermediate distribution medium.

Chillers

Chiller → Airflow ⟹

Chiller

Chiller chills water . . . Water cools air.

Examples:

Cooling tower

Chiller

Air handler or fan coil

Air-cooled chiller

Air handler or fan coil

Direct expansion (DX)

Air-conditioner → Airflow ⟹

Air-conditioner

Air-conditioner cools air directly.

Examples:

Room air-conditioner

Split system

Rooftop unit

Geothermal heat pump

14.05 Types of cooling systems.

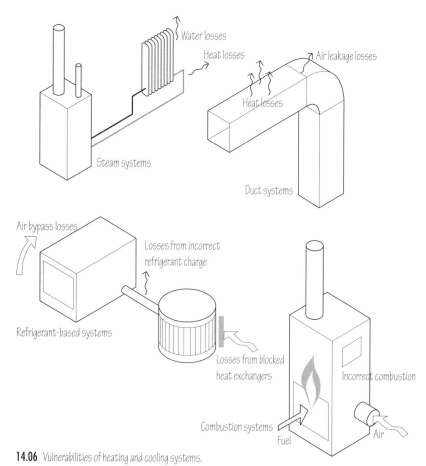

System Vulnerabilities

Different system types have different vulnerabilities.

Steam systems suffer from exorbitant water and energy losses, which are typically over 40%. Forced air systems suffer from air leakage and heat losses from the ductwork, which is typically in the 25–40% range. Refrigerant-based systems, used originally only for cooling but now increasingly used also for heating in heat pumps, suffer from sensitivity to incorrect refrigerant charge, often resulting in losses estimated between 10 and 20%. They also suffer from the effects of heat exchangers being blocked by vegetation growing near an outdoor unit or by dirty air filters and air bypass, either of which will rapidly increase a unit's electricity consumption. Fossil-fuel-fired systems can suffer from incorrect combustion.

Any and all systems can suffer from misapplication. For example, a high-efficiency water boiler will operate at low efficiency if the distribution system is not correctly designed or installed and if the water temperature is too high. A high-efficiency geothermal heat pump will operate at low efficiency if airflow is inadequate, or if the geothermal wells are too small.

Some systems introduce problems into a building that do not relate to the heating or cooling system itself. For example, many fossil-fuel systems require openings in the building, which are needed to draw in the air used for combustion and to vent the byproducts after combustion, typically up a chimney. A chimney typically draws in excess air over and above what is needed for combustion, and this air often ends up itself requiring added heat. Another example is a through-wall air-conditioner, which introduces air leakage into a building as well as conduction losses by thermal bridging.

14.06 Vulnerabilities of heating and cooling systems.

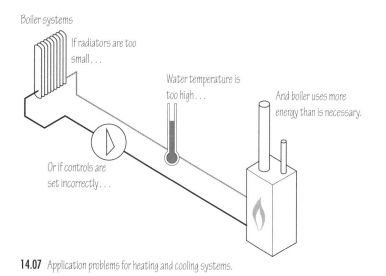

14.07 Application problems for heating and cooling systems.

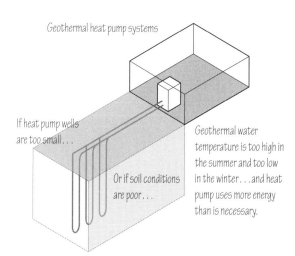

Guidance from the Outside In

The focus for heating and cooling from the outside in is to put the heating and cooling system firmly within the thermal envelope. Locating the system outside the thermal envelope or in unconditioned spaces such as basements is to commit buildings to energy losses of 10%, or more.

Placing heating and cooling inside the thermal envelope simplifies the options for green buildings:

- Avoid locating heating and cooling systems and their distribution systems in unconditioned spaces, such as basements, crawlspaces, and attics.
- Avoid placing heating and cooling systems on the roof or in the outdoors. Here, we are specifically referring to air handlers or packaged equipment, which involve the flow of indoor air to and from a heating and cooling unit. We are not referring to heat rejection equipment, such as cooling towers, air-cooled chillers, or condensing units, which do not involve the flow of indoor air and which, by definition, need to be located outdoors.
- Avoid combustion systems that introduce holes in a building that communicate with the building interior. In other words, avoid combustion systems other than sealed-combustion systems.
- Avoid through-wall or window-mounted equipment, which introduce air leakage into buildings.
- Avoid supplying heat just inside the inner envelope, such as below windows; on an outside wall; or in the floor above an unconditioned space or on grade.

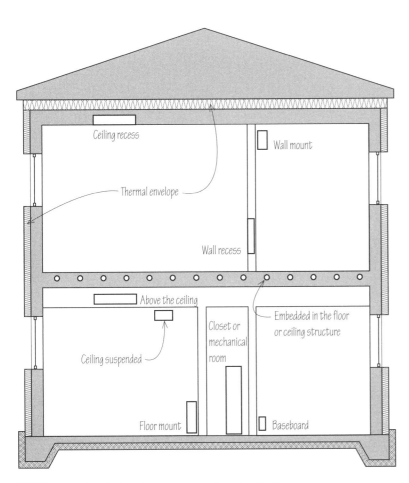

Ceiling recess

Wall mount

Thermal envelope

Wall recess

Above the ceiling

Closet or mechanical room

Embedded in the floor or ceiling structure

Ceiling suspended

Floor mount

Baseboard

14.08 Locations within the thermal envelope for the heating and cooling delivery systems.

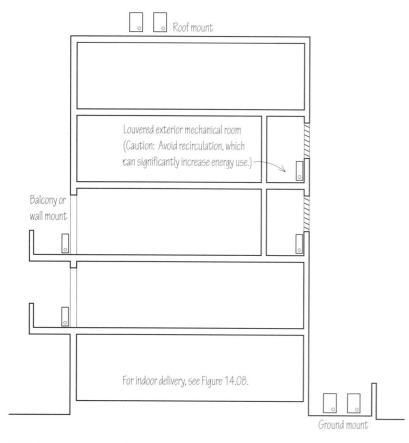

Above-ceiling location for heat pump raises ceiling and is more difficult to service.

Heat pump located in closet

Other options for distribution include radiant heat floors and ductless fan-coil units.

Geothermal well field is quiet and out of sight.

14.09 Geothermal heat pump system.

Roof mount

Louvered exterior mechanical room (Caution: Avoid recirculation, which can significantly increase energy use.)

Balcony or wall mount

For indoor delivery, see Figure 14.08.

Ground mount

14.10 Air-source heat pump locations.

Despite narrowing the field, these simplifications still leave many options.

Geothermal heat pumps, with the heat pumps located well within the thermal envelope, are probably the most efficient heating and cooling option. It is always preferable to avoid placing the heat pumps outside the thermal envelope—on a roof, in a basement, in a crawlspace, on the ground outdoors, or in an attic. If using a forced-air distribution system, the ductwork should be well-sealed. Attention should be directed to where the heat pump is located to avoid transmission of compressor noise and vibration into the occupied spaces and for ease of servicing. Closets are a good location for ducted heat pumps, providing a combination of noise isolation and ease of access for service. They can also be located above ceilings but this makes them more difficult to service and can force an increase in the above-ceiling dimension and so increase the height of the building. Geothermal systems have significant outdoor aesthetic and noise benefits. Because the outdoor heat exchanger is buried, there are no cooling towers, condensing units, rooftop units, or other unsightly equipment taking up space or making noise on the ground or on the roof.

Air-source, ductless heat pumps are another option. Widely used around the world, these systems are gaining acceptance in the United States. Variable-speed versions of these systems have boosted their efficiency and raised their capacity at low outdoor temperatures, allowing their application in northern climates. Heat recovery versions allow efficient simultaneous heating and cooling of buildings with interior core spaces or other cooling-intensive spaces. Distribution losses from the refrigerant piping are lower than losses from ductwork or from water or steam piping. The ability to transport energy at low parasitic power (i.e., the power for pumps and fans) is excellent. Design of these systems tends to be easier than central applied systems, such as boiler and chiller systems.

Because they are typically manufactured in smaller capacities, multiple units are required for large buildings. However, these small sizes provide installation flexibility. The heating and cooling system can be installed modularly, without cranes, because no single component of the system is too big to fit in a typical elevator.

The most significant limitation with current ductless heating and cooling systems is that there is a maximum length, currently 500 feet (152 m), between indoor and outdoor units. Similarly, there is a maximum vertical height, currently around 300 feet (91 m), between indoor and outdoor units. An appropriate location also needs to be found for the outdoor units.

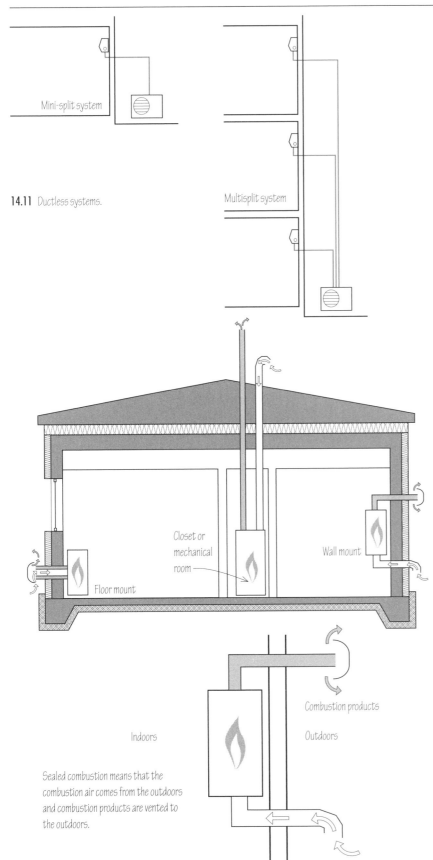

Ductless systems come in two types, the mini-split, in which one outdoor unit is matched with one indoor unit, and the multisplit, in which one outdoor unit is connected to multiple indoor units.

Some kinds of fossil-fuel systems are another option. These include sealed-combustion boilers or furnaces, installed in closets or mechanical rooms within the thermal envelope, and gas-fired room heaters.

For boiler systems, the preference is for radiators to not be installed on outside walls, where they can lose heat directly through the wall assembly to the exterior of the building. Radiant floor distribution is an option, albeit one not well-suited for a building that needs rapid response to indoor air temperature changes or one that depends on significant temperature setback during unoccupied hours. Radiant floors also carry a risk on the ground floor slabs of buildings because of heat loss through the slab, even if insulated.

Sealed-combustion, gas-fired, vented room heaters are another option. It is important not to confuse these with unvented heaters, which look and work the same as vented heaters, except that they exhaust their combustion products right into the living space. Unvented heaters are undesirable in green buildings due to the humidity and combustion byproducts that they deliver to the building interior. Like electric-resistance heating systems, none of these options provide cooling.

For almost all candidate systems—boilers, furnaces, and heat pumps—variable-speed fans and pump motors should be specified wherever possible. These are available as options for most sizes of equipment, from large to small systems. In large systems, these are referred to by the control device that adjusts the speed—variable-speed drives (VSD) or adjustable speed drives (ASD). In small systems, they are referred to simply as variable-speed motors. Variable-output heating and cooling systems, such as modulating furnaces, boilers, and heat pumps, should be specified. For a more affordable alternative, two-stage systems, which still provide efficiency advantages over constant-capacity systems, can be considered.

14.11 Ductless systems.

Mini-split system

Multisplit system

Closet or mechanical room

Floor mount

Wall mount

Combustion products

Indoors

Outdoors

Sealed combustion means that the combustion air comes from the outdoors and combustion products are vented to the outdoors.

Combustion air

14.12 Location options within the thermal envelope for sealed combustion systems.

Electric-resistance heaters, such as electric baseboard heaters or cabinet unit heaters, can be placed in each room. This is atypical in green buildings, as electric-resistance heat has historically been viewed as an expensive and inefficient form of heating. Depending on the source of the electricity, electric resistance heat can also be high in carbon emissions. So it may not be a first preference for green buildings. However, if the electricity can be provided with renewable energy, such as wind or solar photovoltaic energy, and if the building has been designed with a low or near-zero need for heat, then electric resistance heat presents an option that provides low distribution losses, no impact to the building envelope, low installed cost, and convenient control.

Are rooftop heating and cooling systems, so commonly found on single-story buildings such as retail box stores, appropriate for green buildings? Rooftop system energy losses have been found to be significant. It is difficult to build an airtight rooftop heating and cooling unit. Because the air in these units is either at a positive or negative pressure relative to the outdoors, air leaks in and out of these systems through cracks and holes. Both the outdoor air and the indoor, conditioned air flows through these systems, yet only one thin piece of sheet metal, inside the equipment, separates the indoor air from the outdoor air. This partition has many potential air leakage sites, such as penetrations for piping and power and control wiring; joints where the top cover seals the unit, on the side panels, and where a sheet metal divider rests on the bottom of the unit; and the many screw fastener penetrations. In addition, the indoor compartment is surrounded by the outdoors, with more sheet metal joints, access panels, and other penetrations allowing air leakage in and out of the units. The insulation used in these units is typically only between 1 and 2 inches (25.4 and 50.8 mm) thick, thinner than what is used in building walls and roofs. Additional losses occur at duct connections, in exposed ductwork above the roof, and in ductwork in the building below. Over time, the condition and efficiency of these systems deteriorate further, perhaps because they are out of sight on the building roof and less apt to be maintained, and because they are exposed to wind, rain, and sun. In short, rooftop mechanical systems present many energy risks for green buildings.

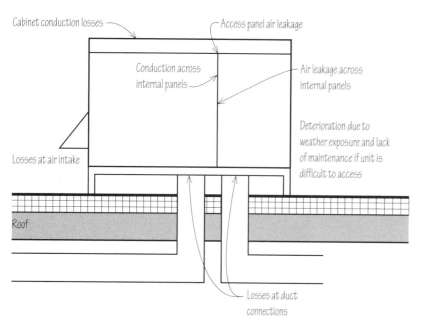

14.13 Rooftop system vulnerabilities.

Cabinet conduction losses

Access panel air leakage

Conduction across internal panels

Air leakage across internal panels

Deterioration due to weather exposure and lack of maintenance if unit is difficult to access

Losses at air intake

Roof

Losses at duct connections

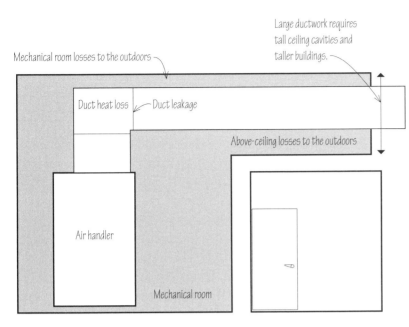

Mechanical room losses to the outdoors

Large ductwork requires tall ceiling cavities and taller buildings.

Duct heat loss — Duct leakage

Above-ceiling losses to the outdoors

Air handler

Mechanical room

14.14 Vulnerabilities of large air handlers and mechanical rooms.

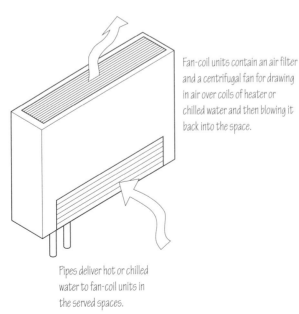

Fan-coil units contain an air filter and a centrifugal fan for drawing in air over coils of heater or chilled water and then blowing it back into the space.

Pipes deliver hot or chilled water to fan-coil units in the served spaces.

14.15 Water-based fan-coil unit.

Large central heating and cooling systems, using central air handlers in mechanical rooms, are likely more efficient than systems installed on the roof, in the attic, or in the basement, but they still present multiple energy issues. These include uninsulated or inadequately insulated ducts and piping, leaking ducts and piping, and losses even if the ducts and piping are well-insulated and not leaking. The required fan power is also high, due to the need to deliver large air quantities over long distances from the mechanical room to conditioned spaces. Central air handlers also require large ductwork. As a result, cavities above ceilings need to be tall, increasing the overall building height and costs by as much as 10% to 20% or more, as well as inflating energy losses through the building envelope. Ceiling cavities with ductwork introduce another set of losses that occur between the mechanical room and the conditioned space.

These challenges of heating and cooling systems that depend on central mechanical rooms and large ductwork suggest the better alternative of placing distribution and delivery systems inside the spaces that need heating and cooling, where there is almost no potential for equipment and distribution losses and no dependency on insulation and air-sealing. A number of systems provide this option. Ductless, split heat pumps are common around the world in many types of buildings, including vast high-rise buildings. Geothermal heat pumps frequently approach the same level of efficiency, although most systems are still ducted and so have duct losses as well as require power for the geothermal water pumping system. Certain kinds of fossil-fuel-fired room heaters also provide room-based heating, although without cooling. Water-based fan coils are another proven option, providing low fan power, no duct losses, and good zone control, although still retaining pumping and piping losses.

As discussed earlier in the context of compartmentalization, central air handlers are disproportionately large consumers of fan power. The energy advantage once held by variable-speed motors in large air handlers (referred to as variable air volume, or VAV, systems) has been reduced as many of the smallest fan coils now can make use of variable-speed motors. Small, distributed systems use significantly less fan motor power than larger systems. The use of large air handlers to integrate ventilation is itself problematic, as discussed in the review of ventilation options. The integration of ventilation in large air handlers causes unnecessary fan power use, prevents the separate and more efficient heating and cooling of ventilation air, and frequently results in over-ventilation. For these reasons, large central air handlers are likely not as efficient as distributed systems, such as ductless heat pumps, geothermal heat pumps, or water-based fan coils.

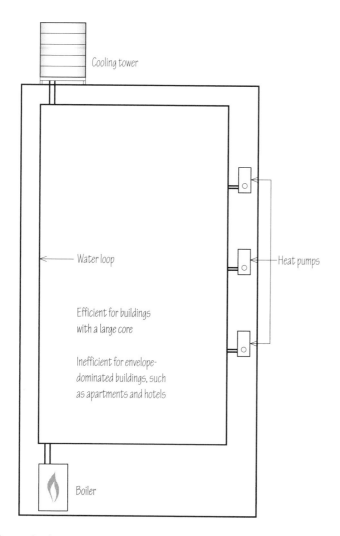

Cooling tower

Water loop

Heat pumps

Efficient for buildings
with a large core

Inefficient for envelope-
dominated buildings, such
as apartments and hotels

Boiler

14.16 Boiler-tower loop heat pump system.

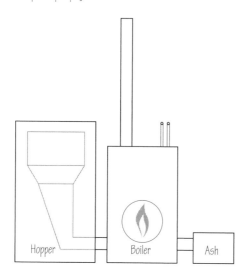

Hopper

Boiler

Ash

14.17 Biomass boiler system.

Another option is boiler-tower water loop heat pump systems. These use boilers as a source of heat and cooling towers as a source of heat rejection outdoors, in conjunction with heat pumps that deliver heating or cooling to the conditioned spaces. The boilers, cooling tower, and heat pumps all add or withdraw heat from a water loop.

However, boiler-tower water loop heat pump systems have been found to be low in efficiency unless installed in buildings that have a significant core and thus are not envelope-dominated. In other words, boiler-tower water loop heat pumps are best suited to buildings that have excess heat year-round originating from a central core of the building, which can be used to heat the perimeter of the building in winter, in climates with a significant winter. For envelope-dominated buildings that form the vast majority of built work, such as homes, apartments, most hotels, single-story retail stores, and small office buildings, boiler-tower water loop heat pump systems have significantly higher energy use and carbon emissions when compared to all the other major available options, such as fossil-fuel heating systems, geothermal heat pumps, and air-source heat pumps. Because boiler-tower water loop heat pumps in envelope-dominated buildings do not obtain any heat from the outdoors, from the ground, or from spaces with excess heat, they inadvertently result in partially fossil-fuel-heated and partially electrically heated buildings, with the higher cost and energy consequences of using electric heat.

A common development with green building projects is to first design the buildings with geothermal heat pumps and then change to boiler-tower water loop heat pumps when the bids come in too high for the project budget. This is a mistake for envelope-dominated buildings, committing them to one of the least efficient and highest carbon-emitting systems available.

Another heating option is biomass-fueled systems. Biomass includes such fuels as wood pellets, wood chips, and logs. The advantage of using biomass as a heating fuel is its low impact on carbon emissions, when the carbon absorption capacity of growing the biomass is accounted for. The typical older-style wood stove, however, is an open system and requires air for combustion and venting. This means that infiltration is being induced unnecessarily. Newer wood stoves have a direct connection to outdoor air and can be considered to be a sealed combustion system. Biomass hot water boilers have been introduced in recent years, although they are typically not installed within the heated core of a building, as they need to be located where the biomass fuel can be loaded. Ash also needs to be removed and disposed. Finally, biomass systems provide only heat, not cooling. Still, the low net carbon emissions of biomass systems warrant their consideration for some buildings.

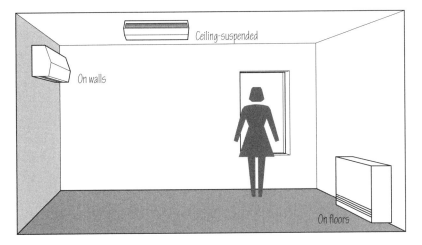

14.18 Locating fan-coil units within rooms.

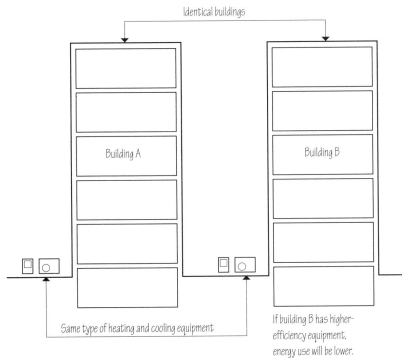

14.19 Higher-efficiency systems save energy but cost more to install.

14.20 A simple formula for estimating energy costs.

The savings for high-efficiency equipment may be expressed as:

$$1 - (E_{low}/E^{high})$$

where E_{low} is the lower efficiency and E^{high} is the higher efficiency. For example, a 95% efficient furnace, when compared to an 80% efficient furnace, will save $1-(0.8/0.95) = 16\%$.

An important heating and cooling decision facing the green design community is whether to locate equipment within rooms. This applies specifically to small fan coils that are either wall-mounted, floor-mounted, or ceiling-mounted. The benefits of locating equipment within rooms are many: the elimination of distribution losses; a reduction of distribution fan power; the provision of local temperature control for zoning; the possibility of eliminating the need for cavities above the ceiling or below the floor for ductwork; and a reduction of installation costs. Possibly the only drawbacks to locating equipment within rooms are noise and aesthetics. Nonetheless, there is a long history of placing equipment within rooms. For example, floor-mounted cast-iron radiators were a fixture in earlier heating systems and are still widely used. As another example, schools frequently use under-window heating and cooling systems. Outside of the United States, in-room ductless fan coils are prevalent in many countries. And if in-room fan coils are unacceptable for a specific building, ceiling-recessed fan coils are another option, as are ducted fan coils in closets or other hidden locations. One form of in-space system to be avoided is through-wall systems, such as through-wall air-conditioners, packaged terminal air-conditioners, or similar heat pumps. The large penetration they require in the wall has been shown to both cause air infiltration and conduction losses.

System Efficiency

Heating and cooling systems are available in varying efficiencies. In general, higher-efficiency systems save energy but cost more to install. Typically, the incremental first cost of higher-efficiency systems is justified by the energy cost savings over time, but this should be confirmed by energy modeling.

Minimum equipment efficiencies are mandated by energy code requirements, many of which themselves have been harmonized throughout the United States through federally mandated efficiency requirements. Higher equipment efficiencies are recommended or required by high-performance building standards such as ASHRAE 189 and the International Green Construction Code and encouraged by programs such as ENERGY STAR as well as state and utility energy programs. The installed cost and operating cost tradeoffs of high-efficiency equipment are readily examined during design through computer modeling. Simple estimates of energy costs are also possible.

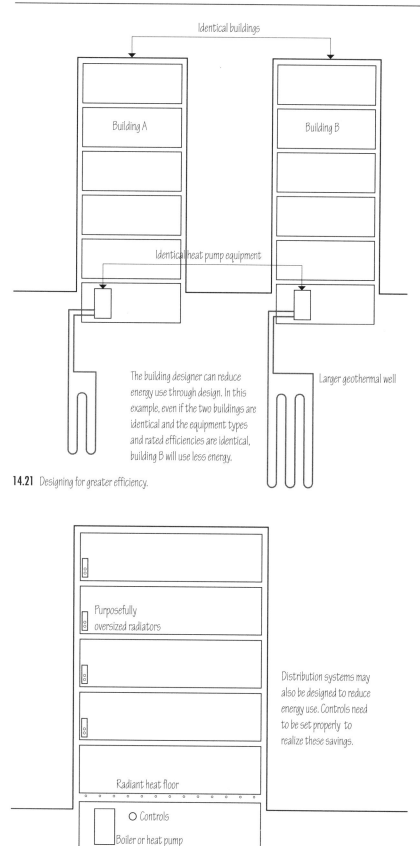

It is important to note that the rated efficiency of a particular piece of equipment does not always translate into performance at that rated efficiency in a particular building located in a particular climate. Moreover, the building design professional has significant control over the actual operational efficiency of equipment in a variety of ways. For example, a geothermal heat pump operates more efficiently if the geothermal well field is larger or if conductive soil conditions are present, allowing more heat transfer in the ground. Conversely, if soil thermal conditions are poor or if the well field is smaller, the system will operate less efficiently. Similarly, a chiller system will work at a higher efficiency if the cooling tower is oversized.

Heating equipment that circulates water in a building, such as a boiler system or heat pumps that supply hot water, will operate at higher efficiencies if the distribution systems are sized large enough such that water temperatures are lower. Certain types of distribution systems, such as radiant floor systems, intrinsically offer the large surfaces required to lower the water temperature, if properly designed. The key is for the water temperature returned to the boiler or heat pump to be low.

To fully reap the benefits of these low-temperature strategies, the system controls need to be set accordingly. The potential efficiency gains are significant. A condensing boiler that operates at 130°F (54°C) return water temperature and 87% efficiency will have its efficiency raised to over 95% if its return water temperature is lowered to 90°F (32°C) by using larger radiators or a radiant floor. For a heat pump, the efficiency gain is even more pronounced. A heat pump that operates in heating at 104°F (40°C) return water temperature and a coefficient of performance (COP) of 3.1 will have its efficiency raised to 3.8 COP at 90°F (32°C) return water temperature, a 23% efficiency gain.

Identical buildings

Building A

Building B

Identical heat pump equipment

The building designer can reduce energy use through design. In this example, even if the two buildings are identical and the equipment types and rated efficiencies are identical, building B will use less energy.

Larger geothermal well

14.21 Designing for greater efficiency.

Purposefully oversized radiators

Distribution systems may also be designed to reduce energy use. Controls need to be set properly to realize these savings.

Radiant heat floor

○ Controls

Boiler or heat pump

14.22 Designing distribution systems for greater efficiency.

A wide variety of efficiency enhancements are available for heating and cooling equipment. Many of these are required by energy conservation codes, especially for larger equipment, but they can be equally well applied where not required by code. These include:

- Free cooling. Also known as economizers, these systems use cool outdoor air or water cooled by the outside air to air-condition a building at times when it is cool outside but warm inside, typically during swing seasons in buildings with high internal gain.
- Outdoor reset of chilled water, hot water, and supply air temperatures. System efficiency is increased by varying the temperatures of heating and cooling systems, as for example, by raising the temperature of water in a chiller system when the outdoor temperature is mild, or lowering the water temperature in a boiler system.

In recent years, it has been determined that oversized heating and cooling systems result in energy losses. These losses arise because oversized equipment short-cycles. Energy codes and green building standards increasingly require that equipment not be oversized. As or more important is to specify variable-capacity equipment, which is less oversized both at full load and at partial load.

Also, the vulnerability of green buildings to failures, as noted previously, should be kept in mind. Just because over-sizing is bad does not mean that undersizing is good. An undersized heating or cooling system will result in an uncomfortable building, one that is too cold in winter or too hot in summer. Heating and cooling systems should preferably be neither undersized nor oversized, but rather right-sized.

Fuel Selection

An important decision in any green building project is the selection of the heating fuel. This fuel selection often has other ramifications, as it often becomes the fuel chosen for other applications, such as heating domestic hot water, cooking in buildings with kitchens, and clothes drying in buildings with laundries.

Heating fuels include solar thermal heat, electricity for heat pumps or electric-resistance heat, natural gas, fuel oil, propane, kerosene, biomass, and coal. In cities or campuses with district heating systems, purchased steam or hot water are other options, although these are still ultimately heated by one of the above fuels. A number of industrial systems derive free waste heat from industrial processes. Cogeneration is another source of heat, in which both electricity and heat are generated by a single process and, again, the process is still fired by one of the above fuels.

When the outdoors is cool or cold . . .

14.23 Free cooling.

And the indoors is hot due to solar gain, lighting, appliances, or activity . . .

Economizers bring in outside air for free cooling.

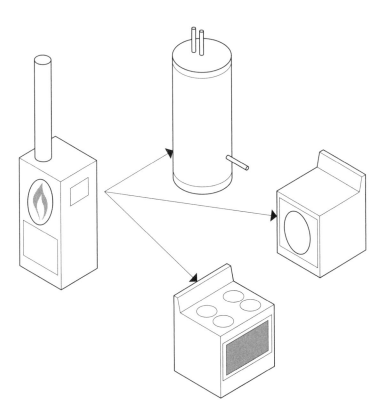

14.24 The selection of heating fuel often impacts the fuel selection for such appliances as water heaters, clothes dryers, and stoves.

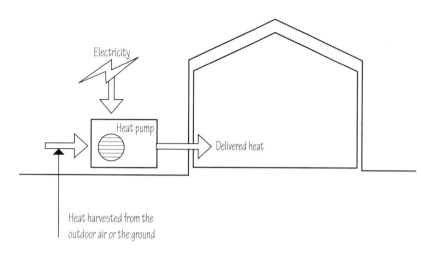

Electricity

Heat pump

Delivered heat

Heat harvested from the
outdoor air or the ground

14.25 Heat pump system.

14.26 Natural gas burns relatively cleanly but is a finite resource.

14.27 Biomass products are rapidly renewable sources of
combustible fuel and are considered to be carbon neutral.

Because of their high carbon emissions, some fuels are less likely to be considered for green building projects. These include fuel oil, kerosene, propane, and coal. This leaves solar thermal, electricity, natural gas, and biofuels as the most likely candidates for heating fuels in green buildings.

Solar-thermal heat is addressed separately in Chapter 15, Renewable Energy. In this chapter, the focus is directed on nonsolar forms of heat.

Electricity in the form of electric-resistance heat should be ruled out in all but close-to-net-zero-energy buildings or in rooms that have a very low heat load. Electric-resistance heat is a high-cost way to heat a building. Electricity is a high-grade source of energy. It is not an appropriate application for heat, which is a low-grade form of energy consumption.

When electricity is used with heat pumps, the system efficiency is amplified by harvesting free heat from the outdoor air or from the ground or groundwater. Heat pumps are probably the most widely used approach for heating in green buildings today. As indicated previously, the one exception is boiler-tower heat pump systems, which are not recommended in green buildings unless used specifically in buildings having a large core area or substantial internal gains.

Natural gas is used in some green buildings. Combustion is relatively clean and high-efficiency options have become available in the past few decades. Disadvantages include the fact that natural gas is a finite resource and recent developments in the extraction of natural gas, including high-pressure hydraulic fracturing, have been found to have significant adverse impacts on the environment. These include air, water, and soil pollution; noise and light pollution due to the drilling and generators required at drilling sites; disturbance of view sheds; and the impact of hundreds of trucks each day required to remove contaminated water from a typical drilling site.

Biomass fuels include wood, wood pellets, wood chips, and a variety of other rapidly renewable sources of combustible fuel. Advantages of biomass include its low impact on carbon emissions—biomass fuels absorb carbon from the atmosphere as they grow. Combustion appliances are increasingly clean although particulate and other combustion emissions have historically been a problem. Disadvantages of biomass include air pollution if combustion is not clean and the need for loading the fuels, although automatic augurs have made the process easier. Traditional fireplaces and many traditional wood stoves are not considered green because of their incomplete combustion, low efficiency, and the amount of combustion air that they draw into a building as infiltration.

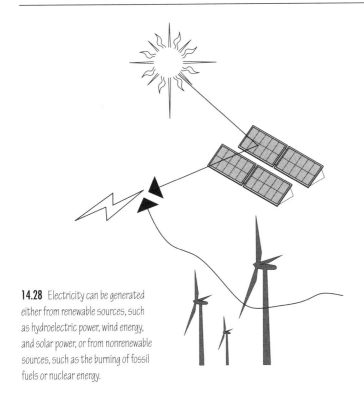

14.28 Electricity can be generated either from renewable sources, such as hydroelectric power, wind energy, and solar power, or from nonrenewable sources, such as the burning of fossil fuels or nuclear energy.

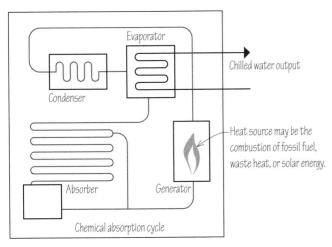

14.29 Absorption cooling.

Fuel choices typically relate to the specific building at hand, a fuel's availability, and its appropriateness to the building. A larger, society-wide case can be made for or against specific fuels. The case is made that electricity is increasingly obtained from renewable sources, such as wind, solar energy, and hydroelectric systems. In other words, a portion of the electricity we use is already renewable, and this portion is growing. Fossil fuels, on the other hand, will never be renewable, and depletion of fossil fuels makes mining ever more difficult, increasing its negative environmental impacts.

After a fuel is selected for space heating, fuels may be selected for the smaller fuel loads in a building. The second important choice is the fuel for heating domestic hot water. A building that uses electricity for space heating will likely choose electric appliances—stoves, clothes dryers, and the like—which is another consideration in both the space-heating fuel selection and the appliance selection.

Advanced and Emerging Systems

A variety of advanced and emerging systems are available to provide specialty heating and cooling. Absorption systems provide cooling through the use of a chemical absorption cycle, requiring the input of heat rather than an electrically driven compressor. Power is still required for fans and pumping. These systems are of interest when a free source of waste heat is available, such as the heat from an industrial process, from the production of electricity, or from solar energy. Absorption cooling, fired by fossil-fuel heat sources or purchased steam or hot water, is generally not competitive or energy-efficient when compared with conventional cooling unless the heat source is free waste heat.

District heating and cooling are provided by a central plant, typically using steam or hot water for heating and chilled water for cooling. Steam should be avoided for green building projects due to its propensity for leaks and for these leaks to go undetected as well as heat losses due to its high temperature. Benefits of district heating and cooling are enhanced when combined with the generation of electricity (combined heat and power, or CHP). Disadvantages of district heating and cooling include distribution losses.

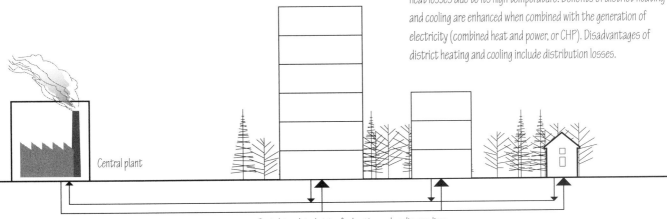

14.30 District heating and cooling.

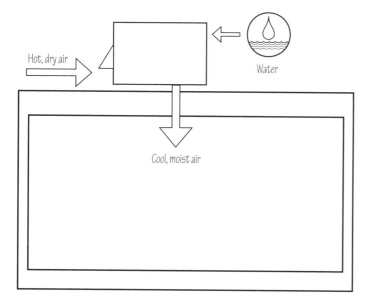

14.31 Evaporative cooling.

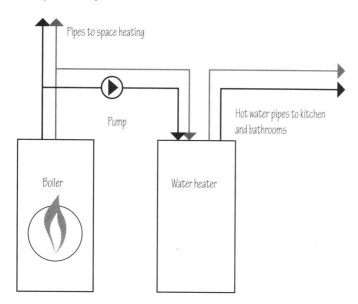

14.32 Integrated systems.

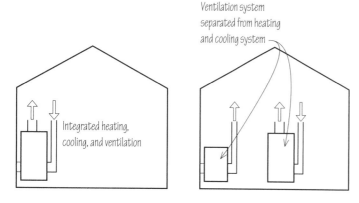

14.33 In green building design, it is likely prudent to separate functions like ventilation and domestic hot water heating from space heating and cooling.

Evaporative cooling is provided by the evaporation of water. This system works in dry climates and uses less energy than conventional cooling but consumes water.

A variety of thermal energy storage technologies are available. Ice storage is commonly used to shift peak electric loads from daytime to the night. Rather than saving energy or reducing carbon emissions, the focus of this technology is to reduce peak summertime electric demand and thereby reduce peak demand charges. Depending on the site, ice storage can in some cases reduce energy and carbon emissions, but in other cases, it will increase energy use and carbon emissions. The substantial embodied energy of the storage vessel, which is often concrete, should be accounted for in the analysis.

Other emerging technologies include chilled beam cooling distribution, dedicated outdoor air systems (DOAS), and desiccant cooling and dehumidification. Chilled beam cooling is increasingly used in conjunction with dedicated outdoor air systems to reduce the energy used for cooling by separating the two functions of air-conditioning— reducing air temperature and removing moisture— and delivering each function separately at a high efficiency.

System Integration

It is common in heating and cooling systems to integrate additional functions, such as ventilation or the heating of domestic hot water. Such integration can lower installation costs but has historically introduced complexity and unintended consequences resulting in unnecessary energy use.

The integration of domestic hot water in large boiler systems has been found to often be inefficient, as many boilers operate inefficiently during the summer to provide the relatively small amount of heat required for domestic hot water. There remain questions whether integrating domestic hot water with high-efficiency, condensing space-heating boilers saves energy, as interconnecting piping, pumping, and boiler losses remain.

Integrating ventilation with central air handling systems has also been problematic. Ventilation adds a different type of load to a heating and cooling system, specifically adding a significant dehumidification load in the summer. Separately, when integrated with the central system, the ventilation system requires as much as four to five times as much fan power than if the ventilation system were to be powered by its own fan. The recent development of dedicated outdoor air systems has shown that de-coupling ventilation from heating and cooling has energy benefits.

Affordability and Heating/Cooling

The installed cost of geothermal systems is high due to the geothermal well field required. However, energy savings often justify the added cost on a life-cycle cost basis. Variable refrigerant flow systems, typically as a part of ductless heat pumps, are lower in first cost than geothermal systems but still cost more than low-end heating and cooling systems. The most affordable heating and cooling systems are typically the least energy efficient: packaged rooftop units, through-wall units, and combustion systems that are not sealed.

There are nonetheless opportunities for construction cost savings through green design.

The major cost savings that can accrue for heating and cooling derive from the reductions in load, a result of simpler and more efficient envelope components. The reduction in the heating and cooling system cost is roughly proportional to the reduction in envelope load. However, these savings only fully accrue if sizing of the heating and cooling equipment and distribution occurs after the envelope design is complete.

Other factors in the design of green buildings allow heating and cooling to be removed from many spaces, further lowering construction costs. Improved interior temperature distribution, both horizontally (near the building envelope) and vertically (within a space, due to reduced stratification, and from floor-to-floor), further allows heating and cooling to be removed from some spaces. For example, it has been shown that bedrooms in some apartment buildings can be comfortably heated if heat is supplied to living rooms only.

By locating heating and cooling inside the thermal envelope, construction costs can be reduced by the decreased length of distribution piping and ductwork. For example, in a conventional hydronic system design, the main piping is typically routed around the perimeter of a basement and the distribution piping and radiation is run around the perimeter of each floor. With better temperature distribution due to improved envelope design, radiation no longer needs to be run around the perimeter of a building and can be located instead on interior walls. Therefore, the supply and return main riser piping can be located in the building core, and piping to radiation in each space need only be routed the shorter distance from a shaft in the building core to radiation on an interior wall, rather than to exterior walls.

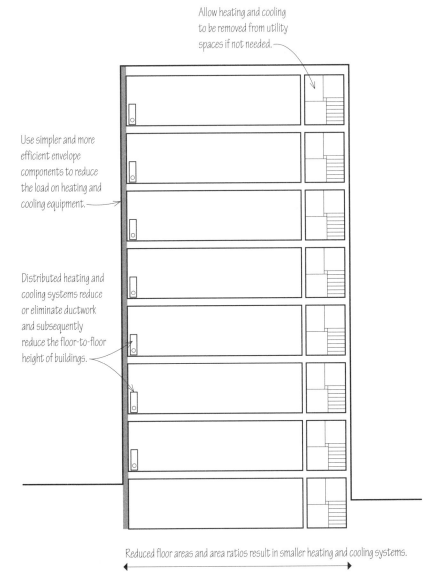

Allow heating and cooling to be removed from utility spaces if not needed.

Use simpler and more efficient envelope components to reduce the load on heating and cooling equipment.

Distributed heating and cooling systems reduce or eliminate ductwork and subsequently reduce the floor-to-floor height of buildings.

Reduced floor areas and area ratios result in smaller heating and cooling systems.

14.34 Opportunities for cost savings with heating and cooling systems.

One of the largest potential reductions in construction cost from small, high-efficiency, distributed heating and cooling systems derives from the reduction or elimination of ductwork. In most buildings, a critical dimension—the floor-to-floor height—is dominated by the above-ceiling height required for ductwork. By reducing or eliminating ductwork, this dimension can be substantially reduced. In many buildings, this dimension is between 1 and 2 feet (305 and 610) and often is as high as 3 to 4 feet (915 to 1,220) where main duct trunks are routed.

15
Renewable Energy

Renewable energy is energy that is provided by renewable sources, such as the sun or the wind. Renewable energy is contrasted with energy generated by fuels that are subject to depletion, such as oil, natural gas, and coal, which were formed over millions of years and which society is consuming at a rate faster than the rate at which the fuels were formed. Renewable energy is also contrasted with the energy generated by fuels that create pollution that will have a lasting effect, such as nuclear energy.

15.01 Alternative energy sources.

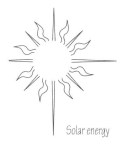

Solar energy

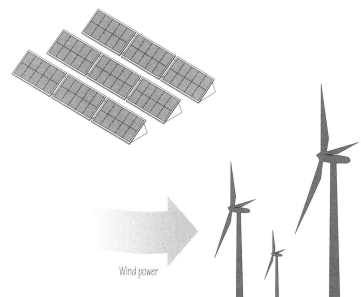

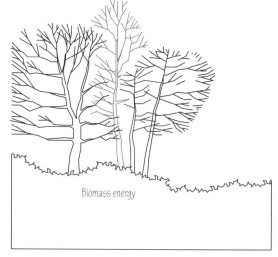

Wind power

Having designed a low-energy building, attention can now be directed to renewable energy to provide some or all of the remaining energy needs of the building. Renewable energy is most effectively addressed at this point because it generally costs more to install than many building-efficiency improvements and it is frequently more cost-effective to address all building-efficiency improvements first. Separately, renewable energy equipment itself contains the embodied energy of manufacturing and transportation processes and so represents an energy penalty as a partial offset to the energy it produces.

At this juncture in design from the outside in, the building should be receptive to the renewable energy equipment because of prior attention to receptivity, as in roof or site design. For example, the roof has been oriented to maximize solar radiation and obstructions have been removed to maximize the area available for solar panels.

The renewable systems considered here are primarily solar and wind. The use of biomass for heating is sometimes considered to be a renewable energy but was separately addressed in Chapter 14, Heating and Cooling. Geothermal heat pumps are sometimes described as a renewable energy technology but this is a misnomer. Geothermal heat from hot springs might validly be considered renewable whereas geothermal heat pumps rely on electricity just as other types of heat pumps do and therefore cannot be considered renewable.

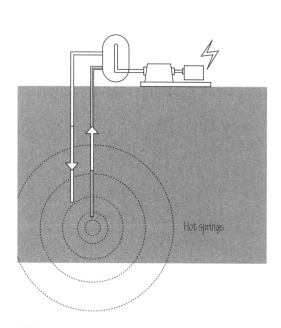

Hot springs

Biomass energy

15.02 Renewable energy sources.

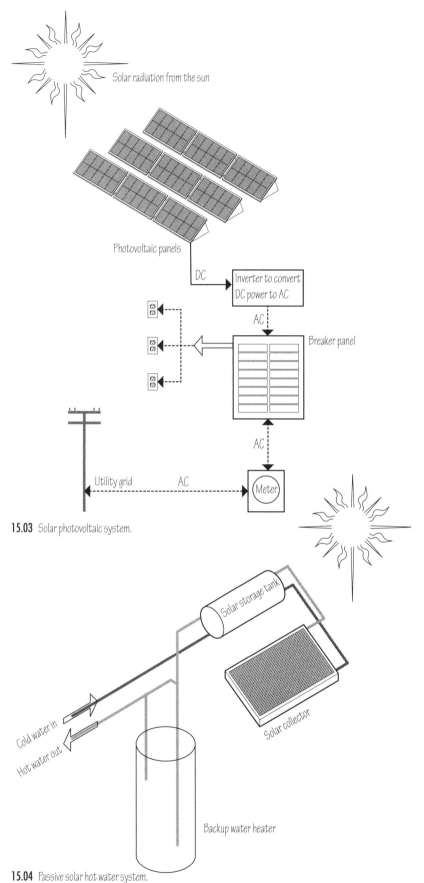

15.03 Solar photovoltaic system.

15.04 Passive solar hot water system.

Solar Energy

Solar energy can be used to generate electricity through solar photovoltaic (PV) systems or to generate heat using solar thermal systems. We have previously discussed the siting of solar panels in the sections on Community and Site (for ground-mounted systems) and Near-Building Features (for roof-mounted systems).

Solar Photovoltaic Systems

Solar photovoltaic panels are commonly referred to as modules. Photovoltaic systems have no moving parts. Electric power is generated in the modules in the form of direct current (DC) power. A control device called an inverter takes this DC power and converts it into the alternating current (AC) power required in buildings. The energy generated by solar photovoltaic systems can alternately be fed back to the electric grid if more power is generated than is needed in the building. A photovoltaic system can either be connected to the electric grid (grid-tied) or use batteries to serve as a stand-alone system, or both, to allow the system to both connect to the grid but to operate on its own in case of a power outage. Most current systems are grid-tied, although batteries are preferred by those who value self-reliance. Benefits of solar photovoltaic systems include a mature and reliable technology and predictability in the amount of electricity that can be generated. The use of solar photovoltaic energy has grown significantly as a result of dropping prices, government incentives, public interest, and new financing options. Reliability risks include damage to modules and problems with inverters, but these risks are generally low.

Solar Thermal Systems

Solar thermal systems can either be used to heat a liquid or to heat air. Solar thermal panels are commonly referred to as collectors.

The liquids used in solar thermal systems are either water in warmer climates or a water-antifreeze mix in cold climates. Liquid systems can either be passive, operating without a pump, or active, requiring a pump. Passive systems are referred to as thermo-siphon systems in which case the storage tank is located at the high point of the system, typically above the collectors on a roof, to allow water to circulate by gravity. These water-based thermo-siphon systems are more common in warm climates where there is no risk of freezing.

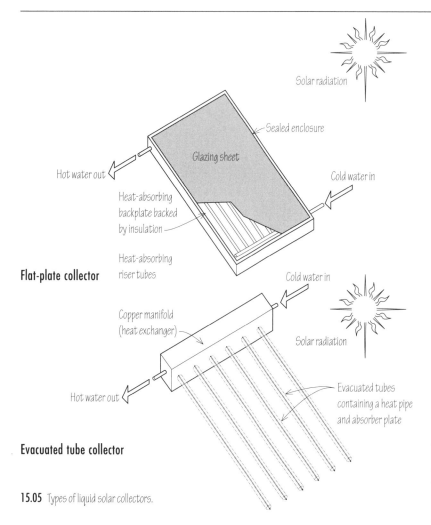

Solar radiation

Sealed enclosure

Glazing sheet

Hot water out

Cold water in

Heat-absorbing backplate backed by insulation

Heat-absorbing riser tubes

Flat-plate collector

Cold water in

Copper manifold (heat exchanger)

Solar radiation

Hot water out

Evacuated tubes containing a heat pipe and absorber plate

Evacuated tube collector

15.05 Types of liquid solar collectors.

Common liquid collector types include flat-plate collectors and evacuated tube collectors. Flat-plate collectors are lower in cost but are also generally lower in efficiency. Evacuated tube collectors are higher in cost but higher in efficiency and can be easier to install on a roof because the collector is field-assembled from modular tubes.

Air-based systems can either heat outdoor air that is being drawn in for ventilation or heat indoor air. The ventilation application is common in a type of collector known as a transpired solar collector, where the air is drawn in through holes in the collector. Systems that heat air can be considered active, using a fan to circulate air, or passive, operating without a fan.

Whether active or passive, solar thermal systems typically have three components:

- Collection, to receive the sun's energy
- Storage, to store heat from periods when the sun is available and deliver it when the sun is not available
- Controls, to initiate collection and storage of solar energy when it is available and to prevent losses when the sun is not shining

These three components are important for the effectiveness of a solar thermal system. Without the three components, a solar thermal system may lose more heat than it gains, as collectors can lose energy as easily to the night sky as they can gain energy from the daytime sun, if not correctly collected, stored, and controlled.

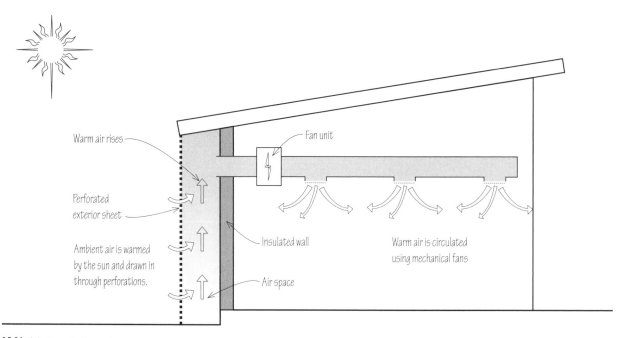

Warm air rises

Fan unit

Perforated exterior sheet

Ambient air is warmed by the sun and drawn in through perforations.

Insulated wall

Air space

Warm air is circulated using mechanical fans

15.06 Solar transpiration system.

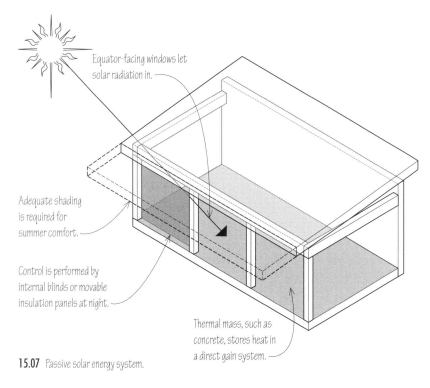

Equator-facing windows let solar radiation in.

Adequate shading is required for summer comfort.

Control is performed by internal blinds or movable insulation panels at night.

Thermal mass, such as concrete, stores heat in a direct gain system.

15.07 Passive solar energy system.

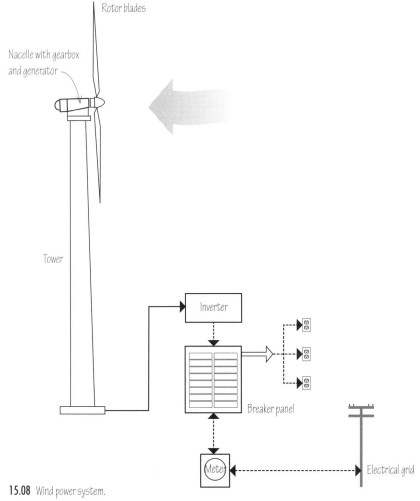

Rotor blades

Nacelle with gearbox and generator

Tower

Inverter

Breaker panel

Meter

Electrical grid

15.08 Wind power system.

Passive Solar Energy

Passive solar energy refers to the harvesting of solar heat without the use of mechanical or electrical systems, such as pumps or fans.

The passive solar energy field in many ways laid the groundwork for much of our current knowledge both in building efficiency and in solar energy. Through hard-earned experience in developing passive solar systems, we have learned how passive-heated buildings need the three elements of a solar energy system, including collection, storage, and control. Collection is performed by south-facing windows. Storage is typically performed by thermal mass. Control is performed by such devices as movable insulation for windows at night. We now know that large equator-facing windows without both storage and control will overheat a building during the day and cause losses at night that require added and unnecessary fossil fuel energy use.

Passive solar remains a viable option for those who are committed to building energy systems with few moving parts, who are willing to accept imperfections such as indoor temperature fluctuations, and who are willing to actively engage in the control of their energy system, as for example, by placing and removing insulation or thermal shades on windows at night.

Wind Energy

Modern wind turbines are used to generate electricity. An advantage of wind turbines over solar photovoltaic systems is the potential to generate power during both day and night. Disadvantages include high cost, dependence on steady winds, and noise pollution. Like solar photovoltaic systems, wind turbines can be grid-tied or stand-alone systems with batteries, or both. Wind turbines are available in a wide variety of sizes—small enough to power a single home or large enough to serve as a power plant with several turbines typically grouped in a wind farm. Wind turbines are best located high off the ground, typically at the top of dedicated wind towers, to reach where the wind blows steadily. Building-mounted wind turbines are available, but are low in both efficiency and capacity.

As with solar photovoltaic systems, wind power systems typically generate direct current (DC) power and use an inverter to convert this power to alternating current (AC).

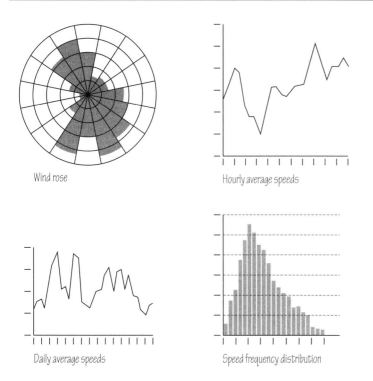

Wind rose

Hourly average speeds

Daily average speeds

Speed frequency distribution

15.09 Mapping wind conditions for wind power systems.

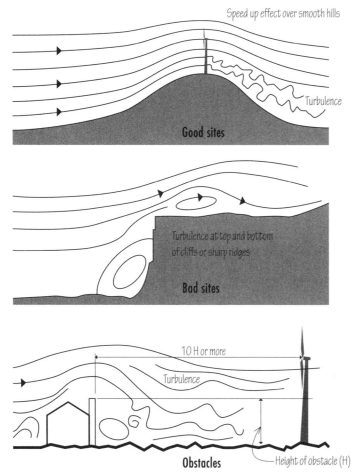

Speed up effect over smooth hills

Turbulence

Good sites

Turbulence at top and bottom
of cliffs or sharp ridges

Bad sites

10 H or more

Turbulence

Obstacles

Height of obstacle (H)

15.10 Wind flow over hills and obstacles.

Wind system design begins by evaluating whether wind conditions are sufficient. Online tools that map typical wind conditions at a site include those provided by the National Renewable Energy Lab or by private companies. More detailed wind inventories require the use of site-specific measurements.

A fundamental variable to consider in the use of wind turbines is wind velocity. If the wind velocity doubles, eight times the energy is available. Therefore, small changes in wind velocity produce significant changes in delivered wind energy. Wind energy is most viable for areas with average wind velocities over 16 miles per hour (26 km/h) at a height of 160 feet (48 m) above ground level. Another rule of thumb is that wind velocities at ground level need to be between 7 and 9 miles per hour (11 and 14 km/h).

Wind towers should be far enough from a building to avoid noise and vibration issues but close enough to avoid high costs in routing wiring from the tower to the building. The impact of the building itself on wind patterns needs to be considered. A hill near a building is a good location. Towers should be as tall as local zoning ordinances allow. The higher the tower, the stronger and less turbulent is the wind. Wind turbines should preferably not be mounted on or to buildings. The wind close to a building tends to be turbulent and weak. Wind turbines mounted near the ground tend to be highly ineffective. A rule of thumb is that the bottom of wind turbine rotor blades need to be a minimum of 30 feet (9 m) above any obstacle within 300 feet (91 m).

Concerns about wind power include bird and bat fatalities, although such fatalities are estimated to be significantly fewer than those from power lines, communication towers, and buildings themselves.

Renewable System Risks

Two risks are common to renewable energy systems.

One risk is that if a renewable system fails, the owner may not know about it because there is typically an automatic backup system in place. In the case of photovoltaic systems or wind systems, the electric grid typically serves as an automatic backup. Therefore, monitoring or metering is essential. In the case of solar thermal systems, there is typically a fossil-fired system that serves as a backup, and this system also can mean that the owner does not know that the solar system is no longer functioning.

Another risk is that if solar systems are installed on nondurable roof surfaces, they will need to be removed when the roof needs replacement. This will increase the cost of maintaining or replacing the roof.

16
Materials

The environmental impacts of building materials result from related energy use and emissions, the depletion of finite material sources, and the undesirable accumulation of materials in landfills. The activities causing these impacts include the mining and harvesting of raw materials, the processing and manufacturing of finished materials, transporting materials, the use of hazardous materials, and the generation of construction waste. Through judicious building design and material selection, we can substantially reduce these impacts.

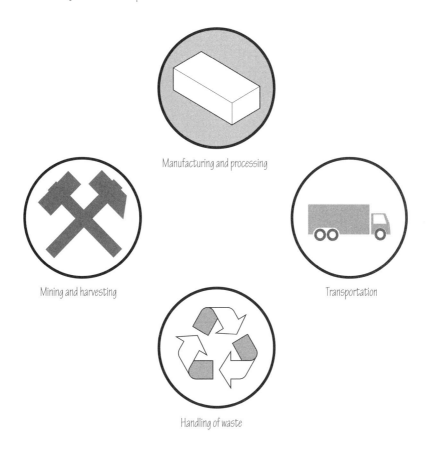

Manufacturing and processing

Mining and harvesting

Transportation

Handling of waste

16.01 Processing of building materials has environmental impacts.

In the process of building design, we can anticipate and are able to support future, reduced impacts of the material waste generated by building operations, as for example through the design of recycling areas in the building, planning for the disposal of hazardous materials, and planning for the eventual deconstruction and reuse of building materials.

The use of energy to harvest and process materials is referred to as embodied energy. It is an important and increasingly quantifiable property that comprises part of the accounting of the environmental impact of buildings. And, as buildings are designed and built to use less energy, the fraction of building use represented by embodied energy increases.

Finally, the impact of construction debris can be minimized through planning during the design phase and thoughtfully applied procedures during construction.

Using Less Material

The greenest material selection is that which minimizes the amount of material used.

Large potential savings in materials can occur during the site selection phase—not to the design of the building itself but rather to its siting and infrastructure. By locating buildings in already-developed areas, one is able to use existing infrastructure materials. Infrastructure such as roads and municipal water systems are essentially reused as they are shared and the potential material consumption of materials for new infrastructure is averted.

Two powerful approaches to green building design were discussed earlier in the context of energy efficiency and also offer savings for material use—reduced floor area and reduced surface area. A building with a smaller floor area will use fewer materials and less embodied energy than a larger building. A building with fewer tall ceilings will use fewer materials and less embodied energy than a building with taller ceilings. A simpler geometrical structure will use fewer materials and less embodied energy than a more complex structure. A single larger building will use fewer materials and less embodied energy than multiple separate buildings serving the same function.

16.02 Shared infrastructure, such as roads and utilities, reduces the impact of new construction.

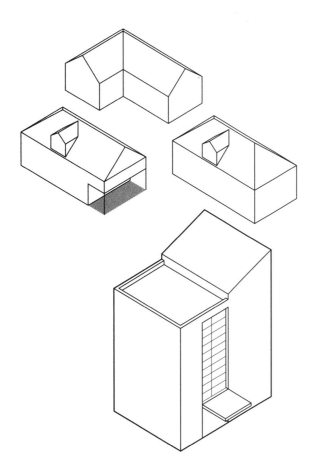

16.03 Reduced floor and surface areas significantly reduce material use.

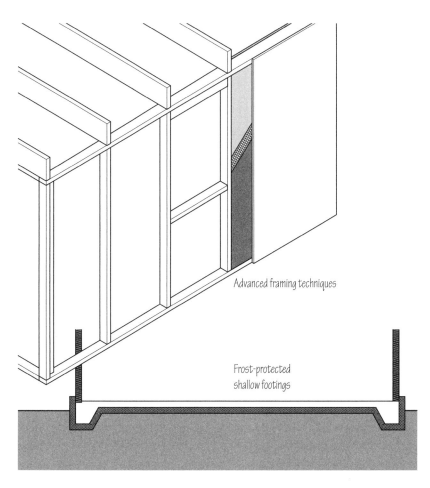

Advanced framing techniques

Frost-protected
shallow footings

16.04 Examples of material conservation through advanced construction techniques.

Another approach to reducing material use is through material-efficient design. Earlier, we discussed advanced framing techniques, specifically in the context of reducing thermal bridging. In so doing, less material is typically used. Examples include using 24-inch (610) stud spacing instead of 16-inch (405) spacing; single headers and single top plates; single studs at window and door openings; and simplified corners such as the two-stud corner. The prior discussion focused on exterior walls and on energy losses due to thermal bridging. For the purpose of material use reduction, interior walls can also be examined. Instead of standard 16-inch (405) spacing for both wood studs and steel studs, 24-inch (610) is allowed by code and can be considered. Another example of material-efficient advanced design is the use of frost-protected shallow foundations instead of regular foundation walls with footings. Frost-protected shallow foundations have been successfully used in the United States and over 1 million homes have been built with these foundations in Scandinavian countries.

Eliminating attics in pitched-roof buildings is another approach to reducing material use, as two structures—the attic floor and the roof—are combined into one.

When detailed structural design is done, rather than using rules of thumb or age-old practices, opportunities for reducing materials may be identified. For example, a 4-inch- (100) thick concrete slab might well be feasible for a particular floor, rather than a 5-inch- or 6-inch- (125 or 150) thick slab.

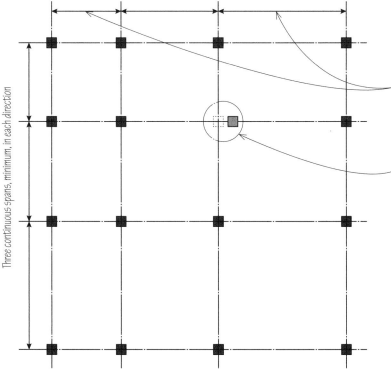

Three continuous spans, minimum, in each direction

Span lengths differ by one-third or less of largest span.
Equal span lengths would achieve greater efficiency.

Columns are offset a maximum of 10%
in one direction only.

16.05 Example of maximizing structural efficiencies to reduce material use.

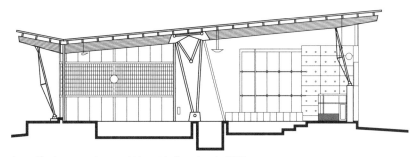

Angus Glen Community Center and Library, Markham, Canada, 2006
Shore Tilbe Irwin and Partners Architects
Halcrow Yolles Structural Engineers

16.06 Exposing the structure to serve as finish.

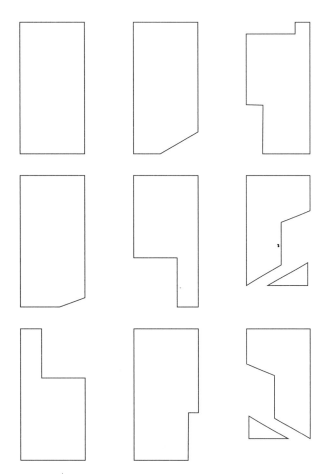

16.07 Planning and designing to reduce material waste.

Another approach to reducing material use is by avoiding finishes where they are not needed. Sometimes referred to as "structure as finish," this approach allows structural elements to serve the dual purpose of structure and finish. Tradeoffs with the need for added lighting should be carefully evaluated if the exposed structure has a low lighting reflectance. Yet another approach to reducing material use is to leave components such as ductwork or piping exposed. This reduces material use for gypsum board and associated furring for chases, soffits, and plenums, as well as finishes.

A final approach to using less material is to generate less waste—in other words, to avoid generating waste. This does not refer to directing waste away from landfills or to reusing waste, which are addressed separately, but rather to generating less waste to begin with. This means planning the design such that lengths of structural members factor into lengths of commercially available structural stock, whether of wood or steel, and similarly with areas of such components as sheathing and gypsum board. It can mean developing cut lists for lumber and sheet stock, which allows placing orders for the correct quantities of needed materials rather than ordering and discarding extra material. It can mean mixing fresh concrete in the correct required quantities rather than in excessive quantities. Prefabricated assemblies, such as structural insulated panels (SIPS), possibly lend themselves to less waste through computer-designed lists of materials.

Design professionals can play a key role in material-efficient design by providing additional information in the construction documents relating to material quantities. For example, noting volumetric quantities of materials on drawings, such as concrete, asphalt paving, and blown insulation, can help contractors prevent waste due to over-ordering. Similarly, providing area quantities on drawings for roofing, sheathing, hardscape, and landscaped areas can facilitate ordering correct quantities. Full detailing of framing further supports accurate takeoffs and further reduces the potential for over-ordering and waste.

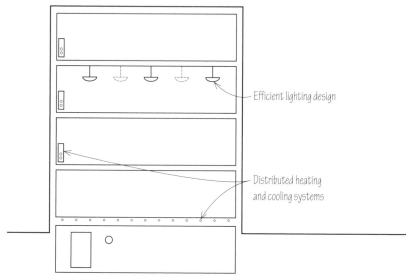

16.08 Optimizing systems to reduce material waste.

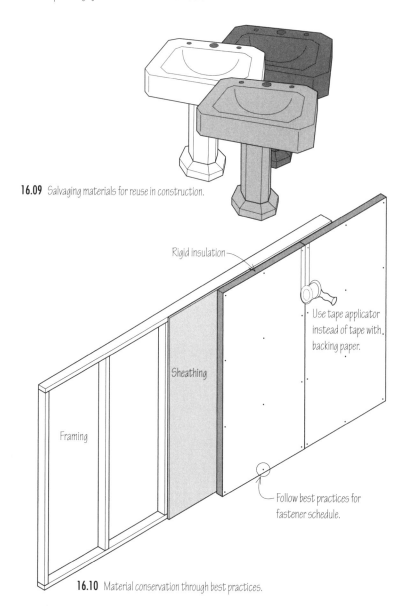

Efficient lighting design

Distributed heating and cooling systems

16.09 Salvaging materials for reuse in construction.

Rigid insulation

Use tape applicator instead of tape with backing paper.

Sheathing

Framing

Follow best practices for fastener schedule.

16.10 Material conservation through best practices.

Using fewer materials through design applies not only to architectural components but also to mechanical and electrical components, such as lighting, heating, and cooling equipment. As addressed earlier, efficient lighting design typically means fewer light fixtures, as design is optimized for the required level of lighting rather than over-lighting by rules of thumb. Other green lighting design techniques also reduce material use. For example, a building with fewer tall ceilings and more reflective surfaces requires less artificial lighting, which means not only less operational energy use but fewer light fixtures as well, resulting in less material use and less embodied energy. Similar benefits accrue to well-designed buildings and their heating and cooling systems. The heating and cooling systems can be smaller not only through efficient building design but also through accurate sizing of the systems. Heating and cooling equipment, such as boilers, heat pumps, and furnaces, can be smaller and the distribution network, such as piping, radiators, and ductwork, can be smaller. Optimally sized heating and cooling equipment and distribution systems require less material and less embodied energy.

Material conservation is also possible through the use of imperfect materials. Select woods, for example, implicitly means that some wood has not been selected and has been discarded. Much rejected wood is structurally sound. Imperfect stone and brick pieces can be usefully applied on a green construction project if they are planned for. Likewise, many other salvaged materials can be accepted rather than rejected, if quality control focuses on integrity of function rather than perfection of form. In a new green aesthetic, imperfection can be exalted as a feature rather than scorned.

Material conservation is facilitated through well-planned design and construction. In this regard, accelerated schedules work against green design, as design professionals tend to fall back on rules of thumb and might not design component-by-component or room-by-room. Green building projects do not need to be synonymous with slow schedules but adequate time should be allowed for the detailed design of each major building component to minimize material use.

Adherence to best practices can substantially reduce material quantities. For example, when fastening rigid insulation to an exterior wall, it has been traditional practice to use 25 to 30 fasteners per 4 x 8 foot (1,220 x 2,440) sheet of insulation. However, it has been shown that 10 to 12 fasteners are more than adequate to fasten such sheets without bowing, bending, or risk of separation. Similarly, taping exterior rigid insulation has been shown to be done rapidly and effectively using a tape applicator rather than being hand-applied by removing tape-backing paper, significantly reducing taping waste.

Reused Materials

To minimize the embodied energy required to harvest and process new materials and to minimize depletion of raw material sources, we seek to reuse materials where possible.

Salvaged Materials

A new industry is arising that deconstructs old buildings, which can provide a source of reused materials for new construction.

Materials salvaged for reuse include much of what is required for construction—dimensional lumber, doors, windows, wall coverings, kitchen specialties, gypsum board, plywood, insulation, siding, moldings, hardware, block, brick, pavers, flashing, roofing shingles, and unused containers of products such as adhesives, caulk, and grout.

16.11 Deconstructing older buildings to supply materials for new construction.

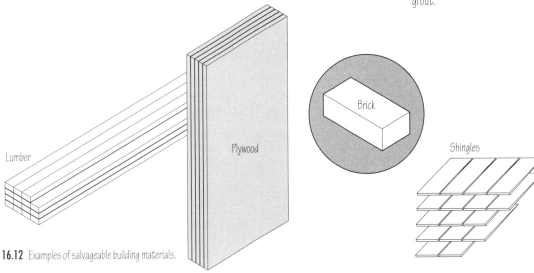

Lumber

Plywood

Brick

Shingles

16.12 Examples of salvageable building materials.

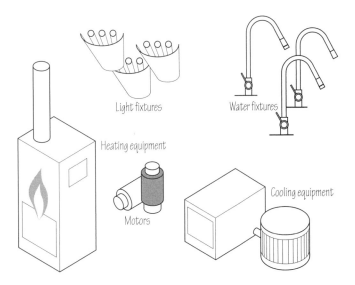

Light fixtures

Water fixtures

Heating equipment

Motors

Cooling equipment

16.13 Many factors go into the decision whether to reuse salvaged energy-consuming and water-consuming equipment and fixtures, including life-cycle energy and water use.

A series of questions arise about the merits of reusing energy-consuming components, such as lighting fixtures, heating and cooling equipment, and motors, as well as water-consuming equipment, such as toilets and faucets. The key environmental issue is whether the embodied energy of such equipment is greater or less than the potential savings from installing new high-efficiency equipment over the expected life of the equipment. There are parallel questions about the financial viability of such reuse, which may or may not give the same answer (yes or no) as the embodied energy question. There may also be legal issues, such as selling low-efficiency equipment that does not comply with federal minimum efficiency requirements. Separately, installing low-efficiency equipment may run counter to some building codes.

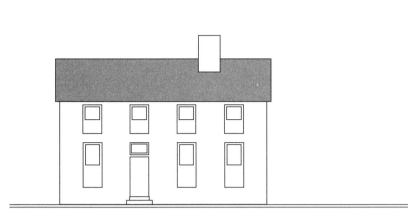

16.14 If a nonhistoric existing building has a window-to-wall ratio of 30% and an area ratio of 2.1, should we reuse it or rebuild?

16.15 Restoring, retrofitting, and rehabbing existing buildings.

A similar question relates to envelope elements, such as old windows. In the case of windows, the assessment should also account for preservation requirements. If there is no preservation requirement, the relative merits of reuse can be evaluated on a life-cycle basis. If preservation is required, a variety of improvements are available that can preserve the window aesthetics while improving energy efficiency, such as weatherstripping, caulking, and storm windows.

Reuse in Place

Another approach to reusing materials is to reuse existing buildings altogether, which further reduces embodied energy use by eliminating the transportation of materials.

Structural elements such as floors, walls, and roofs can typically be reused. Nonstructural elements, such as interior walls, floors, and ceiling finishes, can often be reused as well.

An interesting question arises about the energy impacts of whether to reuse existing buildings or to rebuild. If we assume that the embodied material in a building represents one-quarter of the energy that will be consumed over the life of the building, then a new building need only be 25% more energy-efficient than an existing building to warrant replacing the existing building and still have a lower life-cycle energy use. Many old buildings are intrinsically inefficient, not only in their insulation and airtightness but in a variety of characteristics as well, such as size, shape, and window-to-wall ratio. To be prudent, the comparative life-cycle energy consumption might be assessed as part of the decision to reuse an existing structure.

Another set of questions relates to the merits of reusing existing energy-consuming and water-consuming equipment in a building. The questions are similar to the ones relating to salvaged equipment, although with some differences. In the case of in-place reuse, the legal obstacles are fewer—noncompliant fixtures are not being sold in violation of federal statutes and grandfather clauses will typically prevent any code-compliance issues.

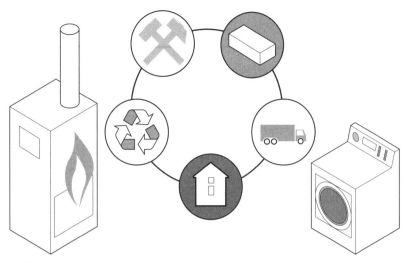

16.16 Life-cycle analysis should be used to evaluate whether or not to reuse existing energy-consuming and water-consuming equipment and fixtures.

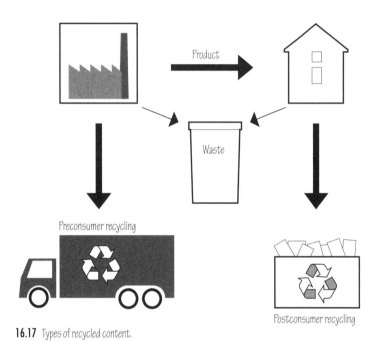

16.17 Types of recycled content.

However, the embodied energy issues become even more pronounced than with salvage reuse, as the fixtures in place are not only typically of low-efficiency but have often been applied in a low-efficiency manner or in a manner that was not intended for the proposed new use. Consider the example of lighting in an office building. An existing building will likely have T12 fluorescent lamps with low-efficiency magnetic ballasts in nonreflective fixtures. Further exacerbating their energy use, the lights will have been configured to over-light the space, perhaps at 2 watts per square foot (w/SF) or higher. Replacement of existing light fixtures with high-efficiency lighting will provide two levels of savings, both through higher-efficiency fixtures and through redesign to readily achievable lighting power densities of 0.8 w/SF or lower. In this example, reusing some of the fixtures in an efficient new layout with new lamps and ballasts may be an option. In short, life-cycle analysis may well be worthwhile in decisions whether to reuse existing in-place energy-consuming and water-consuming equipment.

Materials with Recycled Content

Use of materials with recycled content is encouraged. Preconsumer recycled materials are those that are diverted from the waste stream during manufacturing. Postconsumer recycled materials are obtained from the waste generated by end users.

Concrete is the most-used construction material. Concrete can contain recycled aggregate, which is crushed concrete after the removal of reinforcement and other embedded materials. Concrete can also be specified to contain fly ash, which is a byproduct of coal combustion, or slag, which is a byproduct of smelting metal ore.

Steel fabrication uses a high quantity of recycled steel in its feedstock, reportedly rising above 90% in recent years.

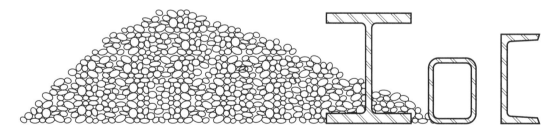

16.18 Previously used materials, such as concrete and steel, can be sorted and processed for reuse. Concrete can be crushed, washed, and graded to produce aggregate for use in the mixing of new concrete. Steel can be collected, separated from other recyclables with large magnets, compressed into large bales, and shipped to a processing plant where the metal is combined with small amounts of virgin steel for use in building products, such as structural steel.

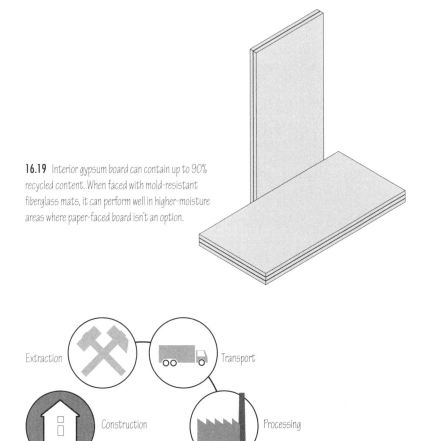

16.19 Interior gypsum board can contain up to 90% recycled content. When faced with mold-resistant fiberglass mats, it can perform well in higher-moisture areas where paper-faced board isn't an option.

16.20 Embodied energy is the total amount of energy used to harvest, manufacture, process, and transport materials to a construction site.

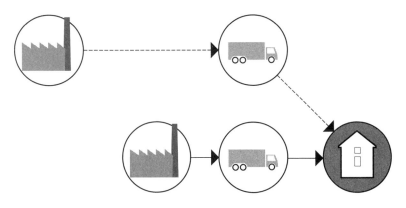

16.21 Green building projects emphasize the value of using locally or regionally acquired materials.

Wood derivative products, such as a variety of engineered wood products, also can contain recycled material.

Gypsum board is available with recycled content, including recycled agricultural materials, fly ash, slag, and other fillers.

Even when a material has some or substantial recycled content, tradeoffs with the chemical content and embodied energy are worth examining. For example, particle board is largely made of recycled materials but its chemical content, including formaldehyde, a known carcinogen, has been significant. And although steel is over 90% recycled, it still has substantial embodied energy.

Selection of Previously Unused Materials

With material use minimized and reused and recycled materials maximized, we turn our attention to selecting previously unused materials. Desirable options include rapidly renewable materials, natural materials, nonhazardous materials of low toxicity, and locally procured materials having low embodied energy.

Embodied Energy

Embodied energy refers to the energy required to harvest, manufacture, prepare, and transport materials to a construction site. Embodied energy generally represents significantly less energy than is used by buildings over their lifetime. However, as buildings are designed to use less energy, the fraction of building energy use represented by embodied energy will only grow. And for zero-energy buildings, the only form of energy consumed is the embodied energy of their materials.

Within the context of embodied energy, green building projects emphasize the value of materials obtained locally or regionally to minimize the energy embodied in transportation. Some green certification codes, standards, and guidelines provide recognition for materials either harvested or processed within a specific radius of the site. LEED allows an optional adjustment based on the type of transportation used for the materials, acknowledging the relative efficiencies of rail and water as compared to over-road transportation.

One solution to the impact of embodied energy is to provide a one-time carbon offset.

Bamboo

Wheatboard is made from straw waste that is finely ground, sorted, and dried, bound with a resin, compressed into sheets, sanded, and cut to size.

Cork

16.22 Examples of rapidly renewable materials.

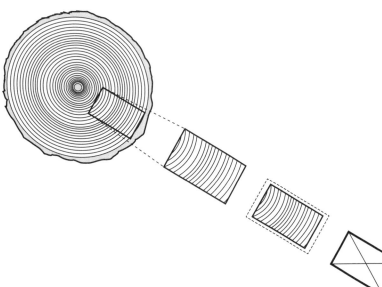

16.23 Wood is relatively low in embodied energy, has no hazardous chemical emissions, is durable if protected from the weather, and can be reused.

16.24 Copyrighted logo of the Forest Stewardship Council.

Rapidly Renewable Materials

Rapidly renewable means materials that grow naturally and can be harvested in a short number of years, such as the ten-year period defined by LEED. Examples include bamboo flooring, cork flooring, carpet fiber derived from corn, cotton insulation, natural linoleum, natural rubber flooring, soy insulation, straw bales for walls and insulation, strawboard cabinetry, wool carpeting, and wheatboard millwork and cabinetry. By using rapidly renewable materials, we reduce the depletion of materials that take longer to grow, such as wood from old-growth forests, or that derive from finite resources, such as plastics derived from fossil fuels. Choosing the right application is important for rapidly renewable materials. Bamboo floors, for example, may not be so durable in high traffic areas or in spaces with excessive moisture.

Other Natural Materials

Wood is an age-old and widely used natural material in construction. Wood is used for structural and nonstructural framing, flooring, subflooring, doors, windows, built-in furniture, wall and ceiling finishes, fencing, and much more. Wood is also used for temporary structures during construction, such as scaffolding and guardrails.

While wood is a natural material, it can be harvested and processed in environmentally destructive ways. These include the logging of old-growth forests, loss of forest cover, logging of threatened tree species, and use of hazardous chemicals. To assure that wood used in construction has been harvested and processed in environmentally sensitive ways, a common requirement is for construction lumber to be certified by the Forest Stewardship Council (FSC).

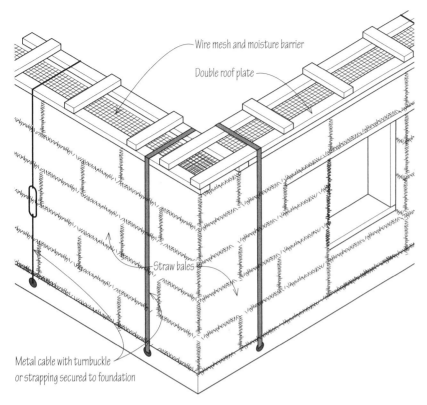

Wire mesh and moisture barrier

Double roof plate

Straw bales

Metal cable with turnbuckle
or strapping secured to foundation

16.25 Straw bale construction.

A natural structural material that also incorporates insulation properties is straw bale. Straw bale construction includes all the most important green material properties. It is made from a rapidly renewable material (and in many cases, a waste product), is nontoxic, has low embodied energy, and is often locally available. Straw bale construction further combines two functions—that of structure and insulation—into one. Disadvantages of straw bale construction include the requirement to prevent rot and the space required for the construction of its thicker walls, typically 18 inches (455) or more.

An ancient natural building material seeing some renewed interest is rammed earth. Rammed earth buildings are found on almost every continent. The walls are built by compacting earth between forms. Rammed earth walls are strong, natural, made of local materials, noncombustible, and nontoxic, except when cement stabilizers are added. Their thermal mass is high but thermal resistance is low, so insulation is typically needed in addition to the earth walls. Rammed earth walls resist infiltration well and also provide excellent sound isolation. Like other natural walls, such as straw bale walls, rammed earth walls need to be protected from moisture. Their feasibility depends on the availability of appropriate soil. Embodied energy is reported to be low but labor costs are high, and specialty training is required as the technique is not so common.

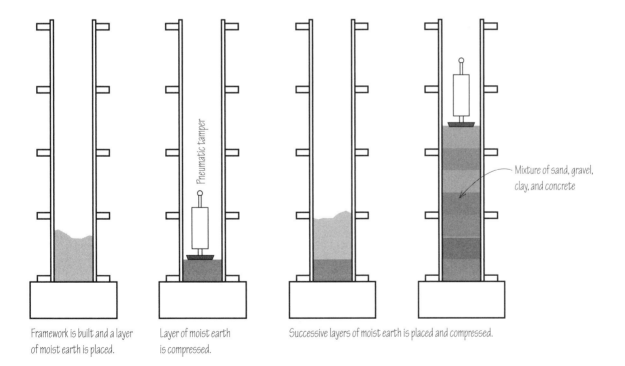

Pneumatic tamper

Mixture of sand, gravel, clay, and concrete

Framework is built and a layer of moist earth is placed.

Layer of moist earth is compressed.

Successive layers of moist earth is placed and compressed.

16.26 Rammed earth construction.

Adobe is sun-dried clay masonry, traditionally used in countries with little rainfall and made near the point of use.

Stabilized or treated adobe contains an admixture of portland cement, asphalt emulsion, and other chemical compounds to limit the water absorption of the bricks.

Exterior walls are plastered on the outside with portland cement stucco to protect against deterioration and loss of strength due to water flowing across the wall surface.

Galvanized metal wire mesh reinforcement

Moisture barrier to prevent the rise of capillary moisture

Wood beams or vigas, the traditionally rough-hewn beams supporting the roof in adobe construction.

Reinforcing rods

Interior plaster

16.27 Adobe construction.

16.28 Not only do we seek to avoid hazardous materials, we seek to actively identify and remove hazardous materials from reused existing buildings.

Adobe is another natural building material, being made of soil having a 15% to 25% clay content, tempered with sand or straw, and containing gravel or other aggregate. Unlike rammed earth walls, adobe structures are not built with forms but rather are prefabricated into large bricks, which are stacked and then mortared together. Thus, adobe construction is not only limited to walls but can be used for vaulted roofs as well. Characteristics of adobe construction are otherwise similar to those of rammed earth—strong, natural, local, noncombustible, nontoxic, of high thermal mass but low thermal resistance (needing separate insulation), resistant to air infiltration, and providing excellent sound isolation. Adobe structures are reportedly vulnerable to seismic activity.

Cob construction, like adobe, is also made of sand, clay, water, and organic reinforcement. But instead of bricks, cob walls are typically hand-formed, lending them to artistic shapes and decorative windows and door openings.

Stone is a strong, beautiful, natural, and inert building material. Primarily used for fence walls, stone has over time also been used for foundations and above-grade walls. Stone does not have good insulating properties and its weight leads to a high transportation-related embodied energy. Stone may also be limited in availability, depending on the region.

Nonhazardous and Low-Toxicity Materials

Green building design professionals seek to avoid the use of hazardous materials. For example, the Living Building Challenge's Red List of banned materials includes:

- Asbestos
- Cadmium
- Chlorinated Polyethylene and Chlorosulfonated Polyethlene
- Chlorofluorocarbons (CFCs)
- Chloroprene (Neoprene)
- Formaldehyde (added)
- Halogenated Flame Retardants
- Hydrochlorofluorocarbons (HCFCs)
- Lead (added)
- Mercury
- Petrochemical Fertilizers and Pesticides
- Phthalates
- Polyvinyl Chloride (PVC)
- Wood treatments containing Creosote, Arsenic or Pentachlorophenol

16.29 Trademark for Green Seal, a nonprofit organization that establishes life-cycle based sustainability standards for products, services, and companies.

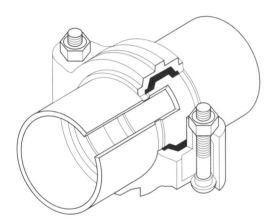

16.30 Avoiding even low-toxicity materials by using mechanical fastenings instead of adhesives and mechanical pipe fasteners instead of welding, brazing, or soldering

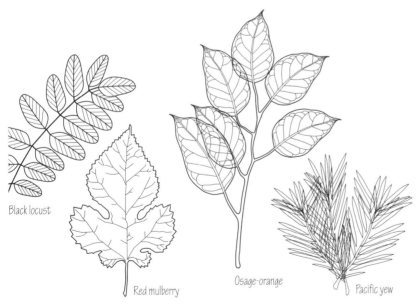

Black locust

Red mulberry

Osage-orange

Pacific yew

16.31 Rot-resistant species of wood.

Beyond the avoidance of hazardous materials, green building design professionals seek to go further and specify materials of low toxicity. Low toxicity usually means materials that are low in volatile organic chemical (VOC) content. These include low-VOC adhesives, concrete curing compounds and sealers, carpets, paints, varnishes, sealants, plastic welding materials, and stains. These are also referred to as low-emitting materials. To qualify as low-VOC, materials must comply with stringent standards for VOC content, such as California's South Coast Air Quality Management District (SCAQMD) rules for adhesives, sealants, sealant primers, clear wood finishes, floor coatings, stains, primers, sealers, and shellacs; or Green Seal Standards for paints, coatings, and anti-rust paints; or the Carpet and Rug Institute's Green Label program.

Going beyond the use of low-toxicity materials are approaches that use no chemicals at all. For example, mechanical fasteners can be used instead of adhesives; unfinished wood can be used instead of applying wood finishes; and mechanical pipe fasteners can be used instead of welding, brazing, or soldering.

A class of materials for which chemicals have long been used is wood treated with preservatives, primarily for outdoor use. As an alternative, outdoor structures and fences can be fabricated from rot-resistant wood instead of chemically treated wood. The United States Department of Agriculture lists four domestic wood species as being exceptionally rot-resistant: black locust, red mulberry, osage-orange, and Pacific yew. Nondomestic tropical hardwood species that are exceptionally rot-resistant include angelique, azobe, balata, goncalo alves, greenheart, ipe (iapacho), jarrah, lignumvitae, purpleheart, and old-growth teak. Not as resistant as these but still classified as resistant or very resistant are the domestic species of old-growth bald cypress, catalpa, cedar (either eastern or western red cedar), black cherry, chestnut, junipers, honey locust, white oak, old-growth redwood, sassafras, and black walnut. Finally, the following domestic species are moderately rot-resistant: second-growth bald cypress, Douglas fir, eastern larch, western larch, old-growth eastern white pine, old-growth longleaf pine, old-growth slash pine, and second-growth redwood. In many cases, these species are not commercially raised as crops and may be difficult to find. It is also safest to select wood that has been certified by the Forest Stewardship Council to ensure that the wood was harvested and processed in a nondestructive way.

Refrigerants

A group of refrigerants that are particularly harmful to the environment are either discouraged or banned from green buildings. These refrigerants are either high in ozone depletion potential (ODP) or are high in global warming potential (GWP), or both. Chlorofluorocarbon (CFC) refrigerants, including R-11 and R-12, were banned in the 1990s and equipment containing these chemicals are actively sought to be replaced when found in buildings undergoing renovation. The chlorine in these chemicals reacts with oxygen to destroy ozone. Two common hydrochlorofluorocarbon (HCFC) refrigerants, R-22 and R-123, have lower ozone-destroying potential than CFCs, but are currently being phased out because they still destroy ozone. Current preferred refrigerant choices, all of which have zero ozone depletion potential, are the hydrofluorocarbons (HFC) R-410a, R-407c, and R-134a. All three may ultimately be phased out due to their global warming potential.

Of added relevance for green buildings is the strong trend toward using heat pumps for both heating and cooling. These include geothermal heat pumps, air-source heat pumps, and boiler-tower water loop heat pumps. All heat pumps use refrigerants.

In the short term, green buildings should limit their refrigerants to ones with zero ozone depletion potential. We direct our discussion to the global warming potential of refrigerants. We note that the impact of these chemicals is not on a continuous basis but only when they leak. So a relevant question is the relative impact of leaks on global warming as compared to the continuous impact of energy use. Energy losses still have a bigger impact on global warming than do refrigerant leaks. For example, the impact of typical leaks of refrigerant R-410a on global warming is less than 3% of the impact of the energy use by a heat pump containing R-410a.

16.32 Refrigerants and their potential effect on the environment.

Refrigerant	Ozone Depletion Potential (ODP)	Global Warming Potential (GWP)	Type	Notes
R-11 Trichlorofluoromethane	1	4,000	CFC	Phased out in the 1990s
R-12 Trichlorofluoromethane	1	2,400	CFC	Phased out in the 1990s
R-22 Chlorofluoromethane	0.05	1,700	HCFC	Widely used for many years but phase-out due to high ODP and GWP. New equipment no longer manufactured with R-22 since 2010. Production of R-22 for servicing existing equipment to end in 2020.
R-123 Dichlorofluoroethane	0.02	0.02	HCFC	Widely used as a replacement for R-11. Equipment containing R-123 to end production in 2020. Production of R-123 to end in 2030.
R-134a Tetrafluoroethane	0	1,300	HFC	Widely adopted for use in chillers, refrigerators, and automobile air-conditioners. Consideration of phase-out is beginning due to its global warming potential.
R-152a 1,1 Difluoroethane	0	124	HFC	Under consideration as a replacement for R-134a.
R-290 propane	0	3	HC	Under consideration as a replacement for R-134a.
R-407c (23% R-32, 25% R-125, 52% R-134a)	0	1,600	HFC	Widely adopted as a replacement for R-22. Consideration of phase-out is beginning due to its global warming potential.
R-410a	0	1,890	HFC	Widely adopted as a replacement for R-22 in the United States. Consideration of phase-out is beginning due to its global warming potential.
R-717 Ammonia-NH3	0	0	—	Toxic. Used in some absorption cooling equipment.
R-744 Carbon Dioxide-CO2	0	1	—	
R-1234yf	0	4	HFO	May see use as a replacement for R-134a.

In seeking to limit the impact of refrigerants on global warming, for buildings that use heat pumps, best practices include:

- Require robust leak testing prior to adding refrigerant charge to systems, as when, for example, positive-pressure testing with nitrogen and deep vacuum draws over a period of time to ensure no leaks, with written reports of the results.
- Require provision for leak detection in mechanical rooms.
- Provide an overall efficient building design. Buildings that are as energy-efficient as possible will use smaller heating and cooling equipment, which means less refrigerant charge. The smallest heating and cooling equipment is possible if the equipment is sized after the envelope and lighting design are complete and if the Owners Project Requirements are accurate with regard to occupancy, schedules, and other owner requirements.
- Avoid heating and cooling spaces that do not require heating and cooling. This again reduces the required system capacity, and so reduces the amount of refrigerant needed.

16.33 Provision should be made for the collection and storage of recyclables; the collection and redistribution of products and equipment to be reused; and for composting.

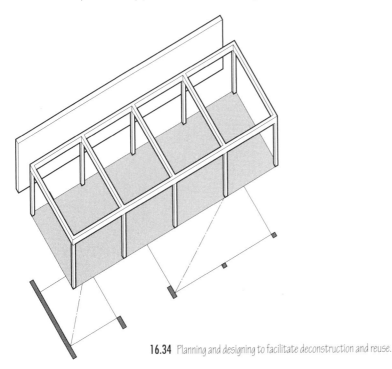

16.34 Planning and designing to facilitate deconstruction and reuse.

Designing for Reduced Postconstruction Material Impacts

During the design of new buildings, provision can be made for reducing postconstruction material impacts; for example, through reducing material use after the building is built.

For example, rooms or space can be provided for an integrated system of solid waste management, including areas for collection and storage of recyclables, areas for collection and redistribution of products and equipment to be reused, and areas for composting. Such provisions make it easier for occupants to divert waste from landfills by recycling, reusing, and composting.

Further, materials used in construction can be documented so that replacement can be minimized. For example, if product details for paints, such as manufacturer, paint color and number, and local sources for purchasing, are well-documented in an owner's manual or in product submittals, it is less likely that an entire room will need to be repainted if touchup painting is required; only small quantities may need to be ordered. This applies to consumables such as paints and wood finishes, as well as to window and door trim, molding, blinds, shingles, and minor furnishings.

Designing for deconstruction facilitates the eventual reuse of building materials when the proposed building reaches the end of its own life. Principles of designing for deconstruction include using modular construction; simplifying connections; selecting fasteners that allow for easier deconstruction; reducing the number of fasteners where possible; selecting durable and reusable materials; and reduced building complexity. The building-specific documentation of design for deconstruction can facilitate such deconstruction in the future.

Construction Waste Management

A major focus of construction waste management is to reduce waste to avoid filling landfills.

Less Waste through Material Use Efficiency

The process of construction waste management was previously begun through attention to material efficiency during design and procurement. By identifying material quantities in more detail, efficient procurement is facilitated, which results in less waste.

Protecting Construction Materials before Use

Priority is also given to protecting construction materials onsite, before use. Our goal here is not only to prevent damage to materials that would diminish their function but also to prevent moisture damage that could lead to indoor air quality problems due to colonization by fungi, and to prevent material waste due to rejected materials. In the latter context, over time we will likely see additional attention to material shipping to prevent damage during shipping that might lead to the rejection of materials. Quality control practices will perhaps also become more forgiving to allow acceptance of materials with very minor or superficial damage, leading to reduced material waste without compromising a building's integrity.

Diverting Waste from Landfills

A main focus of green building waste management is to divert waste from landfills. One strategy to accomplish this goal is to include up-front planning during design, as when, for example, specifying materials to be diverted for recycling or reuse. Goals may also be set for waste diversion, either by weight or volume; provision for the collection, separation, and storage of recyclable waste; and specifying the requirements for tracking and quantifying of waste to meet waste diversion goals. Over time, we expect increased efforts to prevent waste from even reaching a construction site. This might be accomplished, for example, through reduced packaging.

16.36 German manufacturer Ziehl-Abegg recently introduced a fan blade modeled on the serrated edges of the owl's wing, significantly enhancing its aerodynamic properties and reducing noise and energy use.

Other Materials Issues

Transparency

To allow a balanced assessment of material contents—chemicals, embodied energy, natural and recycled materials, domestic or regional origins, and other desirable or undesirable properties—labeling is emerging as an important component of green building materials.

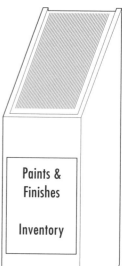

Paints & Finishes

Inventory

16.35 Transparency in the labeling of materials allows for a balanced assessment of materials.

Durability

Durability is a green property insofar as durability delays the frequency of material replacement and the associated material depletion and embodied energy of replacements. Products can also be chosen that do not need regular maintenance, such as resilient flooring that does not require regular waxing.

Biomimicry

Biomimicry is the emerging study of how human-made systems can benefit by examining natural systems. In architecture, natural materials might well inform the energy and material efficiency that are so urgently sought in our structures. Natural shapes such as cylinders and squares, balanced proportions, and efficient area ratios, all can be used to support efficient building design. Nature provides many good models for built-environment processes, such as water purification, heating, cooling, and ventilation. Biomimicry should be applied with common sense, because although many materials, shapes, and processes in nature are intrinsically material-efficient and energy-efficient, some are not.

17

Schedules, Sequences, and Affordability

Schedules and Sequences

Design from the outside in parallels the typical sequence of events in a building project. Construction starts with the site, proceeds to the envelope, and is completed on the interior.

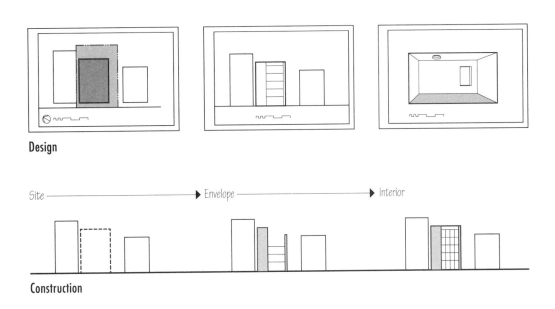

Design

Site ⟶ Envelope ⟶ Interior

Construction

17.01 Designing from the outside in, from site to envelope to interior, parallels the sequence of construction.

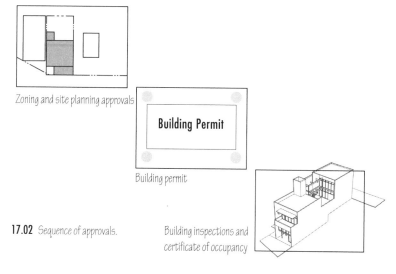

Zoning and site planning approvals

Building Permit

Building permit

17.02 Sequence of approvals.

Building inspections and certificate of occupancy

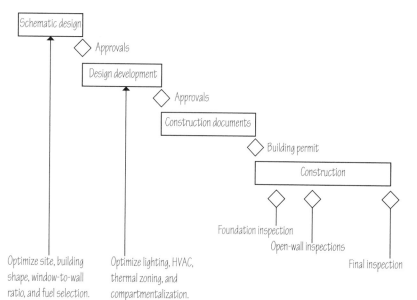

◇ Owner's Project Requirements

Schematic design

◇ Approvals

Design development

◇ Approvals

Construction documents

◇ Building permit

Construction

◇ Foundation inspection

◇ Open-wall inspections

◇ Final inspection

Optimize site, building shape, window-to-wall ratio, and fuel selection.

Optimize lighting, HVAC, thermal zoning, and compartmentalization.

17.03 Green design should begin before relevant approvals are issued.

Consultants

Engineers

Owner

Energy professionals

Architect

17.04 Integrated design involves all stakeholders in the planning, design, and construction process.

Various approvals also follow the sequence from the outside in. Site planning approval typically occurs well before a building permit is issued. Foundation and structural approvals occur before electrical and mechanical inspections, which in turn frequently occur before final interior walk-throughs by the building inspector.

This is not to say that green design should happen in parallel with construction, or even in parallel with approvals. Green design is most effectively launched before approvals are issued. Otherwise, the building facade might obtain zoning approval, at which point aspects such as the building shape or window design can no longer be optimized for low energy use. At the least, the energy system optimization needs to happen before approvals start.

By approvals we mean not only approvals by local authorities but also approvals by the building owner or developer. If an owner chooses a building design before energy systems or impacts have been examined and the design turns out to be inefficient, the architect and the owner are put in the difficult position of having to either defend an inefficient design or having to go through the effort of altering the design.

Proponents of integrated design have advocated for involvement of the entire design team, including energy professionals and the owner, from the beginning of design projects. This has been a positive development. Without integrated design, energy models are sometimes built retroactively for buildings that have been finalized in design, and for which the most significant purpose of the energy model, which is to influence design, is no longer possible. At this junction, only incremental improvements can be made to the design to reduce energy use by an amount that is sometimes so small that it is not measurable in utility bills. Therefore, the owner or tenants are committed to paying unnecessarily high utility bills for the life of the building. They may also be committed to paying for construction costs that are higher than they need to be. Early examination of energy design can prevent these shortfalls.

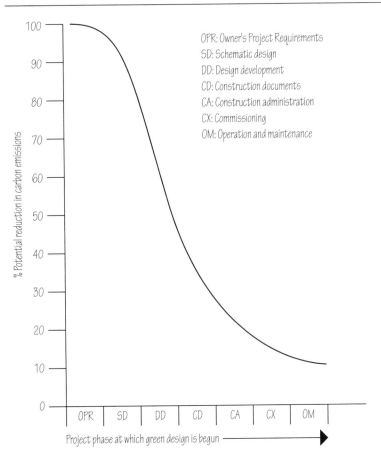

17.05 Reducing carbon emissions by paying attention to green aspects from the beginning of a design project.

OPR: Owner's Project Requirements
SD: Schematic design
DD: Design development
CD: Construction documents
CA: Construction administration
CX: Commissioning
OM: Operation and maintenance

Another lens through which to view design and construction is the potential to reduce carbon emissions. If attention is directed to green design from the very beginning of a project, carbon emissions may potentially be reduced by 100%, relative to a traditional building. Possibilities for affecting carbon emissions drop rapidly during the early phases of design. If green aspects are not examined during schematic design, for example, and the building shape and window-to-wall area ratio are set, with limited roof or site area for renewable energy sources, the potential for impacting carbon emissions is dramatically reduced. If, furthermore, green aspects are not examined through design development, potential carbon emission impacts of building layout, unconditioned spaces, lighting, and HVAC system type are reduced. If green aspects are only begun during the construction documents phase, only minor carbon emissions reductions are possible through incremental and marginal improvements, such as window U-factors or HVAC efficiency. Finally, if no green design is applied, then the potential for reduced carbon emissions represents only those improvements that can be obtained in operating and maintaining the building.

During construction, the contractor sometimes accelerates decisions to keep building activities on schedule and to minimize costs. This acceleration can sacrifice attention to detail, most critically in the area of continuity of the thermal boundary and and in the functionality of the energy systems. This is when added holes creep into the building shell—the gas pipe penetration that is not sealed; the sill plate that is not sealed; the electrical penetration that is not sealed; the floor-to-floor pipe penetration that is not sealed; the window frame that is not sealed; the door frame that is not sealed. Most of these unsealed holes are then permanently covered by finishes. This is where there is need for quality control during construction. Schedule acceleration during and after energy systems are installed, such as the lighting, heating, and cooling systems, can result in increased energy use as well. There are important junctures at which there is need for quality control during construction. Building inspectors and design professionals need to look for these energy deficiencies and must be able to inspect buildings prior to when foundations, walls, windows, roofs, and floors are being finished or hidden from view, and prior to when energy systems are deployed.

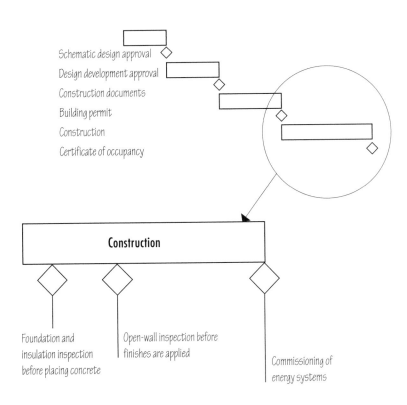

Schematic design approval
Design development approval
Construction documents
Building permit
Construction
Certificate of occupancy

Construction

Foundation and insulation inspection before placing concrete

Open-wall inspection before finishes are applied

Commissioning of energy systems

17.06 Critical junctures in green construction inspections.

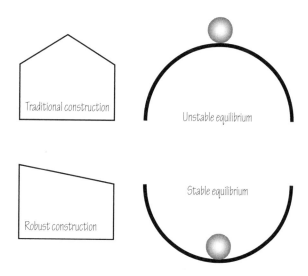

17.07 A metaphor for comparing traditional and more robust construction.

A complementary approach is to design buildings that are more robust—for example, ones that have fewer joints and penetrations, and with the heating and cooling within the thermal envelope. Such buildings are less likely to have construction deficiencies and will have fewer potential air-leakage sites, thermal bridging sites, and distribution losses. Starting from the outside in—simplify the building shape to minimize the number of corners and joints; then minimize the number of penetrations for doors, windows, ventilation penetrations, and combustion penetrations; and use monolithic and strong layers such as SIP panels, insulated concrete forms, and other walls and roof structures which have minimal penetrations, joints, and thermal bridging opportunities. With fewer potential sites for deficiencies, low-energy building performance is less reliant on identifying deficiencies during construction inspection. We might think of a metaphor of a marble in equilibrium on either of two surfaces. On top of an inverted hemisphere, the marble is in a dangerous equilibrium and will roll off if there is any disturbance unless inspected and corrected back to its quasi-stable position. On the other hand, at the bottom of a hemispherical bowl, the marble is in a stable equilibrium. It will always return to its equilibrium, even if there is a disturbance. It is robust by design.

Affordability

Improvements suggested by green design may reduce construction cost, may be cost-neutral, or may increase construction cost. Costs of improvements vary by geographic location, according to local economic conditions, and over time. However, improvements may be grouped according to their overall construction cost impact.

Group I: Improvements that generally reduce construction cost. Examples include:

- Reducing floor area
- Reducing surface area
- Using advanced framing
- Eliminating heating and cooling in spaces not needing it
- Reducing heating and cooling equipment and distribution size due to reduced loads
- Using fewer light fixtures due to reduced lighting loads, resulting from optimized design, more highly reflective walls and ceilings, and avoiding recessed lighting and high ceilings
- Reducing air-conditioning system and distribution size due to reduced artificial lighting
- Eliminating cold water piping and valves from fixtures, such as waterless urinals
- Reducing construction waste
- Using imperfect materials
- Combining multiple uses or tenants in one building rather than in several smaller buildings
- Using structure as finish; unfinished surfaces
- Exposing utilities such as pipes and ducts
- Eliminating attics and pitched roofs
- Reducing number of exterior doors
- Reducing window size and quantity

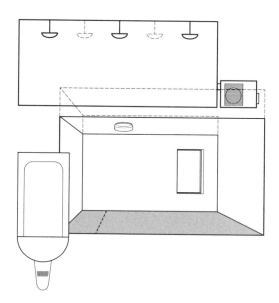

17.08 Group I improvements: Cost saving.

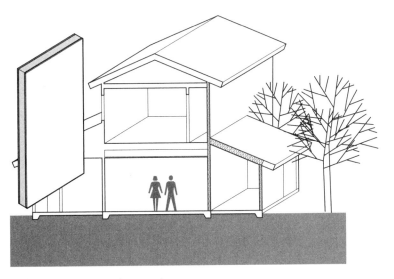

17.09 Group II improvements: Cost-neutral.

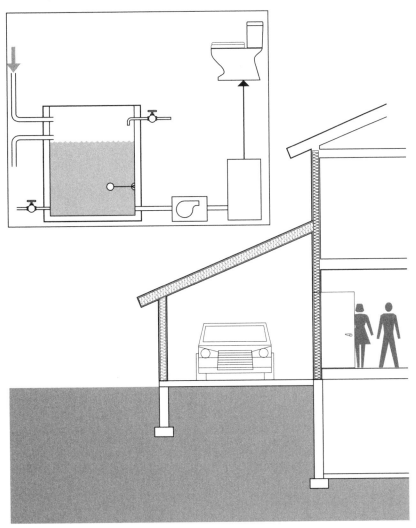

17.10 Group III improvements: Increased cost.

Group II: Improvements that are approximately cost-neutral. Examples include:

- Using prefabricated wall panels, such as SIPs, which have increased material cost but reduced labor cost
- Using trees and other vegetation for shading
- Eliminating basements and crawlspaces, replacing them with attached or interior storage areas
- Moving unconditioned spaces to the building perimeter

Group III: Improvements that increase construction cost. Examples include:

- Added insulation
- Added air-sealing
- High-efficiency heating and cooling systems
- Thermal breaks to counter thermal bridging
- High-efficiency domestic hot water systems
- Using awnings and overhangs
- Heat recovery ventilation or energy recovery ventilation systems
- Harvesting rainwater
- Finishes that promote energy efficiency, such as thermal window shades
- High-efficiency light fixtures
- Energy-efficient lighting controls
- High-efficiency appliances
- Using materials that strengthen thermal boundaries, such as insulated doors between unconditioned spaces and heated spaces
- Adding a second thermal boundary to unconditioned spaces, like garages, by insulating and air-sealing the outer envelope
- Using thermal zoning
- Compartmentalizing building spaces
- Renewable energy systems
- Low-emission materials
- Using appropriate acoustic treatments
- Vegetated roofs
- Using quality control to ensure that building performance goals are met
- Documenting compliance with green building codes, standards, and guidelines

17.11 A building using improvements from Group I and II will cost less to build and will use less energy and fewer materials than the same building without these improvements.

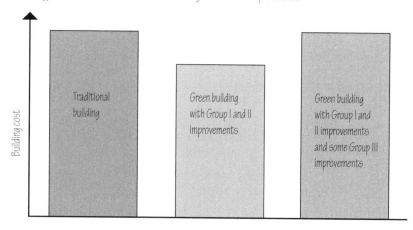

17.12 Cost savings from improvements in Group I could possibly be used to offset the added costs of some of the improvements in Group III.

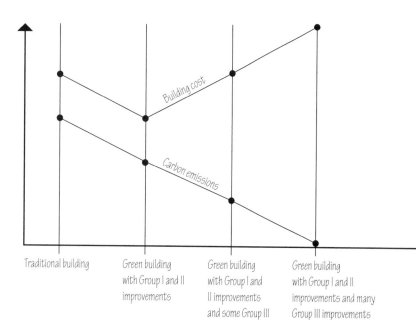

When it comes to estimating construction costs of green improvements, we must be honest with ourselves and with our clients. Many green building improvements will increase the cost of a construction project. Conversely, some potential cost savings may be realized through green design.

Two statements may help to initially characterize the affordability of green buildings:

· If a building is designed using only improvements in Group I (Reduce Construction Cost) and only items in Group II (Cost-Neutral), the building will both cost less to build and will use less energy and fewer materials than the same building without these improvements.
· Cost savings from improvements in Group I could ostensibly be used to offset the added costs of some of the improvements in Group III (Increased Construction Cost). We could envision a building that costs the equivalent of a traditionally designed building but that now uses substantially less energy and fewer materials to be built.

Separately, if a green building does cost more than a traditional building, it is possible to justify some or all of the added construction cost on the basis of future operational savings, primarily the savings of energy costs. This analysis will be addressed in Chapter 18, Quality in Green Design and Construction.

Through the lens of reducing carbon emissions, a building with improvements from Group I (Reduce Construction Cost) and Group II (Cost-Neutral) would have lower emissions and would cost less to build than a traditionally designed building. The same building with some improvements from Group III (Increased Construction Cost) would have even lower emissions while costing the same as a traditional building. Finally, a building with even more improvements from Group III could ostensibly have zero or near-zero emissions while using operating savings from reduced energy use to deliver a lower life-cycle cost than a traditional building.

17.13 Evaluating a building through the lens of lowering carbon emissions.

18
Quality in Green Design and Construction

All buildings are vulnerable to inadequate quality in design and construction. However, green buildings have additional vulnerabilities that relate to their sought-after green features. Indicators of inadequate quality include high energy use, inadvertent use of finishes having high chemical content and subsequent off-gassing, and water penetration resulting in high interior humidity and mold.

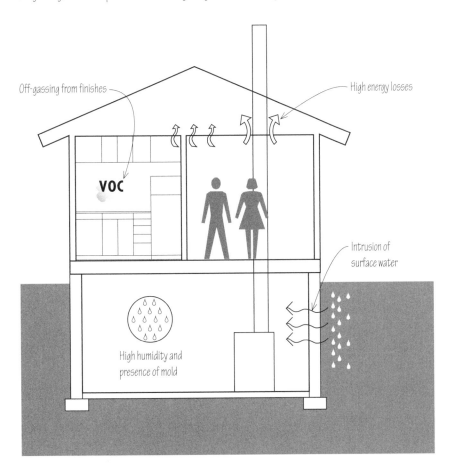

Off-gassing from finishes

VOC

High energy losses

Intrusion of
surface water

High humidity and
presence of mold

18.01 Indicators of inadequate building quality.

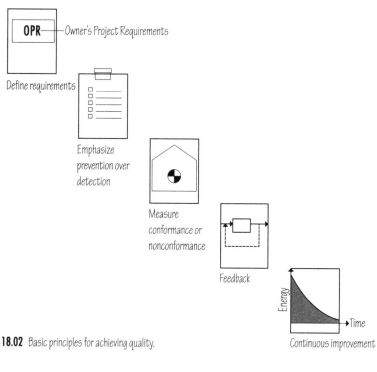

Define requirements

Emphasize prevention over detection

Measure conformance or nonconformance

Feedback

Continuous improvement

18.02 Basic principles for achieving quality.

OPR —Owner's Project Requirements

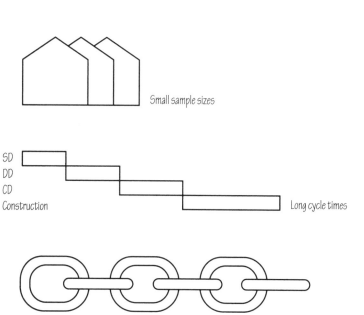

Small sample sizes

Long cycle times

Many parties involved

18.03 Obstacles to quality in design and construction.

Green buildings may be even more vulnerable to certain kinds of failures than conventional buildings. For example, if an air leakage failure of 0.1 air change per hour (ACH) is introduced into a building that was designed for an overall infiltration rate of 0.1 ACH, its infiltration has been increased by 100%. This may result in the heating system having inadequate capacity, resulting in a colder building. The impact of the same air leakage failure on a 0.5 ACH building is only 20% and will likely not be felt at all. Likewise, if a contaminant source, such as high-VOC carpeting, is inadvertently installed in a green building, the indoor concentration of contaminants is likely to be higher than in a conventional over-ventilated or high-infiltration building.

Therefore, the need for quality control in green buildings is high.

The study of quality has advanced significantly over the past few decades. Basic principles of quality include:

· Define requirements
· Prevent defects instead of relying on defect detection
· Measure conformance or nonconformance to requirements
· Feedback
· Continuous improvement

Obstacles to quality in design and construction are many. Unlike other enterprises, such as mass-production manufacturing, buildings are typically built one at a time, with low sample sizes and long cycle times to complete each building. These factors hinder both the measurement and the feedback required for continuous improvement. There are also many parties involved in the design and construction of a building, any of whom may be a weak link and counteract efforts at quality.

Approaches to overcome these obstacles include designed-in quality through the use of robust building elements and adopting a variety of approaches to controlling quality during design and construction. These include defining requirements, inspection, commissioning, measurement and verification, and monitoring.

18.04 Design quality into a building.

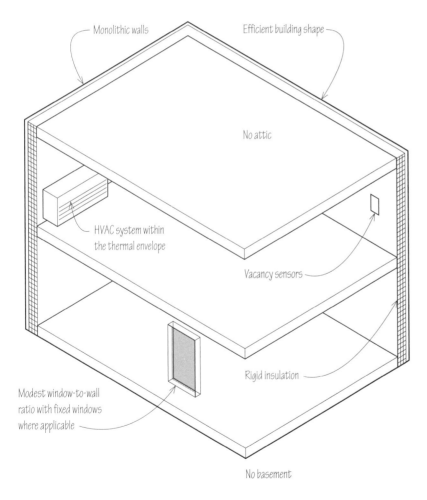

Monolithic walls

Efficient building shape

No attic

HVAC system within
the thermal envelope

Vacancy sensors

Rigid insulation

Modest window-to-wall
ratio with fixed windows
where applicable

No basement

18.05 Examples of designed-in quality.

Designed-In Quality

To minimize the risk of shortfalls, especially in such green features as low energy use, a helpful approach is to design quality into the building. In the classic approach to quality, this is known as defect prevention and is contrasted with defect detection, where failures are sought during inspection. Designed-in quality does not relieve requirements for inspection, but it can reduce the risk of failures.

Opportunities for designed-in quality in green buildings are many. For example, monolithic walls, such as those constructed with ICF, SIP, and similar materials, have few penetrations, are more robust, and are less likely to fail than stick-frame, site-built walls. Rigid insulation board, dense-packed cellulose, and foam insulation are less likely to sag or leave insulation voids than batt insulation or loosely packed insulation types. If an operable window is not specifically needed for ventilation, a fixed window is less likely to fail, especially in terms of air leakage, than an operable window. By placing heating and cooling systems entirely within the thermal envelope, there is less reliance on detecting distribution system leaks and thermal losses and less reliance on systems needed to counter such losses, such as insulation and air-sealing. A recent study of compliance with energy code requirements for duct sealing in nonresidential buildings in California found that the noncompliance rate was 100%. In other words, not a single building examined in the study complied with the requirements. Rather than attempting to boost code compliance, we can guarantee compliance simply by not locating distribution systems in unconditioned spaces.

Some designed-in quality improvements are subtle. For example, vacancy or manual-on sensors reduce energy more reliably than do more conventional occupancy sensors, which often turn on lights unnecessarily during a brief transient occupancy.

Building designs that rely less on equipment efficiency and more on intrinsic efficiency, such as building shape, thermal resistance, and modest window-to-wall ratio, may be more likely to stay efficient over time.

Approaches to Quality in Design and Construction

In addition to designed-in quality, which is intended to prevent defects in construction and building operation, a broad set of quality tools can be brought to green building design and construction to detect and eliminate defects. The approach requires a team-wide commitment to quality and adoption of the language of quality—definition of requirements, conformance to requirements, measurement, feedback, and continuous improvement.

Construction documents themselves serve as an outstanding vehicle for defining requirements. However, in all their detail, construction documents typically do not record the intent of a building's design. Commissioning documents have in recent years begun to serve this function. It is important to document the owner's intent and goals as well as performance requirements and other green building requirements, such as compliance with a specific green certification program, target energy use, maximum air leakage, or defined thermal comfort range.

Quality in Design

One of the benefits of a green building certification, such as LEED, is that the requirement for documentation serves as a form of built-in quality control. In order to document that the heating system is not oversized, a check on the heating system sizing is required. In order to document that the building meets a standard, such as ASHRAE 62 for ventilation, a check on the ventilation is required. This is a benefit for quality control that goes beyond obtaining certification credits.

Quality in Construction

The review of submittals has long served as an invaluable best practice to ensure quality in construction. Submittal review is a form of documenting compliance with requirements and will often serve to identify the substitution of inferior products and, in the case of green building projects, inefficient or polluting products. The practice of reviewing submittals is common in larger commercial and institutional construction projects, but would also benefit projects where it is not common, such as in residential, small commercial, and many private-sector projects.

Quality in construction continues through a variety of best practices, including holding preconstruction and project meetings, where deficiencies are identified and resolved.

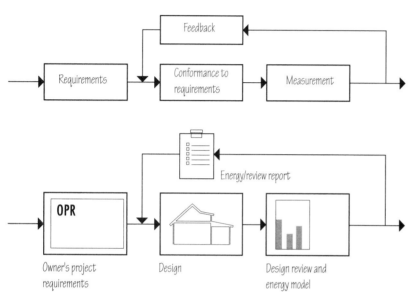

18.06 The language of quality applied to design.

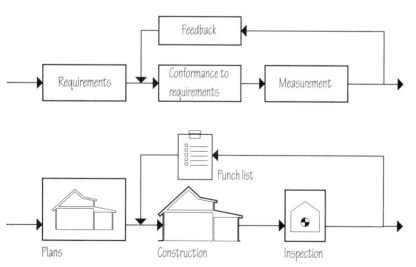

18.07 The language of quality applied to construction.

As simple as it sounds, an important practice in inspection is to reject bad work. Bad work is best found through good inspection. Best practices for field inspection include:

· Allow sufficient time for the inspection.
· Come prepared with a set of construction documents.
· Time inspections so that important green features, such as insulation and air-sealing, are inspected before being hidden in closed walls and other inaccessible locations.
· Take notes and photographs; release observations in a timely fashion.

Of importance is the timing of inspecting air-sealing details. This means inspecting windows and doors before molding is installed, inspecting wall cavities before they are sealed, and inspecting all building penetrations.

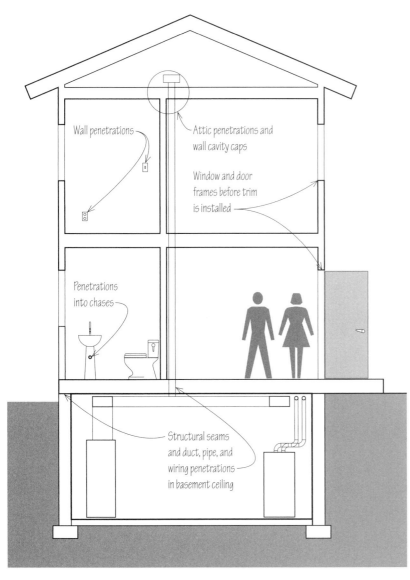

Wall penetrations

Attic penetrations and wall cavity caps

Window and door frames before trim is installed

Penetrations into chases

Structural seams and duct, pipe, and wiring penetrations in basement ceiling

18.08 Timing the inspection of air-sealing details.

Energy Modeling

A foundation of quality in green building design is energy modeling. Energy models help building owners and design professionals to make good energy decisions.

Building energy models are used for several different purposes, including improvement evaluations; energy code compliance; voluntary standard compliance or rating; utility bill and operating cost prediction; tax incentive documentation; and state or utility program incentive compliance. Some models can also form the basis of heating and cooling system design. Advanced uses of the models include refining and optimizing control sequences for heating, cooling, and lighting systems.

The key to effective building energy simulation is to model before decisions are made. If the energy simulation is performed after the building shape is decided, the simulation will not be able to influence the building shape. If the energy simulation is performed after the renderings or elevations are complete, the simulation will not be able to influence the window-to-wall ratio. If the energy simulation is performed after the heating and cooling system is selected, the simulation will not be able to influence the heating and cooling system efficiency.

Schematic design	Design development	Construction documents

Simplified Model
Building shape
Fuel selection

Hourly Model
Detailed improvements

Compliance Model
Energy code
Green certification
Tax and utility incentives

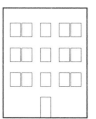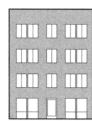

18.09 Types of energy models.

Solar photovoltaic systems

kW/month

J F M A M J J A S O N D
Months of the year

Daylighting strategies

18.10 Specialty energy models.

The different purposes of energy modeling can require creating different models, even if it is appealing to think of one model serving all purposes. Energy code compliance requires an energy model of the final building and energy systems. This is by definition the opposite of what is required for evaluating and selecting improvements, where it is better if nothing is yet finalized and all options are open.

An effective sequence of energy modeling might include:

- Simplified modeling to examine the building shape, ceiling heights, window-to-wall ratio, and preliminary heating and cooling system design, or at least fuel selection. The effort required to create this model is typically from 2 to 4 hours.
- Hourly whole-building modeling. This is referred to as an hourly model because it simulates a building's energy use over a whole year by examining its response to changing outdoor temperatures and sun angles for each hour of the year. Hourly modeling is used to evaluate a variety of improvements—thermal zoning; insulation design including reduced thermal bridging; use of unheated spaces; efficient lighting design; evaluating heating and cooling equipment and distribution systems; design of the domestic hot water system; specifying controls; and design of the ventilation system. The effort required to create this model is typically from 40 to 80 hours, although it can be less for smaller buildings like houses and more for large or unusually complex buildings.
- Compliance modeling. Here, the same hourly whole-building model is modified with the final selected improvements and building configuration for purposes of code compliance, standards compliance, utility bill prediction, and documentation for state and utility incentives if applicable. The effort required to create this model varies depending on the type of building and the requirements of any particular program. It can be a minor edit to the hourly building model, or it can be a more involved edit and re-run of the model.

Specialty energy models and spreadsheets are available for advanced systems and approaches, such as solar photovoltaic systems, daylighting, and combined heat and power (CHP).

Interestingly, most energy models have an add-to-the-building limitation. Most models allow parametric analysis, in other words, the ability to examine the effects of changing one parameter, such as adding to the building's wall R-value or improving the building's window U-factor. However, models often do not allow easy evaluation or reporting of changed parameters that simplify the building. Such changed parameters might include reducing floor area or the height of tall ceilings; simplifying the building shape; removing heat from spaces; and reducing the size or number of windows. Although these building-simplifying improvements can typically be made indirectly in energy models, the changes are often not made as easily as improvements that are added to the building. Therefore, even in energy models, the method of evaluating building energy improvements remains one in which we focus on adding to the building rather than subtracting from it. This is perhaps where building energy design calls for the metaphor of the sculptor, some of whose best work is done by removing material from the sculpture, not just by adding material.

Quality control of energy models themselves is essential to prevent mistakes that can lead to the selection of suboptimal or even energy-wasting systems. Quality control includes self-review of the model by the modeler, supervisor review, and programmatic review by third parties. Review should include inputs compared to building drawings and a comparison of outputs to benchmarks for similar buildings.

For the design of commercial buildings, software programs should meet the requirements of ASHRAE 90 Appendix G, which is required for most code and standard compliance documentation. For residential buildings, RESNET's HERS program is an important reference for compliance documentation.

```
┌─────────────────────────────────────────────┐
│ Environmental Goals                          │
│ [ ]   Architecture 2030                      │
│ [ ]   LEED                                   │
│       [ ] Certified  [ ] Silver  [ ] Gold  [ ] Platinum │
│ [ ]   ENERGY STAR                            │
│ [ ]   HERS _____ Target                   │
│ [ ]   Passivhaus                             │
│ [ ]   Other: _____         │
│                                              │
│ Energy Goals                                 │
│ [ ]   Energy code                            │
│ [ ]   Below code: _____ %                    │
│ [ ]   Net zero                               │
│       Basis  [ ] Site                        │
│              [ ] Source                      │
│              [ ] Carbon                      │
│              [ ] Fossil fuels                │
└─────────────────────────────────────────────┘
```

18.11 Environmental and energy goals for a green building.

Commissioning

Commissioning was originally defined as a form of construction inspection that serves to ensure that mechanical and lighting systems are operating as intended. In an emerging broader definition, commissioning can serve as the vehicle for quality control for an entire green building project, including the definition and documentation of project requirements, inspection of envelope and other nonmechanical/lighting systems, and measurement providing the feedback upon which the building operation can be continuously improved.

Commissioning is typically performed by an independent commissioning provider to maintain an arm's length distance from those involved in design and construction. The commissioning provider usually works directly for the owner. "Commissioning provider" has also been termed "commissioning agent" or "commissioning authority," with some inconsistency applied to the terms, relative to their independence from the design team and relative to the contractor. In this book, we use the general term commissioning provider.

Owner's Project Requirements

Commissioning begins with a document called the Owner's Project Requirements, setting forth the owner's goals, including the main purpose of the building; relevant history; future needs; project budget; expected operational budget; construction schedule; expected building life; intended use for all spaces; quality of materials; acoustic requirements; project delivery method, such as design-bid-build, design-build, or other; and training requirements for Environmental goals are also set forth, including voluntary certifications, such as Architecture 2030 or LEED; energy efficiency for a specific energy utilization index or net-zero energy; carbon emissions; thermal comfort; specialty lighting; and owner priorities for assessing green options, such as lowest emissions or lowest life-cycle costs. Critical decisions by the owner are whether to allow smoking in the building if allowable by law and, if so, in which areas of the building, and near the building, and how this will be enforced, for example with signage or through lease requirements. Green buildings can best set an example in this area by not allowing smoking at all in a building or onsite.

Space: 105	Description: Conference Room		
Hour	Weekday Occupancy	Weekend Occupancy	Notes
12–1 am	0	0	
1–2 am	0	0	
2–3 am	0	0	
3–4 am	0	0	
4–5 am	0	0	
5–6 am	0	0	
6–7 am	0	0	
7–8 am	0	0	
8–9 am	0	0	
9–10 am	14	0	Staff meeting, typical
10–11 am	2	0	
11–noon	2	0	
12–1 pm	10	0	Doubles as lunch room
1–2 pm	2	0	
2–3 pm	2	0	
3–4 pm	2	0	
4–5 pm	2	0	
5–6 pm	0	0	
6–7 pm	0	0	
7–8 pm	0	0	
8–9 pm	0	0	
9–10 pm	0	0	
10–11 pm	0	0	
11–midnight	0	0	

The design professional can assist the owner in defining project goals. There are significant implications to project cost and to the building's energy efficiency, for example, in the detail with which the building's projected occupancy is provided. The owner should preferably identify, on a space-by-space basis, the occupancy (number of people) and type of activity for each hour of a typical weekday, and for weekends. This information is used for sizing the ventilation system and the heating and cooling system, and for energy modeling. Again, the more detail the better. If occupancy information is guessed and is too conservative (too many people assumed), the ventilation system will be oversized, the heating system will be oversized, the cooling system will be oversized, distribution systems will be oversized, the entire system will cost more than necessary, more material will be used than necessary, and more energy will be used than necessary after the building is built. Accurate occupancy information also facilitates quality control through subsequent commissioning tests.

Target light levels should also be discussed with the owner and documented, with the default being the lower end of IES recommendations. Lighting controls should be selected and documented on a space-by-space basis. An example might be "manual on, occupancy off, 3-minute off-delay" or "manual control, multilevel switching to allow one-third and two-thirds the maximum light level that shall be designed to the low end of IES recommendations."

These details should not be presumed to be beyond the ability of the owner to discuss and again, the more detail the better, as these decisions will have substantial impacts on building energy use.

18.13 Example of interior lighting requirements.

Space	Description	Light Level (fc)	Controls				Notes
			Manual	Occupancy	Photocell	Timer	
101	Corridor	10		●			1-minute off-delay
102	Office	30	●				3-level
103	Kitchen	30		●			Vacancy sensor
							1-minute off-delay

18.14 Example of exterior lighting requirements.

Area	Access	Security	Recreation	Decoration	Notes (1)
Parking	Dusk–10 pm				Timer control
Sidewalk	●				Motion control 1-minute-delay
Tennis court			●		
Entrance sign				●	Photocell on Timer off at 11 pm

(1) All exterior lights equipped with photocell override to prevent daytime operation.
Cut-in: 0.5 foot-candle
Cut-out: 1 foot-candle

Outdoor lighting needs should also be identified through a discussion about which lights are required for security, which lights are required for access, which lights are required for outdoor evening recreation, and which lights are required for decoration. Security needs for outdoor lighting should be further explored. Can the use of motion sensors deliver greater security and lower energy use? If motion sensors are not used, are all outdoor lights required for security all night long, or can some lights be turned off at the end of the evening?

Target indoor temperature and humidity should be identified on a space-by-space basis for summer and winter, and for both occupied and unoccupied modes. As part of this process, the owner should clearly identify which spaces need heat, which spaces need cooling, and which spaces need neither heating nor cooling. Further, temperature and humidity control capability should be identified on a space-by-space basis. In other words, which spaces receive control capability? The design professional should spell out the tradeoffs for temperature control so the owner can make informed decisions, as these decisions will strongly impact both energy savings and comfort as when, for example, either facilitating or not facilitating zoning. For each thermostat or control set point, the times of day and week for which temperatures should be set up (occupied mode) or set back (unoccupied mode) should be identified. The documentation of these details promotes clarity in design, equipment sizing, and energy modeling, and also serves as the basis for commissioning tests.

18.15 Example of temperature control requirements.

Space	Description	Heat	Cool	Set Up				Set Back			
				Heat	Cool	M–F	S/S	Heat	Cool	M–F	S/S
101	Office	●	●	70	74	7–5	–	55	90	5–7	24-hr
102	Lobby	●	○	70	na	7–5	–	55	na	5–7	24-hr

Legend: ● Automatic control
◐ Manual control
○ No control

18.16 Prioritization of goals.

Prevent environmental degradation	■	■	■	■
Improved human health	■	□	□	□
Improved human comfort	■	□	□	□
Improved economy	□	□	□	□
Political (e.g., reduced dependence on oil)	□	□	□	□
Improved quality of life	□	□	□	□
Social goals (e.g., fair labor practices)	■	■	□	□
The human spirit (e.g., love of nature, self-reliance)	■	■	■	□

18.17 Example of target reflectances.

Space	Description	Ceiling	Walls	Furnishings	Floor
101	Office	90%	80%	60%	60%
102	Corridor	90%	90%	na	80%

Note: High reflectances reduce the need for artificial lighting, reduces energy use, and reduces the cost for light fixtures.

Examples: | 90% | 60% | 30% |

Bright white:	90%
Off-white:	70–80%
Carpet, typical:	5–9%
Carpet, high-maintenance:	9–13%
Wood:	20–54%
Pale-blue:	80%
Yellow:	47–65%
Concrete, typical:	20–30%
Concrete, polished reflective:	70–90%

The Owner's Project Requirements document also allows the owner to prioritize between green features in case the project budget does not allow all features to be incorporated. For example, the owner might choose from among the green goals listed in Chapter 1, Introduction, and then rank them in order of importance. Further, the owner might rank individual improvements, such as optional compliance credits for LEED or other codes, standards, or guidelines, from high to low priority.

The owner should identify target lighting reflectances for ceilings, walls, floors, and furnishings, preferably by choosing from a color-reflectance chart. Historically, design has been based on default reflectances of 80% for ceilings, 50% for walls, and 20% for floors. The potential for reducing the quantity of light fixtures, reducing energy use, and reducing the window area required for daylighting is so great that the owner's participation in these decisions can significantly reduce both construction cost and energy use.

Because of the energy and capital costs of windows and their associated comfort issues, the Owner's Project Requirements should include an assessment of windows on a space-by-space basis. The owner should answer these questions about windows: Can windows be eliminated in utility spaces such as stairwells and landings, corridors, mechanical rooms, laundry rooms, janitor's closets, and storage rooms? Can window quantity and size be reduced in occupied spaces? In other words, which windows are required for views? What is a minimum acceptable size for windows for views? Which windows should be operable, giving occupants sufficient comfort control, and which can be nonoperable? What is the target window-to-wall ratio? Which smaller windows can be combined into a smaller quantity of larger windows?

18.18 Example of window requirements.

Space	Description	Views	Daylight	WWR (1)	Notes
101	Office	◑	√	15%	
102	Corridor	○	na	na	
103	Lobby	●	√	30%	

Notes: (1) WWR = Window-to-wall ratio
Lower window-to-wall ratio reduces energy usage significantly, except where energy modeling shows gains from passive solar or daylighting.

0–10%	low
10–20%	moderate
20–30%	high
>30%	very high

Legend:
○ No views required
◑ Modest views required
● Panoramic views required
na not applicable

The Owner's Project Requirements should address tradeoffs of building shape and size. Can the height of tall ceilings be lowered to reduce energy use and construction cost? Can attics, basements, and crawlspaces be eliminated? Is a flat roof acceptable to reduce the energy losses associated with pitched roofs? Which area ratio improvements are acceptable, such as building height, shape simplifications, and greater perimeter depth?

Future green considerations can also be itemized in the Owner's Project Requirements document. For example, if solar energy is not incorporated into the initial design, is solar energy an option in the future and if so, should the roof be designed to be receptive to future solar collectors?

Best practices in the development of Owner's Project Requirements include:

- Organizing workshops where key stakeholders can participate in a discussion of project requirements and where the importance of the project requirements can be reviewed. A two-phase workshop works well, with distribution of draft Owner's Project Requirements after the first workshop and distribution of the final document after the second workshop.
- Avoid generalities in the Owner's Project Requirements. For example, "to operate at a high level of efficiency to minimize utility consumption" does not provide hard goals for the design team. Rather, specific statements such as "design to meet an ENERGY STAR score of 95" or "design to meet an energy utilization index of 30 kBtu/SF/year" provide clearer targets.
- Focus on the owner's needs and not on topics that will be covered by design professionals, such as outdoor design temperature conditions. Each entry in the Owner's Project Requirements should be understood by the owner. This promotes owner involvement in developing the requirements and reduces the risk of the document simply being completed by the design professional or commissioning provider.
- Allow for iterations to allow the owner to evaluate tradeoffs and make informed decisions. For example, the Owner's Project Requirements might change after energy modeling provides the projected performance of key design alternatives. Document and date revisions to the Owner's Project Requirements.
- Rank options from green to less green with tradeoffs clearly identified, such as construction cost, energy use, and health and safety issues, so the owner can make an informed choice among the options. For example, choices for outdoor lighting control might be presented first as motion sensors only (with photocell override to prevent daytime operation) and then as photocell-on/timer-off (with time of night specified for lights to be turned off), and finally as photocell-on/photocell-off (all-night operation). As another example, when offering options for types of lighting, differentiate higher-efficiency options, such as linear fluorescent fixtures, from lower-efficiency options, such as recessed downlights.

18.19 Building shape considerations.

Judicious design of building shape is a powerful way to reduce energy use, material use, and construction costs. Check all that apply.

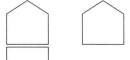

_ Tall ceiling heights can be reduced.

_ Attic is not needed.

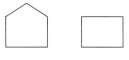

_ Basement is not needed.

_ Roof may be flat.

_ Depth of perimeter spaces may be increased.

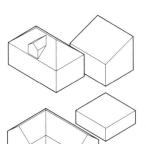

_ Roof design should be optimized for solar collectors in the near-term or in the future.

_ Building shape simplifications may be considered.

With the Owner's Project Requirements, the more detail the better. It is a rare opportunity for the owner to learn, to understand, and to choose among important design options. It is an invaluable vehicle for the design professional to communicate these options to the owner. The Owner's Project Requirements document forms the foundation for the greenest possible design and construction, as well as the foundation for quality control during design and construction.

Basis of Design

Commissioning continues with documentation of the design professionals' approaches and assumptions in a document called the Basis of Design. The Basis of Design typically describes the systems to be commissioned and fills in any design assumptions that might not be provided either in the Owner's Project Requirements or in the construction documents. Examples of what might be included are main heating and cooling design assumptions, such as climatic design conditions, safety factors, and so forth; design noise criteria by space; design illumination in foot-candles by space; occupancy gains—latent and sensible per person—by space; infiltration assumptions or targets; the assumed entering water temperature used to size domestic hot water; stored water temperature; delivered water temperature; plumbing fixture counts; wall and roof assembly R-values; window U-factors; and internal gains such as appliance power levels.

The purpose of the Basis of Design is to confirm that the Owner's Project Requirements have been effectively translated into the construction documents. The Basis of Design also allows another step of quality control, as the commissioning provider can check the Owner's Project Requirements against the Basis of Design, against the construction documents, and finally against the as-built building.

Best practices for the Basis of Design include:
- As with the Owner's Project Requirements, avoid generalities in the Basis of Design. For example, rather than show an assumed power density for lighting in watts per square foot, the actual lighting power density should be shown on a space-by-space basis to confirm its use for cooling system sizing.
- Include reports on all inputs and outputs for critical system sizing, including heating, cooling, ventilation, photometric (lighting) design, daylighting, and specialty systems, such as solar photovoltaic power.
- Include reference codes and standards to which design is compliant. Beyond specifying the codes and standards, spell out the selected compliance path, as most relevant codes and standards allow multiple paths for compliance.
- Include reports on inputs and outputs of energy modeling.
- Avoid repeating items that are in the Owner's Project Requirements or in the construction documents.

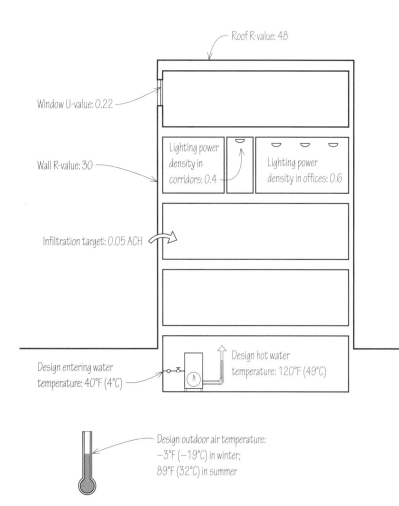

Roof R-value: 48

Window U-value: 0.22

Wall R-value: 30

Lighting power density in corridors: 0.4

Lighting power density in offices: 0.6

Infiltration target: 0.05 ACH

Design entering water temperature: 40°F (4°C)

Design hot water temperature: 120°F (49°C)

Design outdoor air temperature: −3°F (−19°C) in winter; 89°F (32°C) in summer

18.20 Example basis of design elements.

18.21 Commissioning responsibilities.

	OW	AR	EN	GC	MC	EC	PC	CX
Project requirements	◉	⊔	⊔					
Basis of design		◉	⊔					
Design review								◉
Foundation inspection		⊔						◉
Open wall inspection		⊔						◉
Final envelope inspection		⊔						◉
Testing and balancing					◉	⊔	⊔	⊔
Functional testing					⊔	⊔	⊔	◉
Owner's manual		⊔	⊔	◉	⊔	⊔	⊔	⊔
Follow-up testing								◉
Training					⊔	⊔	⊔	◉

Legend:
◉ Prime responsibility
⊔ Supporting role
OW Owner
AR Architect
EN Engineer
GC General contractor
MC Mechanical contractor
EC Electrical contractor
PC Plumbing contractor
CX Commissioning provider

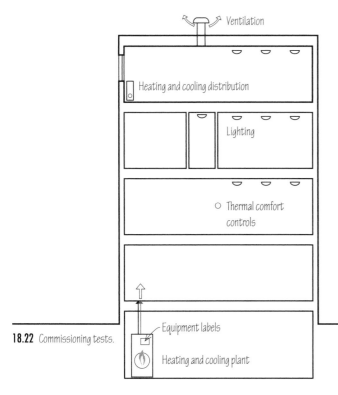

18.22 Commissioning tests.

Other Commissioning Issues

Commissioning requirements themselves should be captured in the construction documents. Bidding contractors need to know what will be expected for commissioning. Requirements should list responsibilities for different aspects of commissioning, including responsibilities for the general contractor, mechanical and electrical contractors, testing and balancing subcontractors, the commissioning provider, and design professionals.

Because commissioning is a relatively new discipline, we must allow for education of all stakeholders, many of whom may not be familiar with procedures, terminology, roles, and expectations of green building projects.

Commissioning Tests

During and following installation, the commissioning provider coordinates and supervises a series of tests to ensure that the building's energy systems are installed and working properly. These tests include system performance tests, such as checking that when a space is intended to be heated the space temperature increases; when a ventilation fan is turned on that it is working; that water flow and airflows are as designed; that combustion efficiencies are per manufacturer specifications; and that air and water temperatures are within the designed ranges. The commissioning provider frequently goes beyond performance testing to ensure that documentation is complete, including labeling of equipment and piping. The results of these tests are detailed in a commissioning report, which also offers recommendations for any deficiencies identified.

The type of problem that commissioning identifies can be illustrated by the following example. Temperature control devices, such as zone dampers, and temperature sensors in two adjacent spaces are mistakenly cross-wired. When the occupants in one space raise the temperature set point on their thermostat, this inadvertently warms the adjacent space. Occupants in the adjacent space now feel too warm and lower their temperature set point, which makes the first set of occupants too cold, who in turn again raise their temperature set point. Energy is wasted and occupants in both spaces are uncomfortable. Methodical checking of each control device in commissioning can prevent problems like this. However, without commissioning, control problems like this often persist for years without resolution.

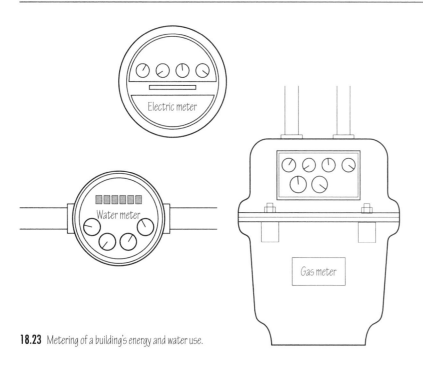

18.23 Metering of a building's energy and water use.

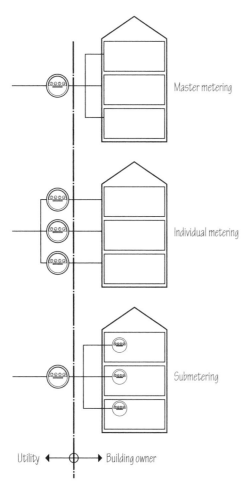

18.24 Metering options.

Training and Documentation

The commissioning provider ensures that the owner is trained in the correct and efficient use of the building's energy systems. The commissioning provider also ensures that the owner has and understands the documentation of all the building's energy systems, including operation and maintenance manuals, equipment warranties, as-built drawings, and control sequences.

Follow-up Testing and Monitoring

Commissioning can include follow-up testing some months after the building has been put into service to ensure that all systems are still operating as designed. Commissioning can also include monitoring, such as continuous temperature and humidity measurement, infrared thermography to ensure continuity of the thermal envelope, blower door tests to assess airtightness, and surveys for occupant feedback and thermal comfort.

Metering and Metrics

Metering

Metering of a building's energy use can be used to obtain information to ensure a green building's efficient operation. Metering choices can also significantly impact a building's energy use over its life. In any discussion of metering, it should be recalled what is not measured, such as embodied energy, and the associated impact of design decisions on such nonmeasured quantities.

Metering can be used as a form of monitoring and so can form the basis for feedback to the owner, operator, and design professionals. Programs such as the EPA Portfolio Manager allow a building's utility use to be tracked and compared to other buildings through the process known as benchmarking.

There are many options available for metering. The most common form of metering is done by the local utility and so may be referred to as utility metering. The most common energy flows that are metered are electricity and natural gas. Water metering is also typically done by a water utility or authority if the water is not provided by a well. A single utility meter for a building or complex is known as a master meter. Metering with multiple utility meters, each serving a tenant within a building, for example, is known as individual metering. When a single master meter is provided by a utility but the building owner then performs separate metering of tenants on that meter, it is referred to as submetering.

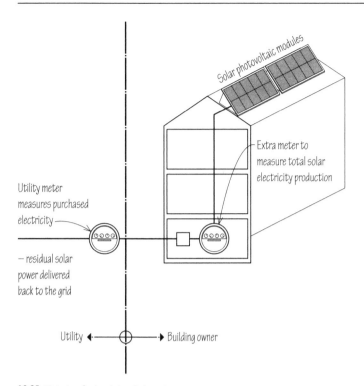

18.25 Metering of solar photovoltaic systems.

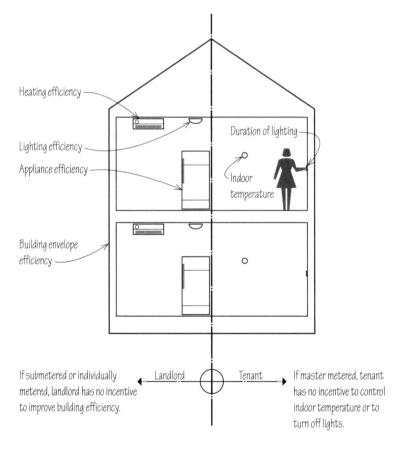

18.26 The split incentive.

For green buildings, further metering can allow feedback that is useful for gauging consistent performance of the building and providing early warning of any problems. These include the use of water meters on systems that should not be consuming water, such as closed boiler/hydronic systems, and where the measurement of water consumption will serve as a warning of water leaks. Metering of electricity from renewable systems, such as solar photovoltaic and wind systems, also can be used to ensure correct operation and to prevent persistence of a failure that might otherwise be undetected if a building continues to receive electricity from the grid.

Tenant submetering of electricity by a landlord is another option, as is submetering other energy flows, including natural gas, hot and cold water, and steam.

Metering can also guide behavior to conserve energy. The classic view is that if, for example, the tenants pay the utility bill, they will be less inclined to waste energy. Unfortunately, a simple shift of metering from landlord to tenants, whether through utility individual metering or through submetering, can have the unintended consequence of removing incentives for the landlord to maintain and improve the building's energy infrastructure. This is referred to as the split incentive.

For example, in an apartment building, the tenants control how long the lights are left on but the landlord controls what types of light fixtures are in a building. If the building is master metered, the landlord has an incentive to maintain and upgrade the light fixtures to more efficient fixtures but the tenants have no incentive to turn off the lights when not in use. If the building is individually metered, the landlord has no incentive to upgrade the light fixtures to more efficient fixtures but the tenants are more likely to turn off the lights when not in use. Individual metering also results in higher overall utility costs due to the multiple monthly meter charges unrelated to energy use. There is no simple answer to the split incentive issue. Perhaps, over time, approaches will be developed to resolve this problem. Meanwhile, we should not assume that individual metering or submetering is necessarily greener than master metering.

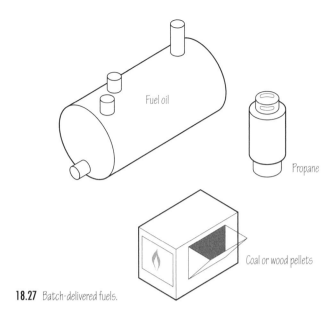

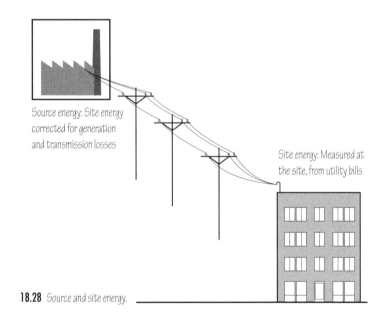

A different form of metering is through the delivery of bulk fuels—heating fuel oil, propane, kerosene, coal, and biofuels, such as wood, pellets, and wood chips. This measurement has important differences from the metering of electricity, water, and natural gas. Most pronounced is the fact that these fuels are measured before they are consumed, whereas electricity, water, and natural gas are measured as they are consumed, which is equivalent to being measured after consumption. Bulk fuel deliveries, often referred to as batch deliveries, can be less frequent, which can mean that the use of the deliveries for tracking energy use is more sporadic and more difficult to be used for energy consumption feedback. Deliveries by multiple vendors can confuse the issue and make tracking more difficult. If a tank is not completely filled, for example, then the actual subsequent consumption over the ensuing period before the next delivery is not known. Furthermore, disaggregation of use—for example, wintertime space heating versus summertime hot water use—is also more difficult with bulk deliveries. In short, the consumption and tracking of bulk fuels presents additional challenges when used for monitoring and feedback purposes.

Metrics

Various metrics may be applied to green buildings.

Site energy, sometimes called secondary energy, or delivered energy, is energy used by a building, typically as measured by utility meters onsite, or by deliveries of batch fuels such as oil or propane. In other words, site energy use is what is reported on the building's energy bills.

Source energy, sometimes called primary energy, is energy used by a building, with a correction for energy used in generating or harvesting the fuel, and transporting it to a building. To calculate source energy, we apply a large correction factor to electricity bought from the electric grid. Smaller corrections are used for other fuels. Source energy is viewed as most closely reflecting the overall environmental impact of energy use. The correction factors vary by geographic location and over time, as they represent the local and current mix of fuels used to generate electricity and harvest and transport fuels.

Different codes, standards, and guidelines use either source or site energy, and some use both.

18.27 Batch-delivered fuels.

18.28 Source and site energy.

18.29 U.S. national-average correction factors for converting site energy to source energy.

Energy Source	Source-to-Site Ratio
Electricity	3.340
Natural gas	1.047
Propane	1.010
#2 fuel oil	1.000

18.30 A summary of conversion factors used for common fuels.

	Units	Factor to Obtain Site kBtu	Factor to Obtain Pounds of Source CO$_2$ Emissions
Electricity	kWh	3.4	3.2
Natural gas	therms	100.0	12.2
Propane	gallons	92.5	13.0
#2 fuel oil	gallons	135.0	21.7

As an example, a 1,625-square-foot (150 m^2), high-performance building uses 540 therms of natural gas per year, and 5,390 kWh/year in electricity. Its site EUI is calculated as:

540 therms/year x 100 kBtu/therm = 54,000 kBtu/year
5390 kWh/year x 3.4 kBtu/kWh = 18,326 kBtu/year
(54,000+18,326)/1625 = 44.5 kBtu/SF/year

This compares favorably to the 2010 U.S. average of 107.7 kBtu/SF/year for commercial buildings. This high-performance building is using almost 60% less energy than the national average.

The United States Environmental Protection Agency (EPA), in its online database program called Portfolio Manager, uses source energy based on national-average corrections for each fuel and electricity to obtain source energy from site energy. The units of consumption of fossil fuels, such as therms of natural gas, or gallons of oil or propane, and electricity in kilowatt-hours are all converted into kBtu (thousands of Btu) and then added together and divided by the building area to obtain kBtu/SF/year.

In its national databases for buildings, the United States Department of Energy (DOE) uses an energy utilization index (EUI), also expressed as kBtu/SF/year. Statistics are maintained for both site and source energy.

The energy utilization index is also referred to as energy use index, energy use intensity, energy usage intensity, or sometimes energy consumption intensity.

Passivhaus's requirement is a maximum of 120 kWh/m^2/year in source energy use. Passivhaus's heating and cooling design demand requirement is 15 kWh/m^2/year for each in-site energy use.

Such metrics come into play in discussions of net-zero buildings. Specifically, we need to clarify whether we are referring to net-zero site energy buildings or net-zero source energy buildings. The metrics are also the basis for discussing the relative energy efficiency of buildings.

Carbon emissions offer another measurement against which buildings can be compared, both in terms of operations (annual emissions) and in terms of one-time emissions as a result of embodied energy consumption captured in building materials. Units for carbon emissions are typically tons/year. Other units include pounds/year and internationally, kilograms/year and metric tons/year are used. The measurements most often refer to carbon dioxide (CO$_2$) emissions but sometimes they are used for equivalent emissions of pure carbon (C).

Energy costs ($/SF/year) are a sometimes useful folk quantification, being expressed in units more familiar to people than kBtu, kWh, or carbon emissions. $1/SF/year is low. $5/SF/year is high.

Metrics are also used for water consumption, such as Kgal/SF/year or gal/person/year.

Metrics for electric-generating renewable energy, such as wind and solar photovoltaic, are typically provided as kWh/year. These are subtracted from onsite electricity use in assessing a building's net energy usage, its energy utilization index, and its carbon emissions.

A building's energy utilization and carbon emissions can be expanded to include transportation use to and from a building.

As a measure of the energy efficiency of a building's envelope, the heating energy use of the building can be extracted from utility bills and calculated by examining seasonal use. A metric known as the heating slope is often calculated. Frequently, a correction for heating use is made based on a specific winter's weather conditions to correct for either a cold or mild winter.

Similarly, other metrics can be obtained by utility bill analysis, such as air-conditioning use and baseload (nonheating and noncooling) use for different fuels.

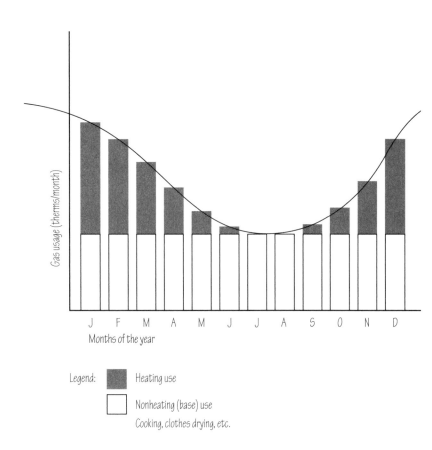

Legend:
Heating use
Nonheating (base) use
Cooking, clothes drying, etc.

18.31 Calculating heating use.

Values and Tradeoffs

Designing green buildings requires many decisions. These decisions are inextricably woven into the hundreds and sometimes thousands of decisions that need to be made to design and construct any building.

Most of the green building decisions involve prioritizing improvements to a building that make it greener, use less energy, reduce other impacts on the environment, and improve the built environment in myriad ways for the benefit of human health. Thicker wall insulation is an improvement. Fewer or smaller windows are an improvement. Bike racks are an improvement. Solar energy systems are an improvement. Sustainably harvested wood and low-VOC paints and reflective walls are improvements. The number of potential improvements is many. How can we prioritize these many improvements?

Energy improvements may be easier to prioritize because we can project savings and estimated construction costs. We therefore have a variety of performance metrics against which different energy improvements can be compared.

An old but still widely used energy improvement metric is the simple payback, which is the estimated added construction cost divided by the estimated annual savings of an improvement. For example, if added wall insulation is estimated to cost $2,000 and the insulation is projected to save $200/year, the payback period is 2,000/200 or ten years. Lower paybacks are better. The payback, however, cannot account for the expected life of the improvement. Wall insulation might have an expected life of 50 years but a similar lighting improvement, such as an efficient lamp, arbitrarily with the same simple payback of ten years, may only have an expected life of five years. The simple payback is not able to tell us that the added wall insulation makes more sense because it lasts longer. Thus the payback is increasingly viewed as being too simplistic.

Another group of metrics falls under the general term "life-cycle costing," which can account for such factors as the expected life of the improvement and any expected inflation in fuel cost. The future energy savings are aggregated and transformed into an equivalent present value using generally accepted economic principles and compared to the added investment. This approach results in any one of several metrics, including net life-cycle cost, savings-to-investment ratio (SIR), or return on investment (ROI).

Increasingly, carbon emissions are being used as a metric, and this can also account for the embodied energy effects of different design options.

In this book, we have discussed many approaches that reduce construction cost, including reducing floor area and using simpler building shapes, advanced framing techniques, reflective interior surface finishes that allow fewer light fixtures and fewer windows for daylighting, smaller or fewer windows, and linear lighting fixtures. These improvements make immediate financial sense, their payback is zero, and their return on investment is infinite. Therefore, these improvements may deserve early evaluation and higher priority.

As previously mentioned, in prioritizing energy improvements, building efficiency improvements should generally be assessed before renewable energy because of the still-high cost of renewable technologies and the associated embodied energy and use of materials to make the renewable energy products themselves. Still, there is no harm evaluating renewable energy alongside building efficiency improvements, as long as efficiency improvements are not ignored.

A major set of decisions arise when we move beyond energy improvements and evaluate nonenergy improvements. What is more important, a $100 investment in energy efficiency or a $100 investment in low-VOC paints? A case can be made that as long as the specter of climate change hangs over us, improvements that reduce carbon emissions deserve higher priority. Others might prioritize human health first. LEED implicitly advocates balance in green building improvements. Other codes, standards, and guidelines prioritize reductions in energy use and carbon emissions reduction.

Several criteria are perhaps worth deemphasizing as we select green building improvements:

- Visibility. Sometimes, it seems that green building improvements are chosen for their visibility or conspicuousness but we make the case that visibility should have a low priority.
- Status. Like visibility, some green building improvements, visible or not, appear to be favored for the status they confer on a building.
- Vendor-driven improvements. Many equipment or construction material vendors approach owners directly with a sales pitch. While vendors should be a part of the overall discussion and their voices should have currency in the conversation, their voices should not dominate in selecting improvements.

It should be noted that government incentives, such as tax credits or deductions for energy efficiency or renewable energy, intrinsically form part of the prioritization process. The government can support emerging technologies and use incentives to reflect and promote the societal benefit of green buildings. It is interesting to note that, similar to green standards, government incentives generally favor improvements that add to a building (for example, add insulation or add solar energy) rather than support economy and modesty, improvements that reduce load rather than add efficiency. Government incentives nonetheless can play a vital role in reducing the pollution from buildings that is harmful to all of society.

In prioritizing green building improvements, we keep returning to the definition of a green building—a green building is one that has a substantially reduced impact on the natural environment and that provides indoor conditions conducive to good human health. The exploration of values that arises when we prioritize green building improvements leads to more questions: Are green buildings desirable for all? Should green building standards be voluntary? Should green energy standards be above-code, or should we raise our energy code to reflect a shared consensus for what is green and important in buildings? If human health is one aspect of green buildings, why are these standards not mandatory, or in other words, written into our construction code? Many of these questions will form an important part of the discussion of green buildings in coming years.

One thing is certain: We must move beyond green buildings as demonstrations, or as trophies, or as tokens of our interest in the environment. The urgency for reducing climate emissions is too great for green buildings to remain limited to a small portion of our building stock. We must take our collective experience and use it toward making green design a part of all design. Quality in design and construction is an important means to this end.

18.32 Prioritizing improvements.

	Energy Use	Material Use/ Embodied Energy	Construction Cost	Environmental Quality
Smaller building	○	○	○	○
Simpler shape	○	○	○	○
Lower window-to-wall ratio	○	◑	○	○
Reflective surfaces	○	○	◑	○
More insulation	○	●	●	○
High-efficiency HVAC	○	●	●	○
Solar energy	○	●	●	○
Rainwater harvesting	○	●	●	○

○ Strongly supports

◑ Partially supports

● Does not support

19
Conclusion

Green Buildings and Beauty

Beauty has great importance in building design. This holds true in green building design and, in some ways, may be even more important. As green building design professionals, we may have to hold ourselves to a high standard to demonstrate that we will not sacrifice beauty as we strive for greener buildings.

19.01 Beauty: The quality or combination of qualities that pleases the aesthetic senses, gives deep satisfaction to the mind, or uplifts the human spirit.

19.02 Beauty for buildings should be more than skin deep.
Casa del Fascio, Giuseppe Terragni, 1931–1933

Why must buildings be beautiful? Beauty brings calm. Beauty brings pride. Beauty brings a sense of order. Beauty can facilitate our connection with nature. Beauty speaks to the great possibilities of finding harmony within and between ourselves and with the world. We leave any further defense of beauty to the poets. We proceed with the assumption that beauty is important.

Beauty is also often in the eye of the beholder. In reflecting on old and new views of beauty, we might add another criterion to the mix—the beauty of building performance. Perhaps a building that uses little energy is beautiful. A building that does not have ice dams hanging off its roof in winter is beautiful. A building that is quiet is beautiful. All of these are characteristics of high-performance green buildings. Beauty for buildings should be more than skin deep.

Green design brings with it new components, such as solar panels, that need to be aesthetically integrated into buildings. For many of us, these components are a thing of beauty, but this may not be the case for all. As design professionals, we need to ensure that these components are integrated in an aesthetically balanced fashion.

Green design will likely change the way buildings look. We have suggested a variety of building shape simplifications that reduce energy and material use. These simplifications, to some, might feel constraining. However, they could also direct our creativity to a new green aesthetic, new forms, and new shapes. We seek to add form to function, rather than function to form. Rather than seeing this as a constraint, we suggest that this may be a glorious opportunity for creativity, as we engage building design on a foundation of high-performance using the vast tools of beauty, such as color, patterns, texture, balance, proportion, and shape.

19.03 Add form to function rather than function to form.

Green Buildings and Nature

In considering building design, it is informative to return to our initial discussions of the natural forces from which buildings provide shelter—sun; air (wind, air leakage, drafts); water (rain, surface water, subsurface water, and humidity); animal life (insects, rodents, birds, and others); temperature extremes; and contaminants (dirt, dust, mud, and airborne pollutants). It is vital to recognize these forces, to respect them, to honor them. The site and building design can work to not only enhance the layers of shelter, and so improve protection from these elements, but also to offer ways in which building occupants can choose contact with the natural world.

Rather than promoting artificial contact with nature through building weaknesses, such as the large windows through which people simply look outdoors, the design professional can seek deeper ways in which to promote these connections on the site with all the tools of landscaping—vegetation, water, views, paths, fences, outdoor furniture, structures such as gazebos and pergolas, and even unusual features like mazes and tree-houses. Perhaps the site can emphasize the sun with a sundial or water with a pool. Even urban buildings offer endless possibilities for meaningful, if modest, connections to nature.

19.04 Connect with the natural world.

We speculate that some aspects of building design have attempted to meet people's vital need to connect with nature indoors. Vaulted spaces may give us a sense that we are outdoors under an open sky, unconstrained by a ceiling. Large rooms likewise offer the spaciousness to simulate the outdoors. Windows and glazed doors intentionally give us views to the outdoors and natural light from the outdoors. However, when these characteristics are taken to extremes, we suggest that they can result in artificial connections with nature, which can ultimately hurt the natural world with which we seek to connect, by polluting it and depleting it through overuse of energy and materials.

Nature presents its vastness as a paradox for people. People need protection from the forces of nature, but people as deeply also need a connection to nature, even for the hardened urbanites among us. Buildings can support meeting both needs, to protect and to connect. But, historically, our hole-ridden, moisture-laden, oversized, overlit, overglazed and energy-intensive buildings have provided neither adequate protection from nature nor adequate connection to nature. We are beginning to do better. Greener buildings offer the promise of greater protection from temperature extremes and the other forces of nature, with less pollution, greater comfort, and a greater connection to the beauty of nature.

19.04 *Choose contact with the natural world.*

Closing

The specter of the many impacts of climate change and other environmental threats calls for a new architecture, a green architecture. Energy use relating to buildings has been identified both as a major cause of greenhouse gas emissions and as a major opportunity to reduce these emissions. We in the design and construction field face a choice, to either bear the responsibility for climate change impacts from buildings or to lead the change that is necessary to mitigate the impacts of buildings on climate change.

The need for green buildings is moving beyond being a fad or being optional. In coming years, it will likely become as essential as fire safety and other forms of life safety in buildings. And so there is an urgent need to move green buildings beyond demonstration, beyond the boutique, beyond serving as a status symbol and to, instead, draw the enterprise of green buildings within the very fabric of architecture, construction, and building ownership.

It is possible that the beginning of the green building movement in the United States marks the end of the frontier movement, where every prairie and every hill called to be explored and settled, and viewed for what it could be turned into rather than for what it simply was. The end of this seemingly open abundance may itself feel hard and constraining. But as the unique human spirit is so able and drawn to do, perhaps this end and this challenge can be turned into a glorious beginning. Instead of being the mirage of an endless but actually limited frontier, the reality of green buildings can be truly boundless.

LEED® 2009 Green Building Certification Program

For New Construction & Major Renovations
Available for optional use through June 1, 2015

Sustainable Sites (26 Possible Points)

SS Prerequisite 1 Construction Activity Pollution Prevention (Required)
SS Credit 1 Site Selection 1
SS Credit 2 Development Density & Community Connectivity 5
SS Credit 3 Brownfield Redevelopment 1
SS Credit 4.1 Alternative Transportation – Public Transportation Access 6
SS Credit 4.2 Alternative Transportation – Bicycle Storage & Changing Rooms 1
SS Credit 4.3 Alternative Transportation – Low Emitting & Fuel Efficient Vehicles 3
SS Credit 4.4 Alternative Transportation – Parking Capacity 2
SS Credit 5.1 Site Development – Protect or Restore Habitat 1
SS Credit 5.2 Site Development – Maximize Open Space 1
SS Credit 6.1 Stormwater Design – Quantity Control 1
SS Credit 6.2 Stormwater Design – Quality Control 1
SS Credit 7.1 Heat Island Effect – Non-Roof 1
SS Credit 7.2 Heat Island Effect – Roof 1
SS Credit 8 Light Pollution Reduction 1

Water Efficiency (10 Possible Points)

WE Prerequisite 1 Water Use Reduction—20% Reduction (Required)
WE Credit 1 Water Efficient Landscaping 4
WE Credit 2 Innovative Wastewater Technologies 2
WE Credit 3 Water Use Reduction 4

Energy & Atmosphere (35 Possible Points)

EA Prerequisite 1 Fundamental Commissioning of the Building Energy Systems (Required)
EA Prerequisite 2 Minimum Energy Performance (Required)
EA Prerequisite 3 Fundamental Refrigerant Management (Required)
EA Credit 1 Optimize Energy Performance 19
EA Credit 2 On-Site Renewable Energy 7
EA Credit 3 Enhanced Commissioning 2
EA Credit 4 Enhanced Refrigerant Management 2
EA Credit 5 Measurement & Verification 3
EA Credit 6 Green Power 2

Materials & Resources (14 Possible Points)

MR Prerequisite 1 Storage & Collection of Recyclables (Required)
MR Credit 1.1 Building Reuse – Maintain Existing Walls, Floors and Roof 3
MR Credit 1.2 Building Reuse – Maintain Existing Interior Nonstructural Elements 1
MR Credit 2 Construction Waste Management 2
MR Credit 3 Materials Reuse 2
MR Credit 4 Recycled Content 2
MR Credit 5 Regional Materials 2
MR Credit 6 Rapidly Renewable Materials 1
MR Credit 7 Certified Wood 1

Indoor Environmental Quality (15 Possible Points)

EQ Prerequisite 1 Minimum Indoor Air Quality (IAQ) Performance (Required)
EQ Prerequisite 2 Environmental Tobacco Smoke (ETS) Control (Required)
EQ Credit 1 Outdoor Air Delivery Monitoring 1
EQ Credit 2 Increased Ventilation 1
EQ Credit 3.1 Construction IAQ Management Plan, During Construction 1
EQ Credit 3.2 Construction IAQ Management Plan, Before Occupancy 1
EQ Credit 4.1 Low-Emitting Materials – Adhesives & Sealants 1
EQ Credit 4.2 Low-Emitting Materials – Paints & Coatings 1
EQ Credit 4.3 Low-Emitting Materials – Flooring Systems 1
EQ Credit 4.4 Low-Emitting Materials – Composite Wood & Agrifiber Products 1
EQ Credit 5 Indoor Chemical & Pollutant Source Control 1
EQ Credit 6.1 Controllability of Systems – Lighting 1
EQ Credit 6.2 Controllability of Systems – Thermal Comfort 1
EQ Credit 7.1 Thermal Comfort – Design 1
EQ Credit 7.2 Thermal Comfort – Verification 1
EQ Credit 8.1 Daylight & Views – Daylight 1
EQ Credit 8.2 Daylight & Views – Views 1

Innovation & Design Process (6 Possible Points)

ID Credit 1 Innovation in Design 5
ID Credit 2 LEED Accredited Professional 1

Regional Priority (4 Possible Points)

RP Credit 1 Regional Priority 4

To receive LEED certification, a building project must meet certain prerequisites and performance benchmarks or credits within each category. Projects are awarded Certified, Silver, Gold, or Platinum certification depending on the number of credits they achieve.

- Certified 40–49 points
- Silver 50–59 points
- Gold 60–79 points
- Platinum 80 points and above

LEED® 4 Green Building Certification Program

For New Construction & Major Renovations
Introduced November 2013

Integrative Process

IP Credit 1 Integrative Process 1

Locations & Transportation (16 Possible Points)

LT Credit 1 LEED for Neighborhood Development Location 16 or
LT Credit 2 Sensitive Land Protection 1
LT Credit 3 High Priority Site 2
LT Credit 4 Surrounding Density & Diverse Uses 5
LT Credit 5 Access to Quality Transit 5
LT Credit 6 Bicycle Facilities 1
LT Credit 7 Reduced Parking Footprint 1
LT Credit 8 Green Vehicles 1

Sustainable Sites (10 Possible Points)

SS Prerequisite 1 Construction Activity Pollution Prevention (Required)
SS Credit 1 Site Assessment 1
SS Credit 2 Site Development – Protect or Restore Habitat 2
SS Credit 3 Open Space 1
SS Credit 4 Rainwater Management 3
SS Credit 5 Heat Island Reduction 2
SS Credit 6 Light Pollution Reduction 1

Water Efficiency (11 Possible Points)

WE Prerequisite 1 Outdoor Water Use Reduction (Required)
WE Prerequisite 2 Indoor Water Use Reduction (Required)
WE Prerequisite 3 Building-Level Water Metering (Required)
WE Credit 1 Outdoor Water Use Reduction 2
WE Credit 2 Indoor Water Use Reduction 6
WE Credit 3 Cooling Tower Water Use 2
WE Credit 4 Water Metering 1

Energy & Atmosphere (33 Possible Points)

EA Prerequisite 1 Fundamental Commissioning & Verification (Required)
EA Prerequisite 2 Minimum Energy Performance (Required)
EA Prerequisite 3 Building-Level Energy Metering (Required)
EA Prerequisite 4 Fundamental Refrigerant Management (Required)
EA Credit 1 Enhanced Commissioning 6
EA Credit 2 Optimize Energy Performance 18
EA Credit 3 Advanced Energy Metering 1
EA Credit 4 Demand Response 2
EA Credit 5 Renewable Energy Production 3
EA Credit 6 Enhanced Refrigerant Management 1
EA Credit 7 Green Power & Carbon Offsets 2

Materials & Resources (13 Possible Points)

MR Prequisite 1 Storage & Collection of Recyclables (Required)
MR Prequisite 2 Construction and Demolition Waste Management Planning (Required)
MR Credit 1 Building Life-Cycle Impact Reduction 5
MR Credit 2 Building Product Disclosure & Optimization – Environmental Product Declarations 2
MR Credit 3 Building Product Disclosure & Optimization – Sourcing of Raw Materials 2
MR Credit 4 Building Product Disclosure & Optimization – Material Ingredients 2
MR Credit 5 Construction & Demolition Waste Management 2

Indoor Environmental Quality (16 Possible Points)

EQ Prequisite 1 Minimum Indoor Air Quality Performance (Required)
EQ Prequisite 2 Environmental Tobacco Smoke Control (Required)
EQ Credit 1 Enhanced Indoor Air Quality Strategies 2
EQ Credit 2 Low-Emitting Materials 3
EQ Credit 3 Construction Indoor Air Quality Management Plan 1
EQ Credit 4 Indoor Air Quality Assessment 2
EQ Credit 5 Thermal Comfort 1
EQ Credit 6 Interior Lighting 2
EQ Credit 7 Daylight 3
EQ Credit 8 Quality Views 1
EQ Credit 9 Acoustic Performance 1

Innovation (6 Possible Points)

I Credit 1 Innovation 5
I Credit 2 LEED Accredited Professional 1

Regional Priority (4 Possible Points)

RP Credit 1 Regional Priority: Specific Credit 1
RP Credit 2 Regional Priority: Specific Credit 1
RP Credit 3 Regional Priority: Specific Credit 1
RP Credit 4 Regional Priority: Specific Credit 1

To receive LEED certification, a building project must meet certain prerequisites and performance benchmarks or credits within each category. Projects are awarded Certified, Silver, Gold, or Platinum certification depending on the number of credits they achieve.

· Certified 40–49 points
· Silver 50–59 points
· Gold 60–79 points
· Platinum 80 points and above

Glossary

ACH Abbreviation for air changes per hour, a measure of infiltration. ACH50 represents the infiltration rate when a building has been pressurized or depressurized to 50 Pascals air pressure, typically in a blower door test. ACHn represents an estimate of the natural time-average infiltration rate.

advanced framing Framing techniques that reduce thermal bridging and material use.

air barrier A membrane, sheet, or other component intended to reduce infiltration; air barriers may or may not be vapor permeable.

air-conditioning The process of altering the properties of air, primarily temperature and humidity, to more favorable conditions.

air handler A device incorporating a fan and one or more heat exchangers, which delivers heating and/or cooling to a system of ductwork for distribution to a building.

air source heat pump A heat pump that draws or rejects heat to the outdoor air; see geothermal heat pump.

albedo The ratio of reflected solar energy to incoming solar energy over wavelengths of approximately 0.3 to 2.5 micrometers. Also known as solar reflectance.

area ratio The ratio of the surface area of a building to its floor area.

artificial light Light delivered by light fixtures, typically by consuming electricity.

Basis of Design A document prepared by design professionals that describes the building design assumptions; used for quality control to ensure consistency between the Owner's Project Requirements, the construction documents, and construction.

benchmarking The process of comparing energy and water use between a building and similar buildings, utilizing such metrics as the energy use index.

boiler A device that heats hot water or produces steam from water.

boiler/tower heat pump system A heating/cooling system that uses a main water loop; heat pumps piped to this loop to deliver heating or cooling to spaces in a building; a boiler that delivers heat to the loop and the building if there is a net deficiency of heat; and a cooling tower that rejects heat from the loop and the building if there is a net deficiency of cooling.

breathing zone The space around people from which people draw air to breathe; important to reach with fresh, ventilating air.

brownfield A site that has been contaminated.

building performance A broad descriptor of a building's ability to meet goals of efficient energy and water use, as well as those for comfort, environmental, and durability.

certified wood Wood from trees that are certified to have been harvested and processed in environmentally sensitive ways, typically under the guidance of the Forest Stewardship Council (FSC), complying with sustainable forestry practices, protecting trees, wildlife habitat, streams, and soil.

chiller A mechanical device that produces chilled water, which is in turn used for air-conditioning via air handlers or fan coils; see direct expansion system.

climate change The long-term change in atmospheric air temperatures and associated impacts, such as the melting of polar caps. Climate change is attributed to human activities, such as the large-scale combustion of fossil fuels, releasing hydrocarbon chemicals, and the interaction of such combustion products and chemicals with the atmosphere.

cogeneration The simultaneous generation of electricity and heat in a process that can be far more efficient than just generating electricity. Also referred to as combined heat and power or CHP.

commissioning A process for verifying that aspects of a building that consume energy, impact energy consumption, or affect indoor environmental quality are working properly. It is a holistic process that serves as the primary vehicle for quality control in building design and construction, from the initial definition of the Owner's Project Requirements to verifying the performance of the building after construction.

compartmentalization The physical separation of areas of a building to reduce unwanted airflow between these areas.

continuity A property of the thermal boundary that prevents sites for infiltration and thermal bridging.

cooling tower A device that rejects heat from buildings to the outdoor air. Cooling towers typically are used as part of a chiller system or a boiler/tower heat pump system. They serve the same function as the well-field in geothermal systems or the outdoor units in split-system heat pumps or air-conditioners but cannot serve as a source of heat.

daylight Light from the sun used for illuminating the indoors during the daytime.

demand-controlled ventilation A control approach to limiting ventilation airflow and thereby reducing energy use when the maximum quantity of airflow is not needed. It is most commonly applied on the basis of carbon dioxide as a surrogate measurement of human occupancy but other quantities, such as the humidity in spaces having significant moisture sources, can alternatively be used. It can also be applied by simply opening and closing operable windows.

dense pack insulation Insulation blown into a wall cavity or other building cavity under pressure to prevent void spaces and provide resistance both to heat flow and air movement.

design for deconstruction Planning for the eventual reuse of building materials when a proposed new building reaches the end of its own life.

direct expansion system A system for delivering conditioned air directly to an airstream from a vapor compression mechanical system rather than by first cooling water. See chiller. The system is used in many types of common air-conditioners, including room air-conditioners, split-system air-conditioners, most heat pumps, and packaged rooftop systems.

distribution losses The unproductive loss of energy from piping and ductwork in heating/cooling and hot water systems, typically when such distribution systems are routed through unconditioned spaces or outdoors. The term includes heat conduction losses, air leakage losses, and water or steam leakage.

disturbance boundary The area of a site that is disturbed during construction.

drip irrigation Irrigation using the controlled and slow delivery of water directly to individual plants through a network of tubes or pipes. Also called trickle irrigation.

dual flush toilet A toilet that uses a lower amount of water for flushing liquid waste, and a higher/typical amount of water for flushing solid waste.

embodied energy The energy used to harvest, process, and transport materials and building products.

energy model Any of various computer simulations that predict a building's energy use.

energy use index (EUI) The total annual energy use of a building divided by the building floor area. EUI is used for benchmarking and for tracking progress toward lower or zero energy use.

fan coil A small air handler, typically without ductwork.

forced air A system comprising an air handler and ductwork to convey heated, cooled, and/or ventilation air to spaces in a building.

fossil fuel A hydrocarbon fuel, such as natural gas, oil, and coal, derived over millions of years from the decomposition of living organisms.

full cutoff luminaire A light fixture that emits no light above the horizontal plane and limits light intensity within 10 degrees below that plane to 100 candela per 1,000 lamp lumens. Typically, the lamp is not visible at all when the fixture is viewed horizontally.

fully shielded luminaire A light fixture that emits no light above the horizontal plane. This type of luminaire is not as restrictive as a full cutoff luminaire because there is no limit on light within 10 degrees below horizontal.

furnace A device that heats forced air.

geothermal heat pump A heat pump that draws heat from the ground to heat a building or rejects heat to the ground to cool a building. See air source heat pump.

global warming potential A measure of a material's or a system's deleterious contribution to global warming; most commonly applied to refrigerants and other chemicals.

gray water Wastewater from sinks, showers, and washing machines that can be collected and treated for reuse, such as the flushing of toilets or watering of landscape, or from which heat can be recovered for use in a building.

green building A building that has a substantially reduced impact on the natural environment and that provides indoor conditions conducive to good human health.

greenfield Previously undeveloped areas. The term may also refer to previously cleared, farmed, or forested lands.

greensplashing The design of buildings that are nominally green or even certified to be green but are inefficient because of their excessive surface or window area, use of too much artificial light for show, or a single, conspicuous green improvement.

greenwashing An artificial claim to being green.

greyfield A previously developed area, uncontaminated but with a visible residue of development.

hardscape Paved areas, such as streets and sidewalks, where the upper soil profile is no longer exposed to the atmosphere.

heat island effect The absorption and retention of incoming solar radiation, resulting in local temperature increases.

heat pump A device that transports heat from one body, such as the ground or outdoor air, to another body, such as the air inside a building, in a process that is reversible.

heat recovery The process of extracting heat from one flow, such as the exhaust air from a building, to heat another flow, such as the intake air for building ventilation from the outdoors in winter.

HERS Index   Home Energy Rating System Index: a standard by which a home's energy efficiency is measured. A score of 0 represents a net-zero energy home; a score of 100 represents a standard new home; and a score of 150 represents a home that is expected to use 50% more energy than a standard new home.

hydronic system   A hot water system used for space heating.

indoor air quality   The overall measure or absence of indoor airborne contaminants, such as particles, tobacco smoke, carbon dioxide, hazardous chemicals, odors, humidity, and biological contaminants.

indoor environmental quality   The aggregate quality of the indoor environment, encompassing indoor air quality, thermal comfort, noise and acoustic conditions, and water quality.

infiltration   The exchange of air between the outdoors and the interior of a building.

inner envelope   The inner shell of a building, including such components as the attic floor, basement ceiling, and inner walls of unconditioned spaces; components that are in contact with conditioned indoor space.

insulated concrete forms (ICF)   A system of formwork for reinforced concrete consisting of modular, interlocking units of rigid insulation.

integrated design   A collaborative approach in which a broad group of stakeholders, such as the architect, engineer, owner, building occupants, and more, are holistically involved in a project from early in the design process.

layer of shelter   A building component that protects against loads.

LEED®   Leadership in Energy and Environmental Design, a green building certification program.

load   An outdoor element, such as temperature, that exerts stress on a building.

light pollution   The introduction of undesirable artificial light into the outdoors.

light spillage   The unwanted spread of artificial light from the indoors to the outdoors.

light trespass   The unwanted spread of artificial light from one property to another.

luminaire   Light fixture.

motion sensor   A device that controls lights automatically by sensing motion. Also called occupancy sensor.

manual-on motion sensor   A motion sensor that only automatically turns off a light, and requires that the light be turned on manually. Also called vacancy sensor.

motion sensor off-delay   The time period after motion is no longer sensed during which a light stays on before automatically turning off the light. The delay should preferably be set as short as possible.

net zero   The ability of a building to require zero externally provided energy or to not release carbon emissions. Net zero can refer to a variety of different energy consumption or carbon emissions metrics.

outer envelope   The outer shell of a building, including such components as the walls, windows, doors, roof, and foundation; components that are in contact with outside air or the ground.

outside air   Air brought in from the outdoors for ventilation.

Owner's Project Requirements   A document that sets forth the building owner's goals and details about the anticipated building use. The details provided in this document can significantly impact green building design.

passive solar   The harvesting of solar heat without the use of mechanical or electrical systems, such as pumps or fans.

perimeter depth   The depth of perimeter spaces of a building, i.e., the room length perpendicular to the outside wall.

pervious surfaces   Surfaces on a site that allow onsite percolation of water down into the subsoil, including pervious pavers, porous asphalt, pervious concrete, and vegetated landscapes.

postconsumer recycled materials   Materials obtained from the waste generated by end users, which is recycled into the raw material of new products.

preconsumer recycled materials   Materials diverted from the waste stream during manufacturing.

previously developed site   A term used to indicate a site that is not a greenfield but is neither a known greyfield nor a brownfield.

rainwater harvesting   An approach to capturing and using rainwater, typically including a collection area; a conveyance system to route the rainwater to storage; a storage tank; filtering and possibly disinfection treatment; a backup system to provide water for times of low rainwater; provision for overflow; and a distribution system to deliver the water to the water loads.

rapidly renewable   A term describing materials that grow naturally and can be harvested in a short number of years. For example, LEED defines the period as ten years.

reflectance   The ratio of light reflected by a surface to the light that is incident to the surface.

renewable energy   Energy that is provided by renewable sources, such as the sun or the wind.

roof receptivity A property of roofs for supporting the installation of solar energy systems, including such characteristics as freedom from obstructions, contiguous area, unshaded area, orientation to the equator, and adequate structural support.

sensitive site A site that should be protected from development, typically defined to include such areas as prime farmland, parkland, flood hazard areas, habitat for endangered or threatened species, primary dunes, old-growth forests, wetlands, other water bodies, and conservation areas.

sidelighting Daylighting provided by windows on the side of a building.

solar photovoltaic system A system for generating electrical energy from solar radiation using semiconductors that exhibit the photovoltaic effect.

solar thermal system A system that converts sunlight into heat, either for heating water or for heating air.

stack effect The buoyancy-driven flow of air up through a building in winter.

structural insulated panel (SIP) A prefabricated assembly comprising a rigid insulation core sandwiched between two layers of structural board and combining the functions of structure, insulation, and air barrier. SIPs are most often used for walls but they may also be used as floors and roofs.

sustainability The property of things that last.

thermal boundary Surfaces along which insulation is routed around a building.

thermal comfort That condition of mind which expresses satisfaction with the thermal environment. It is characterized primarily by the absence of discomfort due to high or low air temperature, humidity, or airflow, although it may also be influenced by other factors, such as surface temperatures, activity level, and clothing level.

thermal bridging The loss of heat from the building interior to the outdoors by means of conduction through solid building materials, bypassing the insulation layer.

thermal zoning A heating/cooling design approach by which different areas of a building are provided with separate temperature controls.

thermal zoning diagram A construction drawing that delineates different thermal zones on a floor plan.

toplighting Daylighting supplied from the ceiling of a space through skylights or roof monitors.

unconditioned space A space that is neither heated nor cooled.

vapor barrier A membrane, sheet, or other component intended to prevent the migration of moisture through the building envelope.

variable refrigerant flow heat pump A heat pump with a variable speed compressor.

variable speed drive A motor control that varies the rotational speed of an alternating current (AC) electric motor by controlling the frequency of the electric power supplied to the motor. Typically used on larger, three-phase, motors. The term encompasses variable frequency drives (VFD), adjustable frequency drives (AFD), or adjustable speed drives (ASD).

vegetated roof A roof partially or wholly covered in vegetation that is installed over a waterproof membrane. Also called green or living roof.

ventilation The provision of outdoor air into a building. The term is sometimes more loosely used to include the exhaust of air from a building or the use of outdoor air for cooling.

ventilation effectiveness The portion of ventilation airflow that actually reaches the building occupants. Zero percent ventilation effectiveness means no outdoor air reaches occupants, whereas 100% ventilation effectiveness means that all the outdoor air reaches occupants.

volatile organic compound (VOC) Any compound of carbon (with some exceptions, such as carbon dioxide) that participates in atmospheric photochemical reactions. VOCs evaporate under normal indoor conditions and are undesirable as indoor air contaminants.

waterless urinal A urinal that does not require water, typically using an oil-based liquid seal in the drain to prevent odors from migrating back into the building.

window-to-wall ratio The ratio of the area of a facade that is occupied by the glass area and frame of windows.

wind turbine A device that converts wind energy into mechanical energy. When used with a generator, the system produces electricity.

Bibliography

Resources in the green building field are many and are growing rapidly. The following necessarily limited selection of books, reports, articles, standards, and web sites, most of which are primary sources, were found helpful in the preparation of this book and are recommended as potentially useful resources for professionals in the field.

American Society of Heating, Refrigerating and Air-Conditioning Engineers. 2010. *ANSI/ASHRAE Standard 55-2010 – Thermal Environmental Conditions for Human Occupancy.* Atlanta: ASHRAE.

American Society of Heating, Refrigerating and Air-Conditioning Engineers. 2010. *ANSI/ASHRAE Standard 62.1-2010 – Ventilation for Acceptable Indoor Air Quality.* Atlanta: ASHRAE.

American Society of Heating, Refrigerating and Air-Conditioning Engineers. 2010. *ANSI/ASHRAE Standard 62.2-2013 – Ventilation and Acceptable Indoor Air Quality in Low-Rise Residential Buildings.* Atlanta: ASHRAE.

American Society of Heating, Refrigerating and Air-Conditioning Engineers. 2013. *ANSI/ASHRAE/IES Standard 90.1-2013 – Energy Standard for Buildings Except Low-Rise Residential Buildings.* Atlanta: ASHRAE.

American Society of Heating, Refrigerating and Air-Conditioning Engineers. 2007. *ANSI/ASHRAE Standard 90.2-2007 – Energy-Efficient Design of Low-Rise Residential Buildings.* Atlanta: ASHRAE.

American Society of Heating, Refrigerating and Air-Conditioning Engineers. 2011. *ANSI/ASHRAE/USGBC/IES Standard 189.1-2011 Standard for the Design of High-Performance, Green Buildings (Except Low-Rise Residential Buildings).* Atlanta: ASHRAE.

American Society of Landscape Architects, the Lady Bird Johnson Wildflower Center at the University of Texas at Austin, and the United States Botanic Garden. 2009. *The Sustainable Sites Initiative: Guidelines and Performance Benchmarks.* Austin: The Sustainable Sites Initiative.

Anis, Wagdy. 2010. *Air Barrier Systems in Buildings.* Washington, DC: Whole Building Design Guide, National Institute of Building Sciences (NIBS). http://www.wbdg.org/resources/airbarriers.php. Accessed 10/12/13.

Athena Sustainable Materials Institute: www.athenasmi.org/

BREEAM. 2011. *BREEAM New Construction: Non-Domestic Buildings, Technical Manual, SD5073-2.0:2011.* Garston: BRE Global Ltd.

Brown, E.J. 2008. *Cost Comparisons for Common Commercial Wall Systems.* Winston-Salem: Capital Building Consultants.

Building Green, Inc. 2013. http://www.buildinggreen.com/. Accessed October 13, 2013.

Building Science Corporation. 2013. http://www.buildingscience.com/index_html. Accessed October 13, 2013.

California Stormwater Quality Association. 2003. *California Stormwater BMP Handbook*: Concrete Waste Management. Menlo Park: CASQA.

Carpet Institute of Australia Limited. 2011. *Light Reflectance.* Melbourne: CIAL.

Center for Rainwater Harvesting. 2006. http://www.thecenterforrainwaterharvesting.org/index.htm

Center for Neighborhood Technology. 2013. http://www.travelmatters.org/calculator/individual/methodology#pmt. Accessed October 13, 2013.

Ching, Francis D.K. 2007. *Architecture: Form, Space, and Order*, 3rd Edition. Hoboken: John Wiley & Sons.

Ching, Francis D.K. and Steven Winkel. 2009. *Building Codes Illustrated: A Guide to Understanding the 2009 International Building Code*, 3rd Edition. Hoboken: John Wiley & Sons.

D'Aloisio, James A. 2010. *Steel Framing and Building Envelopes.* Chicago: Modern Steel Construction.

D&R International, Ltd. 2011. *Buildings Energy Data Book.* Washington, DC: U.S. Department of Energy.

DeKay, Mark and Brown, G.Z. 2013. *Sun, Wind, & Light: Architectural Design Strategies*, 3rd Edition. Hoboken: John Wiley and Sons.

Durkin, Thomas H. *Boiler System Efficiency.* ASHRAE Journal. Page 51. Vol. 48, July 2006.

Efficient Windows Collaborative: www.efficientwindows.org/

Fox & Fowle Architects et al. 2005. *Battery Park City – Residential Environmental Guidelines.* New York: Hugh L. Carey Battery Park City Authority.

Green Building Initiative. 2013. *Green Globes for New Construction: Technical Reference Manual*, Version 1.1. Portland: GBI Inc.

Gruzen Hampton LLP and Hayden McKay Lighting Design Inc. 2006. *Manual for Quality, Energy Efficient Lighting.* New York: NY City Department of Design and Construction.

Hagenlocher, Esther. 2009. *Colorfulness and Reflectivity in Daylit Spaces.* Quebec City: PLEA2009 - 26th Conference on Passive and Low Energy Architecture.

Hernandez, Daniel, Matthew Lister, and Celine Suarez. 2011. *Location Efficiency and Housing Type*. US EPA's Smart Growth Program, contract #GS-10F-0410R. New York: Jonathan Rose Companies.

Heschong, Lisa. *Thermal Delight in Architecture*. 1979. Cambridge: MIT Press.

Higgins, Cathy et al. 2013. *Plug Load Savings Assessment: Part of the Evidence-based Design and Operations PIER Program*. Prepared for the California Energy Commission. Vancouver: New Buildings Institute.

Hodges, Tina. 2009. *Public Transportation's Role in Responding to Climate Change*. Washington, DC: U.S. Department of Transportation.

International Dark-Sky Association. 2013. http://www.darksky.org/. Accessed October 12, 2013.

International Living Future Institute. 2012. *Living Building Challenge 2.1*. Seattle: International Living Future Institute.

IPCC, 2012: Summary for Policymakers. In: *Managing the Risks of Extreme Events and Disasters to Advance Climate Change Adaptation* [Field, C.B., V. Barros, T.F. Stocker, D. Qin, D.J. Dokken, K.L. Ebi, M.D. Mastrandrea, K.J. Mach, G.-K. Plattner, S.K. Allen, M. Tignor, and P.M. Midgley (eds.)]. A Special Report of Working Groups I and II of the Intergovernmental Panel on Climate Change. Cambridge University Press, Cambridge, UK, and New York, NY, USA, pp. 1-19.

International Code Council. 2012. *International Building Code*. Washington, DC: ICC.

International Code Council. 2012. *International Energy Conservation Code*. Washington, DC: ICC.

International Code Council. 2012. *International Green Construction Code*. Washington, DC: ICC.

International Code Council. 2012. *International Mechanical Code*. Washington, DC: ICC.

Lemieux, Daniel J., and Paul E. Totten. 2010. Building Envelope Design Guide—Wall Systems. http://www.wbdg.org/design/env_wall.php. Last updated October 8, 2013.

Keeler, Marian, and Bill Burke. 2009. *Fundamentals of Integrated Design for Sustainable Building*. Hoboken: John Wiley & Sons.

Lstiburek, Joseph. 2004. *Vapor Barriers and Wall Design*. Somerville: Building Science Corporation.

Masonry Advisory Council. 2002. *Cavity Walls: Design Guide for Taller Cavity Walls*. Park Ridge: MAC.

Munch-Andersen, Jørgen. 2007. *Improving Thermal Insulation of Concrete Sandwich Panel Buildings*. Vienna: LCUBE Conference.

NAHB Research Center. 1994. *Frost-Protected Shallow Foundations, Phase II—Final Report*. Washington, DC: U.S. Department of Housing and Urban Development.

NAHB Research Center. 2000. *Advanced Wall Framing*. Washington, DC: U.S. Department of Energy.

National Renewable Energy Lab. 2002. *Energy Design Guidelines for High Performance Schools: Temperate and Humid Climates*. Washington, DC: U.S. Department of Energy's Office of Building Technology, State and Community Programs.

National Electrical Contractors Association. 2006. *Guide to Commissioning Lighting Controls*. Bethesda: NECA.

Newman, Jim et al. 2010. *The Cost of LEED: A Report on Cost Expectations to Meet LEED 2009 for New Construction and Major Renovations* (NC v2009). Brattleboro: BuildingGreen.

Newsham, Guy, Chantal Arsenault, Jennifer Veitch, Anna Maria Tosco, Cara Duval. 2005. *Task Lighting Effects on Office Worker Satisfaction and Performance, and Energy Efficiency*. Ottawa: Institute for Research in Construction, National Research Council Canada.

O'Connor, Jennifer, Eleanor Lee, Francis Rubinstein, and Stephen Selkowitz. 1997. *Tips for Daylighting with Windows*. Berkeley: Ernest Orlando Lawrence Berkeley National Laboratory.

Pless, Shanti, and Paul Torcellini. 2010. *Net-Zero Energy Buildings: A Classification System Based on Renewable Energy Supply Options*. Golden: National Renewable Energy Laboratory.

Rainwater Harvesting Group. 2013. Dallas: Texas A&M AgriLife Extension Service. http://rainwaterharvesting.tamu.edu/. Accessed October 13, 2013.

RESNET. 2006. *Mortgage Industry National Home Energy Rating Systems Standards*. Oceanside: Residential Energy Services Network, Inc.

Sachs, Harvey M. 2005. *Opportunities for Elevator Energy Efficiency Improvements*. Washington, DC: American Council for an Energy-Efficient Economy.

Selkowitz, S., R. Johnson, R. Sullivan, and S. Choi. 1983. *The Impact of Fenestration on Energy Use and Peak Loads in Daylighted Commercial Buildings*. Glorieta: National Passive Solar Conference.

Slone, Herbert. 2011. *Wall Systems for Steel Stud / Masonry Veneer*. Toledo: Owens Corning Foam Insulation LLC.

Smith, David Lee. 2011. *Environmental Issues for Architecture*. Hoboken: John Wiley & Sons.

Straube, John. 2008. *Air Flow Control in Buildings*: Building Science Digest 014. Boston: Building Science Press.

Tyler, Hoyt, Schiavon Stefano, Piccioli Alberto, Moon Dustin, and Steinfeld Kyle. 2013. *CBE Thermal Comfort Tool*. Berkeley: Center for the Built Environment, University of California Berkeley. http://cbe.berkeley.edu/comforttool/. Accessed October 12, 2013.

Ueno, Kohta. 2013. *Building Energy Performance Metrics*. http://www.buildingscience.com/documents/digests/bsd152-building-energy-performance-metrics. Accessed October 13, 2013.

Urban, Bryan, and Kurt Roth. 2010. *Guidelines for Selecting Cool Roofs*. Prepared by the Fraunhofer Center for Sustainable Energy Systems for the U.S. Department of Energy Building Technologies Program and Oak Ridge National Laboratory under contract DE-AC05-00OR22725.

U.S. Department of Energy, the Federal Energy Management Program, Lawrence Berkeley National Laboratory (LBNL), and the California Lighting Technology Center (CLTC) at the University of California, Davis. 2010. *Exterior Lighting Guide for Federal Agencies*. Washington, DC: Federal Energy Management Program.

United States Green Building Council. 2012. *LEED 2009 for New Construction and Major Renovations Rating System*. Washington, DC: USGBC.

U.S. Environmental Protection Agency. 2011. *ENERGY STAR Performance Ratings: Methodology for Incorporating Source Energy Use*. Washington, DC: EPA.

Wang, Fan, Theadore Hunt, Ya Liu, Wei Li, Simon Bell. 2003. *Reducing Space Heating in Office Buildings Through Shelter Trees*. Proceedings of CIBSE/ASHRAE Conference, Building Sustainability, Value & Profit. www.cibse.org/pdfs/8cwang.pdf.

Whole Building Design Guide. 2013. http://www.wbdg.org/. Accessed October 13, 2013.

Wilson, Alex. 2013. *Naturally Rot-Resistant Woods*. National Gardening Association. http://www.garden.org/articles/articles.php?q=show&id=977&page=1. Accessed October 13, 2013.

Wray, Paul, Laura Sternweis, and Jane Lenahan. 1997. *Farmstead Windbreaks: Planning*. Ames: Iowa State University — University Extension.

Zuluaga, Marc, Sean Maxwell, Jason Block, and Liz Eisenberg, Steven Winter Associates. 2010. *There are Holes in Our Walls*. New York: Urban Green Council.

7group and Bill Reed. 2009. *The Integrative Design Guide to Green Buildings*. Hoboken: John Wiley & Sons.

Index

benchmarking, 247

biofuels, 200

biological diversity, 7

biomass, 188, 199, 200

biomass-fueled systems, 196

biomimicry, 226

blinds, 74, 133

blower door, 85

boiler efficiency, 198

boiler/tower water loop heat pumps, 196, 200

boilers, 115, 188, 190, 192, 196

boundary, 35

boundary, thermal, 84, 170

break rooms, 186

breathing zones, 170, 177, 179

BREEAM, 29, 103, 157, 179

bridging, thermal, 88, 190

brownfields, 41

buffer zone, 40

building boundary, 35

building facade, 81

building operation, 174

building paper, 173

building performance, 11

Building Research Establishment Environmental
    Assessment Method, 29

building science, 10

building shape, 57, 171, 244

building simplicity, 63

bulk fuel metering, 249

buoyancy, 65

C

cabinet heaters, 188

cabinet unit heaters, 194

canopies, roof, 77

capture, contaminant, 168

capture, source, 174

carbon, 42

carbon dioxide, 3, 167

carbon emissions, 3, 9, 44, 229, 232, 239, 250

carbon offset, 219

Carpet and Rug Institute, 223

carpeting, 133, 174, 223

carpeting reflectance, 136

carpools, 45

casement windows, 105

caulk, 86, 127, 131

cavity, wall, 109, 131

ceiling cavities, 195

ceiling plenums, 120

ceiling reflectance, 101, 136

cellulose insulation, 235

cellulose, dense-pack, 126

central air handlers, 183, 195

central laundry, 156

CFC, 224

charging stations, 45

chart, psychrometric, 182

chase, uncapped, 109, 129

chases, 131

chemical filters, 175

chiller systems, 189

chiller, air-cooled, 189

chiller, liquid-cooled, 189

chillers, 192, 198

chimneys, 87, 89, 109, 127, 172, 190

chips, wood, 200

chlorofluorocarbon, 224

CHP, 163, 199, 201

cistern, 165

claddings, 16, 90, 91, 92, 93, 94, 96, 173

cleaning, 174

climate change, 2, 5, 9, 258

climates, cold, 92

closets, 105, 123, 192

clothes dryer vents, 87

clothes drying, 175, 199

clothes washers, 156, 160

CMU, 91

CMU, high performance, 91

CMU, lightweight, 91

coal, 8, 188

coastal flooding, 2

coatings, 223

cob construction, 222

codes, 25

coefficient of performance, 198

cogeneration, 199, 201

coil, fan, 183

cold climates, 92

collector, evacuated tube, 208

collector, flat-plate, 208

combined heat and power, 163, 199, 201

combustion, 190

combustion vents, 87, 172

comfort, 169

comfort measurement, 181

comfort zone, 182

comfort, thermal, 180

commercial kitchen hoods, 177

commissioning, 184, 236, 239, 245

commissioning agent, 239

commissioning authority, 239

commissioning exterior lighting, 154

commissioning provider, 239

commissioning ventilation systems, 177

commissioning, lighting controls, 151

community, 35

community connectivity, 51

community-centered development, 39

compact development, 51

compactness, 39

compartmentalization, 137, 179

complexity, surface, 67

composite window frames, 98

composting, 225

composting toilets, 160

computer simulation, 68, 72, 104

concrete, 218

concrete sandwich panels, 93

concrete washout, 53

concrete, pervious, 51

condensate pans, 175

condensate recovery, 165

condensation, 92, 180

condensing units, 191

conference rooms, 185

conformance to requirements, 234, 236

connectivity, 39

conservation areas, 40

construction cost, 58, 60, 66, 72, 104, 106, 110,
    131, 134, 140, 144, 155, 166, 179, 203, 230,
    243, 253

construction staging, 42

construction waste, 211

construction waste management, 225

consultant, energy, 97

consumer protection, 9

contaminant capture, 168

contaminant source reduction, 168

contaminant, airborne, 167, 174

contaminants, airborne, 167

content, recycled, 218

temperature stratification, 181

temperature, air, 180

temperature, equilibrium, 114

temperature, radiant, 181

temperature, unconditioned space, 124

thermal boundary, 84, 170

thermal bridging, 19, 88, 190

thermal buffer, 119

thermal comfort, 8, 180, 239

thermal conduction, 89

thermal continuity, 111

thermal convection, 89

thermal envelope, 116

Thermal Environmental Conditions for Human Comfort, 182

thermal losses, window, 100, 103

thermal mass, 92, 132

thermal resistance, 59, 88

thermal zoning, 137, 242

thermal zoning diagram, 140

thermal, solar, 206

thermo-siphoned airflow, 129

think as a community, 37

threatened species, 40

three-way switching, 150

threshold, door, 108

through-wall air-conditioner, 87

through-wall systems, 197

through-wall units, 189

tilt, 78

timers, 150

tint, window, 133

Title 24, 27

tobacco smoke, 167, 172

tobacco smoking, 171

toilet lid sink, 164

toilet, composting, 160

toilet, dual flush, 160

toplighting, 99

topology, 90

top plates, 213

topsoil, 7, 42, 51

tower, cooling, 48, 192, 196

townhouses, 107

tracked-in dirt, 55

track-off mats, 172

tradeoffs, energy, 81

training, 247

transformers, 48, 157

transparency, 226

transportation, 44, 51

transported water, 53

trespass, light, 46

trickle ventilators, 178

triple pane windows, 98

tube, light, 101

turbine ventilators, 178

turbine, wind, 209

U

U.S. Army Corps of Engineers, 40

U.S. Department of Agriculture, 40

U-factor, 98

ultrasonic sensors, 151

uncapped chases, 109, 129

uncapped wall cavities, 86, 129

unconditioned space temperatures, 124

unconditioned spaces, 107, 113, 174, 191

United States Botanic Garden, 33

United States Department of Agriculture, 223

United States Environmental Protection Agency, 250

United States Green Building Council, 28

unitized panels, 95

unrecognized unconditioned spaces, 120

urinal, waterless, 160

USDA, 40, 223

use of the roof, 82

USGBC, 34

using less material, 212, 215

utility bills, 11

utility metering, 247

utility spaces, 105

V

vacancy sensors, 152, 235

valley, roof, 77, 109

values, 253

values, owner's, 39

vapor barrier, 112, 118, 173

variable air volume, 183

variable refrigerant flow, 192, 203

variable speed drives, 157, 193

variable speed heat pumps, 192

variable speed motors, 193

variable voltage variable frequency (VVVF) drives, 158

varnishes, 223

VAV, 183

vegetated landscapes, 51

vegetated roofs, 110

vegetation, 55

vegetation, native, 56

vehicles, 45

vent, clothes dryer, 87

vent, combustion, 87, 172

vent, exhaust fan, 87

vent, plumbing, 19, 77

vent, ridge, 109

vent, roof, 109

ventilation, 140, 168, 176

ventilation air intakes, 87

ventilation effectiveness, 177, 179

ventilation energy, 169

ventilation zoning, 140

ventilation, commissioning, 177

ventilation, demand-controlled, 170

ventilation, energy recovery, 176, 181

ventilation, heat recovery, 176

ventilation, natural, 178

ventilation, nighttime, 132

ventilator, trickle, 178

ventilator, turbine, 178

very weak layer, 126

vestibules, 105, 113, 121, 122

view out, 103

views, 103, 104

vision glazing, 101, 103, 108

VOC, 223

volatile organic chemicals, 223

VSD, 193

VVVF drives, 158

W

walkable streets, 39

walk-up stairs, 127

wall cavities, 109, 131

wall cavity, uncapped, 129

wall headers, 87

wall insulation, 92

wall reflectance, 101

wall, curtain, 95

wall, masonry, 91

wall, metal frame, 95

wall, party, 109, 129

wall, poured concrete, 93